Journey Proud

*Recollections
of a Fifties Woman*

Claire King Sargent

Claire King Sargent

OAK TREE PRESS INC. PHOENIX, ARIZONA

Copyright © 1999 by Claire King Sargent

Published by Oak Tree Press Inc.
2201 North Central Avenue - #13-A
Phoenix, Arizona 85004-1417
Tel: (602) 253-5796 • Fax: (602) 251-3920
E-mail: oaktreeaz@aol.com

All rights reserved. Printed and bound in the United States of America. No part of this book may be reproduced in any form or by any means, electronic or mechanical, including information and retrieval systems, without permission in writing from the publisher, except where permitted by law.

Permissions acknowledgments appear on page 361.

Library of Congress Cataloging-in-Publication Data

Sargent, Claire King.
Journey proud: recollections of a fifties woman/ by Claire King Sargent - lst ed.
p. cm.
ISBN 0-9668332-5-2
1.Sargent, Claire King. 2.Women—United States—Social conditions. 3. Mississippi—Biography. 4.Women in politics—United States. 5. Arizona—Politics and government—1951- 6. Arizona—Biography. I. Title.
F815.3.S37A3   1999
305.42'09'791   [B]   98.88513

NOTE TO THE READER
The names of some of the individuals in this book have been changed to protect their privacy.

THIS COPY **SIGNED**

Jeannette King

Journey Proud

For my mother
whose life was a catalyst in mine
and my children
whose lives were changed because of it

The influence you exert is through your own life and what you become is yourself.

—Eleanor Roosevelt

An Epistle of Thanksgiving

To Dave Wagner, possessed of courage and generosity, who slogged through my earliest rough draft, determined that I had the makings of a book, and, urging me on, saw me through as insightful encourager.

To Susan Heath, my editor, who never flagged in her unwavering belief in me and my book. Endowed with infinite patience and grace, affirming me in times of both doubt and clarity, she was sister, friend, and wise guide.

To Mark Sanders, artist and technological magician, who understood my vision and brought it to reality.

To Susan King, who gave me *Writing a Woman's Life*.

To Sherri Chessen and Sam and Maddie Fleishman, who got me on the road.

To Elizabeth Ryan, Dr. Nancy Holland, Shirley Smallwood, and Dr. Martha Burk, believers all, who sparked me with their power.

To Barbara Pigott, Bettye Wilson, Charlotte Larson, and Larry Painter, who, in sharing their observations and suggestions, buttressed my resolve.

To Fran Noone, Shelby Watson, Charlotte Sargent, Catherine Mills, Nancy Spencer, Kathryn Little, Worth Van Zandt, Jeanne Clark, Michael Walters, Suzanne Schutt, Linda Nadolski, and the Dobbses, Frances, Catherine, and William, for their unfaltering support.

To Diana Victor, Esq., Bill Rejebian, Ronda Ridenour, and Jerome Joseph Brown, Esq., for their generous assistance.

To Shelby Watson and Bettye Wilson, once again, for their photos of our early years, and to Jane Goldstein for her photo of Gloria Steinem.

To Roslyn Breitenbach for her usual aplomb in getting the job done.

And, as ever and always, to my husband Henry.

Contents

Preface
xiii

Prologue
xix

PART ONE

Mississippi
1

PART TWO

New York
67

PART THREE

Arizona
167

Epilogue
357

Preface

I've always done everything first and then later found out how to do it—this book being only the latest example of that mode of operation. Since I *finished* the book before I got around to the "setting forth of the scope and intention" part, this could better be called an afterword than a preface. When I think about it, that's the same way I've lived my life.

My generation of women—those who came of age in the fifties—married young, had our children, and became "housewives," a most unappealing appellation, with its implication of being married to a house. (Interesting that the word "hussy" is derived from the root of "housewife"; I once wrote a one-act play in college based on that fact.) It was not until the seventies and the re-emergence of the women's movement that many women of our transitional generation began to feel that after rearing our children, being a housewife just wasn't any way to fill the rest of the days of our lives, and began to look for fulfillment elsewhere—in essence, starting a new life. Having lived the life prescribed for us, in the second half of our lives we set forth in a new direction to another country.

I've been writing all my life, just not for pay. I wrote a weekly column for my college newspaper, and back in the eighties here in Phoenix I wrote for the now-defunct *Arizona Women's Voice*. Our daily newspaper, the *Arizona Republic,* has published my articles when I got a burr under my saddle, and the *Phoenix Gazette* (also now defunct—is there a connection?) invited me (euphemism for no compensation) to write commentary pieces during the 1994 national elections. So I suppose you could call me an unpaid professional, sort of a dollar-a-year person, only cheaper.

Having written nothing much longer than a newspaper column, I discovered what all authors already know: that writing a book is not only not easy, it is extremely tough. Into my fourth year of writing, when I re-read Annie Dillard's *The Writing Life,* I was enormously heartened and relieved to be reminded that she believed that writing a book—*full time*—takes between two and ten years. And I wasn't even writing full time!

The book you have in your hands is not the book I started out to write. The opening lines of my first draft, which haunted me until I wrote them down—"I still sometimes wake up in the middle of the night and remember with searing painful clarity the night in Flagstaff during only the second, and last, debate with McCain and Mecham. I was awful."—aren't even in the final book.

I began writing about my campaign for the U.S. Senate in Arizona against Senator John McCain after friends and relatives asked me to tell them what it had been like. When I realized that they found many of my stories hard to believe (and of course what I saw was only the tip of the iceberg), I compared the reactions of these "real" people with those of the insiders with whom I talked—newspaper people, campaign consultants, business people, and various inside-the-Beltway types—whose response was always, "Everybody knows that." It was clear to me that there was a genuine disconnect between these insiders and everybody else: two worlds existing side-by-side with no overlap. That in fact "everybody" does *not* know "that."

I did a lot of reading after the campaign, and among the books I read was the now almost obligatory *Writing a Woman's Life* by Carolyn Heilbrun. (Does she groan today, I wonder, "Oh no, not again!", every time another woman lifts her pen in tribute?) Heilbrun's book made me understand how important it is for women to write their own stories, since most women's stories have been written by men—as most political insiders are—and are inevitably informed by the male perspective and experience. Realizing that women must define their own experience, I believed I had a unique story to tell. Well, not a unique story, perhaps, but an old story from a unique point of view—mine.

And so I began. But after writing for more than a year, I felt dissatisfied; something I couldn't put my finger on was nagging at me. I took a break, and in my ruminations and searchings kept reading, coming across Anne Lamott's book *Bird by Bird,* an affirmation of writers and their need to write, in which she passes on the advice from an old Mel Brooks routine: "Listen to your broccoli, and your broccoli will tell you how to eat it." Taking that advice, I began to pay closer attention to my own instincts to try to figure out what was going on.

Finally it dawned on me that what I'd written was nothing more than another story of a political campaign, that I had left "me" out of my own story, just as "I" had essentially been left out of the Senate campaign, since political campaigns trivialize and marginalize the candidates by depicting them as one-dimensional cartoon characters. I'd had a life before the campaign. How could I write about my campaign without also writing about that life—how I came to be who I was—the world and the times I grew up in, where I came from, my experiences of a lifetime?

Little boys have always grown up with dreams of being president. Now even little girls are allowed to dream those dreams. But when I was a girl in Mississippi during World War II, at the weekly Saturday double feature I don't ever remember seeing a movie with a woman hero, unless you count *Naomi, Queen of the Jungle,* the serial in which there was always a man around to save her at the last minute. Wait a minute! I do, too: Veronica Lake, in *So Proudly We Hail,* as an army nurse who blows herself up with hand grenades in her shirt to stall the Japanese while the other nurses evacuate the wounded! The point of a woman hero's story, though—if she were allowed to live—would, in the end, I'm sure, always have to be that she got her man.

The idea of growing up to be a United States Senator would never have entered my head. The closest I might have come, if the Senate had ever crossed my mind at all, would have been to be the *wife* of a senator, never the senator. So for me to write my story, I realized I had to begin at the beginning, a long row to hoe to be sure, filling me with trepidation.

And so I started over, writing in a stream of consciousness that turned into a crazy quilt of recollections with no apparent pattern.

After finishing the first draft, I didn't know what to do with it—for even the most abstract quilt has a pattern, recognizable or not—and I was new to this game. Even in its disjointed form, however, I was astonished to discover that everything was connected, and inevitably, I believe, the sum total of my life had led me to run for the Senate.

Once more I began, this time rearranging—connecting—the story chronologically, and filling in some of the blanks.

Writing this book has been a journey of self-discovery and revelation, which I never anticipated, *lagniappe,* "something extra." More in my life has been revealed to me—relationships, patterns of behavior, lifelong traits, growing and becoming—in the writing of it than in the living of it. In the words of poet Sarah Orne Jewett, "The road was new to me, as roads always are, going back."

Though it has been different, my life is emblematic of the last generation whose parents were the children of Victorians (even before Dr. Spock) and the last generation to be able to remember World War II; the generation born "in the depths of the Depression"—many of us suffering as we struggled to reconcile our upbringing with the changes swirling around us in the sixties and seventies. (A contemporary recently remarked, "When we talked about 'the change,' we weren't talking about menopause!")

Finally, I discovered as I wrote that so many times I qualified something with "those were in the days before . . ." Of course, in the span of years between 1934 and 1999, the world is so transformed that most people today can not possibly identify with my experience. So I've made a list of some of the ordinary things that didn't exist during part of my life:

Television
Penicillin
Credit cards
Xerox machines
Electric typewriters
Jet planes
Legal abortions
Computers
Throw-away diapers

Microwave ovens
Electric dishwashers
Freeways
Stereos
Hand-held hair dryers
Air conditioning
Birth control pills
SATs, LSATs, GMATs
Corporation Man

And here are some things that were givens:

Girdles and Merry Widow strapless bras
Polio
Measles
Playing in the clouds of mist behind the DDT truck
Smoking cigarettes
Drive-ins: restaurants and picture shows
Segregation
Anti-Semitism
Discrimination with regard to gender, race, religion, national origin
(sexual preference was still in the closet)
Pollution
Insecticides
Father as head of household, mother as housewife
Women, if they worked, were secretaries, nurses, teachers, clerks
The universal draft and military service
The whole world was not on a first-name basis

In a wholly different context, Robert J. Lifton, author of *The Protean Self*, intrigued me when he observed, "Bearing witness requires the full participation of the self . . . One takes in the pain and recasts it in the retelling of the story. By struggling to contribute to larger consciousness, one calls forth portions of the self that have been slumbering."

Writing *Journey Proud*—bearing witness for my generation—has required such a concentrated participation of the "self" that the six years it took to finish it are like an evening gone.

Prologue

On New Year's Eve 1956, it was getting close to midnight by the time I stepped six hours late from the Chicago and Southern Airlines plane onto the soil of Newark, New Jersey—a strange place to have to land, it seemed to me, to go to New York City.

That morning, as I'd peered through the small window at the crowd of family and friends, pressing against the chain link fence at the edge of the tarmac just outside the tiny terminal of the Jackson Municipal Airport, some crying, some laughing, all waving and yelling good-bye, I couldn't believe I was actually taking off on this great adventure into the unknown.

"If we crash, I'll die happy," I thought, immobilized with fear as the stewardesses sealed the door shut.

I was twenty-two years old and had never before been on an airplane, or north of Lynchburg, Virginia. It hadn't even been a whole month since I'd decided to leave Mississippi.

The first week of December I'd walked into Mrs. Godwin's office and told her that if they needed somebody to go work up in the newly opened New York office, I would like to go. I'd begun working for Mrs. Godwin at the advertising agency she owned with her husband when I graduated from high school four summers before, until I started full-time after graduating from college in May. Even though I was slightly intimidated by Mrs. Godwin, I liked her, admired her. On occasion she would affectionately call me "Bright Eyes," though I was never exactly sure why.

"And leave Mississippi!" she replied, shocked.

"Yes, ma'am."

"Are you really sure about this?"

"Yes, ma'am. I've thought about it a lot. I've worked in every department. They could never find anybody in New York who would understand the way we do things down here and know the people here the way I do. I've worked with everybody in the New York office and know them all well. They need me up there."

"Do you think you could be ready to go in three weeks?"

"Yes, ma'am, I sure could."

"It just never occurred to me. But if you really want to go, I'll try to talk to the boys in New York tonight."

Walking out of her office, my legs were weak and I felt funny all over, especially my stomach. It was almost five o'clock. I went to my desk and called Daddy to see if he could pick me up after work on his way home. I was going to explode if I wasn't able to tell somebody the momentous news of what I'd just done.

"Guess what!" I shrieked as I got into his car. "I may be going to New York!" And proceeded to recount the conversation with Mrs. Godwin.

Daddy was smiling. He seemed pleased. I've heard of fathers who can't stand to have their little girls leave home and do everything they can to stand in their way. Not my daddy.

"New York is real expensive. Do you think you can make enough to live on?" The practical one.

"If they want me to go, I know I won't make enough to live high on the hog. But I don't care. I just hope I get to go."

"Well, I do, too. If you don't like it you can always come home. Not many girls get a chance to leave home and see something different. I'm glad you want to see something besides Mississippi."

PART ONE

Mississippi

One

I remember Pearl Harbor, the day of infamy, though I didn't know what infamy was when I was seven. On a Sunday afternoon, as I was taking a walk with my father along a new gravel road we were inspecting, friends drove by in their car and stopped to talk to Daddy about what had happened in "Hawahyah." (It's hard work for Southerners to say HI-WA-EEE. It doesn't glide easily off tongue and jaw.) I had not heard the news before, perhaps by design. And after they drove away, I remember being afraid, and Daddy holding my hand and reassuring me that Pearl Harbor was far away across the ocean. That we didn't have to worry because it was too far for Japanese planes to fly to Mississippi.

We lived outside the city limits of Jackson—considered by people in town to be the country—on Meadowbrook Road, its name suiting it perfectly, surrounded as we were by land of splendid open fields and woods of oak, poplar, sweet gum, hickory, cedar, and pine—thick with vines so strong and sturdy we could swing across the creek like Johnny Weissmuller in the Tarzan movies, and with brambles so dense that sometimes we had to chop our way through, like the long-ago Choctaw Indians must have had to do.

On the other side of Meadowbrook was a stand of plum trees, in the summertime brilliant with lustrous red-orange fruit; and the low-growing prickly bushes along the side of the road—that we had to thread through carefully before reaching the plums—were laden with succulent blackberries, both of which my brother and I would pick for Mama to make jelly and cobbler. (When I lived in Brooklyn, I was surprised to discover a street in the Bay Ridge section called Meadowbrook Road, since those bucolic words represented the opposite of what I supposed Brooklyn to be.)

I don't ever remember anybody explaining to me why we moved out there, except that Daddy never was one to go with the crowd, and I don't know how he happened to buy the land from Mr. Culley, who owned all the land that ultimately became our neighborhood.

Daddy chose a corner lot with four towering oak trees on about an acre of land. When he built the house, a two-story Colonial with dark green shutters, he sited it so there was an oak tree in both the front and back yards, and one on each side. The house was started in 1939, and we moved in in 1940, the year I entered the first grade. Daddy was an engineer and knew about building things. When we had our first dishwasher put in when I was in high school after the war, the young carpenter told Mama he'd never before cut through kitchen counters that were made with two-by-fours.

New for the late thirties, the Culleys had built a "modern" house, an elegant ranch house, long and low. It faced the graveled lane (now Oak Ridge Drive) that ran by the side of our house—which faced Meadowbrook—also a gravel road then. When the Culleys looked out of the window of their kitchen, which in a modern house was on the front, they could see our driveway and back door, which we always used except when company came.

We didn't have a yard in the traditional sense. We just quit mowing along a certain line and then the woods took over. Just beyond the yard I discovered the perfect hideout, where young oak trees, honeysuckle, sumac, and poison ivy vines all entwined into a thick overhead ceiling, forming a leafy room. Sometimes I would steal away to this secret spot with some fudge cake and a Coca-Cola, a Captain Marvel funny-book or *The Secret Garden,* and at other times I would go there just to be by myself, to daydream.

The Culleys had more of a proper yard, planted in grass and surrounded by a white three-railed fence, which included the "lake"—actually nothing more than a small pond but as big as a lake to us as children—with an island in the middle where a weeping willow grew, chartreuse in the spring, surrounded by jonquils the color of butter and pink azaleas.

Part One - Mississippi

It was a year or two before we were joined by other neighbors, who also bought their land from Mr. Culley. They built back behind us along the lane, which became a dead end (not a cul-de-sac) down past the Culleys' pond. It was the nucleus of our neighborhood, with no paved streets, no sidewalks, no sewers or water. We all had septic tanks in our back yards and got our water from Mr. Culley's well.

Mr. Culley was a "developer" long before I ever had any idea what that was. And to my mind he was also rich.

～

As a child the heat of Mississippi summers never bothered me. But it bothered the adults—just as it bothers me now—giving rise to the Summer Rule: that after dinner (the noon meal) everybody "rested" until two o'clock. All the mothers in the neighborhood united, for naturally if one child were out playing, the others would want to follow. Those were the years when everyone was terrified of polio, the crippling, sometimes deadly disease now mercifully almost extinct (the test to be sure you didn't have it was to be able to bend your head down far enough to touch your chest with your chin), when getting enough rest was one defense for staving it off. The fear of polio was the best weapon in a mother's arsenal to keep us if not in our beds, at least in our rooms.

The only girl in a neighborhood of boys, I was a tomboy. In front and back yards we played softball, football, kick the can, and capture the flag; in the red sand canyons at Cedar Hill Lake we shot BB guns, and occasionally a rifle or shotgun when we were with our fathers (once, grabbing up the BB gun, I took aim at a bluejay who was attacking a mockingbird in our front yard; when he plopped over, dead as a doornail, I couldn't believe I'd killed him and ran and hid, scared to death, under my bed); in the woods surrounding us we built huts of bamboo and, terrified as I was of snakes, I swam in the muddy pond inhabited by fish and frogs and water moccasins. I didn't like fishing because I hated squshing the squirming worm onto a hook and, if I happened to catch a fish, was squeamish about having to twist the hook out of the mouth of the struggling victim fighting for its life.

I loved the seasonal rituals of jump rope, jacks, hopscotch, and yo-yos; red rover, May I?, and sling statue. There was no schedule of these activities in our lives. Everything was spontaneous, improvisational, calling for self-sufficiency, creativity, and ingenuity. And I was usually the instigator.

What I didn't do was play with dolls. At an early age I had been the recipient of the obligatory girls' gift of a duo of dolls, the bride and the baby. And though I admired their beautiful clothes, they languished untouched, unloved, and unnoticed. Nothing gave me more pleasure, though, than opening a new box of Crayola crayons. It was quite a sensuous experience, the smell of the wax, the intense colors glowing like jewels—purple violet and crimson orange—the perfection of the point of each crayon before it was worn down with use.

And my imagination flourished with radio.

Faithful to my favorite programs, *Jack Armstrong—All American Boy* and *Terry and the Pirates,* I would quit playing softball in the afternoons after school to go inside to listen. I sent off to *Terry and the Pirates* for the ring with the secret compartment where I could hide poison and secret messages, and entered the contest to describe in twenty-five words or less why I loved Quaker Puffed Wheat, "shot from guns." If I were sick, I listened in my bed to *Stella Dallas* and *Queen for a Day,* which I dreamed of being.

After supper Mama and Daddy and my brother and I would sit around listening to *Fibber McGee and Molly,* Jack Benny, or *Dr. I.Q., the Mental Banker* ("I have a lady in the balcony, Doctor"), where program contestants might win silver dollars by answering questions. And my favorite: "Mr. District Attorney, champion of the people, defender of truth, guardian of our fundamental right to life, liberty, and the pursuit of happiness. With Jay Jostyn in the title role, featuring Len Doyle as Harrington and Vickie Vola as Miss Miller."

Daddy was a stickler about bedtime, and after ostensibly going upstairs to bed I'd sneak out of my room and sit at the top of the stairs where I could hear *Gang Busters* as he and Mama listened in the living room below.

If we weren't listening to the radio, and if Daddy had finished reading his paper, we'd play Chinese checkers or checkers, Sorry, or a card game called Touring that I got for Christmas. I'll never forget the time I drew a card that said "collision" and I called it "collusion," making Mama and Daddy laugh before Daddy explained the difference. This was all before Daddy left for the War—an idyllic time, wrapped in the cocoon of innocence.

∽

At the picture show every Saturday I took in a double feature—usually a musical or a war story—and a cowboy show starring Johnny Mack Brown (who, my mother was pleased to report, went to Mississippi State College in the town where she grew up), Hopalong Cassidy, or Roy Rogers; a serial (*Naomi, Queen of the Jungle*); a Movietone newsreel; a comedy (as we called cartoons); and a bag of popcorn. All for fifteen cents.

The newsreels and war movies instilled a deep fear and hatred for the Swastika and Hitler and the Rising Sun and Tojo. Steeped in wartime patriotism, I knew and loved all the war songs. "Let's Remember Pearl Harbor," "You're a Sap, Mr. Jap," and "Marching Along Together" were my favorites.

Even in Mississippi we had blackouts, and the neighborhood air-raid warden checked to be sure all of our lights were turned off. My brother and I had airplane cards—similar to baseball cards today—each with a silhouette and description of every plane in the war. We could identify American planes—twin-tailed P-38 Lightnings, P-51 Mustangs, B-17 Flying Fortresses—as well as German Messerschmidts and Japanese Zeros. We were ever on the alert for enemy planes—especially the Germans, so close to us just across the Atlantic, who could make a sneak attack at any moment.

At school everyone brought a dime or a quarter to buy a victory stamp every Friday to fill up a stamp book to equal $18.75, enough to buy a war bond, which one day would be worth $25. On our birthdays and at Christmas my brother and I occasionally received a war bond as a gift as well, ending up with several bonds each by the time the war was over, which without a peep we signed over to our father when he asked us to, to help him get started in his business when he came home from the war.

∽

It was probably in the third or fourth grade that I wrote to every movie star I could think of, asking for their picture. Each day when I got off the school bus I rushed to the mailbox by the side of the road in front of our house to see if the postman had delivered a new treasure for my scrapbook—some "autographed," some not—of Hollywood's heartthrobs. The famous pin-up photo of Betty Grable in her bathing suit, said to be taped in every GI's locker; of Gary Cooper, Alan Ladd, Ann Sheridan, Rita Hayworth, Hedy Lamarr, Greer Garson, Clark Gable, Van Johnson, Van Heflin, Paulette Goddard, Ava Gardner, Tyrone Power. And on and on.

Each time I received a picture, I would immediately check to see if it had been autographed, and if so, closely inspect the signature to see if it had been written in real ink by licking my finger and rubbing it to see if it would smear. When it was real, I would show it to Mama and ask her if she thought Rita or Tyrone had really signed it. "I can't tell," she'd say, studying it carefully. "I 'spect they're so busy they probably have to get somebody to help them sign all their pictures. But it's nice somebody did."

Letting me down easy.

In a departure from Southern tradition I was given no middle name. Because of this oversight, in my early years I always felt that with only one name I had been deprived of one of the essential requirements of life, enjoyed by everyone but me. And at one time in my adolescent years, after seeing the movie *Reveille with Beverly*, starring Ann Miller, for a brief period I adopted the name Beverly Claire. And in an even more unusual departure, I was not named for any ancestor or relative because my parents couldn't settle on a family name. And even though they'd never known anyone named Claire, I was given the name simply because they thought it beautiful (my tenth grade Latin teacher thrilled and embarrassed me when she called on me one day as "Clara, bright and famous," translating my name before the class).

And though I had a temper, and still do (in grade school some of the boys taunted me by calling me "red hot mama"; and one time at church I hauled off and hit a boy with my purse when he just wouldn't leave me alone), I was reserved and shy when I was young.

At Grandmama's my cousins and I would dress up in our aunts' old evening dresses, pretending we were in picture shows, and

Part One - Mississippi

would spend endless hours devising intricate choreography for marches or dances, which we would perform to the music of my Aunt Missy's *Nutcracker Suite* records on the Victrola. Even though I was always the "bossy" one who thought up everything we did, when any of the adults wanted to come in to watch our act, I was too shy, or embarrassed, or self-conscious, and refused to perform for onlookers.

Even as late as the eighth grade, when I had been invited to a dance given in one of the ballrooms in a downtown hotel by a ninth grade girl in my neighborhood, I was mortified when I had to dance with my date, Wade Creekmore, an old friend—supposedly shyer than I was—in front of all those older ninth graders and parents. Wade (who later became a Frogman in the Navy) was willing, and even tried to persuade me, but I dug in my heels. I spent the entire evening—in the new white dotted-Swiss evening dress that Mrs. Ishee the sewing lady had made for me—watching from the sidelines, all the while aching to be out there dancing. I was just so self-conscious I couldn't make myself do it.

Paradoxically, even though I was shy, I was seldom timid. This would appear to be an anomalous quirk given my personality, and I have no explanation for it. They could be the opposite sides of the same coin for all I know. And even though I've always had a sense of humor, I was definitely never a natural ham, a spontaneous emcee type with a line of patter. I could only be myself, whereas actors have the gift of becoming someone else.

༄

My mother's family were music lovers. My great-aunt Jerry, a musician who worked for the WPA (the Works Progress Administration, set up by FDR to employ people during the Depression), was one of the founders of the Jackson Symphony Orchestra. An old maid, as unmarried ladies were called, whenever she came for a visit, she would take my brother and me to Seale-Lily, the local ice cream parlor, for an ice cream cone, and pay us each a nickel if we didn't let the cone drip on the seat of her car.

She always arrived with a gift of books for my brother and me, in what I later realized was an effort at enlightenment and intellectual stimulation. The first book she gave me was a children's biography of Mozart, which mystified me, since I was unable to grasp the fact that anyone six years old could actually write music, much less play the piano. Another was a beautifully bound and illustrated book of *Grimm's Fairy Tales*. When you look back on your life, you become aware of those along the way who were trying to help you, though you didn't know it at the time.

At the age of seven I read my first "real" book, *The Mystery at Lilac Inn,* when my Aunt Frances gave me my first Nancy Drew for Christmas. I became hooked not only on Nancy but on Judy Bolton, Nurse Sue Barton, Penny Parrish, and the Hardy Boys. And I was fascinated to read somewhere after my Senate campaign that many other women who have run for political office had also been Nancy Drew fans as girls.

I turned into a bookworm, through inclination, not parental urging or even the remotest sense of intellectualism. In fact it would be years before I even knew what the word "intellectual" meant. It's not that my family weren't readers; they read newspapers and the popular magazines of the time, such as the *Saturday Evening Post, Time, Life, Look, Colliers* and *Reader's Digest.* Part of the ritual of my father's day was to read the morning paper over breakfast before he left for work (an act as a wife I consider intolerably inconsiderate), and when he got home, to sit down "in peace" before supper to read the evening paper.

It could be that the real reason we didn't have a lot of books was because they cost money. And we had the public library. Being in the country, we didn't have to go down town to the library. It came to us. The bookmobile arrived on the corner in front of our house every two weeks during the summer. The driver would open up the back of a vehicle similar to a van, with an aisle down the middle, and on each side were shelves crammed with books, reaching to the top, like a miniature library. Surrounded by all those books, I brimmed with joy and anticipation, and after all these years I still get the same feeling every time I set foot in a library or a bookstore.

I had no parental guidance in what books to read. No one spoon-feeding me the Classics or Good Literature. I picked whatever I wanted and would head for my room to read on my bed in front of the slowly oscillating electric fan, wholly oblivious of the

Part One - Mississippi

heat. I spent many a hot halcyon summer day thus engaged. (*Halcyon Days* was, in fact, the title of one of the books I once happened to choose, and I remember asking Mama what "halcyon" meant. I've always loved those onomatopoeic, evocative words. I understand why someone once described the words "summer's day" as the most beautiful sound in the English language.)

∞

Every Sunday my brother and I went to Sunday school with Mama and stayed afterwards for church. I don't remember ever discussing religion. It was just taken for granted. However, my mother, who liked to have fun, did recall for us the Sunday afternoons of her youth when she and her brothers and sisters were forbidden to play cards or dance or go swimming—in essence, not to have any fun. Besides the gift of music, my mother's family also contributed a long line of Methodists, including a minister. All of this uprightness, though, did not preclude a love of the grain or the juniper. Our family were Methodists more of the hymn-singing than teetotaling persuasion.

Reader that I was, I loved the Bible stories of Sunday school and vacation Bible school: Adam and Eve and the snake in the Garden of Eden. Cain and Abel. David and Goliath. The good Samaritan. The woman at the well. The prodigal son. Learning the difference between "stature" and "statue" when we memorized the verse for the day, "And Jesus grew in wisdom and in stature."

"Be ye doers of the Word and not hearers only," a fixture in my memory ever since those early days, could be the goad that's been spurring me to action ever since. As well as the condemnation of "mouth honor"—what I later would recognize as "lip service."

Even after studying religion and moving beyond literalness, if I am called a liberal, I trace it to the old stories instilled in me in my early years, to the very roots that are claimed by the religious right today. The paradox for me is how they can claim The Truth, when they refuse to feed those who are hungry, clothe those who are naked, comfort the sick, love their neighbors as themselves, or take to heart the admonition, "Even as ye have done it unto the least of these, ye have done it unto me." It is simply beyond me.

Two

In the summers, with my brother and cousins, I would spend several weeks at my grandmother Hogan's house in Starkville. I say grandmother's house, because that was the way I thought of it, even though my grandfather was there, too. We were always "going to Grandmama's," and Mama was always "going home."

My cousins Bettye and Myra were one year older and one year younger than I and lived in the Delta. My brother was two years younger than I. So we were all stairsteps. Another cousin, William, two years younger than my brother, would visit sometimes, too. And now that I'm a grandmother myself, when I think of what Grandmama put up with, having us all there for weeks on end!

All the men in our family, even an aunt, and most of the fathers of all my friends were in the war overseas or involved in the war effort in some way; and while we were at Grandmama's, we wrote painstaking letters on regulation tissue-thin V-Mail stationery to our Uncle Alex who was a prisoner of war. He was the pilot of a B-17 Flying Fortress when it was shot down over Germany. When he came home from the German prison camp after V-E Day in 1945, he courted a girl from the Delta, and they were married that same year in a Delta wedding, a month before her nineteenth birthday. It was so-oo-oo romantic. I was eleven years old and in seventh heaven.

Summertime in Mississippi was a magical, even mystical time for me as a child. And still is. At Grandmama's, before we went to bed, with our hands cupped around our eyes we would peer soundlessly through the screen of our bedroom windows into the inky firefly-studded night, to try one last time to see if we could catch a

Part One - Mississippi

glimpse of some of the fairies entering or leaving their bowered home in an overgrown patch of honeysuckle a short distance from the sandy driveway just beyond our windows.

In search of evidence of the fairy encampment, during the day we would crawl through a narrow opening to enter the roomlike space, where a stone bench and birdbath green with lichen and moss had stood for years. In an earlier time it had been a place to sit and watch the games on the level grass-covered expanse that Hogan teenagers had once used as a tennis court, where, according to my Aunt Missy, they had played without a net.

One moonlit night as we were watching for fairies, we saw Missy coming home up the cinder path that ran along the other side of the hedge that grew next to the tennis court. When she came in, obviously having spotted us at our vigil, she came back to our room to report excitedly that as she was walking up the path she had seen about a dozen fairies dancing in the moonlight on the tennis court. Even though she stood as still as a statue, the fairies must have sensed her presence and disappeared into thin air. We were enthralled, and we believed. Though on many a night after that, when we thought we caught sight of a fairy, we were never, ever truly sure.

∽

Bettye and Myra's mother died when they were five and three, of peritonitis after an operation. She was buried under an oak tree in the cemetery in our family plot, which was surrounded by a picket fence made of iron. Grandmama called it Kiki's garden, that spot where Katherine, her daughter called KiKi, lay.

Sometimes when we didn't have anything to do we would go find Grandmama to ask her for suggestions, and she might say, "Why don't you go and visit KiKi's garden and take her some flowers." And off we'd go, stopping to pick some althea or cosmos or larkspur from the yard before we left, or Queen Anne's lace or black-eyed Susans from the side of the road along the way. We'd also take some flowers for our Methodist minister ancestor, Uncle Sage, also buried in KiKi's garden, and were quite respectful of his grave where he lay under a weathered tombstone carved into a lectern with an open Bible on top.

Occasionally we would pull some of the weeds that had overtaken the garden or climb the oak tree whose spreading branches formed an umbrella of dappled shade over KiKi. Later we'd wander around the cemetery, stopping to examine the tombstones. Our favorite was the little lamb, which we would stop and pat, and make up stories about what happened to the child who was buried there. When we buried my grandmother almost forty years later, my cousins and I went searching for that baby lamb and found it, still there, steadfast, keeping watch.

On the way home from Kiki's garden, we would stop and play in the sand at some kind of facility, I have no idea what, probably a cement-maker, which used a great deal of sand. Nobody ever said a word to us or chased us away, and we spent hours burying our feet or building castles or simply digging holes. When we got home that first time after our discovery of the sand and excitedly told Grandmama about it, she said, "Aren't you lucky! Let's call it Hogan's Beach." And after that when we went to KiKi's Garden, we'd always stop at Hogan's Beach on the way home.

I don't know whether Grandmama was being ironical or whimsical about calling the sand Hogan's Beach. My grandmother, who had had a hard life, by the time I knew her always found the good, the positive side in everything.

∽

She was called Miss Mamie. I didn't know until I read her obituary when she died at the age of ninety-seven that my grandmother's real name was Mary Elizabeth. Even Papa called her Miss Mamie and she called him Mister Hogan.

The details of her early days are sketchy, and all that is known of my great-grandmother Katherine Flanagan I've gleaned from birth, death, and marriage records. On the other hand, the origin of the family of my great-grandfather William Sage is extensive, as a result of Aunt Jerry's research for the DAR. The Sage family of the Old World was chiefly of French and Saxon extraction. In the New World far-flung Sages have been included "on the rolls of honor on every battlefield of America for 250 years" and "in the ranks of all avocations of life: judges, doctors, professors, congressmen . . ." Congressmen? Congressmen? It was not until after my campaign for the Senate that I found out about all this, discovering as well a Sage coat of arms with the motto *Non sibis sed patriae*—"Not for himself, but for his country"—but even more important, that my Sage ancestors were "self-reliant and independent," and "appeared to have been people of *great will power*" (emphasis mine).

Of course all those ancestors being described were men, but the same blood has coursed for generations through the veins of women Sages as well, and I reckon there's just no getting around the fact that genes will out—regardless of gender—and that *Non sibis sed patriae* could also be translated "Not for *her*self, but for *her* country" just as well.

Somehow, my grandmother, born in north Mississippi in 1882, the fourth girl and seventh child of twelve children—after years of working at the side of her mother in the kitchen and serving meals in the dining room at a girls' seminary in northwest Mississippi—was able to attend Mississippi State College for Women in Columbus (and in her early nineties would be presented with a purple orchid and honored as the longest-lived attendee at the annual alumni meeting).

Leaving MSCW—known as the "W"—after completing a two-year business course (or so it is believed), she moved the twenty miles to Starkville, where she found a job keeping books. She lived with a widowed uncle—the Methodist minister buried in Kiki's garden—who had been married four times, remarkably producing no children. This is when she met Papa, whom she married in 1902, when she was twenty and he was thirty-six.

༄

We have more detail about Papa's family from an account in a biographical history of Mississippi published in the early 1900s. Its prose reads like a page straight out of the nineteenth century (which, of course, it is), reminding me that it was in the Victorian novel that I first encountered the term "bourgeoisie," but it was to be many years before I realized it was us.

After graduating when he was nineteen from Mississippi A & M (later Mississippi State), Papa "engaged in the raising, buying and shipping of live stock, as well as in agricultural pursuits, having a valuable landed estate near Starkville and making a specialty of the breeding of fine Jersey cattle." Further, he was "held in high regard" for showing "his liberality and public spirit" and "establish(ing) himself as one of the representative business men and honored citizens of his native county. . . . In politics he pays allegiance to the Democratic party, in whose cause he takes a lively and loyal interest."

This branch of my family first appeared in Mississippi in 1833 with the arrival of my great-great-grandfather Elijah Hogan from northern Alabama. After becoming "one of the substantial and influential citizens of the county, he was a leader in the Methodist church and assisted in the organization of the first church of this denomination in Starkville."

And the one and only reference I've ever seen or heard about anyone in my family having anything to do with the Civil War reveals that my great-grandfather Alexander Hogan "manifested his loyalty to the Confederacy when the War between the States was initiated by doing all in his power to uphold the cause of the Confederacy. In 1862 [at the age of thirty-three] he enlisted as a private in the Forty-third Mississippi infantry, with which he was in active service until the close of the war, save for the period of his imprisonment. He was captured at the time of the siege of Vicksburg and was taken to camp Douglas, near Chicago, where he was held in captivity until the close of the war, when he received his parole."

One of the fiercest and most terrible battles of the Civil War, where twenty thousand soldiers died, the unspeakable horror and devastation of the siege of Vicksburg ended on the Fourth of July, 1863. My great-grandfather, it would certainly appear, was blessed with good luck, courage, and a strong constitution to have survived—both the battle of Vicksburg and the Yankee prison. And a year after the war was over, Papa was born.

∾

They built their home on top of a hill that took up a whole block, facing Hogan Street. Designed by an Atlanta architect, the two-story house, with a deep spacious front porch and wide center halls, shared the hill with a barn and pasture, a smokehouse, and a vegetable garden. In the spring a profusion of yellow flowers—daffodils, jonquils, butter 'n eggs, narcissus—sprang up bright as stars

Part One - Mississippi

all over the grassy hill (prompting Grandmama to break out in a rash and her eyes to water profusely).

As the children arrived, eight in all—including a set of twins—Grandmama had the help of several "hands," as colored servants were called. She recalled for me toward the end of her life the fine trips she and Papa took on the Gulf Mobile and Ohio Railroad, sleeping in the Pullman car on the way to New Orleans, where they would stay for several weeks at the Monteleone Hotel. When she told me this, I was surprised, because I had never before heard of her doing anything even halfway extravagant or carefree in my whole life. A side of Grandmama I never knew, since it all happened in the more than thirty years of her marriage before I was born.

Even before the Depression times became so hard (Mama always said since hardly anybody had any money then anyway, the Depression didn't make all that much difference in Mississippi), that, taking matters into her own hands, Grandmama closed in a sleeping porch and took in their first boarder. A railroad man from West Point twelve miles away, he spent every other night in Starkville before making the return trip home, and according to my aunt Daisy, referred to his wife as his "ball and chain." Other than the boarders Daisy can recall no other source of income during that time beyond the meat Papa smoked—after killing a steer or a hog—and sold to Mr. George Bryan over in West Point, whose descendant would become chairman and CEO of Sara Lee when the meat packing company that grew out of those bleak days was acquired by the huge conglomerate.

~

Each summer morning around nine o'clock, we would see Papa, who was in his seventies, take up his Panama hat and leave the house to walk up town to visit with his cronies over coffee at the Bell Café, or join them on the bench in front of the Oktibbeha County Court House under a shade tree. Just as the noon whistle blew at the Borden's plant up the street, he would appear on the cinder path leading up the hill to the house in time for dinner.

(I don't know if my grandparents ever owned a car. Grandmama briefly thought about learning to drive after the war started, but since they didn't have a car then, she never got around to it.)

Wonderful things from the garden behind the house were deposited in the kitchen every morning by Will, the colored gardener, who was almost as old as Papa. Corn, tomatoes, peaches, snap beans, butter beans, lady peas and crowder peas, okra, figs, turnip greens. In the barn were cows and hogs and chickens, too. The iceman appeared each day as well, bearing a huge block of ice on his shoulder and depositing it in the top section of the icebox; we had to use an ice pick to chop off ice for iced tea or "ice water."

At every meal we had hot homemade bread, either cornbread or biscuits or rolls. Butter was churned on the back porch, where we would occasionally work at it, getting in the way of the cook, whose job it was. It was hard work, and I don't think we ever stuck with it to the end.

Dessert might be plain white cake with no icing, my favorite, hot from the oven, its vanilla fragrance filling the house, or buttery chess pie. During peach season we made peach ice cream, turned by hand in the ice-cream freezer with ice and rock salt, which would occasionally find its way into the cream. When it finally got hard, we would fight over licking the dasher when it was pulled from the middle of all that goodness.

At the end of each meal, when Papa had finished, he would fold his napkin and announce, "My message is delivered," arise from the table, and retreat to his bedroom for a nap. At a quarter of two the shrill whistle at the cotton mill, 'way down behind the house across the tracks, was Papa's alarm clock. By the time the two o'clock mill whistle blew, his hat already on his head, he was on his way out the front door for his afternoon rendezvous at the Bell Café.

As evidence that the sense of smell is the most acute in evoking memory, the moment I get a whiff of the aroma of coffee brewing in the late afternoon, I'm transported instantly to Grandmama's kitchen, where every afternoon she made coffee to coincide with Papa's return home from his sojourn up town, sometime around four-thirty (it was a known fact that drinking hot coffee made you feel cooler).

After exchanging the day's news with Grandmama over coffee in the breakfast room, Papa repaired to his rocking chair in front of the fireplace in his bedroom. On the hearth was a scuttle for coal, which

Part One - Mississippi

was burned in the grate, and over the fireplace a copy of a detail of the now ubiquitous Raphael's angels. And when I visited Franz Joseph Haydn's home in Vienna, I was quite delighted—if not startled—to find the same familiar cherubs on the wall of his study. Above Papa's bookcase next to the fireplace was his favorite picture, "End of the Trail," the poignant silhouette of an Indian slumped in despair astride his barebacked horse (I was a grown woman before I gave any thought to the significance of this).

Papa enjoyed the solitude of reading his pulp magazine cowboy stories and chewing his tobacco—next to his chair he kept a disgusting spittoon—until we pestered him by sneaking up behind his chair to tap him on his bald head and chew ice in his ear. Then, fly swatter at the ready, he'd get up and take off after us around the house, Gulliver chasing squealing Lilliputians. I know we must have driven him crazy, but he was such a good sport. And we had so much fun.

After all of his children had left home, when Papa was asked if he weren't lonesome, he'd say, "Yes, I am. But it's a happy lonesome!"

ᛰ

My great-aunt Miss Daisy, called DaDa (pronounced day-day), was Papa's never-married sister, another family old maid. I never see a quilt today that I don't think of DaDa. And when I think of the beautiful work she did, never appreciated by any of us until years after she was dead, I am still suffused with guilt. She saved scraps of fabric she had used for dresses she made for herself, her nieces, and Grandmama, and when we were there in the summer we would spend hours carefully cutting out pieces for her next quilt from a cardboard pattern. She taught us how to sew a straight seam with tiny stitches to piece the quilt together, and how to crochet. We crocheted wonderful ruffly round "wash cloths," completely impractical and never touched by water, though taking up endless hours of close work—which was more to the point I think, idle hands being the Devil's workshop.

DaDa kept her scissors with her sewing things locked in a chifferobe in her room, and whenever we wanted to use them to cut out paper dolls, or pictures out of the Sears and Roebuck catalog or magazines, she would unlock the door and take them out with great ceremony, slowly lifting them to her lips and kissing them, before prayerfully relinquishing them into our hands. "Kissing them goodbye," she would say to us, after years of experience of lending her possessions to her nieces and nephews, and now the next generation of borrowers.

Writing of DaDa reminds me of the subject of primogeniture. During all those childhood summers until she died, DaDa would tell us that she was leaving her land—which she'd bought by saving her part of the "milk money" from the cows on the Hogan farm—to our uncle named for our grandfather (then the oldest nephew, after the eldest, Robert, had died at the age of twenty-five of a ruptured appendix), so that the land would always be in the family name.

Which is exactly the way it turned out. Not one of the daughters ever received so much as an acre of land.

As far as I'm aware, the idea of questioning the inherent and flagrant inequality of this arrangement would never have crossed the mind of her four nieces, because they would never see it as having anything to do with being equal or unequal. It was simply tradition, never questioned, accepted as gospel. Just the way things were.

∾

I knew them only after everything was gone. First, the Depression and the loss of Papa's business, the livestock, the land. Then the original house. It burned to the ground the year after I was born; caught fire one Sunday morning while everybody was at church, starting in the kitchen, which stood apart from the main house. When the fire whistle blew and the volunteer firemen bolted from their seats, my grandparents heard the shocking news along with everybody else when it was announced from the pulpit that it was their house, whereupon the pews emptied as every congregant rushed out to help. It's funny though. I never even *knew* there was another house until I ran across a photograph years later. The much-smaller one-story house I knew and loved was built over part of the foundation of the original house, and the old front walk leading up the hill from Hogan Street had become a driveway.

The pecan tree that was in the front yard of the "new" house, planted before the old house burned, became a symbol for me over the years. Quite a mystical symbol, actually. My tap root, as I began referring to the tree when I visited from the North, an allusion to James Street's romantic novel, *Tap Root*.

As a child, embraced in its arms, I climbed nimble as a monkey in that tree. It had a huge branch, about ten or twelve inches around, extending almost straight out from its trunk, maybe eight or ten feet above the ground. One day I climbed down from the crotch in the trunk above the limb, realizing what I was getting ready to do, since I'd thought about it for a long time.

"Watch me!" I yelled to my cousins and brother as I stood contemplating the limb. Feeling like an acrobat on the tightrope at the circus, I stepped carefully, one foot in front of the other, without pause, all the way across the ten feet to the other side, the first one to think of trying such a daredevil act.

There's a yellowed photograph of me from those days. It's shot from the ground, looking up from an angle. I'm out on the limb, all alone, and I'm smiling.

Though both sides of my family arrived in Mississippi in the early 1800s, to my recollection I never heard anyone from either family ever refer to the Civil War as The War Between the States. There were never stories told longingly of the glory days before The War. In fact, no one seemed to dwell in the past, where so many Southerners reside.

Oh, I heard them talking about how we could trace our family all the way back to the Revolutionary War, which to them must have seemed far enough, though it never made a deep impression. It's just the way things were.

Each of my parents came from families of different temperaments. To generalize wildly, the Hogans were outgoing and voluble, while the Kings were more reserved and self-contained. I, as a combination of the two, reflecting them both, sometimes feel as though I have a split personality.

I have two distinct sides: a time for solitude is as necessary for me to survive, to recharge, as food and water; but at the same time, I need the energy and stimulation of interaction with other people. Aren't all families like that, though? Each person a bunch of chromosomes sprouting from new cuttings of branches from every family tree back to the beginning, even *before* the Revolution?

In its own way each family was warm and loving and generous. My father's only sibling, his sister Frances Allen—called Sissy—who was eight years younger than he, often reminds me that my arrival as the first King grandchild was a moment of great rejoicing, and that there never was a child more loved and adored or doted over than I was.

My grandmother King, Miss Corinne, born a Greer in Shuqualak, in the eastern part of the state not far from Macon, was a woman of sweetness and gumption, who commanded great respect. And from her pictures, she was a woman of genteel loveliness. Sissy recalls few details of her mother's life, though remembers that Corinne and her sister Markey went to live with their older sister in Meridian after their parents died. And after Markey moved to Hattiesburg, where she got a job tinting photographs, Corinne joined her there, where she also found a job, and my grandfather as well.

Sissy recently referred to my great-aunt Markey, who twice married rich older widowers, as "an old man's darling." And it was Markey, or Auntie, as she was called, who showered me in my early years with smocked silk dresses (when I was a teenager complaining about not being able to buy a new dress, Mama told me it was too bad I had been too young to appreciate elegant silk dresses when I was a little girl, since I'd never had anything so fine since) and who paid for Daddy to go up North to Cornell University.

Corinne Street in Hattiesburg was named for my grandmother, a transitory memento of a woman lost to time. I'm sure the residents of that street today have never given so much as a fleeting thought as to how the street came to be named, or have ever even been curious about who in the world Corinne was, or even if it were named for an actual person.

Grandmother King was mostly bedridden by the time I was born and died when I was six. I never knew what was wrong with her, but whenever I would go in to see her I was always uncomfortable because she would cry when she hugged me—a trait I would inherit—and I am filled with such compassion for her now, understanding how she must have felt when she took her first grandchild in her arms.

Her bedroom was downstairs, where she spent most of her days in bed. Granddaddy slept on a feather bed in her room, and though I'm sure it would horrify child psychologists today, one of the great joys of visiting them when I was four or five was burrowing down into all that softness in the feather bed with Granddaddy, who wore a nightcap to keep his bald head warm.

Earl Breckinridge King, my grandfather, was in the insurance business, which he had started from scratch after the lumber mill he owned had burned to the ground. He was considered to be a man of the highest integrity when, instead of going into bankruptcy after he lost everything, he paid off all of his debts, even though it took many years. By the time I was born, they had turned their 1908 Bay Street Victorian-style home into a boarding house, with boarders in the three bedrooms on the second floor and a housekeeper in the small turret room on the third (the memory of this as I write conjures up the smell of the red Lifebuoy soap found in the single "unisex" bathroom on the second floor). Chickens scratched in the dirt in the backyard in a coop under the pecan tree, where at a tender age I was an inadvertent witness to my first sight of the act of wringing a chicken's neck, causing me to flee in terror.

After accepting a job in Hattiesburg, Granddaddy arrived in Mississippi sometime around the turn of the century from Glasgow Junction, Kentucky, where he had grown up on the family tobacco farm before attending a business college. Daddy was named after his grandfather, John Breckinridge King. In the eighth grade in American history when I read about Vice President John C. Breckinridge from Kentucky, I bragged to everybody I was kin to him, but to this day I have no idea if I really am.

I remember Daddy crying only two times in my life. The first time, soon after he'd come back from the war, he was sitting on the sofa in our living room in Jackson, tears streaming down his cheeks, after he'd gotten a long distance telephone call that Granddaddy had died of a heart attack. It scared me, and I didn't know what to do. And the second time was as father of the bride, as he was walking me down the aisle to give me away to a Yankee husband. That scared me, too.

Daddy graduated from high school when he was fifteen, the day before his sixteenth birthday, so he started to college at Mississippi A & M in Starkville when he was only sixteen. He graduated at the top of his class, in engineering. Then he went off to Cornell University in Ithaca, New York, to go to graduate school, but came home after only a few months because he was in love with my mother. I've always been curious about that, but I never found out the details beyond the fact that he said it was cold up there and he missed Mama. There's a lot I would have found out more about if Daddy hadn't died before we had a chance to talk about things like that. But we didn't have time.

Three

The first time I crossed the state line to leave Mississippi was to go to Louisiana. My brother and I, at age six and eight, were ecstatic over the prospect of driving with Mama to Alexandria, close by where Daddy was stationed at Fort Polk, to tell him good-bye for the last time before he left to go overseas. The import of the reason of the journey was lost in the fact of the journey itself. The adventure of it all! And we were to stay in a hotel!

Up until that time I had never been farther than either of my grandparents' houses almost equidistant from Jackson: the Piney Woods in the south, the rolling hills in the northeast. And now to go to another state and cross the Mississippi River over the huge high bridge at Vicksburg! I was beside myself and couldn't sleep for the excitement. "Journey proud," Mama called it.

Geography was one of my favorite subjects, reading about all those far away places with strange sounding names, impossible to even dream that I might ever actually see them, a longing that I was not able to recognize. I knew all of the states and capitals and sent away for brochures with coupons out of *National Geographic* and other magazines. I couldn't imagine what a mountain could possibly really look like, and was transported by pictures of Pike's Peak and Glacier Lake and the Grand Tetons and Old Faithful. I just couldn't conceive of the wonder of it all.

To us the trip took forever. Gas and tire rationing were by now a way of life, and we couldn't drive over the 35-miles-an-hour speed limit. I don't know if Mama had to save up her gas and tire ration stamps for the trip, but she was praying we wouldn't have a flat. And all along the way we passed convoys of army trucks.

But the real event came when we reached the bridge over the Mississippi at Vicksburg. As we drove across the river, Mama broke into a rousing rendition of "Mississippi Mud"—keeping time with her foot on the gas pedal so the car "danced," and taking her hands off the wheel to clap when she came to the line about "clapping their hands"—blithely scaring us to death out in the middle of the bridge.

What a disappointment! It wasn't at all the "mighty Mississippi" that I'd been led to expect by story and song. It didn't look much bigger than the ol' Pearl River back in Jackson. But the bridge was so far above it my stomach felt the way it did when I rode the Ferris wheel at the fair as we peered down at the roiling muddy water below. The sign that greeted us at the end of the bridge, "Welcome to Louisiana," elated me. And I noticed the highway markers now read "Louisiana" as well. My first venture onto foreign soil.

I've never returned to Alexandria, and it's just as well because it could never live up to the exalted place my memory bestows upon it. Through the scrim of time I actually only remember grayness, the weather as well as the town—it must have been winter—the soldiers and the trucks and the hotel itself.

After riding in wonderment in an elevator to our floor, my brother and I were at first uneasy to discover we would be separated from Mama in a room by ourselves. We had a room next to, but not adjoining the room our parents would occupy when my father arrived.

Daddy didn't get in until after we'd gone to bed. When he awakened us in our beds before dawn the next morning to tell us good-bye, it was strange to discover him in his uniform, which we'd never seen before. He'd brought for us two engineer's insignia like the ones he wore on his uniform, which he pinned on our pajamas, and after a hug and a kiss, we got up and followed him to the door where Mama waited. One vivid memory remains: my brother and me standing in the doorway of our room watching Daddy, suddenly a soldier in uniform, kiss Mama good-bye at their door, and turning and walking off down the hall with Mama watching him turn the corner out of sight.

Louisiana would remain solitary on my list of "States That I Have Visited" for three more years. But you have to start somewhere.

∾

After the war, for those of us whose lives hadn't been too disrupted or uprooted, life remained relatively seamless. As a child of twelve I was unaware of the historic social and economic upheavals the end of the war had wrought. The biggest change for me was that my father and other fathers came home, rationing ended, and it was on to junior high.

Just as those who had gone to war had tasted a new life beyond their formerly narrow world, so had I on a much different level. While my father was overseas, we rented our house and moved to Starkville. Until then my brother and I had been at Liberty Grove, a county school, spanning grades one through twelve (there was no public kindergarten), for (white) children from all over that part of Hinds County. Some were hardscrabble farm children from deep in the country—children with "cooties" who couldn't come back to school until they were examined by Miss Harris, the Public Health Nurse. After my brother was allowed to start first grade at the age of five (for the simple reason that he was the only one in the neighborhood who wasn't in school), he joined me and the other neighborhood children on the county school bus—smelling in the morning of the baloney sandwich lunches carried in brown paper sacks—which picked us up and brought us home.

In moving to Starkville, and to a different school, I was introduced to a new world. When I left Jackson, I was in the fourth grade. When I returned, I was in the sixth. It was hardly a case of How you gonna keep 'em down on the farm?—Starkville, Mississippi, certainly wasn't Paree—and most people would be hard put to find any difference between a county school in Jackson and the public school of Starkville. But I had seen another world, and when we moved back to Jackson, I wanted no more of Liberty Grove.

Right after I was born in the Baptist Hospital, I was taken home to the little apartment my parents rented in Judge Lyell's home on Bellevue Place; and before we built our house on Meadowbrook, we lived in an apartment on North Street. I'd had a lot of playmates down there, children of the friends of my mother and daddy. But because we went to different schools after we moved to Meadowbrook, I seldom saw those early friends. Then the war came and some of those families left town to live where the fathers were stationed. Now they were back, and everybody was starting seventh grade at the beautiful new junior high school in town. And I decided I wanted to go there too.

When I told my mother, the go-between, what I wanted to do, she said she didn't know if we could afford it, and that I'd have to ask Daddy. He found out it would cost ten dollars a month tuition for me to change schools. A lot of money. But when he said he would do it, I felt like I'd been tapped on the head by a fairy godmother.

∼

I was all alone. I can still see that wide white sidewalk—long and straight as a highway—when I got out of the car after kissing Daddy good-bye. (I could only imagine later, when I was a parent, how Daddy must have felt, his heart so full, watching me from his rear view mirror as he drove off, probably calling Mama when he got to his office.)

In my morning-glory blue pinafore with tiny white polka dots and white drawstring blouse I'd chosen specially for the first day of school, my fine new notebook clutched under my arm, I walked what must have been a mile before reaching the towering front steps of Bailey Junior High School. Never looking back, I carefully climbed the tiers and tiers of granite steps, the huge entrance looming before me. As I pushed against the door into the maelstrom of unknown students, it reminded me of the first time I jumped off the high diving board.

After school I had to take the Number Two city bus to the end of the line, and walk more than a mile to our house. But I didn't care. I was going to Bailey.

∼

There was one thing that Daddy did that drove me up the wall. If he told us once, he told us a million times how as a boy he had to ride the two miles to school every day on his bicycle, rain or shine.

And home to lunch and back to boot. Or how he remembered when bacon was only fifteen cents a pound. When I did the same thing to my children, I heard the echo and knew exactly how they felt.

I think the bicycle experience somehow stuck with Daddy as an important Lesson of Life, a lesson in self-reliance, one that he needed to pass on to his children.

For my thirteenth birthday I received at long last the object of my longing, a shiningly beautiful blue bike. I remember it being in the fall (I can still smell the crisp air of fallen leaves) that a problem developed with my bike, and Daddy had to take it down town with him in our car to have it fixed. As I was helping him get the bike in the car—we had an old prewar 1941 Ford at the time, and it wasn't easy—he told me that when it was ready I was going to have to ride it home.

"From down town? I can't ride my bike from down town!"

"'Course you can. It's not that far," Daddy replied as he shot out of the driveway.

I had no idea how far it was in miles, but it might as well have been the moon. *Nobody* would think of riding a bicycle that far. Certainly nobody I knew. I just was not going to do it.

Now I know that I'm willful—Mama called me "bullheaded"—but I come by it naturally. From my daddy, who got it from his mother, Miss Corinne (and from other branches of my family tree as well, as it now turns out). So the return of the bicycle became a battleground, albeit silent. As usual, Mama was caught in the middle. I would throw myself on the sofa and sigh and moan about how mean Daddy was to make me ride so far. Nobody else's daddy would make his daughter do such a hateful thing! What if I get hit by a bus! What if I have a flat! What if I'm kidnapped! What if I fall! What if it rains! My imagination for disasters knew no bounds.

Mama told me if I didn't hush I was going to drive her nuts, that I should save my melodramatics for Daddy. I never said another word about it to Daddy, though, hoping he'd change his mind and give in. I just lay low, keeping out of his way, hoping Mama would try to change his mind, knowing how soft-hearted she was. (This episode reminds me that our generation of females dealt with "confrontation" in the time-honored way—and still does—and that the then unheard of term "conflict resolution" was an oxymoron. When I recently asked my husband how his family resolved conflict when he was young, he said, "It was easy. There was never any conflict, because if my father said to do something, that's what we did.")

To no avail. One night Daddy announced at supper that my bike was ready and I could go get it any time I wanted.

"Go *get* it! How am I going to go *get* it?"

"On the bus after school. It's just a block from Capitol Street."

"I'm not going to do it."

"Well, your bike's not going to ride itself home. If you want it, you're going to have to go get it."

For days I fumed and sulked and skulked. Finally, accepting the inevitable, I decided to get it over with. The next morning at breakfast I asked Daddy if he would call the repair shop and tell them I would be there after school to pick up my bike. He tried not to look surprised as he lowered his morning paper to look at me, said he'd be happy to call them, and then proceeded to help me work out the best route home, away from the most heavily trafficked streets. When he dropped me off at school he told me not to forget to call Mama to let her know when I was leaving the bicycle shop.

The man at the bike place couldn't have been sweeter.

"Your bike's good as new and ready to go. You sure are a brave girl to ride home all by yourself," he greeted me.

"Yessir. It'll be fun," I lied. "Can I please use your phone to call my mother so she'll know to be looking out for me?"

"Right over there, sugar."

After I hung up, I got my books and put them in the basket on the front of the bicycle and walked it out the door onto the sidewalk. All day long I'd been dreading this moment, and now the time had come to get on that bike. There was no way out.

Off I went, sailing by places I'd never been able to see so clearly from the window of a car or bus. Past Smith Park, and my church, Galloway Methodist, the New Capitol, and down the hill past Greenwood Cemetery. On out West Street, up the long hill past Millsaps College at the top, zooming along downhill, free as a bird on the wing. I was exhilarated! There was nothing to it! Across

Woodrow Wilson. The scent of burning leaves as I passed the small houses along the way, boys playing football in a yard, then out North State to Meadowbrook and E.B.'s Drive-In on the corner, the aroma of barbecue and hickory smoke filling the air. I'm almost home! Past Jackie Pierce's and James Trawick's, just up the hill I can see the Culleys' fence!

As I come into sight, Mama and my brother and all the boys in the neighborhood who've been watching for me let out a cheer and rush out to meet me and almost knock me off my bike.

Hail the conquering hero home from the wars!

∞

My father was not a sophisticated man, though he was elegant in his own unpretentious way. However, after returning from the war, when he was in England, France, and the Philippines—I believe he was the only father in our crowd to go overseas—he had been exposed to the wider world and, I believe, hoped that someday my brother and I would be able to experience more than what Mississippi had to offer, not that he ever told me that, of course.

Occasionally Broadway touring companies would come to town to play at the Jackson Municipal Auditorium, though I had never seen one. When I was in the eighth grade I was unprepared for an extraordinary occurrence: Daddy's invitation to go with him to see the musical *Oklahoma!*, and to invite one of my friends to go with us. It wasn't that he wasn't kind or thoughtful, but I had never heard of him exhibiting the first sign of interest in music of any kind, except when Mama played the piano. Unless Mama had mentioned it to him, I'm sure he had no idea that I knew by heart the words to all the songs in *Oklahoma!*, after my cousins and I had spent a whole summer at Grandmama's listening to my aunt Missy's *Oklahoma!* records.

Reflecting on it, I've wondered if he and Mama, after putting their heads together, decided he needed to do something with me, just the two of us, since he spent time with my brother doing boy things. No matter. For whatever reason he did it, that evening, the evening that Daddy escorted my friend Catherine Lotterhos and me to my first Broadway play, was a momentous event of my life.

∞

Though he was not inclined toward leading a life in "society," Daddy wasn't in the least antisocial. He was simply secure in who he was; he never bragged or put on airs. His friendships were quiet, deep, long-standing. He had been handsome as a young man, and still was. And he was awfully smart.

"He's a civil engineer," a distinction I would always make whenever I was asked what my father did, the fear of the snobbishly insecure that someone might think he drove a train. Since the first grade, all the way through college, for sixteen years I had carefully filled in the blank "father's occupation" with the two words: "civil engineer." Never just "engineer." And it was years before I learned that engineers were inclined to have particular personality traits, as in, "Isn't that just like an engineer . . ." would think? or act? or be? And come to think of it, he fit the profile pretty well. He tended to taciturnity, or more precisely, he was not loquacious; he was great at numbers; he had a self-deprecating, low-keyed sense of humor; he seldom showed his emotions; he was reserved and dignified, not what you'd call a people person; a man of his times.

He liked girls who were "ladylike" and "refined"—what else? Even when I was twenty-two (working, but living at home after I'd graduated from college), I was taken by surprise and embarrassed when he put his foot down when I told him I was going to be in a Radio City Music Hall Rockett-like chorus line with some other girls to raise money for a perfectly respectable men's organization, like the YMCA. "No you're not," he said. "It wouldn't be ladylike." And that was that, since all through my life, one of Daddy's most frequent admonitions to me had been, "And don't dispute my word."

∾

By high school, what was valued above all else was being "popular," by definition popular with boys, with being "cute" topping the list of qualities necessary to achieve that elevated status. Beauty queens, Miss America being the ultimate (Mississippi, I believe, once produced two in successive years), were our role models. Cuteness constituted a combination of looks, sex appeal, friendliness, flirtyness—in essence, nothing about it had anything to do with brains. In those instances when girls with brains filled the cute bill as well, they were smart enough to play down the brainy part.

A senior girl's secret dream at Central High School was to be chosen by the boys in the ROTC to be one of their four Company Sponsors, with the ultimate honor being selected Battalion Sponsor. It couldn't be touched by anything else: not Miss Central High, not Most Beautiful, not even being a cheerleader, and certainly not Most Intellectual. It was the zenith for a girl at Central. Every Friday the ROTC came to school in uniform, with the five sponsors sticking out in the halls and classrooms like American Beauty roses in a patch of roadside weeds. Seeing them in their uniform—below-the-calf pleated wool gabardine skirt the color of cream, khaki Eisenhower jacket, white shirt and black tie, topped off with an officer's hat complete with bill—every other girl was consumed with longing, coveting even their white orthopedic oxfords, a sacrifice any girl would have cheerfully given her life for.

Popularity among girls was in another realm, where completely different qualities were prized: sense of humor, trust, kindness, reliability, generosity, thoughtfulness, even intelligence.

Our crowd of eight had started out at Bailey together, flown up from Brownies to Girl Scouts, gone to summer church camp, taken dancing lessons, passed our driving tests—all the rites of passage. We overlapped the cute crowd, with whom we were good friends and with whom we participated in larger scale events. When we were left without dates for the football games, our mothers would tell us: "Don't worry, your time will come." And we'd wail, "But WHEN?"

My time has finally come. I just never realized it would take a lifetime.

∽

In reality most people don't keep up with the friends they grew up with, and once they leave the place they were born, or even if they don't, taking different paths and pursuing different interests, they grow out of touch.

Not so with our crowd of eight girls, with one exception all born in the Baptist Hospital in Jackson in 1934. Out of those eight, there's only one with whom we have no contact, who after she left Mississippi deliberately cut all ties to us. And as I write this, it's the first time I've realized that it was she who was born elsewhere, albeit the South. Is there a connection? Each of us at various times in our lives tried to see her, to call her, to write to her, but after being rebuffed at every turn the light finally dawned. One must really be determined to deter someone hell-bent on devout friendship, and she must have breathed a sigh of relief when we finally got the message that she wanted nothing more to do with either us or her past life. At first we were hurt, then sad, and finally let it go. Ironically, she's worked in Washington for over thirty years on Capitol Hill for a Republican senator.

The rest of us—Catherine, Charlotte, Kathryn, Nancy, Shelby, and Worth—are as close as sisters and through almost all of our years on this earth have grieved and laughed together and loved and supported each other as each of us has been both assailed and blessed by life.

Of us all, I'm the one who's lost most of my Southernness, but then I'm the one who left. It took me more than twenty years to kick over the traces of the ladylike Southern-wife life of sacrifice, the Junior League, staying pretty and sweet and kissing men's feet. I'm not saying that I'm right and they're wrong. I'm just saying I can't do it.

In a way I hate it that I've lost the graciousness, the gentility, the hospitality, the loveliness of the ladies I left behind, and many times over the years I've been asked how I happened to leave Mississippi. For the longest time the answer was always that I left because I had a job.

Because it took me a long time to understand why.

∽

Though certainly never a Simon Legree when it came to having fun or a good time, Daddy was a true believer in the value of work over indolence. When we got to be teenagers he believed that both my brother and I should be able to help supplement our allowances if we needed extras.

So in junior high, my brother took up that time-honored occupation of boyhood: the paper route. Of course, as with a family and its dog, the unspoken understanding of everyone involved with a boy and his paper route was that it's not the boy who has the paper route, it's his mother. The only job available to me as a girl was that other time-honored occupation: baby-sitting, which I hated equally as much as my brother hated being a paper boy.

As the final days of high school dwindled to a precious few, sometime during those spring weeks of endless senior parties, teas, and dances leading up to graduation, Daddy mentioned to me that it was time to get down to thinking about a real job during the summer to help pay for incidental expenses when I began college the next fall. Far too preoccupied with the festivities of a graduate's life, his words went in one ear and out the other.

A seismic change, which transformed our lives, had occurred in our family when I was fifteen. To my complete mortification, my mother had given birth at the age of forty-one to twin girls, which today doesn't seem old to be having a baby, but at that time, it was *old*. As well as an openly public display that she and Daddy still *did* it! By the time of my graduation three years later, however, they were beloved and cherished additions to our family and adorable toys to my friends. You can imagine, though, how Daddy's financial picture changed with the advent of two new mouths and the cost of two college educations looming on his immediate horizon.

It was a week or so before graduation. Daddy was driving me to a party and asked if I'd given any thought to what I was going to do about a job after graduation. Of course I said no. Then, in the most serious discussion we'd ever had, he asked if I really felt that I needed to go to college. I could feel my skin begin to prickle from my scalp to my toes as he continued this disturbing conversation. He said he wasn't sure he could swing two college educations at the same time, and that since I had taken typing and shorthand in high school (he'd insisted on that), I would be able to get a job without going to college. That if he had to make a choice, he felt it was my brother who should go, since I would probably be getting married in a few years anyhow.

I couldn't breathe. I couldn't speak. Then, when I did, it was with complete self-centeredness.

"What do you mean, not go to college? I can't *imagine* not going to college? What in the world would I *do*? *I'm* the one who's made almost straight A's all my life. Isn't there some way we can *both* go?"

I'd always made good grades, and without too much effort. At the last assembly at the end of ninth grade, I couldn't believe my ears when they called my name out to stand up and be recognized as one of the ten students with the highest grades through our three years at Bailey. Daddy beamed when there was even an article about it in the *Jackson Daily News*. It was the only time I was ever to receive so much attention for being smart, though in my early grade school years I would get a quarter from Daddy for every A I made.

Since a girl being smart was not valued by the larger world, and with no understanding of my own intelligence, I never even thought about it as being important, or even necessarily a good thing. In fact I didn't think about it at all, though I was always curious, loving school and learning new things.

If Daddy was using shock therapy, it worked.

"Why don't we give it a try, and see how things are next year, when your brother will be graduating? If you can get a good job this summer, and get a part-time job at MSCW, maybe we can work it out."

He continued, "Have you ever even thought about what kind of job you'd want after you graduate from college? Which courses have you enjoyed most?"

"I've liked everything, but if I had to choose one, I think I've loved English most of all."

"What kind of job do you think you can get if you major in English?"

"I guess working for a newspaper, or advertising, something like that, where you use words. I'm really not sure."

"I don't know the people at the newspaper well enough, but I know somebody who owns an advertising agency. Would you like for me to call him and see if they hire anybody for the summer?"

"Yessir, that would be real nice, Daddy. Thank you."

And that was how I landed my first job, setting me on the path that would change the course of my life.

Part One - Mississippi   37

It was the summer of 1952. General Eisenhower and Adlai Stevenson were nominated for President, and Nat King Cole singing "Unforgettable" was number one on the Hit Parade.

∽

Without recognizing it at the time, of course, I received an important lesson that first summer with Dixie Advertisers.

The agency was owned by a husband and wife team, Genie and George Godwin, and I worked for Mrs. Godwin. Apart from the main creative offices, in a small separate building peopled only by women and thereby earning the sobriquet "Genie's Girls" (and much worse from the boys on the creative side), she ruled over accounting, bookkeeping, and billing. No matter who you were, from account executive down to the porter—even, perhaps, and especially, Mr. Godwin—when Genie spoke, people listened. Or quaked, depending on one's constitution. And at the age of eighteen, I was petrified.

My job for those three summer months was to type the name and date of a newspaper clipping on a little form and paste it to the clipping. Also to pull the "tear sheet," the page in the newspaper on which an ad had run, providing proof for the client. In addition our office was in charge of typing the orders and the shipping of mats and plates for the ads to the newspapers.

That was the Stone Age, even before copy machines, when we used carbon paper in our typewriter to make copies, a page of carbon paper over a sheet of onion skin paper for each copy you needed, which meant you had to erase all those copies whenever you made a mistake, a job I seemed to spend more time at than typing. If we needed a lot of copies, we typed stencils to be run off on the mimeograph machine. It was cheaper, though, to use the ditto, a process in which you used a form filled with quivery purple gelatin that produced copies in purple ink. Can you imagine what it was like not to be able to make a copy of *anything*—a clipping, or an article in a magazine, or pages from a book, even a photograph? We had to send all of that out to a blueprint company to be Photostatted. I'm not sure that it wasn't a blessing in a way. You only got copies when it was necessary, not the mountains of irrelevant paper you get today.

The exception to all these duties were the two hair-raising weeks when Mrs. Godwin's secretary was on vacation, and I filled in for her.

During those two weeks I'm sure there was an up-tick in the cost of Dixie Advertisers stationery. I messed up so many letters and memos on bond and onion skin, and was so panicky that Mrs. Godwin would see how inept I was, that I stuffed the reams of paper I'd ruined into my purse so that the evidence of my incompetence wouldn't be discovered in the waste paper basket.

I'm sure Mrs. Godwin was as undone as I was in her deprivation of having to cope with such inexperience, but she was magnificent. She held me to a level of perfection and professionalism that has influenced me to this day. She was kind but firm, demanding but patient. She was slim and trim, wore the best-looking, most elegant clothes I'd ever seen, and had not a hair out of place. I'd never before known a "working woman" who was the boss. I was in awe, in fact, intimidated.

I loved working there, the esprit de corps. I loved Mrs. Godwin and all the women, which included a party-loving divorcee who was frequently unreliable, sailing in sometimes close to noon, regaling us with tales of her nocturnal escapades (but who they put up with because she could type like the wind); a grandmotherly widow, who quietly but firmly kept everything and everybody on track; a girl four years older than I, Mrs. Godwin's secretary, who became a good friend; another divorcee with twinkly blue eyes who dyed her hair an iridescent carrot red; and Walter, the good-natured and knowing colored porter, who shuttled between the two offices.

On my last day of work before I left to go off to college, Mrs. Godwin called me into her office. One of the things I admired about Mrs. Godwin was that she didn't beat around the bush, and after she asked me to sit down, which made me kind of nervous, she said she wanted to tell me what a good job I'd done and how much they enjoyed having me work there. And then, to my surprise, because I hadn't thought about it before, she said since having me there to fill in for people on vacation had worked out so well, she hoped they could count on my coming back the next summer, and wished me good luck in my freshman year. Overjoyed but caught off guard by such unexpected praise from this woman I admired so much, I thanked her awkwardly and said I would love to come back.

It was the first time I'd ever had any recognition, apart from school or family, for a job well done. And it felt mighty good.

Four

If you lived in Mississippi and went to college, you went to college in Mississippi, except for the enlightened few, who, if they were able, sent their children out of state. In those days of "college boards"—before SATs—unless you were applying to the most prestigious schools, schools that I was essentially unacquainted with, being accepted didn't amount to much more than applying.

When the time for me to leave for MSCW was imminent, Mama, who had been to a women's college, proffered this advice: To get along in life you need to be able to get along with other girls, to have good women friends. If you can't get along with girls, you'll never be able to get along with men, either. And so with that seed sown, I arrived at the W.

And, oh, how I loved it! Even with curfews and rules that today seem positively Victorian. Which they were. MSCW is in Columbus, where Tennessee Williams was born. Does that tell you something? In every small town, especially in the South, particularly in Mississippi, legendary stories abound. But the fantastical Gothic tales of the goin's on of Columbus topped any I'd ever heard. I think Tennessee was about three when he moved away, but by then he had already been tainted. It was in the water.

Rooming with Shelby Thompson, one of my oldest Jackson friends, across the hall from Shirley Brown, another old friend I'd known since the first grade at Liberty Grove, we lived in the oldest dormitory on campus in what today could only generously be described as a cubicle. (Since this was the nation's oldest state-supported women's college, you need to understand that ours was a *really* old dormitory.)

To formal dances in those days we wore net evening dresses over hoop skirts, which we had to cram along with all our other belongings into only two narrow closets or under the bed. There was a communal bathroom down the hall; no telephone; no TV (there *was* no TV)—an existence that today almost compares with Prince Charles's days at that Spartan Scottish school where he was so deprived. And we thought it was all perfectly splendid!

It didn't take long to settle into the routine of dormitory and college life. And if I have one memory above all else of that first year, it is laughter. We were so silly and had so much fun we would ache, bent over, and wet our pants from laughing so hard. This is not to say that there weren't hard patches, petty disputes, blue funks, the usual intrusions of dormitory life. With one of the biggest intrusions being our studies. It was just real hard to find time to work them in.

Nobody had prepared me for the fact that college was not simply a continuation of high school. Where high school had always been easy for me, college was more of a challenge than I had any idea it would be. I now had to work harder, though not with my nose constantly to the grindstone. And even though girls and boys both got the same education, the saying was that girls went to college to get an M.R.S. degree, since their education didn't prepare them for anything else. Though if you were a man, you could always get a job, just by virtue of going to college.

As a freshman I had only one other elective after choosing French for my language, and, poised to make my second selection, Daddy cut in to save me from myself by telling me, "You can take all the French and English you want, but if you want me to pay your tuition, then the one thing you have to take is typing and shorthand so you'll be able to support yourself when you graduate." And that being that, ended the discussion before my ifs, ands, and buts could spill out to dispute his word.

However, on one level it was exactly like high school. So much of our life still revolved around whether or not we had a date for the weekend football game and the dance afterwards over at Mississippi State, twenty miles away. Popularity with boys, even in a girls' school, was still the ultimate state of grace. There was even the Old Maid's Gate, which you walked through backwards to keep from ending up as an old maid.

Since I knew a lot of people from Starkville, I didn't go too many football weekends without a date, either with someone I knew or a blind date with a friend of a friend. And I hated it. Others may have, too, but they had to go along with it, just as I did, since not to love it would make people think there was something wrong with you.

The weekends were one big party, centered on the football game. Because I had a grandmother in Starkville, I had a place to stay and was always free to take anybody I wanted—there was many a pallet on the floor during those freshman weekends. So whoever was staying at Grandmama's would go by and drop off her suitcase, all gussied up fit to kill in her "game" outfit and high heels, and sometimes, if she was lucky, with a corsage of a single chrysanthemum as big as a cauliflower pinned to her suit. From there it was on to a fraternity house—where there was an unending open house—to check out who was there, to see and be seen, peck at a little food, then on to the game. All of this in swirling mobs of people.

Through a coalition of the Baptists and the bootleggers, Mississippi remained a dry state until the 1960s, when it became the last state in the union to legalize the sale of alcohol. "Legalize" is the key word here. The wondrous thing about Mississippi was that with the sale of alcohol being illegal, you could send any four-year old child to the bootlegger to buy your whiskey, and nobody would think anything about it. Some of the parents of my friends even had their booze delivered to their houses on a regular basis by their personal bootlegger. The state legislature went so far as to pass a "black market tax" on the sale of illegal whiskey, which always led to a spirited race for the office of State Tax Collector, who was able to take home about $100,000 a year, after taxes, as it were.

What I'm getting at is that on these college weekends the alcohol flowed like water, though a strict protocol of keeping the bottle out of sight in public places (a brown paper sack constituted camouflage) was observed to maintain the hypocrisy. And it was a "shipping" offense for an MSCW girl to drink if she had not formally

Part One - Mississippi

checked out not just to leave campus but to leave town.

It took a long time, actually, before the reality of the fact that I hated this whole scene began to seep into my consciousness, for wasn't this the way college was supposed to be, what it was all about? So why wasn't it fun? Why wasn't I having a good time? There must be something wrong with me. But then the game was over, and it was back to the fraternity house for more crowds and booze, then home to Grandmama's to change for the dance.

It was the dance that I really looked forward to because I loved to dance. And when Ray Anthony's band broke into "One Mint Julep," or the Red Tops, the colored Dixieland band from the Delta—the most popular and in-demand band in the state—let go with "Lawdy, Lawdy, Miss Claudie," winding up with "When the Saints Go Marchin' In," everybody just cut loose, rocking to the Memphis Shuffle like crazy, transported.

Sometimes I'd get "stuck"—when nobody broke in and you were with the same partner for more than two or three dances—and I'd cast my eye around for someone I knew to come and rescue me. Charles Slade McElroy, called Charles Slade until he got sophistication and became "Pap" in high school, and his older brother, Buddy, who all the girls swooned over because of his blue "bedroom eyes," grew up across the street from Grandmama, and I'd known them practically all my life. So when I got to MSCW I counted on Pap (Buddy by then was in the army) to dance with me when I came over to State for the dances. But by then he was a Big Man on Campus with more glamorous fish to fry than the girl across the street. He'd give me a dutiful whirl, I'll give him that—he had *good manners*, after all—and then he was off to dance the evening away with his choice of a bevy of beautiful belles, avoiding my eye, pretending he didn't see my plea to bail me out.

The last time Grandmama and I had a real conversation before she died, she told me that Charles Slade had been to visit her and told her to be sure and tell me hello. "I sure did always love Claire, Miss Mamie," she was pleased to quote him as saying.

"Grandmama, if that's not the biggest tale I ever heard." (Even at that late date, I wouldn't use the word "lie" in front of Grandmama, since from childhood I'd been taught that it was a "bad word.") "If he loved me so much, why didn't he dance with me at all those dances when I needed him to cut in and save me?"

After the dance, it was back to Grandmama's to change into something comfortable for the dreaded Blanket Party, when everybody converged on an open field where there was a bonfire and more booze. Each couple had its own blanket, to which they repaired, the more amorous couples choosing a spot the farthest away from the light of the fire. I can't describe how much I despised this obligatory ritual with its implicit promise of much more than toasting marshmallows, no matter who you were with, whether you hated or loved him, or even just liked him as a friend. Needless to say, since I was never with anybody I loved, I tried to stick as close to the fire as possible, an atavistic act of self-protection.

Finally the fire burned down and I was returned to Grandmama's, where, worn out from the strain, I fell into my bed. Another great college weekend behind me.

As part of Orientation every freshman was routinely tested in English and later grouped into English classes according to the test scores, though we weren't told that at the time we took the test.

On my first day in English class, I discovered that I was among those who had scored in the top one percent on the English exam and that in this class were the highest scorers. We were thus informed by the head of the English department, who was to be our professor, kind of a gnomish little man, small and rather elegant, who spoke with an accent (a foreign accent), which gave him an air of cultivation and erudition, except for the fact that he spoke it through pursed, wet lips. He was exotic for Mississippi, not like anybody I'd ever encountered before, and I was daunted. Not just by him, but by the other girls in the class. To tell the truth, this was the first time I'd ever been in a class where everyone was my equal, or better. The first time I'd ever really been challenged, and after twelve years it was a long time in coming.

As the freshman year was drawing to an end, my English professor announced that he would be in need of a secretarial assistant the following semester if any of us were interested. Thinking that working for him would be more interesting than the strictly clerical job

I'd had that first year, I waited to see him after class. When I told him I would like the job, that I could type and take shorthand, he seemed delighted and hired me on the spot. How propitious it all was.

By our sophomore year school had become more routine and we were now no longer the greenhorns. I was much more interested in my studies, and worked harder, though don't get me wrong, never was I a grind. I just took it all more seriously.

My world was beginning to open up. I was only dimly beginning to sense a conflict between the world I was living in, the way life was lived even right there at MSCW in a woman's world, the things that were most important—boys, dates, popularity, getting married—and the world of ideas I was beginning to explore, and where I fit in.

∞

After my mythology class on a gorgeous bright blue Friday afternoon in late September, it was like a summer day as I walked to the English professor's office to put in two hours of work. Because it was so hot I wore a sleeveless light blue cotton dress, trimmed with navy blue rickrack around the scoop neck and the bottom of the skirt, a dress I'd made myself. I remember the rickrack because I never got it completely straight. Funny how you remember the smallest details of some things so vividly.

The professor hadn't showed up when I arrived, but I had a key and let myself in and had begun typing his vocabulary list for the next week when in he walked, spirits high, step spry, "Miss King, Miss King, Miss King!" he sang out jauntily, obviously infused with the beauty of the day, as everybody had been. Matching his mood, "Doctor, Doctor, Doctor!" I lightheartedly acknowledged his greeting, and then paid no further attention to him as he puttered around his desk while I attended to typing my stencil.

Engrossed in my work, I was suddenly aware that he had shut the door and was standing behind my chair, watching me type. I immediately made an error and told him to go away, that he was making me nervous looking over my shoulder, and began correcting the mistake.

I can still feel his hands on the top of my bare shoulders, cool and smooth, but nervous fingers twitching slightly. I could smell him as well. I didn't know what was going on. I had no idea what to do. I began to type again, thinking, please Lord, let him go away. But he didn't go away. He remained standing there and began slowly moving his hands, his fingers all quivery, down my chest, until the tips of his fingers were just at the edge of my blue dress. My adrenaline was surging, my head spinning, and I held my breath, paralyzed. When I understood that this was not a dream, but the real thing, I shrugged my shoulders and brushed his hands away as though being annoyed by some insect.

Not a word was spoken as I took to the typewriter and he strolled nonchalantly back to his desk and sat down leisurely in his chair to look over some papers.

With my stomach in knots I raced to finish my work, gathered up my things, and acted as though nothing had happened. But as I told him good night and walked out the door I could not look him in the eye.

As the year wore on I was filled with vague feelings of discontent. Of being in limbo. Of waiting for something to happen, to change. And it never did. It was just more of the same, a treadmill.

I began looking at college catalogues with the wishful thinking that somehow I might be able to swing the tuition to an out-of-state college. I had begun to think about how much I loved to write and that maybe a degree in journalism was what I should be pursuing, and got a bee in my bonnet to go to the University of Kentucky. When I saw how exorbitant the out-of-state tuition was, I knew it was beyond anything we could afford, even with a real part-time job. I talked to Daddy anyway, and he said there was just no way he could do any more than he was doing. Though I was disappointed, I wasn't surprised.

Each time I went to my job in the English department, one place I should feel secure since it was what I loved most, I was overcome with anxiety, with dread and foreboding. I had decided to stick it out until the end of the semester and then try to find something else.

My relationship with the professor was just as though nothing had ever happened, though I resorted to long-sleeved, buttoned-to-the-neck shirts and jackets and avoided sweaters—especially Angora or cashmere—on the days that I worked. Weeks passed without incident. And my guard had dropped.

I hadn't thought about skirts.

In the fifties we wore straight skirts and when you sat down your knees showed. One warm day I had pulled my chair to the end of the professor's desk closer to the open window, placing me on the professor's side of the desk, facing him, without a barrier, as he dictated a letter. As he reached across the desk to pick up a paper to refer to, his chair rolled closer to mine. It made me uncomfortable, but I kept on taking notes as though I didn't notice. Then his hand was on my knee. I looked down and saw his hand was covering my whole kneecap, his fingers pressing into my flesh just above it.

It's so easy now to say, Why didn't you punch him in the mouth, scream, run, tell him to go to hell? But when you've been conditioned to be NICE, not to OFFEND anyone, especially a MAN who was my PROFESSOR, to be DEFERENTIAL, I was thrown for a complete loop.

I moved his hand, got up, and moved my chair to the other side of the desk, and we resumed the dictation as though nothing had happened.

Not long after that, it was discovered that my sophomore roommate Douglas Fox—a tall, elegant, dark-haired, doe-eyed Delta beauty—had tuberculosis. We were all devastated when we learned that she would have to leave school and go to the sanatorium in south Mississippi, which could be for months, even years.

With the addition of the pall cast by the plight of Douglas on top of my situation in the English department, I decided to ask Daddy if I could come home and go to Millsaps College in Jackson. I knew it would be easier financially with me living at home, and though I'd never really thought of Millsaps as anywhere I'd want to go—since I would have to live at home—some of my good friends were there and loved it.

I simply needed out.

Several years after I left the W, I heard that my English professor was asked to leave, after a girl far braver than all who preceded her blew the whistle. But because of my embarrassment and humiliation, even shame—that somehow what my professor had done had been my fault—I've never breathed a word about it until now.

∽

I was happy at Millsaps, a small Methodist liberal arts college. It was comfortable and low-key, and I had so much more freedom. I hadn't realized how oppressed I'd really been at MSCW until I was out. I felt like I'd been sprung from a convent. And living at home I was no longer bound by dormitory rules, though there were some antiquated rules regarding campus life: no drinking anywhere—period—and on campus there was even no *dancing*, which meant that all the dances had to be held somewhere else. Chapel was required twice a week. More than two cuts and there were dire consequences, though I forget now what they were.

Smaller than the W, with about a thousand students, Millsaps was like a big family. When you walked across campus, even the president (who had married a girl from Sherard whose family were neighbors of my Delta cousins) would call you by name when he said hello as he passed you on the sidewalk. Which had its good points as well as its bad. It was a real small town, with hardly any anonymity.

Nevertheless, attending a church school unquestionably grounded my education in a deeper experience for me. My sense of idealism was reinforced as well, and I'll always be grateful for that.

At mid-semester when I transferred, there was no rush season by sororities, since it was held only in the fall, and it seemed to be taken for granted anyway that I would become a Chi Omega since I was a "legacy," meaning that my aunts and cousins had been Chi Os, as were most of my close friends as well. I really never gave any thought to joining anything else, whenever I thought about it at all, and when they called to ask me if I wanted to join, I said yes.

It was because of my experience in the Chi Os and the Lockhearts social club I joined at the W that I realized that basically I don't like organizations for which you have to be approved to join (even though I realize the Senate has been called the most exclusive club in the world). I'm just not comfortable when it comes to sitting in judgment of others as to who is "acceptable" and who isn't.

For years after I left college, I was opposed to sororities and fraternities as snobbish and discriminatory, causing more pain and

Part One - Mississippi

harm than good, after seeing so many girls—boys too—scarred for life by not being found "acceptable" by those in what they considered the "right" sorority or fraternity. But as I've mellowed over the years, I suppose I've come to recognize that cliques, organized or informal, will be forever with us in some form or another, on or off campus, from the street gang to the sylvan gang in the Bohemian Grove, among both the young and the old. So I've just adopted the attitude of the French shrug . . .

⁂

In many ways I thrived at Millsaps. Majoring in English naturally expanded my world and whetted my appetite and curiosity for more. And there were new creative outlets from which I derived a great sense of satisfaction and camaraderie. The Millsaps Players, an exceptional college theater group that produced three or four plays a year under the direction of Lance Goss, became a crucial part of my life. I was immediately drawn to the people involved because they were the most fun, interesting, and "far out," everything being relative in terms of time and place, of course.

Years later I would compare a political campaign to putting on a play: Both are finite operations, with a fixed date, taking a dedicated crew of disparate groups working together in a close sense of esprit and commitment, all equally important and necessary to the whole. They both have their star, who can't look good or give a peak performance unless the script, the director, the scenery, the props, and the financing all mesh smoothly. There is the same sense of manic obsession with everybody working toward the same result: opening night and getting elected. And the letdown after it's over.

Another experience that enriched my life and expanded my world both literally and figuratively was becoming a member of the Millsaps Singers, a choral group that performed sacred music. I had to try out to get in, but after all my years of singing alto in church choirs, I was sufficiently prepared. I still count being a Singer under the direction of "Pop" King as one of the high privileges of my life.

In the spring of my junior year the Millsaps Singers, filling two Greyhound buses, embarked on a three-week tour, with Denver as our farthest destination. Since Pop had friends all over the country, we sang in Methodist churches across America from the Mississippi

River to the mountains of Colorado, in the cities and towns where his friends were, and stayed as guests in the homes of church members.

Our first stop after crossing the Mississippi River was in the big downtown church in Little Rock, Arkansas. From there we rolled on through the oil country of Oklahoma, to Hutchinson, Kansas, where Pop had Mennonite friends in whose church we sang and in whose homes we stayed. Our boys joked that the Mennonite girls who wore little white handkerchief-like things on their heads were virgins, and those who didn't, weren't. Isn't it wonderful what passed for humor?

The drive across the flat monotony of Kansas (neither the world's largest ball of twine nor the deepest hand-dug well now found there had yet been dreamed of) made me realize how excited the pioneers must have been when they first spotted the mountains of Colorado. And how crushed they must have been when they got over Pike's Peak and discovered they were still only half way to California, with yet another mountain range to cross. Until you drive it you have no idea how really gigantic America is. And I was pleased to notice I wasn't the only one open-mouthed over seeing my first mountain. Everybody was ga-ga. Two Greyhounds full of rubes, and just as proud to be there.

In Denver four of us stayed with a couple who were both Millsaps graduates and former Singers, the husband then an officer in the Air Force stationed at Lowry Air Force Base. They'd gotten all of us dates with debonair friends of theirs ("older men," two or three years older than we were), dashing in their uniforms, who took us to the Officers' Club for dinner and dancing. Quite a stretch from the sweet, pious Mennonites to *Springtime in the Rockies*.

From Denver we turned south to the verdant farm country of the beautiful San Luis Valley, where the same four of us stayed in the farmhouse of old friends of Pop's, among the most generous, decent people I've ever met. And after that came the shock of the white sand moonscape of New Mexico, about which I recorded in my diary, "No wonder they used this place to practice with the atom bomb."

∽

As I look back, I am astonished at how much I accomplished,

even making the Dean's List occasionally. Because among other things, I spent a *lot* of time playing bridge. (Those were the days when I said things like: "I'll never marry anybody who doesn't like to dance or play bridge.")

Today hardly anybody learns how to play bridge. Actually, hardly anybody learns to play cards of any kind. Probably because of TV.

I picked up bridge by osmosis, watching my parents and their friends. In high school our crowd played bridge all the time, with a lot of time on our hands on those football nights when we didn't have a date—there were always at least four of us available. By the time I got to college, if I was going out with a boy who liked to play bridge, we'd occasionally play with my parents. That must sound extraordinarily unusual to today's generation.

At Millsaps there was always a bridge game in the grill and we had our regulars who knew generally when everybody was going to be around. Many a time we'd have four hands dealt and waiting at the end of a class, and before you knew it, somebody was cutting a class to stay in the game, and many a time that person was me. It *is* an obsessive-compulsive game. One time the *Jackson Daily News* sent a photographer out to take our picture after my partner picked up a hand containing thirteen diamonds, and she momentarily became a celebrity.

Probably because some of my bridge partners were war veterans, the subject of bridge brings me to something that was common after World War II, and that picked back up again when I was in college: men returning from the Korean War who went to college on the GI Bill. Notice I said "men," when I've been calling my classmates "boys." Well, the returning soldiers *did* seem more like men to me. They were more serious, usually married, many with children, and they were older. And though I'd always had friends who were boys, this was the first time I experienced friendships with married men. There was just no occasion for single women to have platonic relationships with married men in those days. If women worked, their jobs were never as equals with men. But in college a married man was just another student, and some of them became good friends of mine.

In the middle of my senior year two of those friends were

named editor and business manager of the college paper. I hadn't heard about it until one day the business manager, whom I knew better, asked me to meet him after classes for a cup of coffee in the grill, that he had something he wanted to talk to me about. Well, I couldn't imagine what it could be, so formal and all, and was dying of curiosity. You could have knocked me over with a feather when he asked me if I would write a weekly column for the newspaper, to replace someone who had graduated. He said the editor had sent him as his emissary to try to persuade me to do it.

Intriguing as the idea was, I was already greatly overextended, though enormously flattered at being asked. Not wanting to take on such an obligation without having the time I would need to give it my best, I told him I just couldn't possibly do it, and tried to help him think of someone else for the job.

"Aw, c'mon, Claire. You're the one we want."

So after I persuaded him to help me recruit someone to take turns, with each of us writing a column every other week, I accepted.

And so "Clairvoyant" (clever, eh?) was born. Karen Gilfoy, my funny, talented friend, took on the other column, and we had more fun than the law allows.

The boys in the art department at Dixie Advertisers where I worked in the summers loved me, so I went down to talk to them about coming up with a caricature of me for my column, and within minutes I had exactly what I wanted.

Working hard to make my first column different from my predecessor's, I used a Latin quotation I'd just come across in an English class, which I thought would be quite impressive and erudite. Soon after my column was published an editor from the *Jackson Daily News* came out to critique the entire paper, the first under the new editor's regime.

"Please," he said to me, "don't try to show off with those highfalutin' Latin phrases. Nobody has any idea what they mean but you. You don't want to write over the heads of your readers."

I could feel the red blush heating up my face. I was so embarrassed I never wanted to write another word. Then, "But I like the caricature. Nice and clean."

Taking what he said to heart, I abandoned Latin phrases forever.

Well, almost.

Several years ago I had occasion to be on the Millsaps campus and, overcome by nostalgia and curiosity, on the spur of the moment dropped by the library to see if I could dig up any of my old columns. Unfortunately I could, and did, and was horrified to discover a smart-alecky overwrought example of glorified campus gossip.

But upon closer inspection, on reading all of my columns in their entirety in the context of the time and place that they were written, I discovered that I had been aware of things that I hadn't remembered I was aware of in 1956. And I discovered something else. I discovered potential, and was fleetingly filled with a deep sense of loss, a flash of "If only . . ."

Finally, like someone sneaking a peak at a pornographic magazine, I glanced furtively around to see if anyone was looking and, putting the papers back as surreptitiously as I could, stole out of the building.

∽

The men in my life for the most part have been older, and there's no explaining why some of my first, most agonizing, painful infatuations happened to be Yankees.

The seventh through the ninth grades were excruciating years, of course, only when you're that age you don't know it's excruciating. We thought it was wonderful. Though we thought most of the boys were "fruits," the disparaging term we used for today's geeks or nerds (at that age, though we had no idea, our parents must have known of its connotation, but didn't want to have to explain to us about homosexuals)—or for any boy we deemed unattractive or "repulsive," another descriptive word then in great favor.

It was the summer between eighth and ninth grade—I would have been fourteen—that some of our crowd went with Shelby to visit her grandmother, who still lived in the house in which Shelby's mother, Evana, had grown up, in the small town of Port Gibson, where the Presbyterian Church has a steeple in the shape of a hand, with the index finger pointing straight up to Heaven. I believe Port Gibson, which is north of Natchez, was also at one time on the Mississippi River, before it changed its course, leaving behind smaller tributaries and streams adorned with glorious sand bars and gullies.

As it happened, the son of one of Evana's girlhood friends, who had married and moved to St. Louis, was visiting *his* grandmother as well; and when the gentleman caller stopped by to visit the afternoon we arrived, even though he *did* have a Yankee accent, he was definitely neither a fruit nor repulsive, but tall and dark-haired, and though not handsome, quite nice-looking, and sixteen. I was taken with him because he was different from the boys we knew in Jackson, and I felt shy in the presence of his natural poise, never thinking he'd pay any particular attention to me, with all of us there for him to choose from.

I recall few details, but somehow a moonlight picnic on the locals' favorite sandbar was arranged, and though there must have been other boys, I don't remember any of them. Because somehow I ended up in the company of Bobby Whitfield, the worldly, easy-going Yankee, who in the soft light of the silvery moon whispered in my ear, "You are the most *provocative* wench."

Never having heard that kind of exotic talk before, and though not exactly sure what he meant (I looked it up in the dictionary when I got home), I fell heart-stoppingly, dizzyingly, can't-get-your-breath in love. But in that time and that place, it was nothing more than a brief interlude of sweet romance and unnamed longings never expressed.

Though I continued to pine for him for many months, I never saw him again. And it would be two more years before I received my first kiss, from a different Yankee.

He drove a yellow convertible. I met him the summer I was sixteen.

∾

So many of my most enduring memories are those of Starkville summers. The boys we knew, whose families were friends and even cousins of our family, were older than the boys I knew in Jackson, and even if they really weren't, they enjoyed appearing to be protective of my cousins and me because we were "Miss Mamie's" granddaughters.

Though the reputation of the good-looking, cool Northerner preceded him, I don't remember the exact occasion when Tom Casey and I met in that summer of 1950. It may have been a casual

Part One - Mississippi

encounter in a gathering at somebody's house. But everything I'd heard was no exaggeration. He was taller than I, and quite tan, with light brown hair and blue eyes that crinkled at the corners when he smiled, like a Jon Whitcomb illustration, which defined the heartthrobs of the day. (An explanation as to why it seems I was always so particularly attuned to a boy's height: because I am five-feet-eight, and it was considered to be simply awful to be taller than the boy you were with, resulting in many a stoop-shouldered, bent-kneed girl. [And unaccountably, the short boys always seemed to be terrific dancers.] The height of your heels depended on how tall your date was. You wouldn't be caught dead in anything but flats if heels would make you even a hair taller. So in those long-ago days I fretted over my height and always rejoiced when I met someone taller than I. Of course now I couldn't care less, and adore being tall, but it took me a while to get there.)

On a Sunday afternoon I went with Casey, as he was called, and some other friends—in great style, with the top down on his yellow convertible—to the public swimming pool in West Point, an even smaller town close by. Lean and tan, he was a low-keyed natural athlete and a superb swimmer, and though he was attentive to me, he wasn't at all obtrusive. At eighteen, his relaxed, confident manner was the exact opposite of the way I was feeling, though I hoped it wasn't showing. Surpassingly aware of him, I thought my heart was going to thump right out of my chest. (I know it's a cliché, but sometimes it's the only thing that will do.) I was unaccustomed to being treated in such a way—in such a mature way—by a boy, and wasn't sure how to respond, bursting as I was with joy from the novelty of this new sensation, which had been so long awaited, and so long in coming.

I was spending the night with Georgianne Long, one of my girlhood pals. When we drove up in front of her house, the top still down on a fragrant, lightning-bug, star-filled night, there were other cars, and we could see a crowd inside. Our friends got out and walked on up the grassy hill, leaving us behind. I busied myself with getting my things together, and as we always did in the olden days of the fifties, Casey got out and came around and opened my door. When he put his arm around my waist to walk me up the hill I thought I might pass out, and then, still in the shadows, before we reached the lights of the porch, he stopped, and put his other arm around me, and kissed me. I was self-conscious, knowing that everybody in the living room was probably watching us from the open windows, but I just closed my eyes and let the ecstasy of that sacred moment wash over me. It was exquisite. Tender but passionate. How lucky I am to have been kissed for the first time—in a way that I've never forgotten—by someone who really knew how a girl wanted to be kissed! Because no matter how many times I'd seen it done in the movies, or read about it, the first time is still the first time. And of course I wondered if he knew it. (I realize how quaint all this seems by today's standards, but there's a lot to be said for romance.)

My memory is hazy about our relationship after that, but I believe I was heartsick that he was leaving to go out of town almost immediately, and I went back to Jackson. After he graduated the next year he went off to the Korean War, as did so many of the Starkville boys I knew and loved.

But that's not the end of the story.

When I was a sophomore at the W, Sarah Yount, one of my new friends I'd made there—smart as a whip and majoring in English as I was—was pinned to Red Dot Anthony, a boy from Starkville I'd known for years. One day close to the Christmas holidays she stopped by my room with the stunning announcement that Casey, a friend of Red Dot's, was home from the wars, had heard from Red Dot that I was at the W, and wanted to call me for a date.

At first I was thrilled with the news, then filled with trepidation. We were three years older—there was a lot of difference between being sixteen and nineteen—and curious as I was, even interested in rekindling the old flame, I realized we were different people. And after a year-and-a-half of dating college boys who were friends of friends, I knew I needed something more in common with a boy than mere proximity. Also, I was on the verge of transferring to Millsaps in a few weeks.

When he called me, though, I got that old feeling, and couldn't wait to see him again, to see what was in store for us.

He looked different—not as lean?—older, which of course he

Part One - Mississippi

was. But his eyes still crinkled when he smiled. We double-dated with Sarah and Red Dot, no longer in the yellow convertible but in the back seat of Red Dot's car. We both worked hard at trying to make conversation to bridge the gap of time, and though we didn't say anything about it, I'm sure he realized as well as I did that it just wasn't the same. We had nothing really to talk about. Of course he had to kiss me, and I'd been waiting for it, looking forward to it, to see if the old magic would suddenly appear. He was still a sublime kisser, but the spark was gone. I knew I didn't—couldn't—love him. And I was sorry. It would have made life so much simpler if I had.

I believe I heard years later that he married a girl from West Point, but I never saw him again.

I'll always be beholden to him, though.

∾

Now Sonny was another story entirely.

Doesn't every woman have at least one man in her past, the memory of whom makes her squirm?

It was in my Victorian novel class that I first became aware of him; a small class, no more than a dozen, and if there were two other boys in there besides him, I'd be surprised. So it would have been hard not to notice him, even if he hadn't been arrogant and argumentative, qualities not often displayed (though no doubt devoutly desired by some professors) in the classrooms of Millsaps. But rather than being chastened when our elderly professor, the head of the English department—not accustomed to being challenged—belittled his ideas, he seemed to enjoy the fray, being contentious. It didn't bother him a whit. I'd never before encountered anyone like him in a classroom, especially in the English department. And, of course, while being put off by his, for Mississippi, bad manners, his "otherness" interested me, and I was curious about who in the world he was, where he'd come from, out of the blue, into an upper-level English class.

His hair was pitch black, straight as an Indian's, though cut short, and smallish dark eyes set above prominent cheekbones produced a stark round moonscape of a face that showed no expression. Except for the eyes. His eyes, wary though defiant, were the eyes of someone who had been wounded, which had the effect of drawing me to him immediately, while at the same time my intuition was warning me to keep my distance. Even before the days of James Dean and Montgomery Clift (it would be many years before I learned that both were homosexuals) I had always been a sucker for the troubled, "sensitive" type, moving Daddy to say to me, "I sure do wish you could take up with a boy you don't feel you have to mother, somebody who could take care of you for a change," which a few years later I was able to do, though it wasn't in Mississippi.

I decided to go with my intuition, but that didn't bother him. He was in no hurry. So for the life of me I don't know why he singled me out—I don't think I went out of my way to encourage him, to be nicer to him than I was to anyone else: everybody at Millsaps was friendly, except for Sonny and one or two others like him, who could sail across the campus without speaking to a soul while everybody else was hey-ing people to death.

He began by sitting next to me occasionally in class, and we'd exchange comments about the assignment, or, if he hadn't read it, he'd ask me to give him the gist, which wasn't much help to him since we read a novel or two a week with a test every Friday. Then he was there more frequently, but not too obviously, and by the end of the semester he had begun to wait for me when class was over.

I found out that Sonny had been at Millsaps a few years earlier for two or three semesters, but dropped out, either because he enlisted or was drafted into the army in the Korean War. He didn't complete his full tour of duty, the circumstances surrounding his early discharge remaining vague. Even so, when he returned to Millsaps he did so on the GI Bill, his only source of income. He lived off campus in a boarding house across the street from the college, and had no car. Two years older than I, he was majoring in English, and, widely read, he was in a way terribly worldly without ever having seen the world. His *fierce* goodness, which scared me sometimes, resulted in an utter lack of hypocrisy or of any need whatsoever to be "nice" to anybody merely for the sake of being nice. Those he believed to be decent, honest, earned his respect; the fakes his total disdain. On the other hand, he was inordinately kind. But you had to get beyond the surface to discover all this.

We didn't date much in the conventional sense, since he didn't have a car. We'd have lunch sometimes between classes with the regulars at the Adelle Grill next door to his boarding house where he could run a tab, and Elvis sang "Heartbreak Hotel" day and night on the jukebox. And, amazingly, one day he asked if he could go to church with me. I was never sure if it was because he actually liked going to church, whether he thought it would give him respectability, or if it was to be with me. Since I was driving, I had to pick him up on the way down town to Galloway Memorial Methodist, and sometimes he'd invite a fellow boarder to come with us, one illustration of his fierce goodness. He never judged people by their station in life, nor even by their affinity for soap and water, and as a result we were the occasional bearers to the fold of some mighty stout-smelling lambs. I learned a lot about humility and tolerance from him.

He was from a town north of Jackson, in the central part of the state on the way to Memphis, the only child of devout Methodists, an old and respected family in straitened circumstances. Home, for him, he said, was where when he had to go there they had to let him in, paraphrasing a line from Robert Frost's poem, "The Death of the Hired Man." I don't remember what his father did, a farmer perhaps, and his mother, who kept the family on the straight and narrow, was or had been a schoolteacher, I believe. Because of his difficult relationship with his stern and disapproving mother, Sonny was deeply sympathetic to his taciturn father's plight as her husband. I believe at the core of his being he ached for their affection and approval, their love. But in those days of distant relationships, such things went unmentioned, unspoken. No talk of "feelings," seldom even of love. (Those people longing today for the fifties need to remember this. And while I'm at it, I need to put in a word for Sonny's mother, whose side of the story I never heard.) After I got to know him, I realized that he was one of the few truly brilliant people I've ever known, though I could also see that his brilliance had somehow become tragically twisted, perverse. And I knew that it was his tortured soul that both attracted and scared me.

Whenever we went out together at night, I was in the awkward position of having to take my car, unless he could find somebody to double-date with, always putting him in the situation of being dependent upon and beholden to others—with no way to return the favor—which I knew humiliated him but about which he said nothing. And this car business became a bone of contention between Daddy and me, especially when I'd take Sonny home after we'd played bridge at my house with Mama and Daddy, which we would often do.

Invariably it would be late when I got back after taking him home, since we usually took a little time for necking, often up on campus in the parking lot close to the old telescope observatory. I wouldn't have been caught dead in that boarding house, not only because it just wouldn't be fitting, but because in the back of my mind there always lurked a sense of unpredictability about Sonny. And even though I trusted him, I believed he had this rage, I guess I'd call it, deep inside, from some sort of wound in his soul. And of course—Miss Goody Two Shoes, Miss Fix It—I thought my accepting him, uncritically, would change that.

Even so, I wasn't about to set foot in that boarding house. And since I always had to let Daddy know when I got back from taking Sonny home so he wouldn't worry (though I thought then it was his way of showing his disapproval, now I wonder if it was his only means of trying to protect me), it became a thing, and it was because I knew—though he never said a word—that Daddy would just die if he thought I was ever going to marry Sonny. Although Sonny did talk about it vaguely—about my being the wife of a college English professor—but of course I never said a word to Daddy about *that!*

It took longer for me to realize that Sonny was an alcoholic than it would have with somebody else. Because Mississippi was a dry state Sonny had to get his liquor from a bootlegger, or from somebody who'd been to one, and beer wasn't sold on every street corner either. Being poor and without a car, and at Millsaps where alcohol was prohibited, even those times we'd go to the show and out somewhere later with another couple in their car, the times that Sonny and I drank together were infrequent and of relatively short duration. It was those times, in fact, when I wasn't with him that bothered me, when he was out drinking with a buddy or a bunch of folks, and he'd call me on the telephone, obviously drunk. It was as though he lived a Jekyll and Hyde existence, and I lived with a deep sense of unease over something I couldn't put my finger on.

I don't remember the first time he got drunk when I was with him, but I was disgusted. With some people alcohol makes them more fun, with others they become sullen, mean. I don't know if it reveals their true side or not, but Sonny didn't become a happy drunk. He became a silent, surly, almost malevolent drunk. It did something to me in such a way that I never felt the same way about him again. So for me our relationship was downhill after that. But he was so contrite, so ashamed, so convincing, I thought, well, maybe it was just an isolated event. He had never been drunk with me before.

In the fifties it was thought that all a man needed was a good woman to straighten him out. Both sides of the equation—men and women—believed this. That's why so many girls married boys who weren't fit to marry. They were bound to just be sowing their wild oats and would settle down once they got married to the right girl. In our generation there was no such thing as a long-term relationship. That doesn't mean you might not have known somebody you grew up with all your life, but it also doesn't mean you had a relationship with them either. When you started going out with someone, it wasn't any time before it came around to sex (usually in a car), which for a girl was supposedly forbidden. (What did people in New York do without cars?) So what to do? Well, get married of course. For sex. So you could go all the way, rather than fooling around doing everything but the real thing. It was just such a nutty way to live a life! Today I am in such awe of any good marriage that has lasted from the fifties. (Note the qualifier "good." Just because a marriage has lasted doesn't mean it's good. The world is full of long, sick marriages.)

But back to the Sonny conundrum.

It solved itself in a bizarre chain of events.

In the spring of your senior year at Millsaps, a two-part comprehensive examination in your major subject was required for graduation, one written and one oral. On a glorious afternoon of a warm March Friday, a few weeks before our exams in April, Sonny called me up and asked me if I'd like to go with him up to one of the sandbars on the Pearl River and study for the exam. "Who else is going?"

I inquired suspiciously, realizing that if he were already going he had a ride. Oh, three or four others, who weren't majoring in English and who weren't even seniors, who obviously had nothing whatever to do with English comprehensive exams.

From past experience I knew that sandbars were seductive places. I also knew that on such a superb, sun-shiny, sweet-smelling Friday afternoon of a Mississippi spring, with no classes until Monday, that no one but me, and supposedly Sonny, would have even the slightest inclination to study; and that I would have no ally and be completely without defenses once I got there, because I knew Sonny didn't give a hoot about studying. I also knew that it would never occur to the folks he mentioned to even consider traveling to such an inviting spot and not a drop to drink, and that I would be trapped if I wanted to leave. So I told him I was sorry, but I wouldn't be able to study with all those people around. That I was at that very moment immersed in the eighteenth century, with plans to spend the weekend there, and bade him farewell.

Sometime around midnight the telephone next to my bed jangled me awake, and I was sure Daddy as well. It was Sonny. When I heard the sound of his voice, I heard disaster, and though I was surprised, I realized I'd been expecting that call for a long time. Usually so cool, he was completely undone and could barely get the story out.

One of the girls who had gone to the sandbar, a Yankee who lived in the dormitory at Millsaps, had passed out from too much beer and sun. When they got back from the river, because she'd get expelled for drinking if they took her to her dormitory, they took her instead to the boarding house, where they dropped her off with Sonny, who put her in his room and left her there to sleep it off while he went next door to the Adelle to get something to eat. When he got back he found her on the floor of the bathroom, unconscious and bleeding, her wrists slashed. In panicked terror he called an ambulance, which whisked her away to the hospital, where the police were called, the college informed, and everyone involved was in serious trouble.

By Monday the news had swept the campus (though the college was able to suppress it in the local papers), the potential suicide victim was sufficiently recovered to leave the hospital, and the sandbar revelers were facing expulsion. Sonny had one lone champion among the faculty (I don't recall any kind of student government), an English professor, who recognized his intellectual abilities and appreciated him for the misfit he was. (After all, the study of literature—even history—is nothing if not the examination, the exaltation of the "misfit," is it not?) Although the professor's intervention mitigated Sonny's punishment somewhat—he wasn't expelled—he was suspended immediately for the remainder of the semester, as well as the next two following. Though he received the news with stoicism, I knew that his heart and soul were awash in black bile, but what embittered him most was being barred from taking his comprehensives only a few weeks away. In a state of agitation after an appeal on that point by the sympathetic professor fell on deaf ears, he broke down in tears at the home of the professor, and both the professor and I were completely helpless in trying to console him. After all, what was there to say?

So Sonny went home, the Yankee girl returned to the north country, I took my comprehensives, graduated in May, and began my new permanent job at the advertising agency in June.

Sonny and I weren't able to see each other much that summer, though we wrote letters and talked on the phone, though not the way we talk long distance today. It was no more than five or ten minutes a week, though Daddy, who got the phone bill, disagreed with my arithmetic. (In those days when the phone rang, you knew you could answer it when you were walking out the door with your hat on and the car running, secure in the knowledge that even if it were long distance, it would take no longer than three minutes.)

I had a new life that Sonny wasn't a part of, and though I loved him in the *agape* sense, I didn't love him in the *eros* sense, but didn't know how to tell him, how he would react. Well, yes, I did. He would go on a drunk. The last thing he needed now was for me to tell him I wasn't in love with him. He needed somebody who was *for* him.

In the fall Sonny invited me to come up to Oxford over the Thanksgiving weekend to the biggest football game of the year, the

Ole Miss-Mississippi State game. I can't remember if he was enrolled at Ole Miss or, not living far away, if it was just an occasion he wanted to invite me to. He'd made arrangements for me to stay with a darling newly married couple we both knew who had graduated from Millsaps, who were living in Oxford while the husband attended law school. I'd never been to a football game at Ole Miss—it was just something I'd never aspired to—but since it was the Big Game, I might run into a lot of people I hadn't seen in ages that I knew from State and the W, and even Millsaps and Ole Miss (in those days if you grew up in Mississippi and went to college there, you knew, or had heard of, practically everybody in the state who was in the range of four years older to four years younger than you, or knew someone who was kin.)

So I went. And right off the bat I was greeted with an ill wind. Sonny had been drinking, though he wasn't drunk, but it hurt my feelings—let me down—that he would start out the weekend that way. Pretending not to notice, I put on my brightest smiling Miss America face, the requisite for an Ole Miss weekend.

It's all a horrible, sordid blur. And all I remember is walking by myself in the late afternoon light, a solitary pedestrian (in spike heels, remember), as though it were the most natural thing in the world to be doing, along the side of the road leading from the stadium, where hundreds, even thousands of cars streamed beside me. And sure enough, cars full of my old friends I hadn't seen in ages that I knew from the W and State, even Millsaps and Ole Miss, stopped to ask what was wrong, to offer me a ride, which I refused because I didn't want to have to explain why I was there, that I didn't know where I was going. And then there was Sonny, drunk, bolting from someone's car, pulling at me trying to get me to get in, causing such a tacky scene. I'd never been so embarrassed, with all those eyes wide with curiosity staring out at us in the dusty twilight.

I've forgotten now, but I believe that was the last time I saw Sonny. It was just two or three weeks later that I found out I would be going to New York, and when I called to give him the news, he was stunned, crushed, and I don't remember him at my going-away party the night before I left.

Part One - Mississippi

I wrote to him not long after I arrived in New York, to give him my address, but I don't know if he answered my letter. I called him only once, a month or so later, at Ole Miss, where he was in school. He said he was going out with a girl from a small town up around Oxford and that he wanted to go to law school, which of course was perfect for him, only I didn't know it then because I hadn't yet been around any lawyers. It wasn't long before I heard they were married, and that her daddy was a man of some means with a lucrative law practice in the town they came from.

That was the last I heard of Sonny for over thirty years, until my old friend Karen Gilfoy called me in Phoenix some time in the eighties to read me a newspaper article with the shattering news that Sonny had been arrested in New Orleans by federal agents for money laundering in the Caribbean.

I never told Daddy about the Ole Miss football game—it would have just killed him—but I knew one of the reasons he was so pleased I was going to New York was because of Sonny. I recently read the five letters Daddy wrote to me during that first year in New York. I had forgotten, but in the first one I received he wrote:

> . . . so from my stand point [he'd just become a partner in a new business] things look better for the future, especially with your calling off things with Sonny. That made me happy as my greatest desire for you is your happiness and I could never believe that you could have been happy with Sonny. There are many reasons why I believed this and I won't go into them now but I will when you get home if you wish. That is just between you and me tho.

And that was the first time I knew for sure.

PART TWO

New York

Five

From the moment I arrived, I was a New Yorker—never a tourist. I had only the New Year's Day holiday to get myself oriented as well as I could before I began my new job on day two of 1957. And I've often thought how lucky I was to be introduced to New York from the ground up rather than from the top down.

I couldn't hold my new world close enough. Ordinary transactions often became high drama. A novice at being a pushy New Yorker, I quickly learned that there were no more "after you's," and that "please" and "thank you" were treated with rolling eyes, or eyebrows raised in astonishment. It was just that old habits are hard to break. Still, even in my spike heels I was able to speed up my walking to such a clip that as I strode along on my long legs people got out of my way. (Even now in New York I'm still not thought of as pushy, though everywhere else I am.)

I lived at the Evangeline Residence for Women in Greenwich Village. I wore my white gloves to work, even in the summer—especially in the summer—and never, ever smoked a cigarette while walking on the street. My New York was the same New York of Robert Redford, but we didn't run across each other. At least I don't think we did, though it's not impossible. Robert Redford wasn't Robert Redford in 1957 (and he was also *really* short). I don't think I hung out with the writer William Styron in any of the Village bars, either, even though we were practically in the same neighborhood. I didn't know from the Ivy League, nor had I ever heard of the Seven Sisters. When I occasionally had brunch on a summer weekend at the Brevoort on lower Fifth Avenue, it was much later that I discovered that Irwin Shaw had written about that very spot in "Girls in Their Summer Dresses." I had missed him, too.

Back in junior high in Jackson, we were required to write a book report on several books a year, which had to include fiction, nonfiction, biography, etc.

In the closing weeks of the seventh grade, having waited until the last minute—it appears that since an early age I've always worked best against a deadline, as the saying goes—I had read everything but the biography. With the deadline upon me, there were slim pickings indeed in the biography section of our school library.

Having read all of those that interested me, nothing struck my fancy among the biographical crumbs remaining on the shelf. It was a short trip to the "W's," where I pulled out a book about Alexander Woollcott. After a cursory flip through the pages revealed that he was some sort of New York writer, because my back was against the wall I checked the book out.

I might as well have been reading Einstein's *The Meaning of Relativity*. But down to the wire with time running out, I pressed on, never having heard of the *New Yorker* or the Round Table at the Algonquin Hotel, much less *The Man Who Came to Dinner* or Dorothy Parker. With absolutely no frame of reference for the New York literary world, I read the words but they just didn't take. Bored to tears, I could not figure out what this man had done that was worth a book. How could I answer the question, "What did he accomplish?" in my book report, since to my mind the answer was, "Search me," as my mother liked to say.

With the report due the next day, I waited after class to ask my teacher for advice on how to write a report about a book that held no meaning, and curious as to what Alexander Woollcott had done that was so great. When she saw what I was reading, I could tell she was kind of tickled for some reason.

"Where in the world did you get this?" she asked.

"It was all that was left in the library."

"I've never had anybody else read it. Do the best you can and don't worry about his accomplishments. It *is* hard to explain."

Somewhere in my memory was stored a description of a different kind of life, whether I had understood it or not. And I could never have dreamed then that one day I would be living within walking distance of the *New Yorker*.

∾

It was not until I got to New York that anybody had ever asked me what I was.

"What are you?" New Yorkers would ask quite directly and matter-of-factly. For the longest time I had no idea what they were talking about. What *am* I? What did that mean? At first I answered, "American," because that is what I was. Then they would press on, "No, no, where did you come from?" and I would answer, "Mississippi." "No, no, what were you before you came to Mississippi?" Again, I had no idea about that either.

With a name like King, I was informed, I was most likely English, and then if I volunteered that my mother's name was Hogan, the reply would come, "Ah, Irish. English-Irish. Most Southerners are," the pigeonhole to which I was most frequently consigned by these Yankee authorities. English-Irish seemed a rather nice thing to be, so even though it was news to me, if they said so, it suited me just fine. In all my twenty-two years no one in our family had ever mentioned anything about being either English or Irish.

It was also the first time I heard someone described as "first generation" or second or whatever generation, which was sometimes spoken of, especially first generation, with disparagement, and other times, if it were more than one generation, with admiration or pride. What possible difference could it make, I wondered? I had no earthly idea what generation I was—how long was a generation?—nor did I care. I had never before heard anyone referred to as *shanty* or *lace curtain* Irish except in books, nor *frog* nor *wog*. During the war we hated Japs and Krauts because we'd been brainwashed that they were evil, but as far as any other ethnic groups were concerned, that was it.

Except for Negroes, of course. I heard *niggah* all my life, but my brother and I were told that it was a "bad word," and not to say it.

In the South the wickedness of prejudice was not only as clearly defined as black and white, there were laws protecting it. In New York I was introduced to new, subtle prejudices that I'd never encountered. Having known only two Jews in Mississippi and probably twice as many Catholics, I was unprepared for the prejudice against them, of the acute awareness of whether someone was Jewish or not. This was the time when Puerto Ricans were having a hard time of it as well, the time of the musical *West Side Story,* which preceded the next wave of Hispanic immigrants.

Leaving Mississippi before the years of open warfare over desegregation, I've often wondered what I would have done had I been there. I was in Brooklyn where it was easy to be holier-than-thou and self-righteous under the protection and comfort of distance, while at the same time knowing the agony everybody at home was suffering. Would I have had the courage to take a stand had I been there, fought the good fight? Dr. Selah, my minister at Galloway Memorial Methodist Church where I grew up, resigned when my old church wouldn't desegregate. I like to think I wouldn't have been found wanting, but it's something I'll never know.

One brave friend had kept her six-year-old-daughter in the newly integrated neighborhood public school from which whites had fled. After two years of her daughter hating school, and leaving home in tears almost every day, begging to go to school with her friends, her mother capitulated. She simply could no longer sacrifice her only child's life on the cross of her principles. So she fought the battle in other ways, as many of my friends did. Though many resisted on the other side, even old sweet friends, and some in my own family.

Of the handful of colleges I could have gone to in Mississippi, I believe Millsaps was the most enlightened. It aroused suspicion and criticism—Communist! Subversive! Liberal!—among the populace as the civil rights movement intensified. In the last month of my senior year, I was aware of a small—one can only call it guerrilla—group, who were clandestinely establishing a liaison with Tougaloo College, the Negro college just outside Jackson. The first time I ever felt my blood run cold with raw fear was when one of my friends who was involved told me what could happen if they were found out. After I left Mississippi, those students went on to become part of a broader group of activists working quietly behind the scene.

I only discovered in retrospect how news was controlled in Mississippi. We lived behind a "paper curtain." The newspapers

Part Two - New York

slanted everything in favor of segregation. Primarily, much of what was going on simply wasn't reported. Since the Jackson papers were the only ones we had (except for the Memphis *Commercial Appeal* or the New Orleans *Times Picayune* which we bought at Mr. Brent's drug store in the Standard Life Building after church every Sunday), and as a student I spent little time reading even them, I was ignorant of the way the rest of the country viewed what was going on in the South, having no perspective about it at all until after I left. It's hard to understand what it was like before television, which in the end is what turned the tide of the country against the South and the evils of segregation, depicted on the small screen in the starkest, most pitiless light.

∞

After the war, when I would occasionally answer the phone and hear a man's voice ask for "Colonel King," I knew it was someone from the war on his way through Jackson. Daddy would come to the phone and have a quiet chat and that would be the end of it. Once or twice I asked him why he didn't invite them to come over, and he just gave me some excuse. One time when he got one of these calls, I pressed him for an explanation. "It would make us both uncomfortable," he said, "because neither one of us would know which door he should come to."

My father had been in command of a corps of engineers, all of whom were Negroes, and all of those men who called were colored. He didn't know how to deal with having them come to either the front or the back door. It could put each of them on the spot either way.

My first questioning of racial injustice. I was twelve.

Mollie Ivins believes that "all Southern liberals come from the same starting point—race. Once you figure out they are lying to you about race, you start to question everything."

In the Mississippi public schools we had free textbooks, and each book had a sticker in the front showing who had used it each year. When the form was filled up, it had been used six years, and by that time you can imagine what shape a book was in, broken spine, tattered, dog-eared, pages missing. It was not until I was in the tenth grade, in an American history class, that I was astonished to hear from our teacher that when we finished with these books, they went to the Negro schools.

Out of sight out of mind, I had been only dimly aware of the colored schools. But when I heard this shocking statement, I sarcastically asked if they got our old desks too. Probably so, he answered evenly. I knew that it wasn't fair, and I wondered what it must be like to have a whole school full of old, broken-down, second-hand furniture, what it must be like never to have anything new, as much as I loved the smell of a new book, a new notebook, new pencils at the beginning of each school year. But then I forgot about it.

And then there was Colored Town. Down by the fairgrounds, in the low ground down by the river. The part of town that was always underwater when the Pearl River overflowed, the first ones to get flooded out. As a child I envied where they lived because they were so close to the state fair that came to town every fall, not realizing that they weren't allowed to go.

Through all of the inhumanity and hatred that has been the result of the evil of slavery and oppression and segregation, you can call me patronizing, condescending, call me anything you want. But I have the feeling of a deeply shared spiritual bond with Southern black people, their heritage, their religion, their music, their food, their language, their rage. There are those who don't understand that many of us who are white who grew up under segregation in the South suffer from that grievous psychic wound as well.

∾

And so I arrived at the Evangeline, on West 13th Street, run by the Salvation Army. A modern sixteen-story building where a room and two meals a day cost me $16.45 a week, and where men were allowed only in the lobby—which had its advantages. (I could tell a date, if he were obnoxious, that I had a curfew, and would make him take me home. He never knew the difference.)

A democratic place, it was rich in a diversity that included several Negroes. For a time one of them who lived across the hall avoided me after she heard my accent. I often got that—reverse prejudice—which I got used to. But another neighbor from Queens, who had the most delicious New York accent ("*Oy* have an accent?" she exclaimed to me), became a good friend—the first professed atheist

I'd ever met—and brought us together.

I was self-conscious back then about my accent when I was around black people. But things are different now. Sometimes, when a black hears my accent, instead of the old hostility I used to get, he or she will smile and ask me where I'm from; and where I used to be embarrassed, I'm not anymore, and the person will smile and tell me about relatives in the South, or how though they might not want to go back, they miss it. And I tell them I feel the same way.

I was brought up with my grandmother listening to the sermons of Dr. Harry Emerson Fosdick and Dr. Ralph W. Sockman on the radio. Dr. Fosdick preached from Riverside Church in New York City, and Dr. Sockman from his pulpit in Christ Church Methodist on Park Avenue, and sometimes I would sit with her to listen.

When I joined Dr. Sockman's church on the first Easter I was in New York, I had reason to become quite self-conscious about the race issue when about fifty of us stood down at the chancel to be accepted as new members in the church.

Among Dr. Sockman's great gifts was his ability to remember everybody's name and where they were from without the first note to refer to. There were two or three Negroes in our group that Easter Sunday, and after he had introduced us all by name and what church we had come from—my Mississippi origins waving like a Confederate flag, or so I thought—I may have been imagining it, but fixing me squarely in the eye to make sure there would be no slackers, he pronounced, "We are all God's children, one family, brother and sister, and this church shall be your home, your refuge."

And verily, I believed him.

It was also when I got to New York that I first began to notice people speaking of class, as "He's really just so middle class," or "What an upper-class accent she has," when I had never thought in terms of class before. Wasn't that why we fought the Revolution? If I had been asked to define class, I would have to have said where I came from there were only two: white and black, with no gradations, except for those whites who were "trash" or "common," words my mother would never use, though occasionally she would refer to someone as "just real ordinary."

Anyway, I wasn't sure where I fit into the class situation.

It was when I read *Auntie Mame* that I was left with no doubt. When her nephew became engaged to a girl who went to college at Sweet Briar, Mame considered that just too middle class and lowbrow for words. To me, in Mississippi, when two of my friends got to go off to Virginia to Sweet Briar, I thought it quite grand, the ultimate privilege, and longed to go there, too. Making matters worse for the fiancée of Mame's nephew, her family had bought all their furniture at W. & J. Sloane's, of all places, the thought of which moved Mame to shudder in revulsion. "So middle class!" she railed. What did she mean? Sloane's was one of the finest furniture stores I'd ever been in.

At first I didn't get it. And then when I did, I laughed in recognition at just how hopelessly middle class I must be.

When you're ignorant, you just don't know what you don't know.

ର

One of Mama's oldest friends from Starkville had moved to New York before the war and married a girl from an old family from Greenwich, Connecticut. They had two daughters before they were divorced right after the war, and I'm not clear why Mama's friend William had an apartment in New York during the war, but he did. And Mama and her youngest sister, Daisy, whose husbands were away in the war in Europe, were thrilled when he offered it to them so they could go and stay there for their first visit to New York, in April 1945. William worked with an international agency helping to bring war refugees into the country, and Mama said you just never knew when you walked into the bathroom if you were going to find somebody sleeping in the bath tub, or on the floor in the hall, many of whom couldn't speak English. I don't think there was a lock on the front door, so people would just come and go. There was a big turnover, and nobody stayed for very long, Mama said.

That was one of the most memorable times in Mama's life, for it was when she was in New York that President Franklin D. Roosevelt died, and she said she'd never forget the crowds of people in the street, weeping over the news.

Anyway, William was a gracious, old family friend, so when I arrived, he naturally felt some responsibility for my welfare and well-being. By this time he had been working for years with American Express, I believe, escorting rich ladies of a certain age on cruises around the world. He was off on a cruise when I arrived, but called me upon his return and invited me to go with him by train up to Greenwich to his former wife's house to meet her and their two daughters, who were in high school, not a whole lot younger than I was.

I had never before been in a house where there was a butler, so when I caught sight of the man who opened the door for us in a morning coat, or so I supposed, I know I must have stared in wonder, but William took no notice, and I was welcomed warmly by mother and daughters. Apparently he had told them he was bringing their Christmas gifts, since he'd been away over the holidays, for they pounced upon a small suitcase he'd brought with him, though he was able to hold them at bay long enough to get it open and lay it on the floor so that he could display his largesse. The girls ooh-ed and ahh-ed over the elegant array of items, bought in ports-of-call while on his cruise, when a dollar in foreign lands was a fortune, and, unbelievably to me, he shared with them how cheaply he was able to buy each item. I was fascinated to hear him say he was allowing each of them to choose just one. (Since they were all so cheap, I was thinking, maybe he'd give me one too.) All this while the butler and a maid served tea (an English tea, not a cup of tea) and I remained as silent as a mummy, taking it all in, feeling like the Little Match Girl. (I believe this was the first time I'd ever known anybody with white servants.)

Suddenly, looking at his watch, William observed that it was time to catch the train back, whereupon he collected the unchosen items and replaced them in his case, the butler appeared with our coats, and we were off to the station in the older daughter's convertible, with the top down—she wore a fur coat—in January.

On the way back, William apologized for the fact that he was not going to be able to see me home when we got back to the city, as he was going to have to leave the train at 125th Street so as not to be late in meeting Mrs. Post when her ship docked; that he was so happy to see me, and that he wanted me to join him next week for a piano recital at Town Hall and would call with details. The minute the train doors opened, he was off at a trot.

There are those who called William a social climber, and if that was true, he did all right. It was Marjorie Merriweather Post, the heiress to the cereal fortune, he was meeting, but I acted like I didn't know who she was when he told me her name, because I knew he was trying to impress me.

William did call the next week, only a day before the day of the recital, and told me he'd pick me up to have dinner before the performance. I don't think he realized I already knew how to get around the city, and that his arrival by cab to get me was a rare occurrence at the Evangeline, though William seemed to take the Evangeline in stride. After all, he'd opened his door to refugees, and maybe he thought that's what I was, too.

In the taxi after he collected me—I wore a long shocking pink velveteen coat, which in Mississippi we deemed heavy but which was like being wrapped in a Kleenex against the cold of New York—William told me we were having dinner at a club, and I don't remember which one it was because it didn't mean anything to me. I do remember the room as small and comfortable, the way English clubs looked in the movies, and the people we were with said they played bridge there. After we were all introduced, we sat down at a round table for five, and I was unnerved to see before me a half-dozen raw oysters on the half-shell, prettily arranged around a little cup of tomato sauce on a bed of ice.

I am allergic to shrimp, which sounds rather benign when stated so simply. But my allergic reaction is that I throw up, throw up so violently that I couldn't believe what was happening to me the first time it happened. And though I'd never eaten an oyster, I wasn't about to take any chances, because when you've been as sick as I have, you never in your life want it to happen to you again. So not wanting to cause any commotion, which such a declaration inevitably invites, I said not a word, picked up my little oyster fork, and gently piercing one of the slimy disgusting blobs, dipped it into the sauce, where I let it remain, toying with it. Then quickly raising my fork to my mouth, pretended to chew, or swallow, or roll it around in my mouth, whatever it is you do with oysters. One down, five to go.

After disposing of the next three, the sauce cup was getting crowded, beginning to run over, coloring the ice red, and becoming brazen with success, I dispatched the last two beneath their shells, burying them in the ice. If anyone in our party noticed, they had the good manners not to let on. Later I couldn't help but wonder if they had a good laugh in the kitchen when it was discovered what I'd done.

When we arrived at the concert, a boy about my age was waiting for us, who turned out to be William's nephew, Sam—whose mother, I knew well, since she was one of Mama's closest friends—in town from his home in California for a short time. Obviously it was William's plan that Sam would be my date for the evening, as he provided us with two tickets, saying that he would meet us afterwards. Right off the bat it was clear to me that our rapport quotient was zero.

After the recital by a Russian pianist—it was my first by anyone professional, since I'd only attended piano recitals that I was in myself, or those of my friends, or the monthly recitals of the Junior McDowell Club on Saturday mornings—William rejoined us and herded us into a taxi to go uptown to a reception. I was having a lot of "firsts" with William, I was thinking, as we whizzed uptown in the frigidly cold night.

The hostess welcomed me with warm, gracious hospitality, qualities not necessarily shared by the rest of the growing crowd now pouring into her commodious Park Avenue apartment, which contained a grand piano at one end of the huge living room overlooking the lights on the north and east sides of the city.

Knowing how to do, after we'd relinquished our coats Sam stuck with me until he ordered us two drinks from the bar and led the way to the dining room, where an enormous table and sideboard were laden with late supper comestibles. When we entered, a chic, pretty blond in a black dress, much more his style than a hicky girl from Mississippi, was helping herself, and spoke to Sam, which is when I lost him for the rest of the evening.

Just then there was applause when the guest of honor entered, promising to play something for us after he had a bite to eat.

Hearing this, I drifted over by the piano, the better to be able to see when he began. And also, because it was on the fringe of the crowd, who all appeared to know each other and who were uninclined to waste time on a stranger in their midst. I was on my own, which actually didn't bother me that much, because I was so engrossed in observing the scene, watching everybody. This was what I'd dreamed of doing, after all, only I'd thought it would be more fun.

When the Russian made his way to the piano, the crowd shifted that way too, and I found myself being pushed up into the piano's curve, where I knew I must be glowing like a neon light in my red dress, feeling terribly self-conscious right up there in the front, practically face-to-face. When he sat down, he couldn't avoid me, and smiled, and I, of course, smiled back. He played one or two short pieces and then, to my astonishment, asked me my name. When I told him, he announced that the next piece was dedicated to me. And in the hush of the room, I almost died when I heard the delicate, opening strains of *Clair de lune,* and stood there with a frozen smile while he played the whole thing. When he finished to wild applause, he got up and took a bow, signaling the end, and came over to me. Sitting together over a cup of tea on the piano bench we talked animatedly of many things, a blessedly far cry from my date, who, with the party breaking up, suddenly loomed over me with my coat.

Down on the street Sam put me into a taxi and sent me on my way back down town—Cinderella going home after the ball—while he took a taxi in another direction. I never saw or heard from Sam again. But I still have the card I received from the Russian on my next birthday, reminding me that he'd played *Clair de lune* for me.

Chance meetings have added to my life's savor.

༄

Only days later, out of the blue I was invited to go to the opera, as well as to dinner beforehand at Charles's French Restaurant, now long gone. Beyond anything I'd ever imagined, I learned only the day before I was to go that we would be sitting in the center box. What did people wear to sit in a box at the opera, or even in the highest balcony? I had no idea, and even if I did, I was sure I didn't own it. At least I'd finally found a new warm black coat that I'd bought on sale at Altman's for $88, but I still had to wear my red wool uniform.

When I walked out of the Evangeline, planning to hotfoot it to the restaurant only a few blocks away, I was dismayed to discover that it was snowing heavily, and sticking. Bootless and hatless, how could I possibly make it to the restaurant without looking like anything in the world except something the cat dragged in? Just as I decided to head out to Seventh Avenue, realizing that even there it would be nearly impossible to find a cab, miraculously a taxi drew up to the curb, and the driver leaned across the seat to shout, "Hey, lady, can you tell me how to get to the Cherry Lane Theater?"

Without hesitation I told him, "Yes, I'd be glad to. But you'll have to let me show you, and then take me to Charles's French Restaurant on Sixth Avenue. Okay?"

After turning around to confer with his fare, a woman, he shouted, "Sure, get in."

I didn't know exactly where the Cherry Lane was, but I remembered seeing the side of a building with the name painted on it and an arrow pointing the way, somewhere down 7th Avenue, and I soon spotted it. "Over there," I said decisively.

When I arrived at the restaurant, not only on time, but dry and kempt as well, I was quite pleased with myself and my newly acquired New York know-how.

So much of my early New York has disappeared, even including the ornate skyscraper where my office was—the Singer Building, for eighteen months in the early 1900s the tallest building in the world until the Woolworth Building just up Broadway was completed—from whose windows I perilously watched and strewed torn-up paper in ticker tape parades, once rushing down to stand on the sidewalk, the better to see Queen Elizabeth and Prince Philip up close in an open car. Bestowing on us a royal wave of her white kid-gloved hand, the Queen in coral velvet cloche was surprisingly pretty, with the clearest peaches and cream complexion I'd ever seen.

The old Metropolitan Opera House at Broadway and 39th Street is also gone, of course. As beautiful as the Lincoln Center Met is, the old one, built in the late 1800s—I remember lots of Old World red and glittering crystal chandeliers and wall sconces—was exactly as I'd expected it to be, as I wanted it to be, only more so. In my red dress I blended right in as we walked up the stairs to find the box. With each step I kept thinking, "I can't believe I'm really at the Metropolitan Opera in New York City getting ready to sit in a box!"

Our party were the only ones occupying the box, and just as we got ourselves settled, the lights went down. Suddenly, a distinguished-looking man in white tie and tails stepped out from between enormous curtains, and like a wave an audible dismay swept across the audience, followed by an expectant hush. It was Rudolph Bing, the general manager of the opera company.

"Ladies and gentlemen," he began, "it is my great sorrow to announce that Arturo Toscanini died this evening." And as the shocks of "Who?" "What?" "When?" "How?" arose in muted cacophony from the collective mouths of the audience, Mr. Bing asked us all to please stand for a minute of silence, and to remain standing as the orchestra played the overture of a Verdi opera—I forget which one—Toscanini's favorite.

When it was over, overcome with the emotion of the dramatic announcement and the lyrical beauty of the music, the audience fell into their seats.

As magnificent as *Madame Butterfly* is, as tragically sublime as Dorothy Kirsten was as Cio Cio San, it was all an anticlimax. My first night at the opera will always be remembered as the Night Toscanini Died.

∞

Movie lover that I was, I loved the theater as well, even before I knew it was "the theatre." I was hooked after I saw my first play, a colorful, rambunctious children's theater production based on Jean LaFitte and his gang of pirates staged by an all-woman cast of Jackson matrons when I was six or seven. At Liberty Grove I had played the queen in a third grade pageant, and at Bailey was awful as the mother in a one-act play, and was smart enough to realize it. After that I was strictly a spectator, until I got to Millsaps and joined the theater group—loving the smell of the crowd, the roar of the greasepaint, as us real thespians liked to say—finding my niche backstage, among the props. And when you've worked with props, you can never see a play without always noticing the smallest detail—a handkerchief, a match, a key, a stamp for a letter—which, though in and of itself is no big deal, can kill an actor having to improvise around its absence.

To absorb the full force of my first Broadway show, I went alone to the theater in Times Square, having avoided that famous crossroads on the night I arrived in New York, when everyone in America knew there would be throngs of revelers in Times Square on New Year's Eve. Not wanting to be "taken for a ride" by the fabled unscrupulous New York taxi driver, I had consulted a map and had seen that the trip to the Roosevelt Hotel, where I would be staying on East 44th Street, would be almost a straight shot from the West Side Terminal through the Times Square area near 42nd and Broadway. So as I entered the cab, employing my best Yankee accent I had told the driver, "Please take me to the Roosevelt Hotel, and don't take me through Times Square."

Not missing a beat the driver turned around and, after giving me the once-over, said, "Well shut my mouth. How long youse been in town?" There was just no disguising the hayseeds in my hair.

It wasn't many weeks later that, washed along in the human tide of theatergoers in Times Square, hayseeds still in abundance, I gawked in wonder, utterly intoxicated.

I saw the musical *Most Happy Fella,* which I'd never heard of, and though it has never been my favorite, it was exuberant and joyous, perfect for my first Broadway play.

My Fair Lady had opened a few months before I arrived, and was sold out so far in advance the only way you could get a ticket was to know somebody, which, as it turned out, I did. A girl I'd met at the Evangeline was dating a boy named Hemion (I can't remember if it was Dwight or his brother, one or both of whom went on to become prominent television producers) who worked at CBS—one of the backers of *My Fair Lady*—who came up with three center orchestra seats for her at box office prices, which at that time was seven or eight dollars. When I think of all the musicals I've seen, that production of *My Fair Lady* is still my favorite. As much as I was enchanted by the transformation of Julie Andrews's Eliza and Rex Harrison's incomparable Henry Higgins, it was Stanley Holloway as Mr. Doolittle who stole the show for me. He was peerless. Though I prefer drama to musicals, that was an era of musicals that today have no equivalent. I feel privileged to have been around to see, off the top of my head, *West Side Story,* '*Bye, 'Bye Birdie, L'il Abner, The Boy Friend, The Music Man,* and a revival of *Three Penny Opera,* down at the Theatre de Lys with Lotte Lenya.

A big event for me was when a theater pal from Millsaps blew into town and we went together to see Jason Robards as Hickey in *The Iceman Cometh,* directed by José Quintero, at the old Circle in the Square near Sheridan Square, a few blocks from where I lived. After I saw *Look Homeward, Angel,* on a late weekend morning from my window on the ninth floor I would look south over the rooftops to 11th Street where Thomas Wolfe once lived and wrote, and wonder how this displaced Southerner must have felt. I saw Fredric March and Florence Eldridge in *Long Day's Journey Into Night;* Henry Fonda and Anne Bancroft in *Two for the Seesaw;* and Pat Hingle and Teresa Wright in *Dark at the Top of the Stairs.* One of my all-time favorites was James Agee's *All the Way Home,* with Arthur Hill and Colleen Dewhurst.

No matter how many plays I've seen in my lifetime—countless now—I still feel the old familiar rush of adrenaline every time I see a curtain go up.

☙

Never having had trouble making friends, between my office friends, the girls at the Evangeline, and the friends of friends from Mississippi who lived in New York, it didn't take long to branch out and meet new people. And when you move to New York from Mississippi, you never want for company from home, since everybody you've ever known, as well as all their friends and relations, calls you up when they come to town. People you barely knew at home were practically your best friend in New York. Also, a lot of boys from home were in the service, and when they came through called me and took me to dinner, or a show, and sometimes even dancing.

Poor as I was, with all the visiting firemen, I was luckier than most when it came to what passed for "sophistication" and "glamour" in those days, such as meeting under the clock at the Biltmore Hotel, and having drinks in the Biltmore bar.

Part Two - New York

Which is where I received one of my biggest jolts of disillusionment.

It's true what they say about a small town keeping people on the straight and narrow, at least in public, because everybody knows everybody. Among a majority of Jackson churchgoers, the consumption of alcohol was considered as sinful as a slap in the face of Jesus. The father of a friend from home—a renowned teetotaler—and a colleague were in town for a convention, and had arranged for me and a friend, another transplanted Jackson girl, to have dinner with them, and to meet them in the bar at the Biltmore beforehand.

The father was a pillar of his church and the business community, and his colleague, a real hotshot, had made it to the top by the time he was in his late thirties. They couldn't have been more different in temperament or demeanor. Though I hadn't met the younger man, even though he was married, his reputation as a ladies' man preceded him. But because he was so much older than we were, and because we would be with our friend's father, we accepted.

This was in the days of good manners, when you told the man you were with what you wanted and he would order for you. After the father ordered my brandy Alexander, an old-fashioned for my friend, and a bourbon and soda for his partner, big as life he debonairly ordered a whiskey sour for himself. My friend and I were floored, and couldn't help exchanging astonished glances.

As we started the second round of drinks, I had become uneasy, getting more so as the partner began putting the make on my friend under the table, which she rebuffed as unobtrusively as she could with forced good cheer as the father seemed not to notice. Things were definitely getting out of hand, and I wasn't sure that we couldn't just as easily have daddy to contend with as well as his friend. I was unnerved by being so acutely disappointed—really crushed, to tell you the truth—but mostly they both revolted me.

I gave it another few minutes before I announced that we were really so sorry, but that we weren't going to be able to go on to dinner with them after all, that we had dates with some boys to go to a party.

What I hated most about the whole encounter was that we'd been sucked into their conspiracy, the conspiracy of silence of ol' boy secrets. Perhaps everybody was in on it; perhaps all the world already knew what we'd just found out, faithfully keeping the silence. Just as I have all these years.

∞

One freezing night early in 1957 I was in the Cotillion Room at the Pierre Hotel with Rex Moody, who handled public relations for our office, his wife, Annelle (they had become sort of *in loco parentis,* making sure I wasn't neglected, or in neglect), and Larry Painter, the creative arm of our shop, who was a great fan of Lilo, the French chanteuse who was singing there. The visiting firemen we were entertaining had called it a night and I was dancing with Larry, a wonderful dancer, having a glorious time. By that time we had all partaken of considerable spirits—it might very well have been the same night that Larry introduced me to the bourbon mist with a twist.

Anyway, we closed the place down, and as we were walking out of the Pierre, fortified by the glow of bourbon against the biting early morning air, we reached the corner of 60th Street and spied the Copacabana, where Frank Sinatra was singing, and all of a sudden Annelle says, "Claire, you love Frank Sinatra. Rex, let's go see if we can get in so she can see him." It was two o'clock on a week night, and I protested, honestly protested. But Annelle would have none of it.

As we squeezed into the foyer of the Copa, the two-o'clock show was just about to begin, and they weren't letting anybody else in. The place was packed, people stacked up against the walls. Suddenly, there appeared before us a man parting the crowd like Moses at the Red Sea, gesturing to us to follow him, which we did, wading through sardined tables wedged with people to find ourselves standing smack up at the edge of the small dance floor where Frank would be singing. Then, miraculously, what appeared to be a table, its top no bigger than a large pizza, was being passed over the heads of the crowd into the hands of Moses, as his colleague produced chairs and a white table cloth while at the same time taking our orders, as smooth as any Houdini.

As Sinatra strolled nonchalantly out onto the tiny space that remained for a stage, decked out in a wool sports coat the color of vanilla ice cream over an open-collared black silk shirt—cigarette in

Part Two - New York

one hand and glass of Jack Daniels in the other—the room exploded. And when he broke into "It Happened in Monterey," an allusion to his stormy relationship with Ava Gardner, we raised the rafters.

I don't know what it cost Larry and Rex, but they must have had to cross the palm of Moses with enough to pay my rent for at least two or three weeks.

All this must sound as though I led an extravagant life. Which was not the case at all. I lived from paycheck to paycheck, and weeks would go by that I wouldn't see a play or go out to fancy places, but New York being New York, I was never without something to do or somewhere to go that didn't cost a lot of money. In fact, even though everything is relative, in those days you didn't have to be rich to be able to buy a ticket to a Broadway show (Off Broadway was in its infancy). But above all, even though there were disadvantages, I could afford to do more of the things I liked to do by living at the Evangeline. Besides making more money than many of the other girls my age, the other advantage I had, or so I thought at the time, was that I didn't work in midtown for a publisher, magazine, or television—the poorly paid so-called "glamorous" world overrun with girls subsidized by their parents.

Before I left Mississippi, Mrs. Godwin had asked me what I thought I ought to get paid when I got to New York. She seemed to be genuinely in the dark on the subject. Everybody else on the payroll in the New York office was an account executive, except for the only other woman, the receptionist, and naturally I didn't fit into any particular slot. As friends of my parents, I'm sure the Godwins didn't want to send me off to New York to struggle and barely scrape by on a subsistence salary. On the other hand, they wouldn't want to be considered extravagant, either. I had talked to some people about the huge difference in the cost of living and somehow came up with $350 a month, which seemed fair, with a raise to $400 a month after I'd been there a year. Before she agreed, she questioned whether I was sure that was really enough, and I assured her she could count on me to let her know if I were starving and couldn't make it. Thus it was that after making what I considered a modest but fair proposal, on my arrival in New York I was surprised to find that so many other girls my age made considerably less than I did.

It's hard to comprehend, I know, but there were no bank credit cards then. It was strictly a cash world. The only credit cards were those issued by department stores. Diner's Club started up around that time, with American Express not far behind. Business lunches and dinners were either on house accounts or paid by cash or check.

One of the things I learned immediately is that when you live from paycheck to paycheck, a banker is a girl's best friend. With only a nickel-per-check service charge for a checking account—before even "special checking" accounts—many a payday would arrive when I literally had no more than a nickel or a dime in the bank; and cashing a check from out of town could sometimes take as long as two weeks. So I made it my business to introduce myself to the vice president at the Chemical Corn Exchange Bank who handled our agency business. He would be charmed, I was assured, to assist me with any problem that might arise. I felt like such a plutocrat.

∽

You need to realize that after all these years I still speak in my native tongue. I simply never had any reason to change the way I talk. (Though to their credit they have always denied it, I'm sure my accent must have been a secret embarrassment to my children when they were growing up in Brooklyn and suburban New York City.)

In fact the opposite was true. In my job at the advertising agency in New York I dealt with an array of outside people with whom, because of my accent, I had instant recognition on the phone, becoming, of course, "Honey Chile" (pronounced "Chy-ul" in New York) to most of them. Realizing no one would ever understand the way I pronounced my first name ("Cly-ah"), no matter how hard I tried to make it come out right, the big surprise to me was that people couldn't even understand me when I said "Miss King."

"Who is this? Miss Cain?"

"No, Miss KING"

"Oh, Miss Keene."

Really.

When I landed in New York, though I thought I was Miss

Part Two - New York

Sophisticate, I had no idea that the rest of the world thought Southerners were country hicks, and that a lot of New Yorkers were innately prejudiced against anything Southern. I thought I was just fine, as bright and smart as the rest of them, especially when I found out I was making more money than most of the other girls my age. Remember, we didn't have women doctors, lawyers, or merchant chiefs in 1957. In the world I lived in, if we hadn't married the day after college, or before, if we weren't housewives, that Holy Grail of occupations, we were secretaries or teachers or nurses, or wore the many hats of that special role reserved only for us, Girl Friday. It was the rare woman who dreamed of moving up in the world.

I've never liked fake people, and when I no longer worked, and the years went by, what I believed was that if I tried to lose my Southern accent, it would be as though I were trying to be someone I wasn't, denying who I was. I would feel like a phony. And for years when I would go home to Mississippi, the great badge of honor I always had bestowed upon me was, "You still haven't lost your accent!" (Now when I go home, I still have my accent but I've lost almost everything else they hold dear.)

My husband said to me recently, "I don't know how you stand it after all these years!" after yet another encounter with a stranger remarking on my accent. I've always found it curious that people will call attention to a Southern accent, though never, ever make an issue of a foreign accent (except an English one, I'm told by an English friend). Simple good manners usually precludes this affront, though this same courtesy is not accorded to Southerners.

I had no idea until I moved to New York that Southern accents were so different. (I was also unaware that Virginians believed themselves to be superior to all other Southerners, and to all non-Southerners as well.) After I became aware of the differences, I developed such a sensitive ear that I became the Professor Henry Higgins of Southern accents, honing the ability to discern the subtle nuances of placing the origin of the speaker.

I was surprised not long ago to discover that I was out of practice, that I'd lost my ear. I was in a shoe store on Fifth Avenue and watched a group of four women as they moved around the store together, a covey of beautiful birds, cooing like pigeons in the most divine accent. It had been years, but the old reflex took over and I said, "I've been listening to you talk and you sound as though you might be from Mississippi." The lead bird, sniffing the air, replied, "Heavens, no! We're from Virginia," and shooed her flock away lest they become contaminated. I couldn't help but laugh out loud in reaction to her obvious snub.

Not until I read Peter Taylor's novel *A Summons to Memphis* in the eighties had it ever occurred to me that even inside the state of Tennessee the people of Nashville look down on their fellow Tennesseans in Memphis. Now that I know Tennesseans look down on other Tennesseans, you can imagine how they feel about people from Mississippi.

Have you ever noticed that no matter where you are geographically—hemisphere, continent, country, state, city, county—it's always the folks in the southern parts who are always looked down on, considered inferior?

༄

I met the man who was to become my first husband when he came to my rescue after an unpleasantness about my Southern accent.

It is after work and I am in Churchill's, a bar with a restaurant upstairs, on lower Broadway just south of Liberty Street, close to my office in the Singer Building. This is downtown in Wall Street, where the ratio of men to women is about a million to one. Most of the women who work here are secretaries or clerks, many from the outer boroughs who still live with their families and don't hang around after work.

Churchill's, one of the few downtown places where the younger crowd meets after work, is always convivial and crowded. I am uncharacteristically early to meet a boy I've been going out with who works for one of the brokerage firms downtown. Today he is uncharacteristically late.

"Nice" girls don't go to bars alone, and "respectable" bars don't even allow women unaccompanied by a man. Since it is freezing outside, after I push through a revolving door that keeps the icy January air out, I stand just inside to watch the door for my date. As I wait there, I can't help noticing a man at the bar, giving me the look, which I ignore, nose in the air.

Finally, this fellow, the soul of a gentleman, very graciously inquires, "Won't you be more comfortable waiting here at the bar having a drink where it's not so cold?"

"No, thank you," I respond prissily, feeling awkward, as well as guilty about being so rude, and wishing Jack would hurry up and get here so I wouldn't have to deal with this.

Literally not taking "no" for an answer, he persists, "Well, you *are* waiting for Jack, aren't you?"

This sort of takes me aback. He must have seen Jack and me here before. But then, anybody can use that old ruse, "waiting for Jack." Mind like a steel trap, I riposte, "Jack who?"

"Sheely," shoots back his reply.

"Well, since you know Jack, thank you, that would be nice," I relent, joining him at the bar. He orders my current favorite, a brandy Alexander, and then, naturally, asks where I'm from. When I tell him, he says: "I thought you were pretty good-looking until you opened your mouth. Why haven't you dropped the accent?"

I am so stung, so taken by surprise by his rudeness, I am speechless. (Don't you always think of things you wish you'd said, even years later, after the moment has passed? This was definitely one of those times.)

Longing to brush it off with a sensational putdown, I come up empty, and so, relying on instinct, I do what any lady would do, I APOLOGIZE.

"Well, I'm just sorry if you don't like the way I talk," and turn away to look up (I have on my three-inch heels, so he must be TALL) into the face of the most attractive man, who has been leaning on his elbows, back against the bar, there next to me on the other side, unable to avoid overhearing the whole embarrassing exchange. "Don't pay any attention to him," he says to me sympathetically, "I love the way you talk. It's wonderful."

Thinking he's a friend of the creep's and is trying to apologize for him, I'm a little cool, but when I understand that he only knows him from seeing him around, I warm up a little. There's just time for him to tell me his name and for him to find out who I am and where I work before Jack finally breezes through the door. After I introduce them, the good Samaritan finishes his drink and says good night.

Ten days later he calls me at work, and the rest, as they say . . .

∾

I can't remember how I happened to meet Jack Sheely. He was from suburban New Jersey, Glen Ridge, I think, close to "the Oranges," as we called all those towns over there with Orange in their name. He'd graduated from Princeton, but didn't wear it on his sleeve. He was easy going and fun, with good manners, though not stuffy or pretentious, and called me "Johnny Reb," as Southern soldiers were called during the Civil War, then simply "Reb." (Now that I think about it, he may have been even more insightful than I realized.)

Having not before been aware of whether someone was a Catholic or not, or what ethnic background someone came from—what someone "was"—after going out with Jack for awhile I came to realize that his Catholicism was important to him, a part of his life, and always would be. Not like a lot of Protestants, who married other Protestants without giving it a thought; that being a Protestant was kind of interchangeable, as long as you went to *some* church.

Jack went around with a crowd of boys who were likable and funny, as he was, who kidded around among themselves in a kind of shorthand language, a cheerful, sometimes hilarious banter, the way guys do who know each other well. And as I came to discover, most of them were Irish Catholics. I must have had an affinity for Irish Catholics, or they for me, because I went out with several others, though I wasn't conscious of it at the time.

One was a guy named Joe, a really good guy, who'd been to Colgate. I was spending the weekend with him at his folks' house in his hometown of Ridgewood, New Jersey, on October fourth, the day the Russians sent up Sputnik—the first satellite—and started the space race. I remember the date, because on October fourth two years later, I gave birth to my first child and read at the time about other important events that had occurred on that date.

And then there was Jack O'Neill. We saw *Love in the Afternoon* together, the enchanting movie with Gary Cooper and Audrey Hepburn. O'Neill was different from the other Catholics I dated,

Part Two - New York

however. He was, he informed me, a Jesuit, an "intellectual," and I forget which Jesuit college he went to. But of course I wasn't impressed because I didn't know beans about Jesuits. He was "faster" than my other Catholic dates, though I don't know if it had anything to do with being a Jesuit.

Jack Sheely had a good mind and a seriousness that many of the boys of our generation seemed to want to disguise. (In Jackson, a lot of the boys in my high school class were really smart, but it was more acceptable for them to want to play football than to make good grades, so they tried to cover up that they were smart.) I sensed an unspoken recognition of these qualities in Jack by the other boys in his crowd, who unconsciously deferred to him when a decision needed to be made.

That first year in New York I got to go some places with Jack that I might have missed otherwise. One golden October weekend we went to a football game at the military academy at West Point, several miles up the Hudson River, the first time I'd ever seen such a vivid display of autumn leaves. We went with his friends and their dates on the Hudson River day liner packed with football fans hanging over the railings. It wasn't the game, of course, but West Point and the Romance of it all that attracted me. (All of the Penny Parrish books I'd read as a girl had been set in and around West Point, and now *I was going to see it*.)

Another weekend Jack invited me to a game at Princeton, and once again, never having seen Princeton, I went. I could have been at Mississippi State, except Princeton had clubs instead of fraternity houses. If I thought there was a lot of drinking at State, Princeton took the prize, the difference being that at State the alcohol had to be kept out of sight, while at Princeton it was flowing like the waters over Niagara. And though Jack got really drunk, at least he was a smiling, happy drunk. But still.

Long-playing records were new in the mid-fifties, and in those days when I was going out with Jack, Sinatra's l.p. "Songs for Swingin' Lovers" was on the air and in the air, everywhere we went. One Saturday night we went up to Suffern, New York, to a party that Charlie (one of the boys in Jack's crowd) was throwing at a house that belonged to his uncle, who was out of town, which naturally made me leery. Charlie had Frank's l.p., and I think it's the only music we danced to, over and over, all night long: "You Make Me Feel So Young"; "How About You"; "You're Getting to be a Habit With Me"; "You Brought a New Kind of Love to Me"; "I've Got You Under My Skin"; "I Thought About You." Whenever I hear those songs, I think of those New York days, just as I do whenever I hear Frank.

As the evening wore on, a couple now and then would disappear from the main party, reappearing maybe an hour or more later. Jack never gave any hint of expecting me to make a trip with him to one of the uncle's bedrooms, and told me just to act like I didn't notice what was going on. It was after four o'clock by the time the party broke up, and after several of the couples left to go home to the suburbs, we had only one car left to take the rest of us back to the city. I don't remember how many of us piled into that car, but somehow I ended up at the wheel, and when the boys told me they had to go to church before they went home, I thought they were pulling my leg. But they weren't. They explained that they'd rather go to Mass then than to have to get up and go later, and asked me to drop them off at a church and take the car and they'd get it later. So I left them in front of St. Joseph's at Sixth Avenue and Washington Place, a few blocks from the Evangeline, and watched them stagger drunk as skunks up the steps and through the doors as dawn was breaking, as though that was the way people went to church all the time. I drove away laughing, thinking about what would happen if somebody ever showed up drunk at church in Jackson, and how they'd never live it down.

That incident drove home to me for the first time just how serious Jack was about his religion. It made me think about our relationship on a different level, whether or not it could go anywhere, something I'd never been faced with. Before, any relationship I'd had with a boy was based on how we felt about each other (or, more precisely, how I felt about him). Religion had never before been part of the equation—and now here it was—and I knew I could never, would never, become a Catholic. Though of course it had never dawned on me that Jack might never consider taking a non-Catholic girl home to meet his mother either.

Somehow, everything works out. Christmas came, and I went home to Mississippi for the holidays. I didn't see Jack until after the first of the year, and though it may not have been the last time I saw him on that night I met him for dinner at Churchill's, it couldn't have been long after that.

He was a good man, Jack was, and having been connected to Wall Street in both of my marriages, occasionally I've wondered over the years if he were still there, too, and what his life has been like.

∽

You must understand that I believed that I had lived quite a worldly life. After all I'd been dancing on the Roof at the Heidelberg Hotel in Jackson, where we took our own bourbon in a brown paper sack to mix with our cokes (which I hated); and to the Buena Vista Hotel in Biloxi where I was introduced to grasshoppers (which I loved). And I'd been to New Orleans on the Panama Limited, to the French Quarter where I drank, among other things, Hurricanes at Pat O'Brien's (which I also loved). So from what I've written about hating all the drinking during my college years and early days in New York I realize that hard drinkers will think I'm a royal pain, that I sound like a disapproving Aimée Semple McPherson.

Which is not the case at all. I was reared in a society of hypocrisy, where drinking was frowned upon but almost everybody did it, where learning to drink in a civilized manner was not part of the culture. My parents had not grown up in families who drank, and only after they were married did they begin "taking a drink" (though my father in all likelihood started drinking in college with his fraternity brothers). Though they drank at parties, they never sat down together for the ritual cocktail at home every evening; and it's the belief in our family that it was the glass of sherry at her weekly bridge club that was the beginning of my mother's alcoholism, though of course no one knows.

I probably had my first taste of whiskey around the time I was eighteen and a senior in high school, and thought it was so vile I could barely get one swallow down. It was a mystery to me how anyone could even drink it, let alone love it. (One morning when I was much younger I had tried some creme de menthe—glowing like an emerald, and fragrant with mint—that had been left out in a decanter in our living room overnight, and was stunned when it was so nasty it made my eyes water.) What I now know is that what we were drinking as high school and college students was of such poor quality, only the impecunious and/or ignorant would be drinking it. Even when I thought I was drinking bourbon, it wasn't bourbon at all; I didn't even learn the difference until I got to New York when I ordered what I thought was bourbon and was startled to learn that I had ordered a blend. Whatever it was—in my college days I had to mix it with Coca-Cola or Seven-Up to be able to get it down—my dates and dances seemed to be a lot more fun when I'd had a few "bourbons" with Coke. By the time our crowd got to college, our parents had sense enough to tell us that if we were going to drink, to do it at home and not to try to sneak around.

What got to me, though—what I really despised—was boys drinking simply to get drunk, which is what went on at college football games and parties in Mississippi, and later in New York as well. Wherever, it was childish and stupid and immature. But most of all, it was just so goddamned boring.

༄

I had been in New York a little over a year when I met the man I married. By that time I'd gotten used to the city, soaked up its energy, immersed myself in "culture," and even taken a course in philosophy at New York University in their Adult Education program, making me feel ancient at twenty-three.

It's hard today to have any concept of what life was like for women in those years. I had had my job with the advertising agency since I was eighteen. When I started that first summer after high school, a job was a job, not a step up a career ladder, certainly not for a woman. I had never, until I was working in New York that first year, really even thought about what advertising was all about. It was the year the movie *The Man in the Gray Flannel Suit* came out, about the world of advertising, and it was the first time I began to think realistically about what it was I was really doing, what I was getting paid for. And it made me uncomfortable. Even though our advertising was "institutional"—we were promoting good will and a positive image for our clients—rather than "consumer"—persuading someone to buy a certain brand of cereal or soap—it was all part of the same ball of wax. And I knew I would never want it to be my life's work (oblivious, then, to the world of non-profit advocacy). Even in the narrow parameters of what "career" meant for a woman in those days—when the idea of progressing much further than I already had I would have thought impossible—it would never have crossed my mind that I might become an account executive, since there was a For Men Only sign over that door, which I never questioned.

Because girls were programmed from birth to become wives, in Mississippi the prevailing sense was that girls who went to graduate school were those who couldn't get a husband. And because I knew I couldn't afford it, I never gave it another thought after I arrived in New York. After the novelty of being in New York had begun to wear off—in a job that wasn't a career and never would be—and a year of dating mostly men who were still boys, my life began to seem aimless, unmeaningful.

It was at this juncture that the chance encounter with the attractive stranger occurred at Churchill's a few weeks after I turned twenty-four.

Six

"I tell you one thing, Claire's not marrying any boy. She's marrying a man," declared Emily Henderson, a neighbor, to Mama after she'd met my Brooklyn-born husband-to-be on his arrival in Mississippi for our wedding, that September in 1958.

He was twenty-nine. We'd had an eight-month courtship, February to September (the football off-season, I was to realize later), in which he'd positively wooed me, sweeping me off my feet.

When he called for me on our first date up at the new apartment I'd rented with three other girls on East 79th Street (1BR, lg LR w/sofa bed), I was surprised to find that he had come in his car, a gray Dodge convertible. It made me uneasy. After all, I knew absolutely nothing about this man, and it had never occurred to me that we would be in a car alone together. As we drove along the East River Drive, a full moon floated in the sky, shimmering in reflection on the river, and I told him how I felt, that for all I knew he could be some kind of werewolf. I thought he would have a wreck from laughing so hard. He wasn't a werewolf, of course, or any other kind of wolf, but wonderful, with a vulnerable sweetness in his eyes, a quick native New York wit, a soft heart, and a lover of jazz. He took me that night to Hickory House for dinner, where we heard Don Shirley, the first of many of the great jazz pianists—Teddy Wilson, Marian McPartland, Billy Taylor—we would hear together during those heady months.

I knew on our third date that he was the man I wanted to marry, when he drove me to West Hempstead, Long Island, to meet his father and brother. His mother had died a few years before, from breast cancer, and he and his brother, twenty months older, had moved into the ranch-style house with their father, who was retired and suffering from heart disease, to keep him company as well as to consolidate their expenses. I was immediately struck by the obvious bond among the three men and was deeply moved by their relationship of mutual respect.

There was a raging snow storm that February Saturday, and a crimson pimple like the eye of Cyclops pulsated in the middle of my forehead as we set out for my first trip to Long Island in his convertible, the first time I'd ever seen tires wrapped in chains. Only the foolhardy or intrepid ventured forth that day, and as the journey began I wasn't sure which he was. Though shaken and drained by the ordeal, by the time we arrived at his house I had experienced the most confident, skillful driving and sheer survival instincts I'd ever seen, and realized that here was a man I could count on, a man who could take care of me for a change, after all the boys I'd gone out with.

The snow was so deep we couldn't turn into the driveway. His father and brother emerged from the house at the top of the driveway, waving to us, waiting at the door. Barney Oldfield had pushed open his door and waded through the thigh-deep snow around to my side of the car to open my door and help me out.

My entrance could not have been better choreographed had it been written by Neil Simon. A neophyte in real snow, as I let go of his hand to precede him up the hill, the snow was so deep I was immediately tripped up, arms flailing the snow for support as I fought to break my fall, and landed full length in a snowdrift, disappearing from view. Rattled, of course, I kept trying to push myself up, fighting in vain to gain a purchase on the top of the snow, which naturally kept giving way as I pushed down. It was pure slapstick, greatly appreciated by father and brother as they broke into laughter and rushed forward to help. They seemed delighted with my "naturalness," and greeted me warmly as all three men lifted me to my feet and helped me inside.

"Pop," as they called their father, was the dominant presence, charming and warm. Though his sons deferred to him, I sensed that they had become the caretakers, the role reversal that takes place when parents age, though they were careful to try not to let it show.

He introduced me to Margaret, their elderly German housekeeper, to whom they had all fondly relinquished rule of the roost.

Pop was a man of low-key style and good taste, and I was quite touched by the obvious but unpretentious details the three men and Margaret had devoted themselves to in preparation for the occasion of my visit: the pretty flowers in the middle of the table set with a white damask cloth and beautiful china and silver. I was overwhelmed by the sheer delight they appeared to derive from simply having me there in their midst, by their genuineness, their kindness. It was also clear that the death of the mother still left a great void in all their lives, especially in Pop's, and that all of them seemed to be warmed by a female presence. I was absolutely dazzled. And during the whole weekend not one mention was ever made, no notice was ever taken—no teasing, nothing—of the third eye glowing in the middle of my forehead.

I was shocked when Pop died three months later. I had not understood how sick he actually was. Other than their mother's brother as their only other relative, his sons were all alone. At this vulnerable, painful time in his life, the younger son needed someone to help him get through it, and I was there. The death of his father, as well as the ordeal of the funeral and burial, was a deeply felt emotional experience that he and I shared together.

It was six weeks after that when he asked me to marry him. After I said "yes," I suggested that together we call my parents so he could "meet" them, at least over the telephone. Just as he was about to pick up the phone, I broke the news to him that Mama was probably an alcoholic and that she might have been drinking when we called, and half-jokingly I added that it wasn't too late for him to change his mind. Undeterred, he dialed "0" for operator.

Since I had not prepared Mama and Daddy for this message of the century, I thought it would be better for me to tell them, and then let my newly-minted fiancé speak to Daddy. My fears were borne out. Mama answered the phone, tying my stomach in knots as she slurred her words. I chirped out the Good News, as though nothing were wrong, and asked to speak to Daddy, which took awhile. Mama had passed the word to him, of course, so when he came on the line and I repeated the story, he sounded as though he couldn't be happier for me, or more pleased. Then the groom-to-be got on the line and introduced himself and told Daddy how much he loved me and wanted to marry me and asked his permission, except it was over the telephone to a father over a thousand miles away. Still, it was meet and proper so to do, after the fact though it was.

Then, covering the mouthpiece, he told me that Mama had picked up an extension phone, and I raced to another phone and we all tried to carry on a four-way conversation, which was so excruciating I wanted to die. I could tell that Daddy was doing his best to end the conversation to spare all of us, and at last we all hung up. Then I burst into tears, feeling sorry for myself, for Daddy, for Mama, and for my fiancé, who had no idea what he was letting himself in for. But then, neither did I. As indeed, who does?

We had known each other four months. He had grown up in Brooklyn, the son of a mother who was Jewish and a father who wasn't, who never talked about his family or background, though the boys did know that he had been a Marine in the First World War. Apparently it was a door he deliberately closed, never to reopen, something his sons respected and never questioned. Pop had been—and still was when I knew him—a dynamic and handsome man, who knew what he wanted and had swept his wife off her feet. He loved and respected her deeply, and brought up his sons to treat her with the same love and respect and consideration. He had a good job, and they lived well until the Depression, when they fell on hard times. Pop was able to provide for his family, though not at the level at which they had once been accustomed, and I believe it affected him deeply.

So my future husband grew up in a small apartment on Eastern Parkway where he and his brother worked after school from the time they were boys. His first job at the age of five, the year I was born, was delivering fish wrapped in newspaper to the customers of a fishmonger. When they were adolescents, their father formed a Boy Scout troop and became its leader to keep his sons and their friends off the streets and out of trouble. He was tough and fair, greatly respected, and almost every one of the boys in his troop became Eagle Scouts.

After passing a demanding entrance exam, my fiancé went to all-male Brooklyn Tech—one of those widely renowned New York City public high schools that produces Nobel Prize winners—whose students specialized in engineering. A natural athlete, he played both baseball and football, and to my amazement he told me they practiced on the roof of the school. And naturally his family grew up loving the Brooklyn Dodgers, his mother included, who at one unforgettable afternoon game caught a foul ball that the whole Dodger team autographed for her.

If we're lucky there are those in our lives who try to help us along the way. In my man's life there was his coach at Brooklyn Tech. By helping to get his athletes into college—those who otherwise might never have had any other prospect of going—he quietly touched more boys' lives than anyone will ever know. He was one of the best men I ever met, a hero in the Brooklyn mold.

Offered a scholarship to Syracuse University for both baseball and football, my fiancé chose football and a major in history, playing football under the newly hired coach, the now venerated Ben Schwartzwalder. After graduation he and another football buddy took off across America making their way to California, to try out with a professional football team. They pooled their money to buy an early model Ford, spending their nights in fields under the stars and on roadsides, their first taste of the bucolic life, and of freedom.

Arriving in California with a recurring dislocating shoulder, which he had acquired during his last year in college, he knew his only chance for making a team was if the team paid for the operation it would take to have his shoulder repaired. After trying out, he was told by one of the teams that if he got his shoulder fixed they wanted him. With no money for the operation, and unable to persuade the team to pay for it, he realized that his dream of playing pro ball was over. Deciding that as long as he was in California he might as well stay awhile and make the most of it, he got a job hooking tuna in a factory in San Pedro, hard physical work that paid well.

After hitchhiking back to Brooklyn a year or so later, he started looking for a job, and through a friend of the family was offered a job as a runner at a small Wall Street brokerage firm. It was only a few months before he was moved to the back office and then only a matter of time before he was on the floor of the American Stock Exchange as their clerk, soon becoming their broker. It was then that our paths crossed at Churchill's.

∞

He had never been south.

Neighbors two houses down were going to be out of town during the wedding festivities and put their house at the disposal of the groom and his brother, who had graduated from the University of Virginia on the GI Bill, and was familiar and comfortable with Southerners and their ways. More so than the groom, who had never been in the company of more than one: me.

We had planned a small wedding for family and close friends. And remembering that September Saturday some forty years ago, one of the little details I recall is that in a closet of the narthex of the chapel in the Methodist church I grew up in, a small radio was quietly tuned to the Mississippi State-Florida football game. When a male wedding guest entered the chapel, and in a whisper asked what the score was, someone was able to tell him.

The bridegroom's brother was his best man and my brother and uncle were groomsmen. Shelby, by then married to an old Starkville friend I'd introduced her to, was matron of honor, with my darling twin sisters, age nine, serving as bridesmaids. And Mama was magnificent. It was a precious time.

As I've said, I only remember seeing Daddy cry twice in my life. This was the second time, just before he had to give me away to my Yankee husband, as we stepped from the little narthex to begin the walk down the aisle. I felt, more than I heard, Daddy catch his breath, and make an almost inaudible sound of what could only be a muffled sob. And in a few more seconds it happened again. Though we had never much talked about love, for the first time it came over me just how much he loved me, and how hard it was for him, this ritual. I was afraid to turn and look at him for fear of embarrassing him, or of crying myself, so kept on smilingly moving forward toward my bridegroom, waiting there for me only a few more steps away.

After a reception in the church parlor where we served punch and cut the wedding cake, my very closest friends and family came out to our house. Under the splendid oak tree in our backyard, the soft September air hung with the perfume of a summer garden: a blend of mimosa, clematis, four o'clocks, jasmine, and gardenias; and Shorty, our yard man, resplendent and proud in his white jacket, helped Daddy pour the champagne.

After I changed into my blue "going-away" outfit (a wool dress and jacket far too hot for September in Mississippi and Jamaica, where we were going on our honeymoon, but practical for New York) and a jaunty, blue fringed-ribbon hat, we dashed through a shower of rice to a waiting highway patrol car, which Shelby's father, the mayor of Jackson, had provided—after I'd sweet-talked him—to make our getaway to the airport. (I've never considered the political implications of such a gesture until this very moment.) The gang was ready. Bob Neill, Nancy's husband from North Carolina, had organized a caravan, which he led in the wildest chase I never want to be in again, tailgating the highway patrolman, who had his foot to the floor and his siren screaming. (I'd introduced Nancy and Bob after I'd met him playing bridge one night, soon after he arrived in Mississippi. As a member of the Army Counter Intelligence Corps, part of his job was keeping an eye on the one known "Communist" in Mississippi, somewhere up around Tupelo.)

Arriving at the airport in record time, needless to say, our cohort of revelers spilled raucously into the little terminal from which I'd departed for New York less than two years before, overflowing out onto the tarmac where the plane waited. Like Ike and Mamie, at the top of the steps we turned and waved to the crowd, feeling deeply loved as everybody hollered and waved and threw farewell kisses.

Buoyant with happiness, here I was once more flying off into the unknown, though now, with my new husband beside me, I was no longer alone. Together we watched the merry band from our little window until they grew smaller and finally out of sight as the plane lifted off into the starry, starry night. It was the perfect happy ending. 'Way down south in Dixie.

༄

My husband loved to tell the story of how he really knew he was married. It was between connections in the New Orleans airport when he was waiting for me to go to the ladies room, and I returned to ask him for a dime to use the toilet. (Pay toilets were just as acceptable and legal in those days as "White" and "Colored" were.)

Actually, I did have twenty-two dollars in my purse, though no change. But if it hadn't been for Mama, I wouldn't even have had the twenty-two dollars.

As I was dressing to leave to go away, Mama asked me if I had any money in my purse. It was something that had completely escaped me. After all, why would I need money now that I had a husband? When I looked, I discovered that I had only two dollars. Mama told me, "You can't leave home with just two dollars in your purse," and went to get her wallet. All she had was a twenty dollar bill, and as she put it into my hand closing my fingers around it, she said, "It's good if every woman has a little money of her own, though I never did. I just wish I had some to give you." That was how I happened to leave home with a dowry from my mother. And it would be a long time before I would understand the truth she was trying to impart to me on my wedding night.

To get to Jamaica from Jackson, we first had to fly to New Orleans to connect with a plane to the Caribbean, which only flew to Jamaica three days a week, Saturday not being one of them (and these were not jet planes). So we had to fly to Havana, Cuba, and spend what was left of Saturday night and all day Sunday in Havana, leaving for Jamaica around midnight on Sunday.

I had read newspaper stories of a revolutionary named Fidel Castro and his band of guerrillas in the Cuban hills, who were said to be on the verge of overthrowing dictator Fulgencio Batista, but caught up as I was in the preparations for my wedding I had not been paying much attention to what was going on beyond the borders of Jackson, Mississippi.

As we stepped out of the plane into the soft Caribbean air, I was quite dismayed, not to say alarmed, to discover that the Havana terminal resembled a scene straight out of World War II, with part of the building bombed out and military jeeps darting about like *cucarachas*, full of soldiers armed with submachine guns.

When we began asking what had happened, we got only smiles and shrugs. Nobody, it seemed, spoke any English. It was already the middle of the night when we took a taxi to the Hotel Nacional, and, except for a small overnight case I'd brought with me, our bags, it appeared, had not arrived with us.

After being graciously welcomed at the front desk—as though all were quiet on the southern front—with a promise that our bags would be delivered as soon as they arrived, we were led to a serenely beautiful room where I was charmed to discover a vase of stunning tropical flowers and champagne, previously arranged for by my new husband. French doors stood open to a balcony overlooking a garden and the Gulf beyond. The lush scents and sounds of the tropical night cast their seductive spell.

It was almost mid-afternoon before we greeted the next day, and still no bags. In those days before air conditioning, with both the temperature and the humidity pushing one hundred, a jaunt in my new wool outfit had all the appeal of a visit to a steam room. Held captive by the idea that our bags would arrive at any moment, as we'd been led to believe, we hung around the hotel. Of course now I'm sorry we didn't take advantage of even the few hours we had there to explore the city, but who could have known that I was enjoying a once-in-a-lifetime visit to Havana? When the bags finally arrived, we changed into summer clothes and set out for a typically late Cuban dinner at the Tropicana, a nightclub built around a giant tree that grew through the roof in the middle of the dining room.

Taking in the huge room as we waited to be seated, I noticed a burly fellow leaning against the wall with his arms folded across his chest, slowly scanning the diners. At a distance of about three tables away from him, another man just like him had positioned himself. He had a pistol in a holster under his arm as he conspicuously stood guard over a table of eight. Mystery and espionage devotee that I am, after the drama of the airport I was instantly caught up in the intrigue, dying of curiosity as to who these people were. When I quietly but excitedly dug my fingers into my husband's arm to call his attention to this fascinating tableau, he had already taken it all in and quietly told me just to act as though nothing unusual was happening. Having been to Havana before, he knew you had to be careful, that it wasn't like home. I was too unworldly to be afraid.

When we were led to our table, I was beside myself when we

Part Two - New York

were seated practically next to the cynosure of all eyes, as they would have described it in the Jackson society pages. Since I was facing their direction, I could easily assess the situation without seeming to be too curious. There were four men and four women; the men, in somber business suits, were all much older than the women, who were sexy and quite swanky. They were seemingly completely unaware of the undercurrent they were creating as they lingered over coffee and brandy and cigars. Suddenly I was aware of a troop of men in civilian clothes converging on the table from each entrance. When they arrived, surrounding the table, all eight occupants arose and, completely shielded by the guards, swiftly departed the room.

As soon as they left, I could barely contain myself until I had a chance to ask the waiter who in the world they were.

"The head of the national treasury," he replied.

Arriving in Montego Bay at two a.m. was a stealth landing that hardly anybody noticed. And besides the occupation that honeymoons are designed for, our days were spent getting sunburned, suffering from cystitis ("bride's disease," so the British-accented doctor informed me as he wrote out my prescription for a sulfur drug), exploring the island, and eating and dancing on the beachside patio in the leafy shade by day and the stars by night. And though we were adhering to the honeymoon script, and everything was perfect, just as it was supposed to be, I couldn't escape the feeling that everything had a sense of unreality. That I was playing a role, and wondered if my husband felt the same way, though of course would never ask him.

Landing in New York after our honeymoon gave me the thrill I get every time I return and see the Manhattan skyline—that I'm home. This was the true beginning of our new life together. The courtship, the wedding, the honeymoon, all the rituals were over.

Seven

I was captivated by Brooklyn Heights the first time I set eyes on it. The beautiful nineteenth-century brownstones, the tree-lined streets, the sense of neighborhood. But most of all I was enthralled with the breathtaking view of the whole panorama of Upper New York Bay from the Esplanade at the end of Montague Street: the wall of skyscrapers of lower Manhattan, the Statue of Liberty, Governor's Island, the Brooklyn Bridge, the constantly streaming Staten Island ferries and stately ocean liners, the bustling warehouses below.

Like many people who haven't been there, I was prejudiced against the idea of living in Brooklyn. Even my husband, who was a native, hadn't been in favor of it. But exhausting and disheartening weeks of apartment-hunting in Manhattan turned up nothing that fulfilled our only two criteria: a) that we could afford it, and b) that we liked it.

A friend kept telling me I should at least go look at Brooklyn Heights before I wrote off the whole borough, that it was lovely, and that there was nowhere more convenient to Wall Street or my office. But I wouldn't listen. It was Manhattan or nothing. Finally, when we were getting desperate and I was getting depressed and frustrated, I asked my fiancé what he thought of Brooklyn Heights, and with nothing to lose, he agreed that it wouldn't hurt to take a look.

Within hours after emerging from the subway in the bowels of the St. George Hotel, we fell in love with an apartment at the end of Montague Street with a knockout view of the bay and lower Manhattan, which would be home to us, and eventually our three children, for the next seven years.

Part Two - New York

I loved Brooklyn, its history. I loved living in a neighborhood where Walt Whitman had been an editor of the newspaper, the *Brooklyn Eagle*. I loved the idea of the Brooklyn Dodgers, for of all the sports, if I had to choose one, it would be baseball—out of nostalgia for all those lazy summer days in Mississippi spent against the background of the sound of the St. Louis Cardinal games as my brother listened on the radio, to the feats of Stan "the Man" Musial, Red Schoendienst, and Enos "Country" Slaughter.

But I hadn't left Mississippi for New York to end up in a small town, which is what Brooklyn Heights was. If you wanted or needed the identity that being a big fish in a little pond offers, it was all there. Even though we were only one subway stop from Manhattan, the psychic distance was far greater. There's just no getting around it. As any Manhattanite knows, when you don't live in Manhattan, you don't live in New York. And I missed it—its immediacy, its energy, its proximity. But Brooklyn Heights was a good place for children.

For after only five months of marriage, at the age of twenty-five, I found that I was pregnant. With mixed emotions that I was cutting the final cord—one being not a little guilt, since the agency had given me two months off for my wedding and brought up someone from Jackson to fill in for me while I was away—I gave notice to my old friends by presenting them with my Diet for Pregnancy, moving them to humorous but gentle solicitude. In those days working when you were "showing" was not permissible, and I had provided myself time for six months of total abandon, encumbered as they would be. And to my mother's relief, I made a commitment to finish my wedding thank-you notes before my baby was born.

Dr. Virginia T. Weeks was our pediatrician. It turned out she was the older sister of Dr. Janet Travell, who would become President John F. Kennedy's doctor, the one who prescribed his rocking chair.

When you lived in Brooklyn Heights you either went to Dr. Weeks or to another long-time Heights resident. Just before I was ready to go home from Brooklyn Hospital, where some of us in

Brooklyn Heights delivered our babies, Dr. Weeks stopped by to see me. (I hate to tell you that at that time four days was the *minimum* stay when you had a baby, and I stayed a week, loving every minute of it. The idea that women today are allowed to stay in the hospital no more than forty-eight hours is inhuman and barbaric, a move in the opposite direction from what women need. Health care has become an oxymoron now that it has become a business.)

After giving me the rundown on the care and feeding of our magnificent new son, she surprised me with the suggestion that one day in the next few weeks, while on an outing with my baby, I should stop by Grace Episcopal Church and sign him up for nursery school.

Nursery school? Now? I asked her.

She said it was the only nursery school in Brooklyn Heights, and if you don't sign them up when they're born, they might not get in by the time they're three. That she would tell them to expect me. I hadn't really given any thought to nursery school, but if Dr. Weeks hadn't prompted me to get with the program, I don't know how long it would have been before I found out that it was already too late. Anyway, I was grateful and realized that I had found a good friend in Dr. Weeks, whose office was on the garden, or bottom, floor of a brownstone on Willow Street where she and her husband had reared their four children.

I believe it was during the very first appointment that she informed me that she was going to give our new innocent baby his DPT shot. When I handed him over—so precious and helpless and trusting—to the mean doctor who stuck him with a needle, and he let out that OOWWAAYYNNHH sound that only a weeks-old baby can make at the top of his lungs, I boo-hooed, "I bet all your mothers cry."

"No, they don't," Dr. Weeks replied. "Next time you'd better wait outside."

One deep winter day, with a snowstorm swirling and already ten inches deep, our baby came down with a high fever; I hated to call Dr. Weeks, but new mother that I was, I called anyway. "I'll be there in about an hour," she said. "Have a cup of hot cocoa ready," and hung up. It took longer, about two hours, and when I opened the door I was delighted, if momentarily startled, to behold her arrayed in a flowing black Franklin D. Roosevelt cape, dripping melted snow, and already in thick wool sock feet after taking off her boots, obviously having made her way on foot. Nobody made house calls anymore—even in those days it was extraordinary—and now here before me was this remarkable woman, I'm sure the first feminist I'd ever met, though I never would have known it, since at that time I'd never even heard the word.

After she'd inspected and dosed my child, we sat drinking hot chocolate together against the raging whiteness. That was when she suggested that I join the junior committee of the South Brooklyn Neighborhood Houses so that I could meet other young mothers in the area, and gave me the name of the person to call. Then she wanted to know what church we belonged to. We had just had our son christened by Dr. Sockman at Christ Church Methodist in Manhattan, where I still belonged, but I told her that just wasn't going to work out, since it was so far away.

She then explained how important it was to take children to church when they were young. Children needed—wanted—to believe in God, a higher Being, and if you didn't expose them to it when they were small they never would be. They could decide when they were older if they didn't want to go to church, but they hardly ever decided to go when they were older if they'd never been.

So that was how I became a Presbyterian. Since there was no Methodist church in Brooklyn Heights, I visited other churches, finding the Church of the Pilgrims—the Congregational church where Henry Ward Beecher, the abolitionist, had been its fiery preacher—quite appealing, though it jarred me when I saw Pilgrims and Indians in the stained glass windows instead of the familiar figures from the Bible. Their hymns were familiar, though, and even after I joined the Presbyterian Church, divided at that time into northern Presbyterian and southern Presbyterian—integrated in the North, segregated in the South—I would occasionally go to the Congregational church because I liked the atmosphere, all that light in its stark white sanctuary.

My husband, who had not been brought up in any faith, a living, breathing example of what Dr. Weeks was talking about, was uncomfortable in church. But to his everlasting credit, when he heard what Dr. Weeks had to say about it, and perhaps because of his own personal experience, whenever I went to church and took our son to the nursery, he would help get him dressed and sometimes either walk with us or meet us afterward. But it was the rare occasion when he joined us inside.

∾

It wasn't until our oldest son decided he wanted to go away to boarding school that I realized why, sixteen years before, all those mothers in Brooklyn Heights had gone to Manhattan hospitals to have their babies: it would never do to have Brooklyn as one's "place of birth" on a boarding school application. From the Eastern boarding school point of view, our son had three strikes against him. Not only was he tainted by Brooklyn on his birth certificate, he was equally blemished with a Brooklyn-born father. And what was bound to be the cruelest blow of all, a Mississippi-born mother.

After we'd been in Brooklyn awhile, when I found out that many Brooklyn Heights residents used that as their return address— to distinguish themselves from the unwashed who lived in just plain "Brooklyn"—I realized that I had been completely oblivious to the social aspects of life in "the Heights," as it was called.

When I was asked to join the Brooklyn Junior League, I was ambivalent. On the one hand I was flattered. Back in Mississippi women would do anything for an invitation to join the Junior League. But on the other, it was like being in a sorority. In the end I was weak, and joined, rationalizing that if we ever moved, it would be a built-in way to make new friends (before "networking"). And to be fair, I met some great women in the Brooklyn Junior League. Because that was the early sixties, we were always considered "wives of," and some of those wives' husbands I've read about in the business sections over the years as they rose to the top of their professions. I've often wondered what the lives of the wives of those men have been, if we'd now have anything in common; if they're still married, if they've found their own identity. Or like so many of my generation, if they *are* still married, were never able to renegotiate their original contract, and remain stuck in the old mold.

It was as a member of the Junior League in Brooklyn that I first heard the word "underclass." One of the requirements of a League member was to devote a certain number of hours a month as a volunteer in the community. And if ever there was a place where you really felt as though you were filling a need and not just doing busy work, it was in the borough of Brooklyn. With an infinite number and variety of ways and places in need of help, Brooklyn was a volunteer's paradise. I had a warm place in my heart for Brooklyn Hospital since, by then, my two sons had made their first appearance in its delivery room; and so I chose to do my volunteer work typing case histories in its social services department. As a twenty-eight-year-old, those reports were my initiation into a world about which I had not the remotest concept, a world of horrifying deprivation and depravity, knowledge from which I had so long been spared and protected. I blinked away tears as I typed unbelievingly of the stark facts of life in its rawest form, fervently hoping that the people I was working for would be able to relieve some of the hopelessness in the lives of these desperate people.

In the end I was to be a Junior Leaguer for only three years, resigning when we moved to northern Westchester County and I was informed that my volunteer job would be to plant flowers at the train station, so far removed from the world of Brooklyn and its manifold needs.

Originated early in the twentieth century by privileged young unmarried women in Manhattan who performed works of charity among the poor, the Junior League's original purpose had been turned completely on its head. Now here we were with young children at home having to pay someone to stay with them while we went out to do good. Which lasted until a woman was forty, when she was then deemed too old, becoming a "sustainer," in essence, "inactive," just at the time she was unencumbered by children and could get out of the house. It was insane. Though I'm a great admirer of its contribution to the community, our daughter grew up completely ignorant of the Junior League. I hope she'll never feel she's been deprived because of it.

༄

The only time I ever remember having any connection with a United States Senator was when my father died. It was 1961. Daddy had been in the hospital for three months with special nurses round-the-clock, who were not covered by his insurance. Even though he thought he had good hospitalization insurance, as it was called then, his last hospital stay impoverished my mother, leaving her in penury for the rest of her life.

Daddy, who at fifty-three claimed he'd never had but one headache in his whole life, began in January to feel puny and worn out, just not himself. The doctor could find nothing wrong. When he went so far as to see a chiropractor for the first time in his life, I became concerned. Then, when he gave up his thirty-year, two-pack-a-day habit of Lucky Strike cigarettes, I realized how desperate he must be, and was now greatly alarmed.

After he was admitted to the hospital in June for a lung biopsy, and found to have pulmonary fibrosis, I went home to Mississippi with our eighteen-month-old son to do what I could to help.

I didn't know what the situation would be when I got there, but I knew it was not going to be good. Over the years my mother had become a full-blown alcoholic, and by that time my twin sisters were eleven years old. It had to be hell for my father, the anguish of lying there helplessly with no one in charge at home, the girls essentially abandoned to their own devices. My heart ached for Mama, too, pretending she was on top of things, when of course she wasn't, and everybody knowing it, including the doctors.

Alcoholism, especially in women, and most especially in women in the South, was a disgrace. It was only spoken about behind one's hand, and behind one's back. It was never confronted, and though we never discussed it, I feel sure my father had tried to do whatever he could. But perhaps he pretended to ignore it, too. He never said the word "alcoholic" to me. Only, "You know your mother's been drinking."

At twenty-seven I had never seen death before, so did not recognize it for what it was as it took my father in its grasp. For almost three months I became mother to my mother, mother to adolescents, mother to my own child, daughter to my father, absent wife to my husband, in addition to decision maker and administrator, as the circle of our lives narrowed around a single hospital bed.

At that time in America the draft was still in effect after the

Korean War. When my brother got out of college he enlisted in the army and at the time of our father's illness was stationed in France.

When you spend every day at the bedside with someone, you lose your frame of reference and become inured to the changes taking place. The shocked faces of relatives and close friends became the barometers on which my father's worsening condition were registered. My father's doctor, who was a "friend" of the family, obviously was most uncomfortable when he had to deal with my mother on the infrequent occasion when I wasn't able to keep her from the hospital. Never giving me a straight answer about my father's condition, he never told me that he was so close to death, and to this day I resent his condescension and the patronizing way he treated my family and me.

The weeks turned into months with no improvement, and on top of everything else, having also discovered I was pregnant, I needed a break, longing to take my child and go home to my husband, the soul of comfort and support.

(In a day when the word "stress" was a stranger to our vocabulary, after I'd been in Mississippi for several weeks, I began having a hard time taking a deep breath, and knowing rationally that it was impossible for me to have in any way contracted Daddy's condition, when I made an appointment with a gynecologist to find out if I indeed were pregnant, I also described to her my breathing symptoms. Not batting an eye, she declared, "It's no wonder!" and whipped off a prescription for Librium, a tranquilizer. It wasn't long after our splendid new son was born [the day after John Glenn's first flight into space] that the malformed and deformed Thalidomide babies began to appear—babies born after their mothers took the tranquilizer drug Thalidomide while they were pregnant—and when I think of how easily my doctor could have given me Thalidomide instead of Librium, it makes my hair stand on end.)

As Daddy's life dwindled, we made the decision to send for my brother in France, to be there with him and give me a rest. I was anxious to get home to my husband, but unwilling to leave until my brother arrived, and with all the red tape there was no telling how long it would take.

If there are six degrees of separation, when you live in a state that doesn't have two million people, and half of those are unenfranchised, between United States Senator John C. Stennis and us there was only one. As a college classmate and friend at Mississippi State of my uncle Robert, the one who died of a ruptured appendix when he was twenty-five, Senator Stennis had spent many an evening in Starkville around the Hogan dinner table. After someone suggested that we see if the senator could help us, I couldn't believe it when it wasn't three days before my brother was home from Europe. I was powerfully impressed.

A few weeks after our father died, my brother suffered a severe breakdown and, at the age of twenty-five, was diagnosed to be a paranoid schizophrenic. With Daddy gone, and my brother severely ill, along with the obligations to my own family in Brooklyn, soon to be increased, I felt responsible for my Mississippi family as well.

Too caught up with the living to mourn the dead, I postponed it for a long time.

∞

One afternoon in the mid-sixties when I was pregnant with our third child, holding one son by the hand and pushing another in the stroller, I was heading to the Pierrepont Street playground with another pregnant mother and her two young boys in tow. As our entourage slowly progressed, my friend asked me what I thought about a new book just out which had raised such a fuss, called *The Feminine Mystique*. At that time in my life, with so little time to read anything but the newspapers, I'd only read a review. Even so, with no frame of reference and no earthly way of yet being able to relate to the experiences the author described, I had summarily dismissed it.

However, my friend, a thoughtful Virginia woman, seemed much more willing at least to consider that Betty Freidan might be on to something, and we continued discussing it until we reached the playground. I don't remember her ever bringing it up again, and after all, why would she, when she realized what a closed mind I had on the subject. In fact that was the only time I remember ever hearing anyone I knew mention the book. I don't believe Brooklyn Heights was a rabid feminist stronghold. Though how would I know?

Eight

Our move to the suburbs came as most moves to the suburbs came, when it was time for your child to enter school. Though there was a good public school in Brooklyn Heights within walking distance, my husband had begun thinking of a house with a yard, the old American Dream, and we began looking at houses in New Jersey, the closest commute to lower Manhattan. I told him that if we moved I hoped we could live in a place that when someone asked where we lived, they would rejoice and be glad, and exclaim, "Oh, how lovely!" instead of the usual rejoinder, "Oh, really?" and a quick change of subject when they heard I had come from Mississippi—a real conversation stopper—or that I now lived in Brooklyn. I felt guilty about feeling that way, as though I were a traitor to my native land and to the place of my children's birth, but sometimes I just got so *tired* of *defending* them. And as we discovered the beauty of New Jersey (even though I'd visited there, it had never been with an eye toward *living* there), I realized how out of prejudice it too had been so greatly ridiculed and maligned.

Not completely happy with anything we saw in the Jersey suburbs, we ranged farther north, on up the Hudson, and though I've now traveled the world over—seen the Alps and the Cotswolds, the Serengeti and Mt. Fuji; the rolling hills and stately oaks of Mississippi; the vineyards and lavender fields of Provence, the Florence countryside, and the grandeur of Arizona—I don't believe there's any place on this earth more beautiful than the Hudson River Valley. And finally, arriving in the town of New Castle in Northern Westchester County, the farthest point my husband wanted to commute from, we bought some land at the end of a cul-de-sac covered with hardwood trees, dogwood, pussy willow, pokeweed, mountain laurel, and crumbling weathered stone walls, renting a house while we built our new home. And when people asked me where I lived, came now the inevitable reply, "Oh, how lovely!" and I would respond with a beaming smile. It's amazing how superficial everything is.

∞

Families moved to Westchester from all over the country, even from foreign lands, and many of those mothers rarely made a trip to the city ("We have branches of all the best New York stores only twenty minutes away in White Plains," was the realtor's cry and favorite selling point), and then only to meet the commuting husband after work for dinner and a show, just as a tourist sees the city, seldom having the chance, or even the desire, to discover New York beyond the tourist sights. More than once I took suburban friends to New York to help them feel at ease there so they'd be inclined to go more often on their own. They loved to go with me—their guide and protector—but remained apprehensive when venturing forth alone. The suburbs were so comfortable, so predictable, so very safe.

As the traditional wife and mother, my life centered around my husband, our three children, and our home. Though families today are child-centered, in those days they were still centered around the husband/father, as they were when I was a child. Outside of my home, with little in the suburbs for me to hook into as a community, I was still much more attuned to the city. Having the luxury of a cleaning woman twice a week, for stimulation and perspective I tried to get into New York at least three or four times a month. Sometimes I had no particular destination—just being there energized me—and if the weather was nice, I'd pick a particular neighborhood to have lunch and then walk the streets and window shop, having my senses bombarded, storing it up until the next time.

∞

Not long after we married, my husband accepted an offer to become a partner in a fine old brokerage firm. When you think of how life works, there's no accounting for how he ended up in a job that was perfect for him. Because there was no way he could have known that he had a natural "feel for the tape," in the parlance of Wall Street, it would never have occurred to him as a boy to dream, "When I grow up I want to be on the stock exchange." It would have been as foreign to him as it would have been for me to dream of being a U.S. Senator.

As a broker on the American Stock Exchange (begun in the early 1800s as the "Curb Exchange," where members met their clients in the streets and orders were literally executed on the curb of the sidewalk, it isn't the "gentlemen's club" that the New York Stock Exchange is thought to be), my husband's hours were ten to four. His family was the center of his life, which is incredibly difficult for a commuting father, and instead of taking the train, he drove each day to Wall Street, leaving quite early in the morning—before it was light in winter—to arrive there in time for breakfast, returning by five o'clock in the afternoon, when he'd play with the children, usually outdoors. And when they were older he was a coach for the boys' Little League games, both football and baseball. I had dinner on the table every night by 6:30, when we all sat down for the evening meal together.

Just as my mother and her mother and her mother's mother before her, I became a terrific cook.

∾

An awakening is only recognized in retrospect. And in retrospect, there were a series of events over a span of several years, at a crucial time in my life, which, taken as a whole, became the distant thunder of the tenpins that began to rouse me out of my Rip Van Winkle slumber.

I believe the first fissure came when I quit smoking and began to take control of my life, though I didn't understand that was what I was doing. I had smoked half my life, eighteen years, and when I stopped, I quit cold turkey. I'd been thinking about giving it up, and occasionally would see how long I could go without a cigarette. Sometimes it was late in the afternoon before I had my first one. The day I quit was the day after we'd spent the evening before at a farewell party for some neighbors who were moving back to Texas. Though I drink only wine now, and hardly even much of that in those days, at that party I drank a good bit more than usual and, caught up in the spirit of the evening, I smoked like a chimney, as we used to say, a *lot* of cigarettes.

The next morning I was hung over more from smoking than drinking, my mouth like the bottom of a bird cage. I was so revolted by the thought of putting one of those disgusting things between my lips, so completely sickened by the idea of a cigarette, that I realized that this could very well be the day that I might be able to make it through without one. Because I felt so bad, it was relatively easy, and I was pleasantly surprised. I didn't mention to anyone that I was trying to quit, in case I wasn't able to do it, not even to my husband, who was at least a one-pack-a-day man himself. I made it all the way through the next day until late afternoon as I had the day before, got through supper, the rest of the evening, and finally made it to bed feeling like the Little Engine That Could. At supper the next evening I told my husband and my children, who all cheered.

The amazing discovery was how much empty time I had on my hands after I stopped smoking, along with the rather disturbing realization of how I had been using cigarettes to fill my days with something to do, or to postpone things I didn't enjoy, like folding the laundry, for instance, and other chores that bored me to tears.

Besides the end of my addiction to nicotine, in the fall of that year our daughter Corinne, the last in the nest, started half-day kindergarten, freeing up my time even more. I had never given the first thought to what I was going to do with my own life since I had fulfilled the only expectations required of me, being a wife and mother. Years after dismissing Betty Freidan, I had never made even a passing acquaintance with the term "personal growth."

Then, the next year, my mother died. When I was thirty-seven.

∽

My mother was a precious fun-loving woman, sweet and thoughtful and generous, happy in disposition. In her senior year in the small all-girl's Methodist college she attended in Mississippi, she was chosen "Most Charming." Featured in a full-page photograph in the yearbook, she is seated on a wicker love seat strewn with photographs of handsome young men, presumably her admirers, while gazing at the photograph of yet another she holds in her hand. I still remember the bolt of white-hot pain that pierced my heart when I came across that poignant picture of her after she died of alcoholism.

Given only the single name, Almyra, after Papa's mother, a descendant of the New Hampshire Ames family who were some of our Revolutionary forebears, for a time Mama called herself Almyra Ames to make up for this deficiency, which was why, with her knowing what it was like, I was never able to figure out how I ended up with only one name. By family and old friends, though, she was always called by the affectionate "Wiwa," which is how her name came out when her young sisters and brothers tried to say it.

I never got to know my mother, woman to woman. Because of her condition, the role reversal that takes place between parent and child in later life occurred prematurely. Mama and I moved from her being mother-to-me-as-daughter to my being mother-to-her-as-daughter when I was still in my twenties.

Whenever they think of Mama, my old friends always tell me, they remember her in the kitchen, and so do I—and I just hate it. Even though cooking was one of her great talents. I don't mean that she was a *cuisinière*, I mean that she had an innate sense of knowing how to make food taste good, which came only with years of experience. She would always remind us that she couldn't boil water when she and Daddy got married. And whenever she burned our toast at breakfast, Daddy always good-naturedly referred to it as "bride's toast" as Mama scraped off the burnt part with a knife. No matter what she fixed for us, it was wonderful. Food was a medium for her the way oils are for a painter, and though she knew she was a good cook, I don't believe she ever really thought of cooking as anything extraordinary, certainly not an art. It was just what wives and mothers learned to do. She just tried to make her dishes taste the way she remembered her mother's tasting. Unless Daddy tried to get her to make things taste the way his mother's had tasted.

Though she never said so directly, I know Mama tired of her role as cook. She became a captive of the kitchen. It was her prison. To provide herself with some bit of freedom from it, she taught our maids how to make all of her classic basics the way Daddy liked them: mayonnaise, which took a lot of time dripping the oil into the electric mixer bowl drop by drop; rolls, biscuits, and cornbread; rice; fried chicken and the gravy to go with the rice; "greasy beans" in the winter when there were no fresh ones, made with canned whole blue lake beans cooked down with onions and bacon grease; all the summer vegetables cooked with ham hock or bacon grease or onions (Mama believed a little onion or onion juice improved almost any dish); fresh corn scraped off the cob. When Mama got home from wherever she'd been, practically all she had to do was go in and pull all of these things together with a few of her added touches—the drudgery and most of the creativity removed.

Forever taking neighbors and friends a pan of rolls (over the years many a phone call would come from her to tell us, "Quick! Take the rolls out to rise!" for our own supper), some of her famous spaghetti, or chocolate chiffon pie or tomato aspic (Sacramento tomato juice, lots of lemon juice, onion juice, pecans, olives stuffed with pimiento, and celery), along with her mayonnaise. Renowned for her shrimp remoulade, after she died several of her friends called to see if I'd come across her remoulade recipe anywhere, if she'd written it down. But of course she hadn't, its secret accompanying her to her grave.

Taking gifts of her food, of her creation, of herself, to others seemed to be her only outlet for a sense of fulfillment or accomplishment, to be appreciated. My brother and I took her for granted, of course. Although every meal ended with "'Joyed my supper"—or dinner or breakfast—as we zipped away from the table, it was a perfunctory ritual, and though true, it was just that, not a real act of appreciation for what she'd given us. Daddy, on the other hand, because she cooked everything the way he like it, displayed far nicer manners and affection in expressing his genuine appreciation.

Whenever I'd have friends over during high school and college, Mama would pull out her toasted pecans or her deep-fried peanuts, which she'd spent countless hours first soaking and then skinning, each and every single nut between her fingers, the best I've ever eaten to this day, bar none; her own cheese straws or garlic cheese roll; or her chocolate fudge and fudge cake, or blonde brownies dusted with powdered sugar. I have her recipes for all of these, and they are typical: "about" a cup, "a few drops," etc. What is most painful to remember is that she would do all this without my ever asking. It was just there when my friends came. I took it all for granted. Just as I took her.

Mama was born knowing how to play the piano. If you could hum it, she could play it. It was a source of pleasure for her, which she loved to share, and many a party would end at no telling what time with Mama at the piano, everybody gathered around singing the old songs.

In the piano lesson phase of my life, when I perfunctorily practiced my "pieces"—plodding through a *Barcarolle* or *To a Wild Rose*—sometimes when she just couldn't stand it another minute, Mama would yell, teeth gritted, I'm sure, from the kitchen (where else?), "It's C-*sharp*, Claire! C-*sharp!*"

She never studied music, and I have no idea why not—even though Aunt Jerry had studied piano at MSCW, as had her sister Frances, only two years younger. Perhaps Granada College was limited in its courses, or—and this is most likely—she simply wasn't interested in *studying* it. She could already play whatever anybody wanted to hear.

Mama loved to dance, and because she could follow the most lead-footed, mud-booted good ol' boy at Mississippi State, making him think he was Fred Astaire, she was every college boy's favorite dancing partner.

She was never without an invitation to whatever was happening, and often would include one or more of her sisters on her outings. Her younger sister, my aunt Missy who became a medal-winning swimmer, said she never would have learned how to swim if Mama hadn't taken her along with her on all her swimming dates to every mudhole and pond in Oktibbeha County.

She loved to go places and see things, and one of her most precious memories was a trip by car with a friend all the way to California to visit Little Sister Sudduth who had moved there from Starkville, and on up to Canada to Lake Louise and Banff, which must have been before she was married. My "foot in the road" spirit came from her, and just as she was the communicator in the family who kept up with everybody, so am I.

Despite her sweetness, without realizing it Mama occasionally could just be real blunt (another trait I inherited from her). An example of this became a classic "Mama" story among my crowd.

During the war, when we lived in Starkville while Daddy was gone, next door to us lived a family who owned a Pomeranian, a nasty little dog, really, called Moo Goo. But I loved her. One day there was a great commotion when a cocker spaniel crashed through the screened-in porch where Moo Goo was locked in while she was in heat. Having only a vague notion of the consequences, I was delighted to find out not long afterwards that Moo Goo was going to have puppies. Horrified that Moo Goo would be producing half-breeds, the neighbors wanted to give them away. I pestered Mama ceaselessly to let me have one of the puppies, and by the time they finally arrived I had worn her down to a nub, and she gave in.

Which was how we happened to acquire Ginger, half Pomeranian and half cocker spaniel, a most unlikely, and unattractive, combination.

Just as a boy's paper route becomes his mother's, so does a child's dog. Born in 1944, Ginger was with me in the move back to Jackson, and on through junior high and high school. With the birth of my twin sisters and my brother and me being caught up in teenage doings, Ginger definitely became lost in the shuffle and was still around when I went off to college. It wasn't that we didn't all love Ginger . . .

The house was empty when I arrived home one fall weekend during my sophomore year at MSCW. As I walked into the kitchen to give the refrigerator the onceover, I saw a note taped to the door of a kitchen cabinet:

Dear Claire,
Don't bother to feed Ginger. She's dead.
Love, Mother

As for calling my mother "Mama," I'm not sure how that happened, because my brother and my father, and almost everybody else I knew, called their mother "Mother"—never, heaven help us, "Mom"—and their father "Daddy." I may have gradually begun to call my mother "Mama" after the twins were born because that's what they called her, at the same time that my young Yankee children were calling me "Mommy," as was the custom in Brooklyn.

(But to this day I've never called my children "kids." I just never wanted them to be thought of as baby goats.)

I recall vividly in the hours after Corinne was born, when I was thirty-one, a scene in my Brooklyn hospital room. Aroused from a postpartum twilight-like sleep, I became vaguely aware of a nurse at my bedside about to give me a shot in my arm. After I weakly inquired why she was doing this, she explained that there was a concern with bleeding, and that she would be giving me a shot every fifteen minutes until it stopped. And, she added, she was sorry, but it was going to hurt. No sooner had the pain subsided from that first one, when there she was again. By the time she arrived with the fifth dose, to be injected in an arm she'd already stuck twice with the pain building up over time, when the needle entered my arm I heard, from somewhere far away, a small primal cry, completely involuntary, issue from my throat: "I want my MA-A-A-ma!" I wonder, do we ever get too old to feel that primeval ache?

There were times in high school and college when I'd breeze into the kitchen to check out what was for supper, and I'd find Mama there sitting on the stool at the kitchen counter, staring into space as she was stirring or mincing something for the evening meal, and as though I'd interrupted a conversation, she'd sometimes say something like, "I wish I'd gone on with my music." Of course I was completely mystified and would beat a hasty retreat back through the swinging kitchen door. Mama was in her mid-forties, but the June Cleavers of the world had never heard of a midlife crisis, and the feminine mystique would fester for many more years as the problem with no name.

By this time, I believe, she had been in despair for a long time. With nowhere to turn for help—without even the language to describe it—the glass of sherry that began with her weekly bridge games gradually increased in number, and then she might have a little bourbon with Daddy before supper, or without Daddy, in the kitchen, while she fixed supper. They say alcoholics are born that way, but it wasn't until I was in my last year in high school that I began to notice that Mama might have a drinking problem.

After she became a full-blown alcoholic, graduating to vodka out of the bottle in a brown paper sack, I remembered with irony something that she told me after I got my driver's license when I was fifteen, when Coca-Cola still came in bottles: "Don't ever drink a Coke while you're driving. People might think you're drinking."

I've come to believe that one definition of original sin is never being able to let your parents know of the abject pain you feel for being unable to tell them how sorry you are that you were so seemingly uncaring and unfeeling, so insensitive and unappreciative for all they did for you. That they die without your ever being able to say, "Ah, now I understand." That by the time you get to that point, it's too late to tell them. Isn't it every generation's guilt?

After Daddy died, Mama was a displaced homemaker, before displaced homemakers had a label: a traditional wife and mother who had devoted her life to the time-honored role of housewife; with little income and two children to support, and her last job outside the home as a schoolteacher over thirty years ago. Her innate optimism and indomitable spirit, along with the belief that her friends would rally around to help her, broke my heart as she struggled to stay sober. Can you just imagine how she suffered, and her friends, too? Of course no one who knew her could recommend her for a job. When they wouldn't even consider her for hostessing in a restaurant, or for a sales clerk in a department store, she had to have been devastated, though she never said so to me. The term "depression" was not yet part of our everyday lives; there was no such thing as "mental health."

She never once acknowledged to me that her drinking was in any way an obstacle, though our oldest, dearest neighbor, Minnie Belle Culley, was her confidante, and she later told me that Mama would come to her and weep in desolation.

The relationship a woman has with her children can never be the same as the one she has with her close women friends. They can't help but be different. She's much closer in a different way to a friend, because they are at the same level of understanding. That's why they're friends. She loves her children because they're her children.

When she could no longer deny reality, rather than being completely defeated, Mama went out to the Old Ladies Home and arranged to play the piano for them two or three times a week. The women loved her, and were always waiting for her with open arms, bestowing affection and a small sliver of self-worth. This endeavor was short-lived however, when she just couldn't keep it up. She had so little to hold on to, even though she believed she had a lot to hold on for, which is what kept her going for another ten years.

My brother was living at home with Mama when he had his breakdown, after Daddy died. Because he was in the army and it was declared service-related, it was in a Veterans hospital that he was evaluated and diagnosed as a paranoid schizophrenic. I still count my blessings every day, because until this very day, he has been under the care of the VA. If that had not been the case, there's no doubt in my mind that today he would be a street person, if he had survived.

Several years after he had been in and out of the VA hospitals, as well as the state mental hospital in Mississippi, I had all of his records sent to a doctor who was a friend and neighbor of ours in Westchester, who offered to have a psychiatrist evaluate them and tell me if there was anything more I could do that hadn't been done. After the specialist had looked at them, he reported back, "You should get down on your knees and thank God every day that he can go to the VA. If he couldn't, you and everybody in your family would be in the poorhouse by now, because nobody can afford the kind of medical bills private care would cost. You just have to accept that you've done everything you can, and that there's nothing else you can do. When somebody finds a cure for schizophrenia, the veterans will be the first to use it because they will save millions of dollars by emptying thousands of beds." (Which, alas, as it turns out, has not been the case.)

And so I accepted it. But acceptance does not cure the pain. The pain just becomes chronic instead of acute.

If home is where when you go there they have to take you in, picture a paranoid schizophrenic man living at home with his widowed mother, a full-blown alcoholic, and his adolescent twin sisters. The house the father built, the family dwelling place for over twenty-five years, where the children had grown up with its familiarity and sweet memories, has been traded, along with a pittance, for a small tract house built in a new development after the war. The mother and her children are now living on social security and a minuscule insurance payment. (Once when I told Mama I couldn't decide whether our family was more Tennessee Williams or William Faulkner, she was not amused.)

I don't know if it was denial or alcohol, or a combination of both, that kept Mama from coming to grips with what a diagnosis of schizophrenia meant. Perhaps nobody really ever took the time to explain it to her clearly, with the way women were patronized and condescended to. Families with schizophrenics had not yet spawned the support groups that proliferate today, so she had nowhere to turn for help in dealing with the disequilibrium wrought by its symptoms.

My brother acted perfectly normal and talked with great insight and clarity about his plans for the future, but she couldn't or wouldn't accept the fact that his brain had a flaw in its circuitry and that he was not, in fact, "normal." That no matter how eloquently he spoke of getting a job, or of his future, there was no way he would ever be able to do it. It was impossible. But Mama believed him, or wanted to believe him, and when he didn't follow through, frustrated and mad, she would fuss at him. An unbearable situation. Disaster waiting to happen.

Naturally the mothers of my sisters' friends wouldn't let them come to our house. Who could blame them? That was one aspect of this forbidding situation. As well as the fact that with practically no supervision or accountability, the twins were essentially on their own. Arriving from Brooklyn, I would take action by waiting until morning when Mama was sober to talk to her when she was more clear-headed, and then take her to the doctor, who gave her a vitamin B shot and Antabuse. That was when I discovered that doctors wanted hands off with alcoholics—since there was no way they could cure them. Alcoholism wasn't cut and dried, an affliction to be treated with pills or shots or anything else. And it wasn't terminal, except like life, in the long run.

She would then go to AA and stay sober until I left, always with a sinking heart for them all, as well as for myself, because I felt so helpless. One time my aunt Sissy and I made arrangements for the twins to go and live with her, but when they found out, they had a fit and fell in it and absolutely refused to go, and said if I made them go they would run away. The only way I could "make" them do it was to take Mama to court as an unfit mother, and Sissy and I just did not have the heart to utterly destroy her by publicly taking away her last tattered shred of dignity. Many years later, when I talked with my sisters about that episode, they believed that they would have been much better off if they had gone to live with Sissy. If that's any comfort in case you're ever faced with such a dilemma.

Life has not inured me to man's inhumanity to man. And when it's carried out under the power of the state, it is at its most egregious: Slavery, segregation, prison conditions, war, the Holocaust, capital punishment, and being placed in jail instead of a hospital for being mentally ill.

The first time Mama and my brother were inflicted with unspeakable inhumanity was the time that my brother had declined into a state of great personal degradation, when for two days he stayed behind a locked door and would neither come out nor let Mama in. She was a wreck.

Her only recourse in this desperate situation was to have him committed to the state mental hospital. Even though Mississippi is behind the times in some ways, the laws about being committed and stashed away on the back forty for life had been changed. But at the time the process for getting someone committed hadn't been touched since the Dark Ages.

Just thinking about this still makes me almost physically ill. The procedure for commitment began with calling the sheriff—the sheriff!—to come and get her only son. What must it have taken for her to do that? It wasn't long before two burly deputies with guns on their hips rang the front doorbell. Mama led them to my brother's bedroom, where one of the men tried the locked door before knocking, and then explained to him who they were and asked him to come out. It took a long time for him to answer before he refused. After a lot of talk back and forth through the door, with most of the talk on the deputies' side, realizing that he was trapped, my brother started climbing out of his window to escape. Hearing the window being opened, the two deputies bounded outside and chased my brother down, tackling and hand-cuffing him in the front yard before they took him off to jail.

Fingerprinted and locked up with criminals, it was two days before he could get a hearing, after which he was carted off to the insane asylum. There he was placed in "hydro"—a snakepit of a place whose horrors I was confronted with at a later time when I visited Mama there—a dim, inhumane labyrinth of doorless, half-walled cubicles, all openly visible to a supervisor and offering no vestige of privacy. On the floor of each cubicle was a mattress on which a patient slept, or sat, after they had been relieved of all possessions—clothes, false teeth, shoes, eyeglasses, comb or brush—and issued a formless uniform, thus reducing them to total helplessness and vulnerability in the most dehumanizing way.

Mama was beyond despair.

As a mother I try to imagine the chilling realization of the nightmare and brutishness she has unleashed on her own child, and her ineffable anguish burns a hole in my soul.

The last thing in the world I would ever want to do is to romanticize alcoholism, but when I contemplate the alcoholics I have known, I've been crazy about almost every one of them, when they're sober. I can't stand being around any of them when they're drunk. Mama disgusted me when she was drinking, and it made it hard for me to love her when she was. I once had a lot of guilt about that. Mothers aren't supposed to be drunks, right? They're supposed to be perfect. How she let me down! And then one day, I was a mother, deficient in perfection as well.

I know that alcoholism is a disease. And this is a huge generalization, but it seems that practically every person I've ever known who's been an alcoholic has been deeply vulnerable. They've been more smart than dumb, invariably good company, and possessed of a fine sense of humor—their tragic flaw their inability to come to grips with life's disillusionment. The world is too much with them, late and soon.

The author Anne Rivers Siddons said of a late acquaintance, "The South killed her on the day she was born. It just took her that long to die. The Junior League and madhouses were filled with a certain generation of Southern women who couldn't find any way to let their vision grow."

It took my mother sixty-three years to die in a madhouse—all alone in the middle of the night—in a ward at the state hospital in Whitfield, Mississippi.

She had never even been in the Junior League.

∾

A parent's death is part of the natural order of things—a time to be born and a time to die. But I don't think anyone is able to realize how unprepared you are for what it's like until it happens. Even when I knew my father was dying, and I thought I was prepared, I wasn't prepared at all.

When Mama died, even though I had never once ever consciously considered her a burden, it was the acute absence of Mama I was so keenly aware of. Where once there had been a huge ominous presence, it was now removed. Where I had once waked up every day with a nagging sense of foreboding, I would wake up in wonder, that something was missing, and then I would remember what it was.

In retrospect, with today's awareness of the process of grieving, I realize that I never consciously had the time to mourn the death of my father. And in truth, it wasn't until after writing these episodes about my early years—in a stream of consciousness—that I was startled to have it so clearly revealed to me what a strong presence my father was in my life. Indeed, until now, I'd always thought that Mama's influence had been greater, because she was the one who was always around. But that is not the case at all.

Now I see that it's my mother who wasn't truly clearly defined for me, and it's only recently that I have been able to recognize myself as a reflection of my mother in those early years of my marriage, always deferring, or at least conditioned to believe it was what I should be doing, just as she had been conditioned to do. I believe my mother was deeply ashamed of being an alcoholic and as a result was never able to speak to me of her inner life, of her hopes and dreams.

I know she believed she failed us—my father, my brother, my sisters, and me—but, oh, who would we have been without her—the whole sense of her that was the bedrock of our lives!

Mama's death, besides freeing me from something I hadn't

known I was burdened with, brought with it as well intimations of my own mortality. As the oldest member of the family, and now of the oldest generation, the awareness that in the scheme of things I was next gradually began to inform my outlook on life. And though I had long before realized that you really can't go home again, I now understood that home is not a place.

∾

I don't remember how long it was after Mama died that I sat down to write a letter to Grandmama. I'd been contemplating and stewing over the plight of Mama's life for some time, and Grandmama seemed to be the only one left I could vent my spleen on. Even though by then she was close to ninety, I knew she'd absorb it with characteristic equanimity into her limitless sponge of life's perplexities.

Writing to her was my declaration of independence from the way the women in our family had had to be since the beginning of time. It was going to end with me, I said, and I was going to see that Corinne's life as a woman would mark a new beginning in the Hogan line. Though I now can't remember what I wrote or that I was specific about a new way of being—I don't know that I had a fixed blueprint for what that might be—I knew only that the old way was over and that I was blazing a new trail.

Nine

Those were years when I was filled with an inner turbulence that I was completely unaware of—feelings that hadn't made it to the surface of my consciousness. Now I understand that I was depressed when I spent all those mornings in bed after Corinne went to kindergarten, getting up at noon to fix her lunch and start my day when she returned. Then when her class switched to afternoon kindergarten for the second half of the year, I'd go to bed after she left and stay there until just before she and the boys came home in the middle of the afternoon. I didn't want them to know. A secret sleeper.

A year or so ago, as a new grandmother, I was interested to see that the author of a just-published book, *Grandparent Power,* was going to be in Phoenix for a book-signing. In my former life in the suburbs, the author had been well-known as a psychiatrist specializing in the problems of adolescence, and over the years I'd read that he had begun to focus on the importance—the need—of grandparents in the lives of children, and also that he was now based in Massachusetts. When I went to buy his book, I asked him why he'd left Westchester. His reply: "It was such a toxic place for kids."

And not just for kids, of course. In those days in the affluent suburbs, with few mothers working outside the home, most of them spent their days in micromanaging their children's lives and chauffeuring their own and other children on an endless round of scheduled activities. I was appalled. It could have had something to do with the fact I had lived in the city without a car for almost nine years, and more, that the suburban version of a child's life had no resemblance at all to my own in Mississippi. First, the children had their lives so programmed for them that they were given no opportunity to be self-sufficient and spontaneous; and second, they were completely dependent on mother as driver. This worked both ways, of course. It gave the mothers something to do, a way to feel needed.

It's an old story. I don't know how the schools stood the inundation of all those mothers breathing down their necks. I figured they had enough otherwise idle mothers without me, but either because of them or in spite of them, the schools were terrific. Since our children didn't have problems at school, my husband and I only went to Open House and for our regularly scheduled parent-teacher conferences. And to show the flag for my children's sake, I volunteered to chaperone the occasional class trip, always quite an eye-opening experience.

It was not until the revolutionary idea of the open classroom was proposed for a new school that two of our children would be attending that I got involved with the PTA, or whatever it was called by then, and became a member of its board. I wanted to support the innovative new woman principal and some of my children's excellent teachers who had volunteered to participate in such an exciting new experiment, which was fraught with controversy since many parents were highly skeptical of such a radical concept and just didn't get it. I became the board's arts representative, working with the school's art teacher and going to the Katonah Gallery, a small jewel of a museum, to pick out a painting every month to hang on the wall in the corridor outside the art room, all of which gave me a great deal of pleasure.

I hated the idea of carpooling when my children were in nursery school—of being so programmed and scheduled and dependent—and later for after-school activities. I tried it once or twice, but when I saw how my children got knots in their stomachs when a mother would be late—for whatever good excuse—making them late, I just couldn't see any reason to have to do it. ("The just must suffer with the unjust," intoned our fellow choir members when my pals and I boarded the bus late on the Millsaps Singers tour.) I encouraged my children to participate in any after-school activity they chose, but I didn't sign them up for all those "make busy" activities. They took piano lessons, which for the boys ended when they were old enough for organized sports in sixth grade. (They took piano out of desire. I was never able to "make" them do anything, and marveled at the way other parents could. The only way we could have made the boys go to dancing lessons when others in their class were doing it would have been to tie them up with a rope, put them in the car, and roll them out on the curb.)

I'm sure I thought that their childhood should be like mine, playing with children in the neighborhood, being self-sufficient in entertaining oneself. And to a certain extent it was. Except for television, which to my great frustration—I know it's a generational thing—became the hearth around which they drew, and were seduced for life.

∾

After a certain point I finally learned that you can't control your children's lives. You have to let them Be. Even though I was an ardent student of Dr. Spock, no one was more surprised than I when I discovered that my three children weren't alike. I thought to be a parent was to treat them all the same. I was not aware that with each child you got a completely new package, and that what had worked with one might be the opposite of what was right for another. In those days when parent was still a noun, before it became a verb, we learned as we went along. And though inevitably the firstborn can never escape being the practice child for beginner parents, I have to put it in context and remember that it's been that way since Adam and Eve (I mean, look at Cain and Abel), and the world has survived, with the firstborn down through history seeming to have thrived as well as the next. When a Jackson friend passed along the "Three L's," advice she got from a child psychologist there, it made eminent sense: First, you give them Love; second, you set Limits; then, you Let them go.

It was hard work, though, taking a hands-off approach, because it went against my nature.

My husband and I had been going out for a month or two when Marion, a friend from Jackson, came up to visit me and my three roommates in the apartment on East 79th Street. She had set her suitcase just outside the door in the hallway when she arrived, and just a beat before my future fiancé reached to pick it up and take it inside, I said to him, "Will you take the suitcase inside?" I was mystified when I sensed a brief, uncharacteristic hint of irritation, but he just picked it up and took it on into the apartment. I don't remember the precise circumstance of the next time a similar incident occurred, when I asked him to do something just as he was about to do it, and I heard him say, "Okay, Puffki."

"What do you mean?" I asked, laughing.

"Don't you know about Puffki the Manager?"

"Never heard of such a thing. Who is that?"

"It's somebody who's always telling people what to do, even when they know what to do, and are about to do it. You do it all the time, and I don't think you're aware of it. I almost said something about it when you told me to take the suitcase in the other night. It drives me nuts."

I blushed in humiliation. "How awful! I'm so embarrassed. I had no idea I did that. Will you help me break the habit?"

"Sure. Whenever you do it, I'll just say, 'Okay, Puffki.'"

It was a lesson in behavior modification. And it worked. Well, most of the time . . .

The first time I thought about it was after I'd been home on a visit to Mississippi, and while I was visiting one of my sisters instigated and oversaw the rearrangement of all of the furniture in her living room during the afternoon. When her husband walked in that night, he looked around and observed, "Well, I see Claire's been here."

I stopped with the furniture, but realized I was like the character in a play whose mere appearance in their midst changes everybody's life. I brought news from afar, tales of wonder, and a different way of looking at things, and left them swooning—though not necessarily happily—in my wake.

∽

After we'd been in suburbia awhile, I found that there wasn't that much for me to latch on to, since I didn't want to be a school maven. So when I joined the church and discovered that it was a real community, it became my small town, a place and people I could identify with. I always knew that no matter how petty people can be or how much they disagree, there was the higher purpose you could always look to—over and beyond the budget, the potluck supper, the disdain for the "C-and-Eers" (those who showed up only on Christmas and Easter)—to keep everybody focused on The Big Picture and what the true bottom line really was.

If the church was my small town, it wasn't necessarily my husband's. Although he didn't embrace any particular brand of religion, I believed he was not without religion in the larger sense of the word. He was deeply moral and ethical. And understanding that it was important to me, and for the children as well, on Sunday mornings he often helped me get them ready for church in the hectic mad dash I was always in as I got the four of us breakfasted, dressed, and piled into the car, driving at breakneck speed on the winding country roads to make it on time.

I'll never forget the look of shock on the faces of two of my Jewish friends in Phoenix—husband and wife; she's a lawyer who always had a nurse or nanny for her four children—when I described the hilarity of the scene of the four of us in the station wagon, the children inevitably squabbling and fighting after the pre-departure chaos, with me fit to be tied, swerving the car as I drove with my left hand on the wheel while I swung the other arm over the seat trying to swat one of them, whoever was within reach (no seat belts on the back seat in the olden days). Getting to church became the most God-less ritual, and I would profanely shout something to that effect as the three of them deftly and gleefully leaped about, dodging my arm, leaving me vainly swatting the air. This, of course, is what they remember most about their church-going experience. But Lord knows I tried.

☙

On weekdays the suburbs were a matriarchal society. The mothers reigned, getting to know one another through the schools and activities of their children. Commuting husbands were like weekend visitors, who, more often than not, were unknown to their wives' Monday-through-Friday female friends. On weekends the absentee fathers, often exhausted from their jobs and commuting, longing for nothing more than to lie on the sofa or in a hammock, felt compelled to throw themselves into a frenzy of weekend togetherness. (My husband was adamant about not planning anything for Friday nights; he just wanted to be at home after a long week, and I couldn't blame him, though sometimes it put me in a tight, uncomfortable spot when I always had to turn down all Friday night invitations.) I was often amused when the fathers who were really Big Deals in fancy, high-powered positions in New York City were nothing more than just another "dad" at the middle school football games, Memorial Day parades, and various children's activities. Strangers in our midst, they were Rodney Dangerfields getting "no respect" on the home front because who knew that they were big shots at the office? Suburbia bestowed no recognition on a man because of his vocation, his profession. There were many big fish, but there was no pond.

My husband's identity didn't stem from his work; it came from his family. He instilled respect for me in our children just as his father had instilled respect for his mother when he was growing up, and he required them to pitch in with chores around the house as he had had to do. Because he was able to get home by late afternoon, he had a much stronger presence in our family than many suburban fathers were able to. He was a deeply devoted father, and beginning with their infancy in Brooklyn, delighted in taking the children on outings, from the buggy (called "carriage") stage on up, to give me a respite. He would take one at a time or all at once, to allow me to have some time to myself; or for each of us to have time alone with each child. When our oldest son started nursery school (thanks to Dr. Weeks), my husband walked with him several blocks out of his way to drop him off before he got the subway to Manhattan. His family was his life.

A former football player, he was a big man; for little boys, just his presence could be intimidating, authoritative—belying the biggest, softest, most gentle heart; underneath he was a marshmallow. But being children, not wanting to take a chance, when he said frog, they usually hopped.

The opposite of their response to me. I was predictable and they knew how far they could go, at times pushing me to the shouting, teeth-gritting stage (just like Mama)—when their father wasn't home.

As I've mentioned, we married during the football off-season, so

Part Two - New York

I had no way of knowing how much football really meant to my husband. During our courtship he said little, if anything, about it; didn't show me one old team photograph or trophy. The year after we were married, he was able to buy three season tickets to the New York Giants games, which now, I understand, have become a legacy to be handed down from generation to generation, family heirlooms. In the beginning I tried to enjoy going, wanting to be a good sport, and would go to two or three games a season, the ones when it was the least cold. When the boys got old enough, the three of them went, and when our daughter got to the game-going age, they would all take turns.

It was because of me that my husband missed "the greatest game ever played," an incident that became part of family lore. My husband and I went to Mississippi to spend the first Christmas of our marriage with my family. As it happened, the day we were booked to return to New York was the day of the Giants-Baltimore Colts playoff game to decide the NFL championship (this was before there was an AFL). Though my husband was disappointed that he would miss it, he didn't make a big deal about it, so I didn't realize its importance to him. Our plane stopped first at Birmingham, and my husband, along with all the other football fans, leaped from their seats and sprinted for the terminal to find out the score. When they returned as the doors were closing, the Giants were winning with just seconds to play, (if you've ever watched football or basketball, you understand just how long a minute, or even a second, can take). Somewhere over Alabama the pilot announced that the Colts had kicked a field goal, tying the game in the very last second, throwing the game into overtime. From the cabin of the plane a collective groan of lamentation from the fans went up in frustration over their absence from this history-in-the-making, hoping beyond hope we would make it to Atlanta before the final whistle. But we didn't. Several minutes later, the pilot came on again, this time to announce the final score, and that the first time the Colts got the ball they had scored the winning touchdown, giving the Colts the NFL crown. Partisan cheers and boos filled the air, and on landing in Atlanta, no plane has ever emptied so fast, with all the men dashing for the nearest bar—thirsty for details.

Every year on television the story of that game is repeated. And on those rare times that I hear it if I happen to be passing the room where my present husband watches a football game (what can I say?), I'm momentarily aware of a frisson of some nameless longing.

As the number of football games expanded, becoming ubiquitous—Monday Night Football, the Super Bowl, and on and on—it became a part of our world, too, as did Little League football, and baseball as well, both of which my husband coached. Then ice hockey. I felt that sports consumed our lives, and I wanted to scream. For awhile, for the sake of togetherness, I would join in for an occasional ice hockey game at Madison Square Garden; at least it was fast, and I liked watching them skate. But finally I just couldn't stand the violence of the game. The children teased me, saying that what I really liked most was watching the zamboni, the magical machine that cleaned the ice during the time-outs. Which was true. It was so graceful and precise, like some extraterrestrial being moving slowly and methodically down first one strip of ice and up the next, until it had made a complete scrape of the whole rink. When I read several years ago that Mr. Zamboni, the designer of his eponymous machine had died, I grieved for him, though probably more for myself and the nostalgic memories of those long ago family outings watching the Rangers at Madison Square Garden.

To do something with me that didn't include sports, when my husband knew there was a play I was anxious to see he'd occasionally surprise me with tickets and I'd meet him in the city for dinner and a show. Every year we would take a vacation together—just the two of us—at some lovely get-away place. And for our anniversary one year, knowing how much I loved Leontyne Price (who was from Mississippi), he paid the resident scalper I hate to think how much for tickets to hear her in the world premiere of *Anthony and Cleopatra* at the brand new Metropolitan Opera House at Lincoln Center.

∾

At my church I was able to achieve a sense of fulfillment, in many ways and on many levels. (For how many centuries have women sought consolation in the church?) One was creative. For a whole year I took on "doing" the flowers for each Sunday church service. I didn't know the first thing about arranging flowers in the formal garden club sense, with those structured, stiff, strictly by-the-rules concoctions. I simply love flowers, and after putting together the occasional Sunday arrangement (is there a synonym for "arrangement"?) over the years, I realized I had a real talent for a natural, free-form, non-stylized "look." And that working with flowers filled me with sounding joy.

With my love of wild flowers, I carried a pair of clippers in the glove compartment of my car, and when I'd spy a particularly wonderful specimen by the side of the road (butterfly weed, now endangered, perhaps because of me), in some ditch or bog (lithrum), or even beyond a fence on private property (interesting, unusual trees for their leaves or twig formation, or an ancient stand of lilacs), I would pull over and leap from the car, clippers in hand. And like one of those formidable, eccentric English matrons, I would plunge intrepidly into or climb over any obstacle to procure the object of my desire. If I ever got caught on private property I had always planned to defend myself as some crazed religious fanatic, with the explanation, "I'm stealing for the Lord!", but to my disappointment the opportunity never arose. I would occasionally enlist my children to help me retrieve some especially hard-to-reach-rarity, though I never asked them to help me steal—they would have been horrified!

Before I became the Flower Lady I had been a member of the church's women's guild, and after a year or so was elected president; and if you ever need someone who must be able to get along with people, who can build a consensus, a church women's group leader is it. And though all ministers may throw up their hands over "the ladies," when they need to get a job done, they know they can always count on them.

Through the years I naturally became friends with the minister, one of the most marvelous men I've ever known. A little younger than my father, he was fine-looking, with a weathered but distinguished handsomeness, mostly bald with a fringe of gray (he even *looked* like my father). Originally from Pennsylvania farm country, he worked his way through college, getting a master's degree in English with the idea of being a teacher, before he decided to become a preacher. Given to quoting the social philosopher Lewis

Mumford, he was also an avid gardener, a man of the soil, which probably helped to account for his deep spirituality.

He loved flowers as much as I did, and was widely renowned as a hybridizer of gladioluses, which had never been a favorite of mine, but which I came to appreciate, well, a little more. He was a good businessman, down to earth, the epitome of common sense. He was the most un-self-righteous man I've ever known, and to tell the truth, he was a much better preacher than pastor, because I think he probably had a hard time with people who felt too sorry for themselves and agonized forever—the hand wringers and breast beaters— and he could only pastor just so much and so long. I liked his style, which is why I stayed with the Presbyterians rather than switching back to the Methodists when we moved to Westchester. We seemed to understand each other, and over the years he encouraged me to be myself, which of course is one of the reasons I cherished his friendship.

The year before he retired, I was elected an elder of the church, the highest honor I've ever had. I was forty-two, and after college, besides the church choir, it was the first time I was ever a member of a group that included men.

Two other (male) elders and I formed a benevolence committee to develop a program to commit our church to an annual contribution to the greater community—local, national, and international— and to identify those who would be the first recipients. This gave me and my two colleagues an enormous sense of satisfaction, and for me it was the first taste of a sense of power, the way men have felt all along without even knowing it.

Actually, now that I think about it, just before that I was on the search committee for our new minister. This was the mid-seventies, when the fact that no women were on the boards that were running corporations and institutions and churches was beginning to become a big issue.

It was on the search committee that I really had my consciousness raised about how women were treated very nicely and graciously, but as though we didn't exist, and the men didn't even notice what they were doing.

It was then also that I was introduced to men's talk, and it took me awhile before I realized that everything was indirect and circuitous, and it drove me crazy. Nobody would ever come right out and say something, except me. I had no idea that was not good form. Then one day after a meeting, as I was walking out with the chairman of the committee, a friend who was a Big Executive with IBM (their world headquarters are in Westchester and IBMers were ubiquitous), he good-humoredly told me that I operated like a bulldozer, and I was completely mystified.

So I dropped by to see my minister to talk to him about the search committee mystique, and the comment the chairman had made to me. I allowed, "If I was a bulldozer, then he was Mr. Smooth. I have never seen anybody operate like that in all my life."

"If he called you that," he laughed delightedly, "then you keep right on doing it. That's how you'll get things done."

Which I never forgot.

And the chairman and I got along just fine. After all, *he* was Mr. Smooth.

At the first meeting of the Board of Elders after I was elected (I think there were two other women, enlightened for the times), the newly installed minister, our former assistant minister, presided. Because of his youth, he was less wise in the ways of elders than our former minister, but wiser than I, because what he lacked in experience he made up for by at least having taken group psychology at Princeton Theological Seminary (this *was* the seventies). Our friendship was based partly on the fact that we laughed at the same things.

The first time I made a comment (the first by a woman at the meeting), it was as though I hadn't spoken. There was no response. Then the next person to speak, a man, repeated what I had just said, in a different way. And then the next did the same thing, and the next. Finally, I caught the eye of the minister and gave him a wide-eyed unbelieving stare of wonder. He could barely keep a straight face, since he knew what he was hearing though the other men had no clue. After they'd all finished re-saying what I'd said in the first place, I couldn't help but ask, "Isn't that what I said to begin with?" and they stared at me in surprise. That was to be the m.o. of the whole meeting, and besides being flabbergasted, I was irritated.

Afterwards I said to the minister, "You remember that old children's game where you sit in a circle and whisper something in a person's ear and tell them to 'pass it on,' and then you see what the original statement has turned into when it gets to the last person? Well, that's what I felt like I was doing in there today. Playing a damn game. Is it always that way?"

༄

One of the most important things that occurred during these years of growth—I wasn't aware that growth was where all that pain and angst was coming from as I was going through it—was getting my relationship with God straightened out. I worked at looking at what I had come to believe as a result of my upbringing—not so much literal as unexamined—and how it didn't gibe with life as I was experiencing it and as I saw it all around me.

I was greatly enriched by my church friendships and activities and benefited from an informal, unstructured biblical and religious education through my search for answers to form a consistent religious philosophy. And apart from the church proper, I took advantage of the prodigious resources right on my very doorstep, like Union Theological Seminary, and, one occasion I'll never forget, when on a magnificent late spring day, a car full of us took off for Princeton to hear Dr. Karl Menninger speak in the beautiful little Presbyterian chapel nestled under the magnificent trees in the middle of the Princeton University campus.

Years later, in Phoenix, Dr. Menninger (by then quite elderly and frail and stone deaf) spoke briefly at a dinner hosted by a local bank in honor of his friend, the great artist Phillip Curtis. I don't know how the doctor happened to be there, but in cocktail conversation before he introduced Dr. Menninger, when I asked the bank president if he'd ever read the doctor's book, *Whatever Happened to Sin?* (in which he wrote about how young soldiers are unleashed to murder legally in time of war, and how they suffer from the experience when they come home), he said he wasn't familiar with any of his books, and wanted to know more about it. When he introduced Dr. Menninger a few minutes later, I was astonished as I heard my words parroted back to me, as the bank president referred to the book I'd mentioned as though he'd read it just yesterday, weaving my words into a deft, informed introduction. It wasn't so long ago that men seldom gave attribution to a woman, unless it was to set up a joke.

Preoccupied with my life as wife and mother of three young children, our existence in the suburbs seemed far removed from the demonstrations and unrest over the Vietnam War, the crucible in which many of the values and view of life of that generation was forged. The closest physical confrontation I can recall were the student sit-ins and takeover of administrative offices at Columbia University in New York City, and some old Columbia grads with whom I talked at a dinner party were completely unsympathetic with the protesters. Foolish consistency being the hobgoblin of small minds, when I didn't believe Lyndon Johnson was telling the truth about the war, I had cast a protest vote for Goldwater in 1964.

I don't remember that I ever heard mention of the war from the pulpit of my church one way or another, though I wasn't surprised, even as I longed for some authoritative declaration beyond the White House, in which my generation until that time had basically trusted. I was torn between believing that the war was immoral at the same time that I believed it was immoral not to support our soldiers—those who had no deferments, those at the mercy of "the system"—who were drafted and sent to fight it (remember the movie *The Deer Hunter?*)

By the time my sons were draft age, the war was long over, though the draft was still in effect. When I told them that if they were ever drafted for a war they didn't believe in, that I would help them if they decided to go to Canada or Mexico, they were shocked. "Mame! (That's what they call me; it's their play on "ma'am." I promise, they'd never heard of her when they started calling me that.) We'd never do that!"

I believe that if mothers were in charge of the world, there would be no more wars. Mothers would not sacrifice the lives of their sons and daughters for the stupidity of war. They would find a saner way to solve their problems.

Ten

I did not get to Europe until I was forty. Today everybody goes to Europe—and to the ends of the earth for that matter—and before they're twenty. Transportation is cheap and fast. In 1974, the year Richard Nixon resigned, to put it in a political context, European travel wasn't exactly rare, but nobody I knew was yet a jet-setter.

We had been to Caribbean islands and Mexico for vacations (spent for me in hairshirted luxury when I observed the poverty surrounding us), but a trip to Europe was my dream of dreams. My first trip was a celebration and observance of my fortieth birthday, symbolic recognition of that rite of passage of demarcation. It was on the same scale as my first trip to New York when I left Mississippi, or my first trip across the Mississippi River to Louisiana when I was eight.

I will only say that it was like peeling away another layer of the onion of life. The greatest impression I brought home from my trip to France and England was a deeper understanding of history, especially of how young America is in the scheme of things, and the obvious distinction between classes. I could better understand when my English neighbors said to me, "But, Claire, there isn't anything really *old* in America," even after I took them to see the home of John Jay (the first Chief Justice of the Supreme Court) close by. Never having given any thought to class until it was brought to my attention when I had arrived in New York almost twenty years before, for the first time in my life I understood as never before why the colonists revolted against the British, and took new pride in my ancestors who had taken up arms. I saw first-hand—not in a book, not theoretically or intellectually, but viscerally—the dividing lines and the results of the class system. And I marveled even more at our experiment in Democracy.

∽

The seventies were hard years for women, quite an unsettled time—a time of transition. Women were trying to find their way from having only one script to read from to the freedom of reading from any script they chose, struggling with new possibilities. And the conventional wisdom had become that if you didn't have a "real" job outside the home, you didn't amount to anything. I read something then that affected me later in my campaign for the Senate, an article that said that when women are asked what their greatest accomplishments are, they always answer, "my children"; though when a man is asked the same question, he always talks about his work. The article wanted to encourage women to look at their larger life, beyond the act of childbirth, to increase their sense of self-worth, for that was the time when if someone asked a mother or a housewife what she "did," she would reply, "I'm just a housewife," or worse, "Nothing."

It's only in the past few years that the whole idea of feminism—that a woman must have the right to choose what's right for her in all aspects of her life—has come full circle. That homemaking and child care have moved from being considered "nothing" back to being valued as a "job" of esteem and importance by society as a whole, and as a result, by women themselves. Because, of course, it now carries a price tag.

It's hard to imagine what life for women was like before the *Roe v. Wade* decision in 1973. Growing up, the act of having an abortion was a mysterious and scary thing that happened only occasionally in some of the fiction I read, never in real life. It was outside my galaxy. Even in my teenage years and in college, abortion as a solution to pregnancy would never have occurred to me or anybody I knew. Of course now I know that worldly white wealthy Mississippians were able to spirit their daughters out of state to hospitals in New Orleans or Memphis, where their money, just as money always has, bought entrée into the nether world of abortion that existed at the time. And that there were Negro women who "had the power," who worked their magic—sometimes successful, sometimes not—to rid desperate women, white as well as black, of unwanted pregnancies.

Fear of pregnancy was the most powerful birth control method ever invented. Back when only "bohemians" (who predated hippies) lived together without benefit of clergy, the swift punishment meted out for straying from the straight and narrow at the wrong time came in the form of a very early marriage, with the subsequent arrival of a bundle from heaven only a few months after the usually "secret" marriage was announced. The alternative to marriage was for the girl to "go away" and spend time with a relative or close friend until the baby arrived and was put up for adoption. Either way, society drew its pound of flesh, and the results of shotgun marriages are represented today in many of the finest families, as well as those that are not. Pregnancy was an equal opportunity event.

So at the same time that my inner life was in turmoil, external events were affecting me as well. The *Roe v. Wade* decision had the same effect, in the sense of freeing me, as the death of my mother. It was a freedom intensely felt in women's collective consciousness, thrillingly liberating. In fact, "liberation" was in the air with the resurgence of feminism, which for me, of course, wasn't a resurgence but an introduction. I was at first skeptical, wary, actually an indifferent bystander until *Roe*. And then the Equal Rights Amendment.

∾

Two years after my trip to Europe, I'd returned from a summer trip alone with many stops, visiting friends and relatives around the country (I'd needed to get away) and dropped by the local travel agent who had booked my trip to turn in part of my ticket for a refund. While I was sitting there as he wrote up the transaction, I said rather idly to him, "You know, Mr. Adamson, you really should hire me to work for you."

And to my complete surprise I heard him say, "When would you like to start?"

"What!"

"I'm serious. You've traveled, you're knowledgeable in a way that people who haven't traveled could never be. I can teach anybody to write a ticket (this was before computers), but it's the traveling itself that's more important."

Over the previous year, finally realizing that I needed a vocation, I had endured great indignities as I tried to figure out what kind of job I could get on a part-time basis so I could be at home when my children got home from school.

One of the jobs I had applied for was to help the restaurant critic for a weekly business newspaper write a book on country hotels and inns in Westchester, Connecticut, and Long Island. I realized the job wasn't going to work out after the restaurant review I wrote as a sample of my writing and reviewing skills was at cross-purposes with him.

He and his lady friend and I went to lunch at one of those upscale franchise restaurants, sort of a pseudo-rustic, inn-type place, which of course I took into account. After taking voluminous detailed notes of the meal, which was mediocre at best, I went home to write it up.

After he read my review, which I thought was quite clever and punchy, he called me to say that it simply would not do. He realized, unfortunately, that he had not made it clear to me that we had dined as guests of the manager. (And, also, without saying so, he obviously had believed that I would be gastronomically unsophisticated as well. Southern accents sometime make ignorant people think you are, too.) Which meant, of course, that I could not be as honest in my assessment of our "dining experience" as I had been. He asked me to rewrite the review in more glowing terms.

I have to admit it. If I was naive to be shocked that this man was accepting meals as a payoff for laudatory reviews, then I plead guilty. But it wasn't so much the dishonesty that surprised me, it was how desperate he must be to be a whore for meals.

I thanked him nicely and told him I didn't believe the job would work out. I was so disappointed, because if the job had been real, it would have been perfect for me.

Because it had been fifteen years since I'd been among the ranks of the employed, after pursuing other dead ends in Westchester, even looking into a women's reentry course at one of the colleges, I realized that because I was over forty I was considered passé. And that there were still very few jobs for women except secretarial. Thanks to good ol' dad I had my typing and shorthand, which by then, though, "older" women were rebelling against. They didn't want the first words out of an employer's mouth to be, "Yes, but can you type?"

Discouraged, I pored over the Sunday *New York Times* employment section scouring the secretarial ads as well—executive secretary, of course—to see if there was anything at all I would be interested in, and how much they paid. What the hell, I thought, I might as well check it out.

Since I'd arrived in New York with a job and had never had to go through the excruciating experience of finding one, I was unaware of the existence of the boiler-room-like employment agencies. Setting out early one Monday morning, after an unprecedented predawn arising, I joined the fathers and husbands on the train into the city before it was light, wanting to be at the agency when it opened, the early bird and all.

Early as I was, it was not early enough. What optimism and hope I arrived with I left at the threshold—All hope abandon, ye who enter here—as I took in a waiting room already smogged with cigarette smoke and practically all the chairs filled with youngish passive-faced people, like those on the subway. It had all the charm and ambiance of a government unemployment office, though at least we didn't have to take a number. My first thought was that I was glad that I wasn't desperate, and then I empathized with my fellow job-seekers who most likely were.

Standing at the desk of the young woman who was busy juggling the constantly ringing phones, I tried to tell her which job it was that I was interested in. Broadly nodding her head up and down at me to let me know she heard me, she handed me a card to fill out and kept gesturing in the direction of the wall behind my back. "The boards, the boards," she hissed. I finally realized she meant the clipboards, which were stacked in an otherwise empty book case. After crossing the room again as though I were on an empty stage, as I picked up the precariously situated clipboard on top, it was like a game of pick-up-sticks, when you moved one, all the others shifted. Suddenly to my horror, about a dozen clipboards cascaded off the shelf and clattered to the floor like an explosion of a string of firecrackers. Naturally, difficult as it was for my audience to show interest, nobody could not *not* look. It is real hard to be graceful stooping down to retrieve twelve clipboards, pitched on high heels with a purse and a clipboard already in hand, and stack them in an orderly fashion, alternating the clip ends so they will lie flat, which was the reason they had fallen in the first place.

When at last I had everything neatly rearranged, I sidled to a chair to have a look at the card. This was when they still wanted to know your age, but I didn't fill in that blank. Then they asked for my last employment, with the dates, and I didn't fill that one in either, since my old agency had dissolved. (I liked to jolly the boys I'd worked with by telling them it was because they couldn't make it without me.)

Next I was asked to list my skills. Skills? My *skills?* There's a language for every vocation, and this was my initiation into employment-speak. Not wanting to have a card full of empty blanks, I begrudgingly listed my "skill" as typing. I left out shorthand because I'd gotten so rusty I didn't want to have to take a test or anything because I knew I'd fail. I wondered what skills men listed.

Once more I made the trek across the room and turned in my card to the phone juggler. And once more she pantomimed, this time to go back to my seat and wait.

When it was my turn she delivered the news that the job I was there for had been filled (that morning? already? by one of the people I'd been waiting with? which one had it been?). But she would call me if they had anything.

There's nothing like experience. The next employment agency I went to I went on a Thursday afternoon. The waiting room was almost identical in atmosphere and decor, but almost empty of customers. Knowing the ropes, I marched straight to the receptionist's desk, picked up a card and with great poise asked, "Do you have a clipboard?" only to have her point with great attitude to the corner of her desk, where if it had been a snake it would have bitten me.

Actually, I only made this draining, debilitating trek twice. And this time I did get a call back. It was for a secretarial job in the garment district, somewhere around 40th Street, "convenient to Grand

Central." It sounded awful, but I decided I would go for the interview, if only for the experience.

I forget what kind of business it was, one of those ancillary businesses that have sprung up around the garment district. The fellow I interviewed with was quite amiable and nice, and we hit it off. And I liked the woman who worked there. So, depressing as the office was, as well as the building it was in, the experience hadn't been a complete bust.

The next day, to my surprise, I got a call from the employment agency offering me the job. It was a boost to my ego, but I just couldn't imagine working there, getting up every morning to commute into New York, and all that it took to do that. I'm just glad I wasn't desperate. I thanked her warmly, before regretfully turning her down.

Later I learned what many people already knew, that there were employment agencies who screened prospective job-seekers before they would take them, and that they were the ones with all the best jobs. A friend of mine at church owned such an agency, and asked me to come in for an interview. If I'd only known.

And then, one day, just like that, I come home from my wanderings and my travel agent offers me a job. It was all right there under my nose all along and I hadn't even noticed.

∼

It was the perfect job for me at that time in my life. I was an outside sales agent, which meant that I didn't get paid a salary, only commission, and only on the new clients that I brought in, which meant hardly any money at all. But I could work my own hours, which was the best part. One big problem, and I consider it the worst possible problem, is that usually everybody who does business with you is a good friend or a friend of a friend. If you mess up, it's hard to live it down, and even if you don't, because you have no control over airlines, hotels, etc., you still get the blame.

I messed up one woman's ticket right after I started, reversing the arrival and departure times for her to meet her mother, who was coming in on the Concorde *in Washington,* something that embarrasses me still whenever it flicks across my memory. It was a disaster, and there was no way I could ever make up for it. But it never happened again, no comfort to my victim.

I didn't have a problem bringing in new clients. I knew a lot of people, and I guess they trusted me, even though in the beginning I did goof up occasionally. But I was never a hard sell because I wasn't in it for the money, which was certainly a good thing. The first year ("while you're learning") I only got 25 percent commission, and I brought in $50,000 worth of business, which in those days wasn't bad for a beginner. The commission, however, was 25 percent of around *10 percent* of the total, so you can see it didn't amount to a hill of beans. But it was a good feeling to make my own money, no matter how little. Travel agencies didn't make a whole lot of money, and I know the business has changed since then, though probably for the worse.

The travel business is purported to be glamorous, that you get all those free trips to exotic places. Which couldn't be further from the truth, what with all the rules and red tape about who could go and who couldn't; and since I'd seen most of the places I'd wanted to see in the United States, I would pass up most of the familiarization trips in favor of almost anything international, the few times they were offered.

୶

It was through the auspices of Pan Am and the German Tourist Office that the meaning of freedom was brought home to me in the most terrifyingly graphic way. The way the terms "freedom" and "liberty" are tossed around is like words spoken by so many parrots. It's only when freedom is taken away that we can begin to comprehend what its loss means.

In October 1976 I was one of a group of about twenty travel agents who were invited to participate in a familiarization trip to West Germany, which included Berlin. Though Germany had never been at the top of my list of places I wanted to go, the prospect of a visit to Berlin fascinated me, and I decided to make the trip, although these trips were tough. They were usually only for a few days, packed full with seeing everything there was to see, with no time to adjust to jet lag at either end. It wasn't a vacation, it wasn't glamorous, it was hard work.

Our arrival into Germany was through Frankfurt, where we

changed planes for the flight into West Berlin, which took us over East Germany. It was late morning on a crisply clear October day when we lifted off from Frankfurt, and as I looked down at the East German countryside, I got the eeriest feeling as I realized that down there below in that bucolic setting was "the enemy." I wondered if there were anti-aircraft guns hidden in the haystacks, the way they were in the war movies I'd seen as a child. I also wondered where the prison camp was in which my uncle had been held captive after his plane had been shot down during the war. He must have looked down from his bomber at that same countryside just as I was. It could have been Starkville from the way it looked up here. It was hard to believe that I was actually flying over Germany. Who would have thought I would ever be doing such a thing?

As we landed in West Berlin I could only think of the planes during the Berlin airlift ordered by President Truman to keep Berlin connected to the outside world. I thought of Marlene Deitrich singing, "Under the lamplight, by the barracks gate . . ." But most of all I thought of Hitler and the concentration camps. I had wondered how I would deal with being immersed in voices speaking the German language, which I had been brainwashed to fear and to hate the sound of. And I knew that my feelings about the concentration camps would always be in the back of my mind, the vivid, unspeakable descriptions of the newsreels I'd seen as a child forever emblazoned in my memory.

So, approaching my visit to Germany with such tentativeness, I nonetheless was fascinated by the sense that West Berlin was a city with an island mentality, and that many inhabitants, suffering from symptoms similar to island fever, occasionally fled the claustrophobia of the city for short vacations, even a weekend, in West Germany (a change, the English say, is as good as a vacation).

The trip into East Berlin was one of those Defining Moments, just as Nairobi would be almost ten years later in a wholly different context.

Because the German Tourist Office, an arm of their federal government, had arranged our tour to East Berlin, our group was thereby designated "official" in a country that revered all things official. Though once we were on the East Berlin side of the Wall what had been official in West Berlin had no meaning. On the bus before we departed for Checkpoint Charlie, our tour guide, who had told us the day before that cameras were verboten and to leave them behind at the hotel, briefed us on our behavior: Do not say anything that could be construed as antagonistic or critical of East Berlin or of Russia, either to a member of our group, which might be overheard, or to an East Berlin tour guide. Be respectful and courteous. Obey all instructions of the tour guides and do not stray from the group. Questions may be asked, but they should not be political or confrontational. Remember, your East Berlin hosts will be in possession of your passport while you are in their city, for after we pass through Checkpoint Charlie, someone will collect our passports. So when they ask you for yours, you must surrender it if you want to continue on the tour. It will be returned to you when the tour is finished.

Giving up my passport seemed a very ominous thing to have to do, and I was uneasy about relinquishing it. But at least if we were held hostage I wouldn't be alone, which sounds like a flip statement, but it isn't.

It was a perfect day for a trip to the Eastern sector: a sky like ashes, with a cold mist of rain. As we approached Checkpoint Charlie, a sign warning us in four languages proclaimed "You are leaving the American sector." I tried not to appear overly curious, like a spy, but didn't want to miss a trick. First, we stopped at the American checkpoint, where our credentials were studied and approved by armed soldiers, who motioned us through as the gate was opened to the no-man's-land "death strip" between the two sectors. After we proceeded a few yards, we encountered a concrete barrier completely blocking the road, turning to go around it, then turning again to regain the road, where we were then stopped by armed East Berlin soldiers, one of whom boarded the bus while the other stood guard. He studied our manifest with suspicion, and as we all sat there in cowed silence, he finally told the driver to move on, remaining on the bus while the driver maneuvered yet another barrier, coming to a stop in front of the checkpoint on the East Berlin side. We had essentially passed through a maze, so that anyone desperate enough to try to escape in a vehicle from East Berlin would have the impossible feat of trying to crash through not one but two concrete walls, in addition to the two gates.

In front of the Eastern gates a man in civilian clothes, a navy blue suit and white shirt with no tie, small but powerfully built, quietly confident, boarded our bus. He exchanged a few words with the driver, who then, to the consternation of us all, departed the bus. A small discussion ensued with the tour director, and then our new commander began to collect our passports. He started at the front, with the soldier following just behind him, and as he stopped at each seat courteously requesting each passport in perfect English, he then took it, inspected it closely and thoroughly, examining each page. Opening it to the page with the photograph, he studied each face in front of him, then the photograph, then the face again, and when he deemed that they were a match, handed the passport to the soldier, who dropped it into a bag that he carried over his shoulder. This was not a perfunctory process; it was painstaking and deadly serious.

You could feel the nervous tension as we sat in stony silence, giving each other furtive looks. Some in the group decided on a friendly tack, saying hello to the collector, who gave no response; others smiled, but his face never registered any change of expression. When he got to me, I smiled instinctively, and staring into his face to see what I could find, caught a glimpse of eyes that were as old as time, missing little and revealing less.

With their bag full of our passports, the little man and the soldier got off the bus, and a new driver got behind the wheel. We waited expectantly, and then another man boarded the bus and cordially introduced himself as our guide for East Berlin. He sat down next to our tour guide, the gates opened and we rolled through. The whole ordeal had taken almost an hour. If it took that long to get in, I hated to think how long it would take to get out.

The only word for it was Sinister. As we drove down the completely deserted Unter Den Linden—bustling and congested with cars and people on the Western side of the Brandenburg Gate—here on the Eastern end it was as though we were on a movie set of the end of the world, the last people on earth. One-dimensional facades of what had once been buildings loomed vacantly on either side of the avenue, the comparative brilliance of the green of a vine or scrawny tree struggling towards the light out of the thirty-year-old rubble of war—here, from a frameless window, there, at the base of stairs leading to nowhere—caught your eye now and then against the bleakness, a slim glimmer of hope. It was several minutes before we encountered the occasional bicycle rider, and finally a car, which, as the tour guide explained, was an "official" vehicle, and volunteering the obvious, that bicycles were more plentiful than automobiles.

As we moved along, we passed an increasing number of pedestrians on the uncrowded sidewalks, and at one point a throng of people pushing into the door of a storefront. It was explained to us that they had probably heard that there were bananas today, or some other such hard-to-get delicacy.

We spent the next several hours touring the Soviet War Memorial in a serene English-like park setting, a powerful reminder that every soldier is some mother's son, no matter what side they're on; having refreshments is a surreal stage-set café in the middle of another park, which was empty; and tip-toeing through the spooky, partially closed Pergamon Museum.

But one of my most haunting memories still is of the exit from East Berlin.

First of all, it was difficult saying good-bye to our tour guide, hating to leave him behind on the other side of the looking-glass. He had been so kind and knowledgeable, and, I felt, terribly self-conscious as he toed the party line to put a good face on what was so obviously a lie (something I later would come to recognize as "spin"). I attributed this to our finally being able to elicit from him the fact that he had a Ph.D.

After he left the bus, an inspector different from the one we'd had before, this one tall and bespectacled with the addition of a tie, though nonetheless quietly menacing, appeared with yet another armed guard who, we were relieved to see, carried the bag containing our passports slung over his shoulder. This time the inspector, as he drew a passport from the bag, called the name of the owner. As each of us got up to retrieve it, once again face and photograph were assiduously compared before it was handed over, my heart skipping a beat with relief as I took mine from his outstretched hand.

When he had finished delivering our passports, the inspector and the driver stepped off the bus, and our original driver appeared, grinning sheepishly at our welcoming cheers and applause. With that, the gates opened, and one barrier out of the way, we rolled slowly out of the world of Kafka toward home.

But what happened next chilled my blood as nothing ever has, before or since.

Instead of continuing on through the maze of the two barriers, at a word from the guard who was still with us, the driver pulled over, came to a stop, and turned off the ignition. As the bus stood in the no-man's-land between the two gates, with the sun now higher in the sky we could see our surroundings much more clearly than we had been able to on our initial crossing in the gray mist of the morning. Surprised by this unexpected action, we all craned our necks to see if we could find out what was happening, but could see nothing. It seemed that we were just sitting there for no reason, and we were filled with a new uneasiness.

Then someone said quietly, "My God, I don't believe it. Look down there!" pointing down beside the bus. There, stooping down close to the ground, was an armed soldier, holding a long pole that he was moving around slowly under our bus. At first I couldn't figure out what was going on. And then I realized that there was a mirror attached to the end of the pole and that he was sweeping it along the bottom of our bus to see if some desperate person was clinging there in the vain hope of fleeing with us to freedom. I still feel the terror that caught in my throat as I prayed that there would be no one there, knowing full well after the experience of this day that he or she would be shot on sight. After moving with excruciating slowness around the entire bus while we held our collective breath, the soldier finally withdrew the mirror. With that, the soldier on the bus told the driver to open the door, stepped smartly out, and signaled us to move on.

As we moved past the two barricades to the gates of West Berlin, we were all so drained by the emotion of what we had just experienced, we sat rooted in silence for the few yards that remained between us and freedom.

Finally arriving at Checkpoint Charlie, as the gates opened up to let us through, the whole bus suddenly exploded into spontaneous cheers and whoops and whistles, euphoric and exhilarated with the blast of FREEDOM!

That night there was quite a noticeable increase in the average consumption of alcoholic beverages by tourists in the American sector of West Berlin.

∾

My job as a travel agent had given me a great sense of accomplishment. In less than two years, besides building up a huge and faithful clientele, I'd completed many of the courses various airlines offered and was in the process of becoming a member of the Institute of Certified Travel Agents, the industry's professional organization, through a year-long graduate-level course approved by George Washington University. With all of this, I had been greatly disappointed when I had asked my agency owner for more money and more responsibility and been turned down. A short time later, I was flattered and delighted when I was approached by the manager of a new agency, which would become a competitor to the agency I was with, to join them as an agent and assist in the start-up. When I told my boss I would be leaving to join the competition, he then offered me more than I'd asked for before. Too late. I declined and, blowing him a farewell kiss, shook the dust from my feet.

Eleven

At the same time that my children were growing up, I was growing too. Unaware of what was happening to me, I began to feel isolated, that I really didn't fit in with my own family. Interested in completely different things, it was as though we lived in separate worlds. Sometimes, when I'd stayed up after everybody else had gone to bed, I would feel so alone, so lonely, that I'd get in my station wagon and drive aimlessly through the empty roads and streets of New Castle. And after a half-hour or so I'd come home, my family none the wiser, feeling better somehow—I guess because I'd at least taken some kind of action—and go to bed. When I've recounted this in later years, thinking it was unique with me, I couldn't believe it when other women told me they'd done the same thing! In every town they should set up a rendezvous spot where all those women driving around out there can get together and talk to each other.

What I'm trying to say here is that I was married to the sweetest, most thoughtful, kind, generous man. He was a wonderful, caring, nurturing father. And still is. He had worked hard all his life and now could afford to do what he wanted to do. I was happy for him.

But I was no longer the girl he married. It was I who was changing. And I felt like such a cliché. Didn't I have "everything"? What was my problem? How could I be so discontented? Unaccountably, I was becoming an angry woman—there had to be something wrong with me. And I really worked at fighting it by constantly reminding myself how lucky I was.

In the end, though, after twenty years of marriage, my husband and I were divorced.

Those words read so clean and simple in black and white. But they are so replete with pain and anguish and heartbreak for so many that I cherish and hold dear in my heart. No matter how faded the scar, the wound remains. I remember in those days when the pain was almost unendurable, that I would cry out, If only it were ten years from now! It couldn't possibly hurt as much by then! And I'd face the next day, and the next, and when ten years had passed, it was true, it didn't hurt as much—having come to the realization that a marriage of twenty years is not a failure—but we're all different people because of it. Why does it take pain to make people grow? No pain, no gain, they say gaily. Have a nice day.

To some women in my town I was a heroine. To others, I was a home wrecker, and worse, a clear example of what happens when you become a Women's Libber. I just knew what I had to do to save myself, and not having any rules to go by—"there's no dress rehearsal for life"—I did the best I could to hurt those I loved in the least way possible, and of course I inevitably made mistakes. If I had it to do over, I would do it again, but hope to do it differently, better.

I understood at the time that the man I had fallen in love with was a catalyst in my life. And when I gave him a copy of *The Awakening* by Kate Chopin (who now is taught in every women's studies course, but who at the time was just being discovered by women like me), after reading it he said, "This is your story. But thank God you don't have to commit suicide!" At times, however, I felt as though I *was* committing suicide; not literally, of course, but psychologically. On the other hand, spiritually I felt that my soul was being liberated, set free. That I had only moved from a small box to a larger box didn't become apparent until the time came to transcend the larger one as well.

Henry was born in the Baptist Hospital in Jackson, five months after I was. His grandmother, who lived with his family in Jackson, recorded in his baby book that I was among the guests at his first birthday party. As newlyweds, his parents and mine, who were three or four years younger than his, moved to Jackson within a few years of each other and became part of the same circle of friends. Our mothers were in the same bridge club, La Comida ("Come eat a lotta lunch"), and his father, an electrical engineer, started out with the Mississippi Power and Light Company. Too old for military service, he remained on the home front, but through his job with the utility company spent a lot of time in Washington involved in the war effort, with the equivalent rank of colonel, giving him the opportunity to meet and work with utility men from all over the country.

Before the war started, the Public Utility Holding Company Act had been passed by Congress. The new law essentially dismantled the utility business by divesting most holding companies of their subsidiaries. As one of the largest, if not the largest, holding companies, Electric Bond and Share Company had owned utilities all over the country, which included many in the South, among them Mississippi Power and Light, as well as a small company in Arizona, Central Arizona Light and Power Company, called Calapco. When the president of Calapco was looking for a successor after the war, he talked to some old Bond and Share hands who recommended Henry's father. The offer was made and accepted. Henry's family moved to Arizona when he was in the middle of the sixth grade, when I had just returned from Starkville to Liberty Grove. If he hadn't moved, Henry and I would have been in the seventh grade together at Bailey Junior High.

Phoenix in 1946 was a small town, about the same size as Jackson, where everybody knew each other, with those old friendships enduring still. When they arrived, Henry's family was considered "newcomers"; by today's newcomers he is called "old Phoenix," to which the truly old settlers most likely take great exception.

A few months after his arrival, Henry senior was named president of the small utility. Over the next several years his company acquired two other small Arizona utilities, consolidating them into one entity, and he thus became the first president of Arizona Public Service Company, as the new company was called. Three years later he was tapped to be president of American and Foreign Power Company, a wholly-owned subsidiary of Electric Bond and Share Company, and once more Henry's parents pulled up stakes, this time for New York City. (In her waning years, his mother declared that the happiest time of her life was those early days in Jackson.)

Part Two - New York

Operating in alien New York territory, when the new utility president needed to hire an advertising agency, he turned to somebody he knew and trusted: his old friend from Jackson, who opened a New York office to handle the account. Are you getting the picture?

It was Henry's parents, the old friends of my parents, with whom I had dinner and attended that first opera in the center box at the old Met the night Toscanini died. In addition to some of my cohorts from the office, to my complete surprise, also in the party that night were Henry, then a graduate student at Columbia University—whom I hadn't seen since he came back to visit Jackson in the eighth grade—and his wife!

In the next year or so while Henry was at Columbia, I would see him and his wife occasionally at parties and gatherings at his parents' apartment when the "young people" were included. And once they invited me to their apartment in the Bronx for supper with them and their young daughter. We led completely different lives. He was a poor struggling student with a wife and child to support, while I was foot-loose and fancy-free, living the carefree good life, at least in their eyes.

He got a summer job with an investment banking firm downtown in Wall Street, close to my office, and once or twice we met for lunch at the counter of Chock-full-O'-Nuts for a hot dog and coffee, the cheapest meal you could eat—he was paid even less than I was—going Dutch, of course.

The only other time I saw him was that summer during the month that his wife and daughter vacationed in Phoenix. I'd persuaded three friends to come up from Mississippi and find a summer job and stay with me in a brownstone I was house-sitting for a friend of a friend (who turned out to be Palmer Williams, the CBS producer, who with Edward R. Murrow produced the famous documentary on migrant workers, "Harvest of Shame"), so once or twice Henry took the subway down to the Village when we invited him to eat black-eyed peas and turnip greens and play bridge with us. After he graduated, Henry returned with his wife and daughter to Phoenix to begin his lifelong career in the utility business. When I opened the telegram he sent to my husband and me when we married, by then he was divorced, and I confess I had a momentary pang. But quickly and guiltily dismissing it, I put him firmly out of my mind.

My husband and I saw him over the years: at his parents' country home in Connecticut when he visited with a pretty Arizona girl, and at other times with his family and old friends; after he remarried, on vacation in Phoenix we met his wife; at his father's funeral in New York; and again when they visited us a year or so later after his father died; once he stopped by to see us when he was close by on business with IBM. I was also closely connected in another way. After I persuaded Charlotte, one of our old crowd of eight who are still like sisters, to come to New York and share the 79th Street apartment with me and the two other girls after I left the Evangeline, I had introduced her to Henry's brother, whom she subsequently married and to whose daughter I am godmother.

In the fall of 1977, in the winter of my discontent, out of the blue one day Henry called me at my office at the travel agency—he'd gotten the number from whoever answered the phone at home. He hadn't known that I was working and had called to see if I would be able to come into New York to have lunch with him the next week. On the verge of leaving for Portugal on a familiarization trip, I told him I'd have to take a rain check. He said that his job now brought him to New York several times a year and, seemingly kind of impressed that I couldn't meet him because I was taking off for Portugal for three or four days by myself (i.e., without my husband), allowed as how next time he'd give me more notice. Because of the state I was in, and though I was happy to hear from him, I found his call to be rather curious, prompting a vague premonitory flutter.

☙

I was as much a catalyst in Henry's life as he was in mine. To say only that we were both in the deep throes of a midlife crisis utterly trivializes the seismic paroxysms and the sackcloth and ashes that our romance and subsequent marriage produced. To do what we did you have to be crazy. Completely mad—or hard-as-flint sane. It's the only way anybody could get through all the pain and hostility and disapproval, especially from old friends you thought loved you.

Our marriage rocked our families and all of our friends—as

closely entwined as they were with both of us—who were just sick about it. Though my family were all deeply saddened and shocked, they rallied to the side of all parties: mine, my husbands'—former and present—and especially my children. I've always wondered how Mama and Daddy, especially Daddy, would have taken it, or if, indeed, it would have happened—Would I have been the same person?—had they been alive.

∞

The most wrenching thing for me was that I left my children behind. The idea of uprooting our children (by then teenagers, with the oldest in college) from the security of the world of their home, their friends, their school, their community was ludicrous and out of the question on the face of it. Even discounting the wicked things that people always say about a mother who doesn't insist on taking her children with her—no matter what the circumstances, which are usually unknown to these experts—as well as the implied unsaid, evil things; the real act of leaving so contradicts the love and spiritual bond and nature of motherhood that most mothers, in the face of all the other emotional and psychological suffering and obstacles that divorce brings, just do not have the extra reservoir of resources that such an action requires. Which is why so many women remain in dead marriages, living a life of denial, often justifying it "for the sake of the children."

We were married two days before Christmas by an Episcopal minister, a friend of Henry's family who cared deeply about all of those caught up in the eye of our hurricane, in the wee chapel of the Episcopal church Henry belonged to. Besides the three of us, Henry's brother served as best man, and a close friend of Henry's was my best person. I wore a pale gray-blue wool suit I'd bought at Loehmann's, and carried a single lapis blue Dutch iris. The church was decorated for Christmas, and even in the desert, to my surprise, was filled with the fragrance of pine and spruce boughs.

With Camelback Mountain brooding in the background, our wedding brunch was held at a lovely old (for Phoenix) inn in the desert, where our small party was joined by one of Henry's oldest friends, Dino DeConcini. It was a sweet time.

As we set out for Tucson after the celebration I thought I was absolutely going to explode with happiness. Inside, at the age of forty-four, I felt like a girl. I had never before known such blissfulness, nor have I since. But no matter. The intensity can't last, or you would be consumed by it, die from it. But I know one thing. I was given a great gift, something that most people never experience, and that everybody longs for. Something I thought had passed me by: that once-in-a-lifetime grand passionate love.

> *Rise up, my love, my fair one, and come away.*
> *For, lo, the winter is past, the rain is over and gone;*
> *The flowers appear on the earth;*
> *The time of the singing of birds is come,*
> *And the voice of the turtle is heard in our land.*

Late as it was, and with the timing all wrong, I believed my time had finally come. And it was worth everything.

PART THREE

Arizona

Twelve

It is late April at high noon in Phoenix, which, as desert dwellers understand, is an hour that bleaches the color from the landscape. As I drive the three-mile stretch south from Camelback Road down Central Avenue toward our apartment building, my heart sings as I proceed along a corridor lined on both sides with citron-yellow trees, canary diamonds glittering in the sun. Like so many shooting stars the palo breas explode with shimmering lemony blossoms against sculptures of pale jade green trunks and branches. No boulevard could pulse with more magnificence!

I reflect back on how it all looked when I arrived, musing on how the transformation of the thoroughfare paralleled my own transformation, my evolution from middle-aged bride—hayseeds gone, though still a greenhorn in the Ways of the World—to who I am today. Can it be possible it's been almost twenty years?

In spite of myself, Arizona has been good to me, once I got beyond the disillusionment and sense of betrayal. Now I can see that every element of my psyche—intellectual, creative, spiritual, emotional, social—desperate for space and light, had long since outgrown their cramped carapace. In ways I could never have conceived, in the tradition of what the West has always represented—the frontier, a new life—Arizona turned out to be my "growin' place," an expanse as wide, as limitless as the horizons of its Big Sky. A place where you can see both ends of the rainbow at the same time.

I had arrived in Phoenix full of enthusiasm and optimism. After all, I was in many ways starting a new life. I had always been resilient, adaptable—one of my "to whom it may concern" letters of recommendation that I'd brought with me even singled out that quality—and the thought that I wouldn't like Phoenix had never crossed my mind.

Nothing could have been further from the truth. I felt betrayed. Alienated. Depressed. Trying to sympathize, Henry's remarkable secretary, Twyla Hannah, who had moved from Chicago, depressed me even more when she told me, "It took me ten years to get used to it. It has to grow on you." Like a fungus? I wondered. Is there an antidote?

A close friend, who after her marriage to a Phoenician moved from New York in the mid-sixties, remembers vividly her introduction to Phoenix. It was early October, "suit weather" in New York, and she was decked out in her new wool trousseau suit. As she walked down the stairs of the plane onto the tarmac into the shock of the 90-plus degree temperature, the dense heat hit her like a wall. Thinking that it must be from the engine of the plane as they walked beneath it, as she proceeded toward the terminal she realized it wasn't getting any cooler. And on the ride from the airport, as her husband drove her to their new home, an apartment in North Phoenix, there seemed to be nothing but cinderblock buildings. As a world traveler she had never before been in a place that she wasn't able to find some little something that intrigued her, that evoked her interest or piqued her curiosity. But nowhere after they left the airport had she been able to discern the first detail that in any manner she would describe as distinctive.

Arriving at their apartment, she was in such a state that she had to go in and lie down. "Now," she said, "looking back, I realize that I must have been suffering from an anxiety attack. Later, I kept looking for the city. I wanted to go and see Phoenix and walk down its streets but I couldn't find it. At that time the big thing was the new Christown Mall, and there was great excitement that the parking lot was going to be landscaped!"

It could have had to do with expectations. After all, my move from Mississippi to New York had been monumental, fulfilling my wildest expectations, and more. But this was as though I had entered a time machine going backward, emerging into a narrow world of complacency, with no thought of the world beyond, or of even wanting to think of it. Occasionally I spotted a billboard or two still in place beseeching passersby to "Impeach Earl Warren!" and "Out of the United Nations!"

When I told people I'd moved from New York, they took a dim view. "Great place to be *from*," they'd say, believing I was to be congratulated on my delivery from the Sodom of America, their idea of the epitome of iniquity, filth, corruption, and crime. But especially they were so pleased for me that I'd escaped the rigors of the New York weather. Paying no heed to Oscar Wilde's warning that "sunshine dulls thought," most Phoenicians, it seemed, believed that the primary reason for being alive was sunny weather.

There was simply no here here. Every house or building that appeared to have any architectural or historical significance had either already been, or was in the process of being scraped away, then quickly replaced with a "new" monstrosity of pure-d mediocrity. On beautiful downtown Central Avenue sites gracious old two-story colonial adobes were being bulldozed to make way for schlock, which itself has now fallen victim to the Second Scraping, leaving bare, vacant land in the city's center. Everything was expendable, transitory.

Even more depressing was a downtown that was so deserted and desolate it looked like a scene from the last day in the movie *On the Beach*, where a few tumbleweeds and newspapers scattered with the wind through empty, silent streets.

I was appalled that there was a sales tax on food. That there seemed to be a certain pride in the fact that Arizona was the only state in the Union with no health care plan for the indigent. That there were no free text books in the public schools—*Mississippi* had free textbooks! When defenders told me that those who couldn't afford books got them free, it made me crazy when I heard how the "poor children" had to stand in a different line to get their books. And when I discovered that there was no bus service on the weekends (even today there's none on Sunday), I almost went around the bend. Arizona didn't seem to believe it was necessary to accommodate folks of few means. (And if it's possible, that attitude has gotten even worse over the years.) Those are just a few things that come to mind right off the top of my head.

～

Now, here's something important. Never once did Henry and I sit down and talk about what our relationship and our life would be like after we were married. We are from a generation who never talked about things like that. Though it probably would have been helpful if we had, we didn't. We didn't have any kind of an "agenda." The only thing we wanted was to be together, and we would take it as it came. Perhaps because he assumed I knew, which of course I didn't, it would never have crossed his mind to explain to me what would be "expected" of me as his wife in Arizona. And since he never expressed any notion of me being anything other than who I was, and doing whatever it was I needed to do to be fulfilled and a whole person, I naturally made the same assumption.

Neither of us had ever been in any kind of therapy, though once Henry almost was. Believing that he was acting completely out of character when he separated from his wife in preparation for marrying me, one of Henry's close friends nagged him so about "getting help," that to get him off his back Henry finally made an appointment to see the psychologist that the friend recommended. The day before his appointment, the psychologist's nurse called to say that because the doctor was playing in a golf tournament, he would have to reschedule Henry's appointment. "Rejected by my own shrink!" Henry in jubilation reported to his friend, after he'd told the nurse not to bother.

I may have been spurned by many of the Old Phoenix crowd when I first arrived, in support of Henry's genuinely fine, truly lovely former wife; and by Henry's mother, who to our surprise took it all quite badly. However, since I didn't know any of those people, I wasn't aware that I was being ignored, and therefore was never bothered by it. As for his mother's judgment of us, I felt sorry for her for depriving herself of a loving relationship with her oldest son, which she continued to do until a year or so before she died thirteen years later. When the time came that he had to take charge of her life, reversing the role that she had mistakenly assumed was hers—controlling his—they both laughed when she confessed to him, "I'm so glad I'm no longer in charge!"

Part Three - Arizona

On the other hand, many of Henry's old and loyal friends (not a few of whom had found themselves in similar circumstances) rose to the occasion, inviting us to dinner or a party, sincerely sympathetic and kind—Henry was inexpressibly touched—which neither of us has ever forgotten.

At a time when you had "connections," before there was "networking," it's hard for me to believe now that when I moved to Phoenix, essentially the only person I knew was Henry, that I had no connection apart from him. Because his family was so closely tied to the social and business circles of Phoenix, as his wife I was thrust into a world that was alien to me.

Even though the population of Phoenix had exploded after the war, it had remained fundamentally a small town at its core, the civic leaders a product of a mix of both the pre- and postwar business community. I had no preconceived notions of "businessmen" as a genre, but was predisposed to think highly or at least benignly of them. After all, Henry was one.

When we married, Henry had been with Arizona Public Service Company almost twenty years, having worked his way up to chief financial officer, and was widely respected in financial circles in Arizona as well as on Wall Street. President of the board of the Phoenix Symphony and active on the board of the regional Arizona Theater Company, he became its first Phoenix chairman when it expanded statewide from its Tucson origins. A prodigious reader, avid theatergoer, devotee of both classical music and jazz, art lover, and student of history, Henry is a low-key and self-deprecating raconteur with a droll, earthy sense of humor. In other words, a man of enormous breadth and depth; and above all, a lot of fun.

This was before he later took up golf, Phoenix Suns basketball, Phoenix Cardinal football, and Arizona Diamondbacks baseball, which prompted me to remind him that when we married I told him that I believed that twenty years was long enough for any marriage. As Margaret Mead observed, 'til death us do part was okay when a life span was measured at only forty years.

I'd never lived any place so in thrall to the corporate business community. In New York I'd known as neighbors and friends, or from my former husband's position in Wall Street, men at the very top of a variety of professions, and so was possessed with a sufficient lack of awe to be unimpressed by a title. Certainly by a vice president, say, of First National City Bank (as Citibank was known then, and where vice presidents numbered in the hundreds in New York), who had come to Phoenix from New York to be chairman of the home-grown bank. Equally unimpressive was the publisher of the two Phoenix newspapers, a wheeler-dealer egomaniac who, because of his position, wielded such disproportionate power relative to his background and abilities, and who, when it was revealed that he had been living a life of delusion as a military hero for thirty years, was brought down when practically his whole life was exposed as a hoax. These and other "leaders" weren't like Henry at all! To me he was far superior to the whole lot. Putting it mildly, I was floored over the parochialism and lack of vision, and just couldn't figure out how Henry had fit in all these years.

When I understood the narrowness of Henry's milieu, of his world, I was enraged, and accused him of deception and betrayal in bringing me to such a barbaric, horrible place, knowing what I was like and believing I would fit in. I didn't want to fit in, and realized that if I ever did I would be lost. I implored my friends in New York, that if I ever told them I liked it, to come and get me. They'd know I'd had a lobotomy. I realize now that the rage I was feeling was a stage of grief, of mourning my old self and my old life. But be that as it may, I was furious! And after what I'd been through damn it all to hell if my life was going to come down finally to "wife of."

∞

Writing about my early Phoenix years is difficult, and I believe it's because I'm avoiding writing about Henry's and my relationship. I don't want to bring Henry into this because it's not about him and I don't want to be critical of him in any way. However, our relationship has everything to do with the kind of life I chose to live and how I chose the paths I did and became the person I am at this moment.

Early on in our marriage it gradually dawned on me at last that I was not going to be able to rely on Henry to fulfill my emotional needs, that my expectations for our relationship were based on wishful thinking rather than the reality of what he—or our marriage—was able to provide, and that my expectations were a huge burden which I had inflicted on our marriage, exactly as I had on my first marriage. When I realized this, I took it upon myself to compensate, or accommodate, for this incompleteness, to accept responsibility for my own life and sense of purpose. I had placed all of my eggs in one basket—Henry—and there was no way in the world he could ever live up to what I thought he would provide.

Looking back, I think I must have focused all of my rage of disillusionment on hating Phoenix, though there was plenty left over to blame Henry, that I had given up everything for *him* and for *this!* When all along of course, it was my own expectation and assumption—ingrained in me since birth—that one man could provide everything that I would ever need.

It took a long time for me to figure this all out on my own, but when I did it was as though I had finally set myself free. Even though I had issued my emancipation proclamation after my mother's death, I had no idea what a new way should be. In rejecting the traditional role of "wife," I was in foreign territory with no map or pole star to guide me; I was without role models. Because we live life forward and only in hindsight have 20/20 vision, it's clear now that no matter how far I'd come, I still needed Phoenix to make all of the old assumptions clear to me.

And that it would be in Arizona that I became a full human being.

∾

That first year in Phoenix I met one of the new wave of women who'd recently graduated from law school, in the vanguard of women on a "career track" hired by APS with the prospect of moving up through the ranks. She was a feminist and she was ambitious, and though I was flattered that such a much younger woman appeared to find me interesting, I also realized that it didn't hurt that I was the boss's wife. But I didn't care. Though I was quite delighted after meeting most of the wives of Henry's colleagues, who had been gracious and welcoming to me, I "related" more to this young woman.

Another was a young woman who worked in Governor Bruce

Babbitt's office, who was also a stringer for the *New York Times*. She sympathized with me, she said, after reading the book *Desperado*—native New Yorker Grace Lichtenstein's side-splitting account of having to forsake Manhattan for the wilds of Colorado in her new job as the *Times*'s Western correspondent—which she gave me. Through these two women I was introduced to a newly blooming circle of young women, in their late twenties, at the beginning of their careers. At a time when it was relatively rare for a woman to keep her own name after marriage, some of these were women who had. We were on almost the same level of consciousness about the women's movement, except we were coming at it from completely different perspectives.

Today they are the mid-life boomer women, now *older* than I was when I first knew them. As women with both career and family ahead of them—at their age I'd already had two children—their lives were as different from what mine had been as anything I could think up. Just as I at a different stage was struggling with no guidelines, they at the same time were struggling with none as well. It was a time of transition for us all.

So essentially, as my own person, I was involved in a completely different world from Henry, though occasionally it would overlap. For instance, when Henry was interviewing a man to work for him, after he met his wife he told me I would be crazy about her because she was so natural and down to earth, but more, she called herself a feminist. Well! I could hardly wait, and when I met her, it was like long lost sisters finding each other in the wilderness. When Henry hired her husband, I was thrilled. She was the first corporate wife I had as a soul mate.

One of the most genuinely unpretentious and straightforward people I've ever known, she was from a modest Irish Catholic family from Long Island, to my mind the unlikeliest feminist, but in many ways she was more fervent than I was, and her unexpected mid-life pregnancy never held her back. In her ninth month we were at some fundraising dinner when she pushed back her chair and hefted herself up to announce that she had to say goodnight because she and I were marching early the next morning in an ERA rally (prompting meaningful glances around the table). And when she appeared the

Part Three - Arizona

next day she was magnificent in a gigantic T-shirt, which, triple extra large though it was, still adhered like a sausage casing to her huge belly, where an enormous ERA button perched precariously right over the spot where her belly button protruded. See why I loved her?

Thirteen

The most pressing thing I needed to do after I arrived in Phoenix was to get a job. Though I had been urged to do so by my lawyer, my minister, and my friends, I had asked for nothing from my former husband. I brought with me one or two pieces of furniture and some china and silverware, but that was it. From my share of my mother's "estate" (the sale of her little house) I had about ten thousand dollars, Mama once again providing me with a dowry. Between the two of us, Henry's and my net worth came to about $26,000, with our new blended family consisting of six children, my three and his three. I was definitely not marrying Henry for his money, and vice versa. In more ways than one I was *not* a "trophy wife!"

Henry had assured me I would have no trouble getting a job with a travel agency when I arrived in Phoenix, and I had no reason not to believe him. At an industry conference in San Francisco I had met the owner of a travel agency in Tempe who had told me to come to see him when I got to Arizona. And so well-armed with a stack of letters attesting to my superior abilities and sterling attributes from my former travel colleagues and clients, I set out for Tempe.

Naturally he didn't have a job available, but he gave me some contacts at other agencies. After warning me that my experience "overqualified" me for most travel agency jobs in Arizona, he added that most agencies had never heard of the Institute of Certified Travel Agents and that there were only a handful of members in the whole state. "Don't count on it to help you," he warned. "It might even hurt."

Great.

And you know what? He was right. The very next owner I talked to sneered, "*No*body around here cares anything about that." He had that hard-eyed zealot look—you know the look I mean—like somebody who had put up one of the "Out of the United Nations!" signs. The way he couldn't get my letters of reference out of his hands quick enough, you'd have thought he was going to catch some "foreign" germ.

Everywhere else I went the first question was always: "Are you domestic or international?" and I was puzzled at first, until I realized you had to be one or the other, you couldn't be both, as I'd been from the start.

Finally I was hired by a young woman manager for "international" and "vacation," another category, different from "business." My hours were 8:30 to 5:00 with a half-hour off for lunch. I made $220 a week, which after deductions came to less than $200. The principal vacation everyone seemed to want to take was a cruise on the Love Boat. None of the other agents, including the manager, had ever been much beyond the Arizona border, unless it was to San Diego, or Guaymas, a small town on the coast of Mexico.

When I left New York I brought with me the account of a boys' camp situated deep in the wilds of central Canada, where beyond a certain point it could only be reached by canoe. Generations of hardy New Englanders had been sending their children there at least since the turn of the century. I liked the owner, Fred Reimers, who was from Jackson and who had attended the camp as a boy. I loved working with the campers and their families, who came from all over the United States, some even from abroad ("international"). As I began setting up the campers' itineraries, the manager informed me she wouldn't be able to give me my share of the camp business, nor would I be paid for the days off it would take to travel to upstate New York, where I oversaw their rendezvous in Buffalo. At first I was unbelieving at such a breach of ethics, then I was furious. After I got my pitiful, paltry little paycheck that Friday, when I got home I threw it on the floor, stomped on it, and burst into tears. She had given me an excuse, and on Monday morning when I called to tell her I wouldn't be back, I felt like a million dollars after I hung up the phone.

I called a travel agency I'd interviewed with before, whose owner was a friend of Henry's. He had only one agent beside himself, and couldn't afford to hire another one. But when I asked if I could come book my camp with him, he was delighted, and we split it fifty-fifty.

∞

Realizing that the travel business was not going to be my life's work, by summer's end in 1979—not even a year since I'd been in Phoenix—I decided to go to Thunderbird, the American Graduate School of International Management, in Glendale, Arizona, to get a masters degree in international management.

This was a big decision for me. As much as we needed the money, there was nothing available for me on a level that would ever lead to a career, and I figured the only way to change that was to get a master's degree. Also, I could get a student loan to do it. Most of the women who wanted careers at that time were going to law school, but it took three years; at Thunderbird, by going to summer school, it would take me only a year-and-a-half. The world of money and business was all I knew anything about, albeit vicariously through both of my husbands, but it had been interesting, and even occasionally exciting. Women were only beginning to enter the world of business, and there were fewer women going to business school than to law school.

On the other hand, my larger concern was to have as much free time as possible to visit my children and to have them visit me. Having a job that was meaningful that would lead to a career was one thing, but taking some dead-end job that would keep me tied down in Phoenix was just something I wasn't willing to do. I decided on Thunderbird, with its international student body, to help me keep perspective and a grip on reality, to remind me that there *was* another world out there.

With twenty-four years between me and my last college exam, at the age of forty-six and without benefit of one of those courses on how to take the Graduate Management Aptitude Test, I took it cold.

Of all times, those Princeton testing people chose our group to use as guinea pigs for experimental questions, and instead of the usual two or three sections out of six to test verbal ability, there was just one, of only twenty questions. When I met Henry for lunch to celebrate after it was over, the minute I saw him I burst into tears. (I sure did a lot of that in those days.)

I've erased from my mind my cruel score—it was so humiliating—but as bad as it was, I got in (they must have needed middle-aged women). I told the admissions officer that a hundred years ago as a senior at Millsaps I'd been intrigued by Thunderbird, and had even sent off to the American Institute of Foreign Trade, as it was known then, for a catalogue. "It's just as well you waited," he replied sympathetically. "We didn't take women back then."

To every thing there is a season . . .

He was quite impressed, I was surprised to learn, with my transcript, and it was the first I was to hear of "grade inflation."

"You have no idea how expectations and standards have been lowered," he said. "Today your grades from Millsaps would be A's and A+'s. A B back then would be equivalent to an A today, what we call grade inflation. You won't have any problem at all, except for getting back into the routine of studying. Why not take only your beginning Spanish for one semester, and then begin a full load the next semester? I think it'll help ease the transition."

Which is exactly what I did, with January 1980 finding me on the Black Canyon Freeway at 7:00 a.m., Monday through Friday, for an hour-and-a-half round-trip drive.

I was back in school and loving it.

ஒ

Yo soy de Arizona y estudio aqui. ("I'm from Arizona and I'm studying here," apt phrase to describe this chapter of my life.)

In class each day, with a student partner we would alternate speaking each side of a conversation in Spanish that the night before we'd memorized by listening to an audiotape. There was no textbook. I know that every time my classmates, all hot-shot linguists to me, got me for a partner, they would cringe inwardly. And though I'm sure they must have felt sorry for me, they were uptight because they didn't want me to pull down their grade. God forbid that they didn't get an A+. No plain old A for these competitive types; and heaven help them if they got an A-. It was the first time I'd ever known students who wouldn't accept the grade they made, who always tried to negotiate with the professor for a better one.

And it was at Thunderbird that by accident I chanced upon a revelation. In my Asian Studies class the subject that day had been about the problems encountered in moving to a foreign country, and as the professor listed each symptom of "culture shock" on the board, the light slowly began to dawn. I had almost every single one! I had been suffering from culture shock and hadn't known it!

When I realized that practically every immigrant has the same experience, it was like a visit to Lourdes. A miracle cure. It wasn't me! It was CULTURE SHOCK! When your problem has been diagnosed, you can treat it. Others have recovered, and you can, too. (Only in writing this have I recognized myself as an immigrant, both literally and metaphorically, and of all of the implications inherent in the meaning of the word.)

We had a choice between two emphases at Thunderbird, finance or marketing. Even as I liked my accounting class—I had a fine teacher—and though statistics was a language I never learned to speak, economics interested me. Unfortunately, the arrogant, patronizing professor and I had a hate on from the first day, ruining it for me, and I never took more than the requisite two semesters.

In a book I once owned written over sixty years ago, and now forever lost to a forgotten borrower, a Norwegian Lutheran minister applied the four humors, or temperaments—ascribed to by the Greeks and later Shakespeare—to four biblical figures to demonstrate to his Protestant flock how God needs and uses us all.

John, the beloved disciple, personified Melancholy, or black bile, from whom the original, creative ideas flowed; the philosopher, the poet, the artist.

Next came Peter, the Sanguine one surfeited with blood, who took up those ideas, spreading the Good News.

Whereupon Paul (I can't help it if he's considered by some to be a misogynist; there are two schools of thought on this), Choleric with yellow bile, commenced to live the Word day in and day out, counseling others to do the same as he traveled his world over.

Last was the Phlegmatic, and for the life of me I can't remember who it was, though obviously his lot was to make the tough decisions. Like "downsizing," or maybe building a nuclear power plant.

So I thought about these four types, and there's no escaping the fact: I am Peter.

I don't have to tell you that I chose marketing.

As I recall, I believe the average age of the student body was somewhere between thirty and thirty-five—I was definitely pushing the upper end—and remember feeling sorry for the one guy I met who was older than I was. It bothered me at first, with everybody so young and having nothing in common, with nothing but their grades and making lots of money primary on their minds. So different from when I went to college, though perhaps I might have been the same way had I gone to graduate school after college. But I got used to it and toward the end got caught up in their job prospects and interviews, and celebrated if one of my friends got a job offer. (Later, finding myself in the ultimate job interview, during my senate campaign I regretted that I hadn't bothered to learn interviewing techniques at Thunderbird.)

Teaching industrial marketing was an excellent professor who was Chinese, a native of Singapore. He was shy and he was smart. Always intrigued by such a combination, occasionally I would try to draw him out for a few minutes after class as most of the other students shot out of the door. The class had divided into teams of four, and besides me, my team consisted of an Arab from Kuwait; a black Ivorian, as he said citizens of the Ivory Coast are called, whose native language was French; and a Jew from Detroit, all men (and all younger, of course). Aware of my Mississippi origins, and having experienced the discrimination of being Chinese in Singapore, the professor inquired as to how my Southern kinfolk would feel about me "mixing" in such a way, cross-cultural issues being of more than passing interest at Thunderbird. I just laughed and told him I'd never know because they'd never find out from me, though I couldn't be sure that such a notion might not have some of my ancestors spinning in their graves.

I was delighted when a New York City friend, also a transplanted Mississippian from a place so far out in the country that my daddy would have said he came from "out from Lena" (Lena itself being no more than a remote crossroads in the middle of nowhere), took it upon himself to journey to Phoenix to witness my graduation from Thunderbird. As with so many East Coastlings—even though he was in the PR biz, he had retained his down-home touch—his only contact with Arizona had been in flying over it on his way to L.A. So even though his first venture into Arizona territory was primarily an act of kindness, after being entertained by my vivid descriptions of my new world, it was probably provoked as much by curiosity, if not sympathy.

He was pleased with the simple pomp of our little outdoor ceremony in the small quad (this was when only the professors, not the graduates, wore caps and gowns), against the backdrop of a colorful panoply of foreign flags, emphasizing our international flavor. However, the drive up the freeway to the campus, and afterward the joys of downtown Glendale on the way to a Mexican restaurant in an industrial section of town only reinforced for him my characterization of there being no here here.

Returning home to our high-rise apartment in downtown Phoenix—built in 1958, the oldest of only three high-rise apartment buildings in the city—with its spectacular view of Camelback Mountain and the far-flung lights of metropolitan Phoenix, I invited him outside on the balcony. "Be real quiet," I told him. "I want you to hear something."

After we'd stood in silence for several minutes, leaning on the railing taking in the view, he turned to me, mystified, "What is it? I don't hear a sound."

"Exactly," I replied. "A straight line on the EEG. Absolutely no sign of life."

༄

Through sheer grueling hard work, I got more of a sense of accomplishment out of earning that degree at Thunderbird than anything I'd ever done. Though as a forty-seven-year-old fifties woman about to enter the eighties job market, I was never comfortable with the idea of selling myself the way all my twenty-something fellow students seemed to be able to do. It was too much like bragging. But I was sure that my fine new masters degree in international management would be the key that would open the door to my beautiful new career.

Most people might not remember, but there was a recession in 1981, the second year of Ronald Reagan's administration. All businesses were cutting back, and in Phoenix the banks with international departments were cutting them to the bone, if not getting rid of them completely. Slim as the international business opportunities were in Phoenix, I gamely plugged away.

It was close to six months before I had my one and only offer, such a cliché that I hate to mention it. At one of the banks I was told by the head of the international department—consisting of one person, him—that he had an opening for a secretary, which he proffered almost apologetically, realizing (to his credit) how I would feel about it. Henry and some of my friends couldn't believe I didn't take it and "work my way up."

(At a time like this I often invoke the definition of faith from *The Song of Bernadette:* For those who believe, no explanation is necessary; for those who don't, none is sufficient.)

Job hunting is a full-time job in itself. It absorbs all of your energy, emotional and psychic as well as physical. You become a one-dimensional person, completely focused on yourself, and exceedingly boring company. Come to think of it, it's exactly what happens to you when you run for office.

Depressed by feeling rejected, and sick and tired of feeling sorry for myself, I figured the only way to quit focusing on me was to reach out and help somebody else. Remembering the words posted with our final grades in Logic by my philosophy professor at Millsaps, "I cried because I had no shoes, and then I saw a man who had no feet," I picked up the phone and called the Volunteer Bureau.

"Would you like to be on the board of directors of Arizona Action for Displaced Homemakers?" I was asked.

"The board of *what?*" having not the foggiest idea of what she was talking about.

I had no way of knowing it then, of course, but that phone call was to change the direction of my life, taking me on a completely different path from anything I'd ever envisioned for myself. I would never be a captain of industry, or even ever again be among the ranks of the employed for more than a few months. I would forever after be a volunteer.

☙

By spring of 1982, when no job had materialized, at about the same time that I was calling the volunteer bureau, I took a five-day course in learning the new Wang system of word processing. We'd sublet a small New York apartment with friends, and after deciding that I would spend the summer there near my children, drawing upon my vast experience with New York City employment agencies, I gleaned from a business friend of Henry's the name of one specializing in law firms. Landing a summer job at the office of Rogers and Wells at the top of the Pan Am Building over Grand Central Station (one of the few New York firms who had begun using word processing), I labored in the mines so far *below* the first rung of the ladder that not only did the secretaries look down on us, so did the summer law school interns as well, *especially* the interns (the very same age and type I'd been in school with only a year before), who earned exorbitant salaries while being treated like royalty as they were wined and dined all summer in private city clubs and suburban country clubs. Down in the pit, though, where word processors, typists, and proof readers toiled in eight-hour shifts twenty-four hours a day, a strong esprit existed among my new friends in low places (shades of Dixie Advertisers thirty years before, and I hadn't moved a peg!) who in real life were aspiring writers, actors, and other assorted colorful characters found only in New York. And where I was afforded a different perspective on the System. When Labor Day came and my job was ending, I was delighted when I was asked to return the next summer.

And back again in Phoenix, it was then that I joined the board of the displaced homemakers.

Fourteen

At about that same time I got quite excited when I read in the local paper about a move underway to change election of the Phoenix City Council from an at-large to a district system. It seemed that the poorer sections of Phoenix, principally South Phoenix, where the Hispanics and blacks lived (remember what I said about *southern* parts?), had been historically short-changed as a result of always being outnumbered by white council members living in the more desirable parts of town.

The Establishment was naturally against any change in the status quo, and the business community raised a lot of money to fight it. Henry and I were going to be out of town for the election, so with a great sense of occasion before we left I went down to vote absentee in favor. When Henry called his office and we heard that it had passed, I cheered and leaped for joy. It symbolized for me a kind of turning point: it was my first sign of hope. Once more, I hadn't been alone, but had had no way of knowing that there were so many others out there who felt the same way I did.

The initiative drive for the new district system had been led by a thirty-five-year-old Phoenix lawyer, Terry Goddard, the son of a former Arizona Governor, and I couldn't believe my eyes when Terry and the member who brought him sat down directly across the table from me at dinner one night at a meeting of the Phoenix Committee on Foreign Relations, which I belonged to. We were perfunctorily introduced, and I naturally let him know how thrilled I was with the initiative vote. I, of course, had no idea he was even considering a run for mayor of Phoenix.

Phoenix had had a woman mayor for eight years who decided to call it quits. Mayor Margaret Hance, whose office was once described as "the Smithsonian of boosterism," was smart, attractive, witty, Old Phoenix—and a captive of the business community.

It was early 1983, and I was on the displaced homemakers board, where I met Deborah Dillon, a friend of Goddard's. I was completely bowled over after a board meeting one day when she pulled me aside and said, "If Terry Goddard asked you, would you consider managing his campaign headquarters when he runs for mayor?"

Besides being enormously flattered, I could hardly believe my luck in being given such an opportunity to be a part of a fight for change.

Henry was out of town, and when he called that night I gave him the news and asked how he would feel about my working for Terry Goddard. "Don't get your hopes up too much," he said.

Not anticipating such a negative response, I was defensive. "Well, why not? Why would Debbie say that to me if he weren't thinking about it?"

"Because I work for APS [the Establishment, as well as the utility company that built the world's largest nuclear power plant]."

"What difference does that make?"

"I just think it does. And I wouldn't want you to be disappointed if it doesn't work out."

The next day I got a call from Mark Steinberg, an associate of Terry's, who invited me to lunch to talk about the job. At the end of a pleasant meal over which we'd discussed what running a headquarters would entail, I warned him that he should be aware of three of my most glaring faults: "One, I am not a patient woman. Two, I don't suffer fools gladly. And three, I don't put up with bullshit." Apparently he was sold.

And when Terry called me a few days later and asked me to take the job, I accepted.

Relating my latest venture to his boss, the CEO, Henry told him, "I have some good news and some bad news. The good news is, Claire has a job. The bad news is, she's working for Terry Goddard."

∞

The only other time I'd ever been involved in politics was when I was six or seven years old, back in Jackson.

Our neighbor Mr. Culley was running for supervisor, whatever that was. On Saturdays or late afternoons when he got home from work, we'd yell, "Mr. Culley, Mr. Culley, are you going politicking today? Can we go politicking with you?"

And if the answer was "yes," all of us in the neighborhood would pile into Mr. Culley's Buick, or if we were really lucky, the black pickup truck used by Robert, the Culleys' handyman. Nothing beat riding in the back of the pickup truck.

Mr. Culley had stacks of little cards he'd printed up, and he would drive us into town to the end of a neighborhood street. We'd get out and run down each side of the street, leaving one of his cards in every front door. Mr. Culley would be waiting for us at the other end, and off we'd go to the next street. Occasionally he'd let us hang on and ride on the running board, which added a sense of daring, of derring-do, to the business of politicking.

Now that I think about it after all these years, Mr. Culley didn't win. But my memory of politicking was that it was powerfully exciting!

And naturally I took the job with Terry without a doubt in my mind that I could do it.

In addition to a liberal arts education; being a mother, with all of the concomitant skills required for managing a household with three children (comparable to, though far more demanding than running a campaign headquarters); being a travel agent, with its attention to detail; throw in president of the Women's Guild dealing with all kinds of personalities and sub-currents of ideas and beliefs; not to mention my recent degree in international management, with marketing, management, and accounting—even some Spanish under my belt; and, well, just let me at it!

On my desk I had fresh flowers, and on the wall behind my desk I taped up a sign with Einstein's words: "Great spirits have always suffered violent opposition from mediocre minds." And I quickly discovered that what was really required most of all was instinctive: an ability to get along with people, and to get things done. I was forty-nine then, still trying to be "nice," and had not known what a valued commodity follow-through was until I discovered, beginning then, how so few people have it.

In the five months I worked on Terry's campaign I probably learned more about more things than I had at any time in my life until that time. It was my initiation into how the system actually works, which in my entire life I'd never been in a position to have to buy into, or if so, I hadn't been conscious of it. I had only recently become aware of someone being described as "effective," and wondered if a mother ever told her children at her knee, "Now children, I want you to grow up to be effective," rather than loving, or compassionate, or doing what's uniquely right for them, to thine own self be true.

It was my introduction as well to working with lawyers—talk, talk, talking everything to death—and of "process," which as a woman of action, drove me to distraction. And it was the first time I'd ever been so aware of those who were such absolutely blatant self-servers.

∞

The job with Terry was to be the last time I was ever again to be among the gainfully employed. I was paid the munificent sum of $1,000 a month, and mighty proud to get it. In addition to my job, we had only two other paid positions: my volunteer coordinator, Joni Bosh, now a mother of two sons and a national director of the Sierra Club, who earned $750 a month; and the get-out-the-vote coordinator, Alan Stephens, who the next year was elected a state senator. He made $1,200 a month. Some of the friendships I made on that campaign have been the most enduring, perhaps because they were rooted in the commonality of basic beliefs and values.

When Terry officially announced in late June, we were the underdogs, I believe about thirty points down, and the local political pundits and the media practically dismissed him. How could anybody win without the support, i.e. money, of the business community, which was supporting his opponent, a businessman and former state senator? But steadily, steadily, Terry built up steam as he rolled along with his underfunded grassroots campaign. I was constantly astonished at his stamina, though as a young man with no wife or family yet to consider, he had twenty-four hours a day to devote full-time to running for mayor, and he did. A few days before the campaign was over, when he was perilously close to complete exhaustion, I asked him how he kept going, and he told me that he just had to reach down inside himself and find the strength. And I tucked that away.

In my first experience of being on the inside as an observer of what's really happening, and then seeing how it was portrayed by the newspapers supporting his Republican opponent (though this was supposedly a nonpartisan race), I was stunned at the way events were twisted and distorted, then printed as gospel, with no recourse to setting the record straight except a Letter to the Editor, even though the damage has already been done. It's like asking a jury not to remember something that has been said. And if they do print your letter, it's usually on a day that gets the lowest circulation. The devastating editorial will be on a Sunday, with the highest circulation, and your rebuttal on a weekday, when the circulation is much lower, or worse, on a Saturday.

Not only did they beat up on him in the editorials, but in the news pages as well. In subtle ways that the general public may never notice—but which the insiders believe "everybody" knows, since their circle is so small—the newspapers always put Terry's opponent's name first in any story about the two of them. And anything that was remotely positive about Terry was below the fold at the bottom of the front page, with his opponent always above the fold, or at the top, where it's read first—all of which is News Manipulation 101, subtle but devastatingly powerful subliminal messages hammered out by the newspapers every day.

I was also dumbfounded at the ineptitude of so many who were considered "experts," those who passed for "pros" on how to run campaigns and other things. It was also about this time that I learned of all the old enmities between the factions and fiefdoms in the state Democratic Party among the Goddards, the DeConcinis, and the Babbitts. And for those of us who honestly believed in

Terry, who had the old "all for one" spirit, it was also a lesson in idealism confronting the demands of so many hidden agendas. Before it was over, one of my primary jobs came to be that of juggling and mollifying all the competing egos and users.

༄

At the beginning of the last week of the campaign, there's no explaining how or why, but suddenly we sensed a palpable feeling that the tide had turned, as though a switch had been thrown, that Terry was going to win. The day before election day I suddenly remembered that in every campaign movie I'd ever seen there had always been an enormous picture of the candidate as a backdrop for the election night victory speech, so I began calling around to find someone who could blow up a photo big enough to suit me. It wasn't easy, but I finally got it done.

After winning by more than a stunning ten thousand votes, when Terry made his triumphant victory speech it was in a setting that would have done the films *All the King's Men* or *The Candidate* proud. Little did I know that the photo I had blown up for all the world to see was copyrighted by the photographer, who spotted it on television and later threatened to sue because I'd used it without permission.

Through it all, I realized that it had been years since I'd felt so alive, so of-the-moment, had so much fun, or such a shared sense of purpose and connection with people who believed in what I did. I was as completely unaware of the symptoms of that dread disease, political junkiedom, as I'd been of the symptoms of culture shock.

༄

My childhood was a time of innocence, when vulgar language was as foreign to me as the idea of being molested. Or even of sex in general. Euphemisms were used for bodily functions and private body parts.

What I'm leading up to is that I was reared in an innocent time among gentle folk—and have lived essentially a gentle life—but my language has become crude and foul. And in trying to figure out how it came about, I believe I can trace it back to when I first got involved in politics, working on Terry's first campaign for mayor, though be assured that Terry is a model of rectitude, that off-color language offends him as much, or more, than anybody.

I mean the minute I start talking politics, or get together with someone involved in a campaign, I begin hearing profanity flowing out of my mouth that would curl the hair of "normal" people. It just pops out. And there have been times when I've seriously wondered if I might have Tourette's Syndrome, having as one of its bizarre symptoms "an involuntary or compulsive utterance of curses and obscenities," which Dr. Oliver Sacks describes in his book *An Anthropologist on Mars*. (I've empathized with those people I've passed on the sidewalks, just standing there, shouting obscenities at the heavens at the top of their lungs.)

Whatever. All I know is that politics unleashes in me a force that more often than not comes out as four-letter words.

∞

A week after the campaign was over I took off on a long-planned stay in the New York apartment we had sublet, to remain through Thanksgiving and Christmas, until New Year's Day, to enjoy the holidays with my children.

I returned to Phoenix the day before Terry was to be sworn in. I had an invitation to the ceremony at City Hall, and don't really remember if there were any other events, though after he was sworn in I do remember walking with him among a group of marchers through the streets of downtown; but I'm not sure where we ended up, since because of him downtown is so different now.

As I entered City Hall through a mob outside, the air crackled with the energy generated by the throng of crusading true believers whose dream has finally been realized—that the savior is at hand and a new day is dawning. Everybody was there from the campaign, and we waved and hugged and carried on like it was old home week. We had all played a part in the seismic change that was taking place and were filled with the initial unbridled enthusiasm and optimism that's inherent with such a changing of the guard. These were my people. I was one of them. And for the first time—it had taken five years!—I was excited about coming back to Phoenix.

∞

Never having been involved in party politics at any time in my life, I was only dimly aware of how state legislators got elected, and knew nothing of the way state legislative districts had been drawn in Arizona. I think I probably voted for Republicans for the legislature the first time I voted because the candidates were women and I'd seen their campaign signs in my neighborhood. It was during Terry's campaign that I saw the party system at work for the first time.

In this new state of awareness after I returned to Phoenix in early 1984, still pumped up over winning the election and the changes that were taking place as Terry made good on his promise to "open the doors to city hall," out of curiosity I looked into who exactly was representing me in my own state legislative district. They were all Republicans, a senator and two representatives, one of whom was an Old Phoenix woman who had been there for twenty years.

I now had a clearer understanding that it was the state legislators who made the rules that affected the lives of everyday Arizonans—it was they who were responsible, or irresponsible, for the sales tax on food; for the lack of free textbooks; for abandoning the poor without health care. I figured that with the winds of change in the air, twenty years was long enough for anybody to stay in office, and I began to think about running.

It would be the perfect "nontraditional" job for me: four or five months of intense, occasional twenty-four-hour days, followed by a scattering of committee meetings; then essentially time off for the remainder of the year. So when the other representative announced that he was moving out of the district and would not be running, leaving what I would learn is an "open seat"—with no incumbent and considered easier to win—I believed it to be Fate, Destiny. And I decided to go for it.

With all the Democrats I'd met on Terry's campaign, I had a built-in base of support. When I went to talk to the folks at party headquarters with whom I'd already worked on the campaign, they appeared to be delighted, and thought I had a good chance of pulling it off, even though, I learned for the first time, I would be running in a district where the Republicans had a registration edge of 2 percent, where voters had elected a Democrat only once in their last eighteen opportunities. Nevertheless, they thought I'd be perfect as a candidate because I was married to an Old Phoenix Republican business executive, and that I "looked like a Republican." That wasn't the first time I'd heard that from a Democrat—I'd heard it during Terry's campaign—which both bemused and amused me, always leaving me at a loss as to just exactly how a Republican looked that would so distinguish one from a Democrat.

What I hadn't counted on was that I was going to have to persuade the Democratic Party regulars in my district to support me. I had assumed that simply by putting myself in the race the Democrats would be delighted. But that's not the way it works. You have to "prove yourself" a good Democrat to the party people. Earning my stripes working to get Terry elected counted, but it was only a foot in the door because, after all, it was a nonpartisan race. Some Democrats were suspicious of my Democratic lineage, wanting to know exactly how many years I'd been a registered Democrat. Others were suspicious because I was "rich." (As I've fought that stupid battle over the years, I realize it is endemic in the Democratic Party—because of course the Republicans celebrate money—and wonder if people like the Kennedys, or the Harrimans, or the Roosevelts, who were truly wealthy, or the DeConcinis, the Babbitts, or the Goddards in Arizona ever had to deal with such an accusation.) And there was no getting away from the fact that for many Democrats I was "tainted" because of my husband.

It was a real drag to have to deal with such piddling and picayune stuff among your so-called "friends," but I was so accommodating butter wouldn't have melted in my mouth (I've always wondered what that means). One of my greatest friends from that time has been Louis Rhodes, then the director of the state ACLU, whom I met on Terry's campaign. He is a walking data bank of campaign statistics and a respected party regular who rescued me. After advising me to send out a letter to all the precinct committeepersons in the legislative district I was running in—to let them know I was running and to ask for their support—he drew up a campaign plan for me.

After signing up to become a precinct committeeperson myself, I sent out fundraising letters for my legislative campaign to everybody who had contributed to Terry and everybody else I knew. Several friends gave fundraisers for me, and in addition to their substantial contributions, U.S. Senator Dennis DeConcini (Dino's older brother) and Terry spoke at separate fundraising events. I received a contribution from the legislative campaign fund of Governor Bruce Babbitt, now Secretary of the Interior, and was thrilled to receive a letter from my hero Rep. Morris (Mo) Udall, working in Washington with the Mondale-Ferraro campaign, which was read at a fundraiser by Dennis: "If we allow Ronald Reagan to win a second term we will all be the losers. That is also true right here in Arizona—we cannot allow the Republicans to defeat a woman who speaks her mind on the issues. A woman who has the strength to speak for those who have no voice. Who stands for those who have no lobby. Who is strong for those who are weak." It was written of course by some staffer. But still . . .

There was a unique aspect about this race that was just too Freudian for words for me, and I felt when I heard it that it was bound to be bad karma. Besides the twenty-year woman veteran, my other opponent who'd won the Republican primary had the exact same name as my father, for whom my brother and son were named!

I did everything right, and the race was being called a toss-up right up to the election. I had great literature and signs. Plenty of money. Good press, including an article in the paper about the unions having a shouting match over whether or not to endorse me, if to do so would hurt my chances of being elected. And because of the fear that the legislature was going to try to ban abortion, I had strong support from Planned Parenthood. (Though walking door to door in the summer desert sun I almost passed out with heat prostration.) Even the *Phoenix Gazette* Republican political columnist who would later be my nemesis was upbeat, reporting that though Republicans outnumbered Democrats in my district, I was "making a race of it." There was no way I could know then of the foreshadowing when he called me "a tart-tongued political newcomer," after some quip I'd made to him—which he duly quoted—and he'd even laughed, unusual for him. Everything written about me was positive: that I was a strong candidate who appealed to both Democrats and Republicans alike. The alternative newspaper *New Times* ran such a powerful, flattering story about me, "Claire Sargent: The Democrats' White Hope," that friends had it framed and gave it to me after the election.

You may recall that 1984 was the year of the Reagan landslide, which brought out voters in unprecedented numbers in my Republican district, in some precincts close to 80 percent. With the long coattails of such stunning turnouts I didn't have a chance at the bottom of the ballot, and I lost by about twelve hundred votes. As a first-time candidate, though, it was an unbelievable experience to think that almost fifteen thousand people had voted for me. Had actually sought out my name on a ballot. Imagine!

Louis Rhodes, the electoral guru, trying to keep me from feeling so bad about not winning, compared my race to Democratic districts where Democrats won only by a thousand votes out of six thousand, to demonstrate to me that I ran very well; he believed my race to be the harbinger for a Democratic victory in my district, which, indeed, came to pass four years later.

It was an important lesson in politics: you can do everything right and still lose. And the obverse is equally true: you can do many things wrong and still win. In fact, no matter how bad a campaign you run, if you win, nobody remembers it after the votes are counted.

For me the most lasting legacy of that campaign was the magnet that it became to a community of women that I had never met nor even knew existed. Women of every stripe, we were sisters united. And they worked like dogs to help me. Though I lost, knowing that I'd done everything I could I was proud of my race. But I was unprepared for the depth of disappointment of my supporters, who appeared to be far more depressed and disheartened than I was, something that every candidate needs to be aware of.

Reading about that election after all these years, I'm fascinated to see how consistent I've been. In 1984 I wrote: "Arizona has changed dramatically in the last 20 years, but the Legislature has remained tied to old ideas and unworkable solutions," billing myself as running against business-as-usual, an "alternative to rubber-stamp, lock-step thinking," critical of legislators who "don't have the guts" to pass an indigent health care plan. "I know Arizona doesn't want to be last in prenatal care," I was quoted as saying, "last in caring for the chronically mentally ill, or last in providing free textbooks for students. Arizonans want to be first in those categories, but we never will be if we keep electing the same people to office." And presaging neighborhood activism, to improve neighborhoods I called for a home-maintenance deduction on state income taxes.

To tell the truth, the first time I ever voted for myself was when I ran for the legislature. After all, I was brought up to believe that it would be conceited to vote for yourself, that it was good manners to vote for the other person. Which I did at MSCW when I was nominated for freshman house chairman (I lost), and again in Brooklyn, when I was nominated for something called the Model Provisional Member in the Junior League (I won).

In the voting booth on election day, after voting first for Walter Mondale and Geraldine Ferraro, and next for Arizona federal and state officials, I turned the page and became weak in the knees when I beheld under "State Representative" my very own name, "Claire Sargent (D)," the solitary (D) among two (R)'s. As I stared at it, I was filled with such awe that I was hardly able to believe that it was really me, my very own self right there on that ballot. Then, with a firm and steady hand, I resolutely stabbed the pin through the hole by my name. I was fifty years old.

~

I doubt if Nairobi, Kenya, was ever the same after being set upon by twelve thousand women attending the United Nations World Women's Conference in the summer of 1985. When I boarded the plane to leave Nairobi for home that July, so deeply affected had I been by the experience of the previous two weeks, I was a woman transformed. I had been to the mountain top and seen the promised land.

Several weeks after being sworn in as mayor, Terry appointed me to the Phoenix Women's Commission, which during the previous years had become moribund at best. I told him I would work to resuscitate it, but if things didn't turn around I would work to close it down.

Energized with the fire of new members and a friend in the mayor's office, the commission immediately rolled up its sleeves to establish the first child care center for the city of Phoenix and set up the first data bank of women's names from which the city, state, and private corporations could draw when choosing new members of public and corporate boards. We were on a roll. And in the spring of 1985 the commission appointed me to be their official representative at the United Nations Women's Conference.

There's no way I'll ever know, but I don't believe the conference would have grabbed hold of my soul in quite the same way if it had taken place anywhere other than Africa. For it was Africa itself that transcended the event, that elevated it to a higher, spiritual level for me. The minute I stepped off the plane from Paris where we'd had a layover, I had the most uncanny feeling of coming home. I can't explain it. It was like walking upon hallowed ground. Others who have visited Africa to whom I've related this sensation have said they felt the same way, that they too sensed a deep, almost primordial connection to place.

Caught up in the torrent of women from every continent and every country, of every color and every race, in the cacophony of the babel of unknown languages, the power of the bond of sisterhood uniting us was palpable and unmistakable.

If we're lucky in this life, perhaps just once we will be part of a rare event of such significance that we sense that we're in the presence of something extraordinary, something historic. It was just such a moment at the opening of the conference in a room the size of a football field in the building of the Kenyan Parliament. The atmosphere was charged with the thrilling sound of ululation and pulsing drum beat, of choirs of African children and native dancers in brilliant colors swirling around us, whipping up the crowd. A rhythmic clapping among the uncounted multitude brought us as one to our feet as we swayed to the rhythm of the music and spontaneously broke into a chorus of "We Are The World," sisters connected globally. Overwhelmed, I looked around and saw that mine weren't the only cheeks streaming with tears, and I doubt if I will ever experience anything like it again.

With emphasis on the conference theme "Equality—Development—Peace," it was the spontaneous gatherings that produced the most fascinating encounters. It was in the Peace Tent, where heated confrontations between Israelis and Palestinians would finally end, if not in accord, at least in agreeing to disagree, which at that time had never happened in the "real world." And one of the more sinister tableaux that sticks vividly in my mind was that of a small group of young Moslem women seated on the grass in a circle surrounding a portrait of Ayatollah Khomeini of Iran, their heads, faces, and bodies swathed in tents of black, trying to assure us that they were, indeed, treated with equality.

We heard stories from the women of Kenya, primarily a Catholic country, which, despite its dire poverty, had at that time the highest birth rate in the world, five children per family. When the women learned that contraceptives were available, those who could would sometimes walk ten or fifteen miles to get them, keeping it a secret from their husbands, because for a man having lots of children was a sign of virility.

As more and more men left their homes in the countryside to seek jobs in Nairobi, the women were left in charge of the children and the land and the one-room, dirt-floored house. It was the women who began each day searching for water and then carrying it to the house. Following that, they had to collect wood to burn to heat the water; each day the wood source was farther away as more trees were cut (causing desertification, which I was to learn more about at a later time). For food the women had to plant the seeds and then harvest the crop. Their lives were a never-ending cycle of servitude and hopelessness. It would be at the Nairobi conference that the concept of offering small loans to women to start their own cottage industries was introduced.

It was then that I first heard of the millions of women who had been subjected to genital mutilation worldwide, a brutal and painful procedure inflicted on girls at an early age; of the hundreds of thousands of girls in Thailand, sold into prostitution by their parents who received an advance against the girls' future earnings—money that is frequently used to build a house; of "dowry murder" in India—the killing of wives to earn more dowry from a subsequent marriage; and of forced sterilizations and abortions in China.

For the first time I reckoned with the idea that being female— the simple fact of gender—puts a fetus, an infant, a girl child, a woman, in harm's way. That there is a bond connected with that.

Part Three - Arizona

Being female transcends national boundaries, cultural differences, and the color of one's skin. Throughout recorded history no one racial, religious, or ethnic group has known discrimination as consistently as women have.

Attending a seminar featuring women from various countries and regions of the world—which had simultaneous translations in French, Spanish, English, and Swahili—it was in listening to Charlotte Bunch, an American, that I understood for the first time that feminism is transformational. Her very simple definition reduced feminism to its essence for me: equality, dignity, and freedom of choice to control one's own life and body, both inside and outside the home, and the elimination of discrimination and oppression wherever it exists.

Feminism is *not* a laundry list of women's issues; there's not only one sphere for women, but the whole globe. *All* issues are women's issues.

Feminism is *not* about "Add women and stir"—adding a few women into positions of power without changing the nature of the institution.

And feminism is *not* "for women only," since a politics based only on women as a special interest group sets us against other constituencies, separating us instead of linking us in a common struggle.

The hand that rocks the cradle is the hand that rocks the boat!

༄

I hadn't gone half way around the world just to see the campus of Nairobi University and the environs of the Stanley Hotel. After all, I was only a few miles from Kilimanjaro! Never having envisioned myself as Jane to Tarzan, or, especially, Cheetah, and without even the remotest inclination to be as one with nature, I nevertheless embarked with three other women on an overnight safari, with accommodations in a hotel rather than a tent.

After a bone-rattling twelve-hour drive in a van over a deeply rutted one-lane washboard road—shouting and gesturing to each other whenever we spied monkeys and baboons cavorting in the trees, or extraordinary birds on the wing—we arrived pale with dust at our destination in the middle of the grasslands of the Serengeti, where at that time of year great waves of animals migrated north to

Kenya from Tanzania just to the south. Such a splendid hotel, complete with swimming pool, out in the middle of nowhere, made me squirm once more in hair-shirted luxury, but as always I salved my conscience by trying to convince myself that my being there helped to put money into empty pockets.

After experiencing all those animals in Africa born free and at home in their natural habitats, even though I'd never been crazy about animals locked up in cages, the whole idea of zoos has become repellent to me, even the "new concept" ones, though I'm sure they must serve some higher good.

At some time in my life I'd read about the night train to Mombasa, a town on the coast of Kenya on the Indian Ocean. So our same Serengeti safari gang booked passage in the sleeping car on the overnight train bound for Mombasa. Our accommodations were a far cry from the romance of the train travel we had envisioned, and after a fitful night's sleep over a square wheel, early the next morning we were dismayed to discover Mombasa to be nothing more than a crowded, squalid seaport town, hardly the stuff of our rosy expectations. After inquiries, we were told that there were beaches bordered by hotels outside of town that were quite beautiful, so we hired a taxi to take us there.

Unbelievably picturesque, it was straight out of the guidebooks. Mile after mile of wide white sand beaches were ringed with palm trees growing almost to the water, the hotels (containing German tourists at that time of year, according to our guide) set back under the trees. Here again, as everywhere I'd been in Kenya, I never felt that any of the amenities—or even the necessities—the luxuries so plentifully provided for tourists, were ever available to or enjoyed by the Africans themselves. Even though President Daniel Arap Moi had polished up Nairobi and removed the beggars and pickpockets from its streets, I sensed that everything was for "show"; that after the women left, everything would go back to normal. I couldn't help wondering if Kenya would ever really be able to make it, and it was hard to avoid the overwhelming pessimism that pervaded V. S. Naipaul's *A Bend in the River*. But I needed to believe that the ideas, the openness of democracy, the sisterhood of the conference was a wedge of light that wouldn't be extinguished.

Part Three - Arizona

Taking off our shoes and dodging jelly fish, we waded at low tide at least a hundred yards out into the warm waters of the Indian Ocean. With the gentle waves lapping against my legs, I stood contemplating the unbelievable, that over this very horizon, thousands of miles away, lay the shores of Australia. I felt the "phantom sob of awe" the way I always do when I contemplate my tiny speck of space in the infinity of the universe.

Fifteen

When I turned fifty it didn't faze me, just as forty hadn't fazed me either. I remember not long after my fortieth birthday—it was the year I was president of the women's guild at my church in Westchester—telling my old friend Shirley Brown Smallwood that I couldn't remember when I'd felt so happy, so content. And before I knew what hit me, the next four years turned out to be the most tumultuous of my life. The most wonderful thing about life is that you never know what's going to happen tomorrow.

And until I turned sixty I thought my fifties—from the mid-1980s to the mid-1990s—were my richest, most fulfilling years. A time paralleling the search for my own self-identity.

After I quit looking for work, I found opportunities at every turn. Just not for pay. I know that great sport was made of Joseph Campbell's telling everyone to "follow your bliss"—that doors will open to you, and hands will reach out to help you that you never knew existed—but I found that what he said is true. By simply doing what I was naturally drawn to, doors kept opening, and I would step through. I was completely untroubled by living an unplanned life, even as younger women's lives were beginning to become as programmed and as narrow as those of men.

I would serve on a board only if I could make a difference, if it wanted to get things done. After the displaced homemaker organization was founded by Johanna Phalen and Madelene Van Arsdell in the late 1970s, during my term as president of the board it was a whoopin'-and-a-hollerin' red-letter day when we got the funding for a permanent home, and Terry turned out for a photo op to shovel a spade of dirt at the ground-breaking.

Which reminds me, I think this may be the place to spill the beans about one of my most exasperating, embarrassing problems: that one of the crucial things you need to understand about me, is that I cry. I don't mean if I'm physically hurt. I mean at the drop of a hat. And there's absolutely nothing I can do about it. I have no control. I have no idea when it's going to hit me. It's like narcolepsy, that condition where you fall asleep standing up, or talking, or driving—it just overcomes me no matter who I'm talking to or where I am. And that's the most awful part—it's almost always when I'm talking about something close to my heart. I can't remember when this affliction first hit me—it just sort of gradually took over—but it must be in my genes, because my mother used to do it occasionally and embarrass me to death, and my grandmother King did it, too. But they didn't run for the U.S. Senate.

It was like an epiphany the first time I came across the word "lachrymose." It was in an article in the *New York Times* sometime in the 1960s, describing Hubert Humphrey, one of the great criers of all time. Just like Hubert, whom I'd always admired because of his big heart and fighting for the underdog, I was lachrymose, and in good company to boot.

During Terry's campaign for mayor, a volunteer—a woman who was a teacher or a nurse, as I recall, who wasn't at all put off when she saw me beginning to "tune up"—asked matter-of-factly what made me laugh. When I told her the movie *Annie Hall*, a few days later she came in with a small framed picture of Diane Keaton and Woody Allen from the movie and put it on my desk next to my vase of flowers.

"Now," she said, "when you feel you might be getting ready to cry, just look at this and laugh."

I bring this up now, because I remember that before the news conference with Terry and the ground-breaking, I had crafted together a few words to introduce him and to commemorate the occasion. Eloquent and brief, I wanted to say them with no notes, and as I began to practice, I couldn't get through them without a waterfall of tears cascading down my cheeks. In a panic, when I got in the shower to begin getting ready, as the water poured over my head and down my face and body, I sobbed out the words over and over, my tears flowing with the water until the sobs and the tears ran dry and I had been released. And when I got to the news conference, even though my stomach was in knots, nobody would ever have had any idea of what I'd just gone through. I was so natural it was as though those pretty words had just popped into my head.

It didn't always work out that way, though.

∞

Today, everybody has to fit into a category. Because so many women work outside the home now, they know things about themselves that women of my generation never even thought about. They're all tested for where they fit into the scheme of things, Human Resource-wise. They speak a common language that describes their insight into their innate temperament and personality, things like whether they're the Take-Charge type, the Need-Direction type, or Nurturers or Mediators; of if they prefer a Spontaneous or Structured "working environment," or are more Big-Picture or Detail-oriented—things like that, which would never have occurred to us, as wives and mothers of the 1950s, to give a hoot about.

I was floored when a friend of mine, a feminist who works in the city bureaucracy, told me recently that she was distressed when she took one of those tests and found out she was in the Controlling/Take Charge category. "I was embarrassed when my coworkers found out what type I was. Everybody hates women like that—bitches—but I just can't help it. I've tried for years to hold back and be a nurturer, but it just saps my energy because it goes against my grain. If I want to get anything done down there, I just have to take charge because nobody else does." So she finally quit trying to be something she's not, and just let loose, doing what she's been good at all along, now that her natural strengths have been officially "profiled."

I was in my fifties before I gained that kind of insight, and in contrast, I had to figure it out on my own, through a lifetime of on-the-job training with no operating instructions. It took that long for me to come to the realization that I had a catalyst personality and to recognize one of my most natural traits, my vitality—my "life force," as one close to me calls it. In both of my marriages, my husbands—though each has a sense of humor—have been solid, substantial, while I've provided the spark, the spirit. Yin and yang. Just like my parents. (Have I married my father twice?)

At a meeting of the board of a non-profit organization in Phoenix—unconsciously doing my catalyst thing—I had opined that what we needed was more action and less talk to solve the problem of the dearth of low-income housing. When the meeting was over and I was walking out with the president of a major corporation, I expressed surprise when he casually alluded to me as a "bomb thrower." Then, struck by déja vu, I heard my minister in Westchester telling me to "keep right on doing what you're doing, because that's how you'll get things done."

"Maybe what we need," I replied to the corporation man, "is *more* bomb throwers."

But I pondered that. A "bomb thrower" (unfelicitous label, one that made me uncomfortable, that he thought that of me—a big leap from "bulldozer"!) is passionate, confrontational, speaking truth to power, unafraid. The suffragettes marched and picketed and chained themselves to the White House fence, and even after being jailed and force-fed, refused to give up until the vote was won. Dr. Richard Feynman, the Nobel physicist, by-passing the process and hierarchy of the presidential commission on which he served to investigate the explosion of the space shuttle Challenger, demonstrated by dropping a rubber O-ring model into ice water on national television that the O-rings had been in part a cause of the disaster. Martin Luther King, Jr. rejected the pleas of the Birmingham establishment when they beseeched him not to march on their city, warning him that to do so would undermine their quiet efforts even then under way behind the scenes.

Leaders with passion fighting for change—the bomb throwers—seldom bow to the "reason" of the status quo.

༄

In 1986, Dino DeConcini, a founder and former chairman of Arizonans for Cultural Development, a statewide arts advocacy group, and Dick Whitney, its current chairman, asked me to join its board and set up a political action committee to support the arts. In setting up ARTSPAC I met the woman from Tucson, a teacher and mathematician, who was running for state superintendent of public instruction (a Democrat), a strong supporter of arts in education. I held a small fundraising luncheon for her and informally raised money and introduced her to people in Phoenix, generally helping behind the scenes of her campaign.

She won her race, succeeding a Democrat who had stepped down after twelve years. Believing that more than routine attention should be paid to the passing of the baton, I called the head of the state Democratic Party with the terrific idea that the party hold some sort of reception for her after her swearing-in ceremony. "It's never been done before," he said. Next, I called a friend who was the head of the State Board of Regents, appointed by the governor to oversee the state university system, with the same suggestion. "Never been done before," he said. By then, wild with frustration, I called Dick Whitney. "That's a great idea! We'll have it at the art museum." And we did.

No good deed goes unpunished, of course. It wasn't long after she'd been in office that insiders discovered that this woman was Trilby to her husband's Svengali. That she couldn't, or wouldn't, make a decision without his okay, and her second term in office ended with the relevation that he was a batterer as well. Even though a woman has a big brain, it doesn't protect her from being used as a punching bag by her husband.

༄

Simultaneously with my experience stemming from the Nairobi Women's Conference and my growing awareness of the connectedness of the global and the local—"think globally, act locally"— through a mutual friend I met David Parslow, who lived in Patagonia, a hamlet in southern Arizona. And demonstrating how everything is connected, after I got to know his wife I discovered that she had lived in Jackson and went to Bailey Junior High. She was there in the sixties while her father, after he retired from the military, took some summer courses at Millsaps before starting medical school at the University of Mississippi Medical Center, where he was on duty in the emergency room the night civil rights leader Medgar Evers was brought after he was gunned down. Considered to be "nigger lovers" because her mother was a member of a small group of members at St. Andrews Episcopal Church in Jackson who were sympathetic to "outside agitators," a cross was burned in the front yard of her house on the very street where I walked home from the end of the bus line when I went to Bailey.

Anyway, right off the bat David told me that I was just the person he'd been searching for: that the first time he saw me I reminded him of a "cosmopolitan" Billie Dawn played by Judy Holliday in the movie *Born Yesterday*. That I radiated her same innate energy—and on occasion her "fuck-you" attitude—and never failed to startle him by saying what is "real."

Well, with an opening like that, how can a girl refuse! And our association on that venture became the beginning of an abiding friendship that continues to increase my life.

David was setting up—what else?—a non-profit organization to further his idea for a most fascinatingly original and intriguing project. Called the Gaia Network, it was drawn on the analogy of the Gaia hypothesis which, as David explained it, saw the world as a giant biological feedback system in which everything interacts. Indigenous cultures had become holes in the cultural part of the system and could be seen as "drop out," a video term for the black streaks across the screen when there isn't enough information. The world wasn't getting a complete picture of itself because these groups were rapidly losing their identity and uniqueness to the influence of one-way information—by satellite dish in the jungles of Ecuador they were receiving *Mister Ed*, Chinese "Kung Fu" movies, and *Dallas*—whose origin was the industrialized world.

The Gaia Network would train these threatened peoples to use video technology *to record their own lives*—their languages, customs, and rituals—that in the process would reveal and reinforce their own values and sense of self-worth, documenting an alternate vision of the human condition.

After I helped David recruit some Phoenicians for his board of directors, we set about seeking grant money from over a hundred large and small foundations nationwide. We endured almost a year of constant, pleasantly-worded euphemistic rejections, and on the verge of giving up hope, received a grant of $15,000 from a small

New York foundation that specialized in innovative, experimental ideas requiring seed money to get started, recharging us and renewing our faith.

Recently I watched the video that was the result of our two-year effort. For the first time ever, Quichua natives in the Pastaza province of Ecuador in the Upper Amazon were interviewing their own people expressing their own thoughts about their lives. Using video cameras with rechargeable solar batteries, the video was shot by four teenagers with no video experience, who, along with the subject matter, were selected by OPIP, the organization that represents five indigenous nations and 103 communities.

It was the beginning.

∽

In the spring of 1987 Dino invited me to a meeting that would change completely and forever the way I would think about Phoenix.

The meeting was called to announce an exciting innovative project to be unveiled that summer on one of the most inhospitable expanses of concrete in downtown Phoenix: the Civic Plaza, which reaches 126 degrees and higher on its surface each summer. It was called the Solar Oasis, the brainchild of Carl Hodges, native Arizonan and director of the Environmental Research Laboratory at the University of Arizona, which designed the Land Pavilion for EPCOT (Experimental Prototype Community of Tomorrow) at Disney World.

Actually, just the expectations created by the Solar Oasis transformed my consciousness of the city into a different way of thinking about living in Phoenix; that first and foremost, it *is* a desert city. (Most people are unaware, or forget, that Los Angeles is a desert city as well. Remember the movie *Chinatown?* Greater L.A. is the prototype of "desert deniers.") The Solar Oasis would be a metaphor for Phoenix—itself a modern urban oasis—combining the use of ancient and modern technology with traditional, historical patterns for desert living.

It was at this meeting, in the context of the future possibilities that might flow from building the Solar Oasis, that I first heard the words "a conference of international desert cities," and my antennae quivered. However, amidst the cornucopia of all the ideas, the desert cities idea was just one among many, and I left the meeting manic with over-stimulation, a symptom, I thought, of how pathetic I must have become intellectually—a desert myself, barren and thirsty—and wondering if I'd undergone the lobotomy.

When a mini-Solar Oasis was unveiled in mid-June, it was billed, among other things, as a boon to downtown revitalization, to demonstrate its attraction by bringing seasoned, hardened desert dwellers to an event held outside in the middle of summer on the concrete of downtown Phoenix (where of course you can fry countless dozens of eggs).

Numbering in the thousands the public turned out. In filtered light beneath the wings of giant canvas awnings resembling moths in flight, hands-on futuristic environmental experiments and exhibits featuring plants for foodstuffs and flowers, a cool tower, and playful leaping fountains of water—powered by solar energy and using recycled water—captured the imagination of the public. Not only was it informative, it was fun. And it was a hit with those who came to see.

෴

Early in 1988, again at Dino's suggestion, I hied myself down to see Stephen Dragos, president of the Phoenix Community Alliance—an organization of business leaders focused on revitalizing downtown—to hear more about the idea of an international conference to coincide with the opening of the Solar Oasis. Terry and Dino had been fishing around for someone to head it up, but so far no one had bitten.

When I met Stephen Dragos I wondered, Could this really be possible? A guy radiating energy and optimism—overflowing with ideas—who actually wanted to get things done? (I'd come to understand that because most folks were talkers, not doers, they were always surprised that when I said I was going to do something, I did it.)

I explained to Stephen how important I believed the revitalization of downtown to be and that the Solar Oasis could become a symbol and a unique destination for a new Phoenix. I could think of no more fitting or colorful way to draw substantive international attention than to have a gathering of people from desert cities all over the world for the opening of the Solar Oasis.

Whereupon Stephen immediately invited to Phoenix the head of the successful just-ended International Winter Cities Conference held in Canada, to give me his insights and suggestions for a conference that would be the flip side of winter cities. The bottom line was that both were attempting the most difficult thing in the world: to change the way people think.

As the weeks passed and the search for someone to head up the conference fell into limbo, I went to Terry and told him that since he hadn't been able to find anybody else, I was going to do it, working out of the Community Alliance, and that if we were going to succeed I had to have his assurance that he would get behind the idea and support it. After giving me one of his characteristic raised-eyebrows-with-a-blink/wide-eyed looks of surprise, he agreed.

With that, I set up shop in the offices of the Alliance, and with the spirit of an entrepreneur and the soul of a 501(c)(3)—a nonprofit organization—plunged into the cold sea of fundraising.

∽

The conference and the Solar Oasis were connected, synergistic. The two would be completely integrated, with many of the conference activities taking place within the Oasis site at the Phoenix Civic Plaza. The Summer Solstice—June 21, 1990—was chosen for the opening date of the Oasis as well as the conference. From the very beginning I thought of myself as the catalyst to bring together all those who could make the conference a success—the people with the ideas, the expertise, and the money—and spreading the word (I am Peter, remember). The very words "conference of international desert cities" triggered in my mind a vision of such global proportions my imagination knew no bounds, which could have been a throwback to my childhood, of my romantic fancy of the allure and mystery of foreign lands. I felt that the great architect Daniel Burnham, who designed Washington's Union station, was speaking to me when he said: "Make no little plans—they have no magic to stir men's souls!"

My dream was of a desert convocation of the earth's urban desert dwellers, representing a spectrum of cities risen from the most ancient beginnings to the most modern metropolis. The diverse mix of cultures, religions, art, history, language, technology—transcending national boundaries—conjured up a rich petri dish in which ideas and information could be exchanged, and from which new connections and solutions to our mutual problems would grow and, with any luck, flourish.

What was so extraordinary is that not once from the first moment we met did Stephen Dragos ever put the quietus on my dreaming no small dreams, of thinking as big and as grand as I was capable of. "It's never been done before"—the mantra I'd heard so often—never crossed his lips, because, of course, that's what he was counting on.

༈

Until I raised the money for part-time help, as an organization of one I engrossed myself in every aspect, as well as in reading as much as I could get my hands on (The Autodidact) about cities and urban desert ecology. I dusted off Jane Jacobs's *The Death and Life of Great American Cities*, the bible of urban planners I'd read during Terry's campaign for mayor, and wandered through William H. Whyte's *City*. I was introduced to *The Politics of the Solar Age: Alternatives to Economics*, by Hazel Henderson, as well as the concept of "sustainable development," as described in *Our Common Future: The Report of the World Commission on Environment and Development*, known as the Brundtland Report. I read Marc Reiser's *Cadillac Desert* and *Earth in the Balance*, by then Senator Albert Gore. By far, however, the most provocative work was *The Turning Point*, by physicist Fritjof Capra, illustrating and illuminating the new paradigm that had been evolving—something everyone was sensing intuitively, but hadn't come to grips with.

I began to comprehend that by accepting our identity as a desert city, in simply affirming what we are—what is real—rather than always searching for an "image"—the artificial—we could emphasize our natural attributes and resources and quit the futility of trying to hold the desert at bay. That our cities and towns—our buildings and our houses, our downtowns and our neighborhoods—should be sighted, designed, and built in response to the sun and the desert rather than to what people were used to "back home," wherever that was. Additionally, Phoenix—and Arizona—could become the global data bank for urban desert design and living and all the manifestations such data might spawn. In short, desert cities—which by definition imply a scarcity of natural resources—could become leaders in solving the environmental problems of our time. We could build on becoming an oasis in the most traditional sense of the word, living in harmony with the desert, and do it with élan.

I just couldn't understand why somebody "in charge" hadn't figured this all out before.

By the fall of 1989 the conference was the subject of a glowing front-page story—complete with color photo—in the *Phoenix Gazette* (above the fold), an editorial, and a feature article. Also by that time I had help, which included my old friend Joni Bosh from Terry's campaign; had raised $250,000; and had generated a letter of endorsement signed by the entire Arizona congressional delegation—which included Mo Udall, John McCain, and Dennis DeConcini—as well as one from the Arizona Governor, Rose Mofford. And in a special year-end section in the *Phoenix Gazette* on "Leadership in the Valley" I was startled to discover myself—along with two other women and seven men—described as "leaders waiting in the wings." I was selected for my leadership to improve the Valley's global reputation, with the goal of "making Phoenix the world's preeminent desert city."

∞

Then an intimation of Trouble developed: the opening of the Solar Oasis was postponed a year for lack of funding. And when our board voted to push the conference back a year as well, we looked on it as giving us more time for planning and raising money.

As a prologue to the main event, a meeting of mayors from selected desert cities, to be invited by Terry, was planned for April 1990, the year before the actual conference now set for 1991. Terry assigned an experienced conference planner at the city to help us coordinate plans for the meeting and letters and faxes began flying out of the Mayor's office. By the time the conference opened, in addition to those from the U.S., representatives from eleven foreign countries showed up: Alma-Ata, Uzbekistan; Ankara, Turkey; Be'er-

Sheva, Israel; Cairo, Egypt; Ciudad Juarez and Hermosillo, Mexico; Gaborone, Botswana; Lima, Peru; Nouakchott, Mauritania; Riyadh and Ta'if, Saudi Arabia; Safat, Kuwait; and Samarkand, Kazakhstan.

However, between late January 1990 and the opening of the mayors' conference that April, almost simultaneous events created lowering clouds on the horizon: two of the biggest engines powering the conference were gone. Terry resigned as mayor to run for governor, and Stephen Dragos left the Alliance to head up a similar organization in Somerset, New Jersey. Neither the new mayor nor the new head of the Alliance—who made no pretenses about being an expert on urban redevelopment—had a clue what the Desert Cities Conference was all about. And when the Solar Oasis was postponed yet again, I began to feel the rug being pulled out from under everything.

On the surface none of this mattered. In addition to the mayors, we had put together an eminent panel of national and international experts to serve as a task force for the mayors' conference, generating a dynamism between and among the two groups that was thrilling to behold. And in the media coverage the meeting was described as "nothing short of the beginning of a new global partnership."

The stake through the heart of the conference was delivered in August on the winds of the probability of war in the Middle East. With so many of our prospective participants drawn from there and beyond, our board had no other choice but to put the conference on hold. Desert Cities collided with Desert Shield.

Terry and Fife Symington wound up in an unprecedented tie in the governor's race, and when Terry lost to Fife in the runoff that spring, it wasn't long before many of us realized that the new mayor wasn't interested in pursuing any idea or project of any kind that had Terry's signature on it. And so, among other efforts, he effectively killed the Solar Oasis, and along with it—except for decreeing tieless short-sleeved shirts to be the official summer garb for men—any notion that Phoenix was in the desert. It was back to business as usual.

∞

"Of all sad words of tongue or pen, the saddest are these, it might have been," is an apt epitaph for the Solar Oasis.

For rather than a design of vision and uniqueness—a metaphor for a modern Phoenix—what do we have in its stead as the "centerpiece" of downtown? Why, nothing less than the most pathetic bow to mediocrity and expediency ever erected: a grotesquerie that resembles nothing so much as an upside-down Moorish casket, complete with lining of silk. All the more egregious because of what it replaced, as well as the expense incurred, which was far greater than the Solar Oasis would ever have cost. I heard that when this monument to tackiness was conceived only a few years later, the new director of the project had never even heard of the Solar Oasis.

Actually, as you can well understand, the casket is no longer the centerpiece. Our new centerpiece, or more accurately, twin centerpieces, are: the Bank One Ballpark—home of our baseball team—situated cheek by jowl with the America West Arena—home of our basketball team. (Where your treasure is, there will your centerpieces be also.) Now the downtown of Phoenix is just like the downtowns of all the other "revitalized" big cities.

And while I'm at it, because our institutional memory is so dim and getting dimmer—and though many others have been given—and taken—credit for the revitalization of downtown Phoenix—it needs to be recorded that it was the result of the vision and leadership that began with the uneasy alliance between Terry Goddard; Keith Turley, the former chairman of Pinnacle West Capital Corporation; and Stephen Dragos.

Years from now, Terry's term as mayor will be looked on as a Golden Age of accomplishment that bequeathed, among other things, a legacy of arts and cultural institutions—including our superb world-renowned central public library—that are the heart and soul of Phoenix.

⁂

If you view "success" in life as measurable by some yardstick, namely winning or losing, I would never measure up. For almost everything that I might consider an accomplishment was really nothing more than endeavor, of simply being in the game; a contribution to a larger, ephemeral ethos: the butterfly flying off a branch in the Brazilian rain forest causing a hurricane in Louisiana, the end result impossible to quantify, to predict, affecting everything, though you never know how. Chaos theory before I knew of it.

This is by way of leading up to what others might consider an insignificant incident that occurred several years after the Desert Cities Conference was canceled. Through the kindness of an assistant to an interim mayor of Phoenix, I received a copy of a letter to the mayor from the president of the convention bureau in which he enclosed computer mouse pads promoting Phoenix as the "Premier Desert City." (I always preferred "preeminent," but, hey . . .) Only a few years before, the word "desert" had been a dirty word, anathema to valley promoters, economic development types, and chambers of commerce. So for me it was tangible evidence that an idea had taken hold. That for whatever reason, some people had begun "to change the way they think."

The scant remains of the conference, like so many pot shards, have ended up in my file drawer. And since I was the only one involved in all of its aspects, I am the only repository of its institutional memory, which, like one of those old movie titles written in the sand, is slowly disappearing as it's obliterated by the winds of time.

My vision of the conference was a convergence of the facets of all my interests, utilizing all my capabilities, even arousing those that had lain untapped, unknown. It was, as well, an exposure to new ideas—and a different way of thinking about the world—as well as to interesting, and even occasionally, extraordinary people. It stretched me in uncounted ways.

But most important for me personally (though I didn't realize it then), at the same time that I was awakening to the idea of the authenticity of Phoenix—"embracing its desertness"—I was awakening to my own authenticity, and embracing my own unique self as well.

∞

After the 1992 senate election was over I learned that during the campaign a crack investigative reporter from the *Arizona Republic* had taken it upon himself to delve into the financial records of the Desert Cities Conference to try to dig up some dirt on me (while John McCain's $4 million in campaign contributions remained unexamined by this same and other intrepid newshounds). Coming up empty-handed, he asked of one of the staff, "What did Claire get out of this? She didn't even get paid." And when the reply was, "Nothing," such a concept was, of course, beyond his cynical ken.

Though it is correct that I didn't receive one red cent—I forgot to even ask for a dollar a year—it isn't true, of course, that I didn't get anything out of it. In devoting more than two years of my life—and everything I had in me—to the Desert Cities project, there was no sum sufficient to compensate me for what I received.

For the record, I did receive one perk as head of the Desert Cities Conference: a five-day trip to Norway, above the Arctic Circle, in the wintertime—the equivalent of a visit to Phoenix in mid-July—to attend the International Winter Cities Celebration in Tromso, a picturesque, seacoast town on the Arctic Ocean.

There's a story about Dorothy Parker, who hated the suburbs, and was loathe to leave New York City for even a weekend in the country. When some of her friends finally succeeded in breaking her down and persuaded her to accompany them on a weekend out of the city, her city friends sent her a telegram of congratulations, and received the following telegram in reply: "Send cake. Enclose file and saw."

I'm a lot like Dorothy Parker in that respect. I am the City Mouse, a natural urbanist.

Though Tromso wasn't nearly as cold—or as dark—as I thought it would be, and the natives couldn't have been sweeter, the whole time I was there I felt claustrophobic, and couldn't resist faxing Henry the Dorothy Parker message from the press center, knowing how he'd love it.

On my way home I stopped over in New York and Washington to make some fundraising calls for Desert Cities, so it was almost two weeks before I got back to Phoenix, and I'd forgotten all about sending Henry that message.

When I arrived home, our friend Mark Steinberg was visiting, and I was surprised to discover on the dining room table a most elaborately decorated one-layer cake inscribed with "Welcome Home, Claire" in a finely wrought icing script. It was so uncharacteristic that it might ever have even occurred to Henry to make such a hokey gesture, I figured it was something Mark had masterminded. I ooh-ed and aah-ed, sufficiently I thought, giving it all I had, but it was long after midnight on my circadian clock, and all I wanted was to get in my own bed. The last thing in the world I needed was to have to eat a piece of that cake.

As they pleaded with me to stay up for some cake and just a short visit, they lured me with a glass of champagne and thrust a knife in my hand for cake cutting. Realizing that there was no putting them off, not wanting to mess up the design, I carefully, and precisely, cut three small slivers from one corner of the cake. I raved about how delicious it was as we all washed it down with champagne, lingered a few minutes, then thanked them for their thoughtfulness and kissed them goodnight. I couldn't get over how crestfallen they appeared to be.

The next afternoon, to my surprise Mark stopped by after work on his way home. After Henry fixed everybody a drink, Mark said he wanted some more of that cake, which was still on the table covered in plastic wrap. I said, "Help yourself," and handed him a plate and a knife. "You cut it so much better than I do," he protested, "and can I have one of those flowers in the middle?"

I was beginning to get more than a little testy about the stupid cake, so took the knife, cut another piece from the corner where I'd begun the night before, and using the flat of the knife plucked up a flower from the middle of the design and plopped it on top. Finally, Henry came over and asked for a piece, and as I resumed my routine, he said, "Claire, just cut the goddamned cake in the middle!"

Prompted by such downright peevishness, I slashed through the middle of the cake, only to hit something hard. I tried again, hearing a metallic sound as I hit it harder. When I realized what was going on, I almost fell out in the floor from laughing so hard.

Sixteen

On the last day of the year 1990 I put the finishing touches on a call to arms to Phoenicians in a letter to the editor of the local papers. Up until then my years of living in Phoenix had taught me that collective public outrage had been hard to come by, and I was telling them it was not too late to rise up against a deal that had been cut in Washington by the Arizona congressional delegation behind the backs of the people of Phoenix, even the mayor.

The story of the swap of land in the middle of downtown Phoenix for swampland in Florida is a long, and by definition, tortuous, tale, one in which the age-old triumvirate of politics, power, and greed are the essential ingredients.

It all began with the 1986 elections, and went something like this:

Florida Republican Paula Hawkins was up for reelection, running against Democrat Bob Graham, and believing that Hawkins needed to beef up her support for the environment, the Republicans cast about for ideas. With the intercession of Interior Secretary James Watt, a scheme to help "save the Florida Everglades" was hatched. One of Florida's wealthiest families, heirs to the fortune of Barron Collier, an advertising executive who brought development to the Florida county named for him, had owned much of the 575,000 acres the federal government had acquired for the Big Cypress National Preserve in Florida in 1974 during the Nixon administration, when the government had bought only the surface land, leaving the oil and gas drilling rights in the Colliers's possession.

Still in possession of a large addition to the preserve, the Colliers now had their eye on the 110-acre Phoenix Indian School site in the middle of Phoenix. With the school (still operating, still with students) placed on the notorious "excess federal assets" list by the Reagan administration, they saw new opportunities: a land swap. Even though the Florida land the Colliers offered in exchange for the Indian School was not high on the Park Service's list of parcels to acquire, and would not really protect much of the Everglades, it would give the *appearance* of protecting the Everglades (and the Colliers would again retain the oil and gas rights) while delivering to the Colliers—through the family-owned Barron Collier Company, Collier Development Corporation, and Collier Enterprises—one of the choicest pieces of real estate in all of Arizona.

To get the deal done the Republicans knew they would need the approval of the chairman of the House Interior Committee, Arizona Congressman Mo Udall, but were confident he would roll over because of his concern for the Everglades. When they announced the deal without first informing Mo, he responded that it would go forward over his dead body, unleashing a barrage of congressional hearings. That's when the Colliers started hiring every available Democrat to work Mo over; and as his health deteriorated from Parkinson's disease, he was assured by his so-called friends it would all be okay.

Paula Hawkins lost her election, but the land swap had taken on a life of its own.

Nobody seemed to be taking it seriously—Trade the Indian School for swampland in Florida? *Impossible!*—even after Terry set up an Indian School task force and local congressional hearings were held with Mo, Dennis DeConcini, and John McCain—our newly-elected senator—in attendance. At the hearing I went to, I was shocked. Except for campaign debates I had never before seen an elected official act so rude and ugly to another elected official as John McCain did to Terry. His bombastic attack on the mayor of Phoenix discomfited practically everybody in the whole room, as well as symbolizing the power of Washington over a mere city. And McCain made it abundantly clear whose side he was on.

Never having been accused of not being a consummate politician, DeConcini had snagged 20 of the 110 acres for an addition to the Veterans Hospital that adjoined the site—which of course nobody would oppose—as the price for his support of the deal, thus placing several veterans' groups squarely in the Colliers's camp (though later there were times when even the veterans seemed uncomfortable).

Five years after its conception, however, in 1991 the plan began to hit the fan.

∾

As open meetings of the Indian School task force began to attract more and more attention, a rare combination of natives and newcomers, Democrats and Republicans (including former Senator Barry Goldwater), Indians and environmentalists—all in an unprecedented swivet—coalesced against the Colliers and their development in favor of a new public park for Phoenix.

That politics, pure and simple, in far-off Washington, D.C., had sealed the fate of one of the choicest pieces of real estate in Phoenix—without the people of Phoenix ever even knowing about it—ignited long-banked fires of righteous indignation into a glorious phantasmagorical conflagration. One that threw the Colliers and their local henchmen for a loop.

Up until that time the Colliers had been only a faceless, unknown entity to me, against whom I had no real animosity. Until, that is, I was sickened by a crude brochure they distributed door-to-door in the neighborhoods surrounding the Indian School land.

Here's a whiff of its stench:

> **Believe It or Not!** It's hard to believe a small special interest group [n.b.: that meant the citizens!] is arguing to cut out the facilities for our veterans and the educational fund for Native American children because they want to make the property a public park—like *Central Park* in New York City.
> But it gets worse...
> Because by law the federal government is prohibited from 'giving away' the land to be used only for a park, special interests expect the city to pay $80 million for the land—*money Phoenix doesn't have and could only get by raising everybody's taxes!*

Then, after your taxes have been raised to purchase the property and build a park, they'll need more money to maintain and operate it. And, because of its enormous size, additional funds must be found to hire a small army of security forces to keep it safe around the clock so it doesn't turn into a Central Park—a magnet for **muggers, rapists and dope dealers** [emphasis mine].

But even after all the taxes have been raised and scores of security hired, **there's still no guarantee that the unsavory won't spill into our neighborhoods around the park** [ditto]. And no matter how much is spent, we can't control cruisers on Friday and Saturday nights!

'Let's Send Washington DC A Message From Phoenix AZ'
The bureaucrats back east will be surprised when we show them that we don't need them to arbitrate Arizona's affairs.

This piece chilled me, and for the first time I understood how fundamentally ruthless and trashy these people were. It was their first public display—rather than behind the scenes where they preferred to remain—of just how dirty they could play.

I could not believe that if the local business community were aware of the Colliers's tactics they would welcome them as a good corporate neighbor with the open arms they seemed to be extending; and second, I was just so disappointed and sick that the local outfit running the Colliers's lobbying—who, though they were known as whores, until then had been respectable whores—would be responsible for such despicable demagoguery. Finally, it demonstrated that the Colliers thought Phoenicians—not just us, "We the People," but the Phoenix business leadership—had just fallen off the turnip truck; and that all they had to do was just walk in and take what they wanted.

I wrote a memo to the executive committee of the Community Alliance, who hadn't lifted a finger against the Colliers, telling them they were fiddling while Rome burned as the Colliers moved ahead with plans for a development that would dwarf the existing downtown. That they were making a mistake (in a mix of metaphors) to look on the project as being a little bit pregnant. But they were only amused: "You never have to wonder where Claire stands!"

At a marathon city council session I denounced the mayor (Terry's successor) for rolling over for the Colliers, for never drawing a line in the sand; telling him that leadership means taking a risk, and maybe losing sometimes because you did what you thought was right. Countless others—with my friend Joni Bosh as the expert, steeped in every jot and tittle of the arcane swap agreement—were constantly, furiously busy, out front and behind the scenes; and though we weren't coordinated, never having a grand plan, we covered every front, shoulder to shoulder.

∞

"Mystery signs focus on land-swap flap," announced the headline of the story when I opened the morning *Arizona Republic*. "Sinister-looking signs that seem to stare back at you," the article began, "have popped up at strategic locations in Phoenix calling attention to the debate over the Phoenix Indian School site."

With the thrill of a subversive savoring her work, I hooted with laughter. We couldn't have asked for anything finer!

As Joni and I had put up the "Keep Your Eye on The Indian School" signs a few nights before, it had conjured up memories of playing capture the flag as a girl in Mississippi. I hadn't had that kind of fun in years! Except that the 100-plus degree heat of the midsummer night almost done me in as I wielded a massive sledgehammer with a heft far exceeding the job at hand.

We had each borrowed a pick-up truck so that the two of us could work as a team. With no air-conditioning we found scant relief from the heat in the movement of the ovenlike air as we drove, Joni with her months-old son Frank strapped in on the front seat beside her so she could nurse him as the need arose. The Daring Duo-and-a-Half!

In the spirit of activist Flo Kennedy, who asked, "If you were the Establishment, which would you rather see coming in the door, five hundred mice or one lion?" the two of us set out to post as many signs at key spots as we could manage.

Since we were putting up the signs after dark (past nine o'clock in the summertime) in downtown Phoenix (essentially deserted by that hour in 1991), one of us would keep watch from our truck while the other put up a sign.

After scoping out a perfect spot directly across the street from the front door of the *Arizona Republic,* I parked my truck down the block and Joni pulled up diagonally across the street to watch while I attempted to hammer the stake into ground that was like concrete. Nervous because the corner was so brightly lighted, I just knew a policeman or somebody from the paper was going to appear at any minute and catch me in the act.

Barely able to lift the sledgehammer more than a few inches above the stake, I missed it, hitting the sign instead, ripping it off. Dripping with sweat and red in the face from the heat, I was just getting ready to swing again when I was so startled by a quiet voice from behind me on the sidewalk that I dropped the hammer, barely missing my foot. "Ma'am," the voice said, "I was wondering if you could help me out. I'm not a bum. I'm trying to get home."

It was like the movie *Bananas.* Or *Life of Brian.* Here I was, stealthily trying to pound a sign into practically cement in the middle of downtown Phoenix in the glare of streetlights, and I'm accosted by someone who wants bus fare out of town. "Ssshhh!" I hissed, glancing around furtively. "Can't you see what I'm doing here? I don't even have my purse! Two blocks down the street is the Catholic church. They'll help you. Now please go away. I don't want anybody to notice me."

"I've already been there. But they're closed."

As I raised the hammer once more, he continued his spiel. And naturally I was beginning to feel like a dog for not helping him, but I just had to get that sign up and get the hell out of there, and of course his standing there as though he were harassing me made me even more conspicuous.

Joni, who was watching, called out in a stage whisper, "What's going on?" and cranked up her motor.

"Wait here," I told the man, and leaving the hammer behind, I bounded across the middle of the brightly lighted intersection toward Joni, who was nursing Frank.

"Can you lend me some money? He doesn't have enough for a Greyhound ticket to get home."

Digging around in her purse, she was able to come up with enough cash, and I dashed back.

However, curious now, instead of leaving after I gave him the money, he remained, standing there, watching me. "You need to go now," I whispered. "Good luck to you," I said over my shoulder in the throes of my heavy lifting. And after what seemed forever I finally got the stake in the ground and another sign stapled to it.

That accomplished, we went around the corner to the back door of the newspaper to plant another there as well before moving on, Johnny Appleseeds sowing our signs all over town until long after midnight.

With no one taking credit for the signs, it was suggested to the reporter by one of our own that they were the handiwork of the "goddess of public interest."

∾

Well, nobody was more surprised than the Colliers—or their allies, the newspaper editorialists—when for once the little guys won. Or, more precisely, kept the big guys from picking up all the chips. After weeks of wobbling and weaving with a deadline looming, our no-backbone mayor, who never met a developer he didn't like, devised a compromise that provided seventy-five acres for a park. The Colliers got sixteen acres, zoned for office towers, *in addition to two city-owned blocks in downtown Phoenix*, and agreed to contribute $35 million over thirty years to a trust fund for Indian education.

In a stunning denouement, and to the furious mayor's surprise—this was in the waning days of 1991, the year before John McCain's reelection campaign for the Senate—McCain pre-empted the mayor, popping up like a rabbit out of a hat, several hours ahead of the mayor, to take all the credit—as is his custom—for the agreement!

At the end of the day, a columnist in the *Phoenix Gazette* hailed the mayor and two members of the city council for the success in the land swap, as well as the activists who "helped influence policies that will affect the city for a century or more," and singled out the

Part Three - Arizona

"increasingly feeble performances of members of the state's congressional delegation, all of whom should be voted out of office as soon as possible."

◌

In early 1991, on the heels of Governor Evan Mecham's impeachment for failing to report a large campaign loan (he was later cleared on a second charge), followed yet another political scandal that came to be called AzScam. A group of state legislators, Republican and Democrat alike, were forced to resign their seats after taking illegal campaign contributions from an undercover agent, ostensibly representing Las Vegas gambling interests, in exchange for their votes in favor of legalized gambling in Arizona. The smarmy details of the whole sleazy sting—many believed it to be an obvious case of entrapment—were caught on hidden video cameras and played night after night on local television, revealing to the public the naked greed and hubris that until then had been displayed only behind closed doors. Among those forced to resign was a Democrat from my district, the one I had run in in 1984, who was into her second two-year term. The county board of supervisors was in charge of appointing the replacements for the seats left vacant, which would be filled by a member of the same party of the legislator who resigned.

All this occurred while I was preoccupied with phasing out the Desert Cities Conference and fighting for the park at the Indian School. Of course I was as mesmerized and sickened by the tales of undercover payoffs and corruption as the rest of Arizona, but I hadn't given the first thought to getting myself appointed, until several friends and former supporters began to ask if I were going to put my name in the hat. After all, it *was* the seat I'd run for. So I started thinking about it.

It certainly wouldn't take the time or money or energy that went into a campaign. And I believed that because of my work on the conference, as well as the fact that at that very moment I was working with a whole bunch of Republicans in the Indian School fight, I would be able to get bipartisan support, which I believed was important. So when the details of the process were announced in early March 1991, I decided to give it a try. When I called the

Democratic Party headquarters to let them know, they appeared to be delighted. Only a few people, whose names weren't familiar to me, had applied by then, and I was encouraged.

A committee was appointed by the supervisor in whose district the seat fell, in my case a Democrat, one of two of five supervisors, which I thought would be to my advantage. The committee would be composed of members reflecting the percentage of each party registered to vote in the legislative district, and as I recall, there was one more Republican than Democrat, six to five, with a Democrat appointed chairman. Anyone who wanted to be considered could send in a résumé. About fifty people applied, and that number was winnowed down to around five or six, of which I was one. The next step was a personal interview with the committee.

During this time I'd submitted quite a respectable group of letters written on my behalf, including both Democrats and Republicans. I was confident that I had as good a shot as anybody else at getting the appointment.

In light of the temper of the times, with all the corruption and the disgust with the legislature, my message to the committee was going to be one of change, against business as usual. (Sound familiar?) I believed that if change was what they wanted, I would be the one they would pick. If they didn't, they would choose someone else.

And they did.

With the administration of then Governor Mofford soon coming to an end, her director of the department of administration had decided to go for the legislative seat. Since no one had told me she was considering it, I was taken by surprise.

With her connections to the governor, I knew that Cathy Eden would be a strong contender. But I hadn't reckoned on her connections to the Phoenix Firefighters, one of the strongest of the few unions in Arizona, which had helped me put up my signs when I ran in 1984. Cathy had strong, continuous, old-party ties to the Democratic Party through her brothers who were firefighters, and through her father, who many years before had been elected for several terms to the State Corporation Commission, which regulates the utilities. And as luck would have it, the supervisor who was to

Part Three - Arizona

have the final say on who would be selected had won both of her elections with the formidable strength of the firefighters behind her.

On the day of the final interview Cathy and I were in the waiting room at the same time, and, trying to appear calm, we sat together as we waited our turn and wished each other luck. We were a perfect contrast: the career administrator and the activist. I had worked hard on my presentation, and though I felt good about it, was still a nervous wreck. I knew most of the committee, who were gracious and considerate, and have no idea how long it actually took—it was so pleasant and natural it seemed short—but when it was over, I knew I'd done well. As I left, the chairman told me he would call to let me know the results after all the interviews were finished. I'd done my best, and from then on it was completely out of my hands.

When the chairman telephoned, he reported that of the top three, I had come out number one. Cathy was second, with another woman third. He warned me that it didn't necessarily mean that I would be the final choice, though that was the order that would be reported to the supervisor, who would then make the final decision. With that he congratulated me, thanked me warmly for my participation, and wished me luck.

I didn't know the supervisor well, though as fellow Democrats we were friendly enough. She had a reputation for being enigmatic, having a hard time making a decision, remaining aloof, playing everything close to the chest. Prone also to migraine headaches—she was even reported to be suffering from one that had sent her to bed while on county business in Washington, where she had been during the interviews, due to return the next day after taking the red eye back to Phoenix. I could just imagine that if you were susceptible to migraines, what she was facing would sure do it to you.

The next morning when I met with her, sure enough her face had that swollen look of heavy medication and her eyes were almost slits. I felt so sorry for her on the one hand, but on the other wished that she were more on top of things. I had to hand it to her, though. She gave a thoroughly warm and winning businesslike performance, praising me while at the same time telling me what a difficult decision she had to make. It couldn't have taken more than five minutes, and promising that she'd call me first thing the next morning, I was dismissed.

As promised the call came, and again she did a superb job. With care and sensitivity she explained how hard it was for her, why she had chosen Cathy over me. She could hit the ground running. There would be no learning curve. Et cetera. Et cetera. Et cetera . . .

Everybody learns life's lessons in different ways. It was as a young mother that I learned what every mother learns sooner or later: not to be too disappointed if things don't work out the way you hoped. Move on, and start making other plans. Once you have children, no matter how far ahead or how meticulously and down to the last detail you make plans for something, the list of what can go wrong to thwart your arrangements at the last minute is endless. I still prepared for things as I always had, but I changed my expectations, so that when things *did* go according to plan, I was always pleasantly surprised.

And so, disappointed that I had been called but not chosen (this was *politics* after all), after the supervisor hung up I immediately called Cathy to congratulate her and to offer my help as she began her job as my new representative.

This was one of those times when you think about the way life works. And though I'm not a complete fatalist, I do believe that if something doesn't work out, it isn't meant to be, and that there's something else I'm supposed to do.

Seventeen

Inclined toward Jung's theory of synchronicity, that there's no such thing as coincidence, I came to believe deeply that I was the right person, at the right time in my life, in the right place at the right time, to run against John McCain for the United States Senate in 1992. Not a year before, or a year after, but at that precise moment. It's hard to explain, but I knew I was going to do it before I actually knew it, if you can understand that. The same way I knew I was going to walk across the limb of the pecan tree that summer in Starkville when I was six years old. It's clear to me now that the seeds for my decision to run for the Senate, given who I am, were being sown all my life.

"Claire has always had a great feeling that she has a mission in life to change things," quoth Henry a few years after my campaign for the Senate. This statement, though perhaps true, is not necessarily how I would have put it. I have never believed I had a *mission*, though I've always believed my life had *purpose*, which to me are two different things; the former, specific, the latter, general. However, when Viktor Frankl, the author of *Man's Search for Meaning*, says, "Everyone has his own specific vocation or mission in life to carry out a concrete assignment which demands fulfillment. Therein he cannot be replaced, nor can his life be repeated," isn't he saying that both the mission/purpose and a life are one and the same?

As I grew, I felt as though I was moving toward discovering what that purpose might be. Life had favored me with that rarest of blessings, the freedom to make choices and take risks, to speak out and fight for issues I believed were important without fear of retaliation or retribution. But because I was unaware of a self-imposed constraint that I hadn't recognized—the need for permission—this privilege took a long time to sink in. When it finally did, I believed that life demanded more of me because of it.

One of the advantages of taking several years to write a book is that you sometimes gain new insight as you write.

The life-threatening decision to run for office—no matter how much money you have or how much you can raise, no matter how many people urge you to run—just as we are born alone and we die alone, the decision must be made by the candidate alone.

When I first tried to explain how I came to run for the Senate, I thought making the decision to run had required the inner journey to the center of my being that I was aware of only in retrospect. But I had it backwards. I realize now that this inner journey had been under way for several years—the whole thing about authenticity and my own unique identity—as, if they're fortunate, happens in the lives of women of my age. And that it was at the *end* of the journey, coming down the other side of mountain in a car with no brakes— that was the *cause* of my decision to run, not the result. And nothing could stop me!

In my favorite description of her English professor-sleuth heroine, Kate Fansler, Amanda Cross describes me to a T: "She has become braver as she has aged, less interested in the opinions of those she does not cherish, and has come to realize that she has little to lose, little any longer to risk, that age above all is the time when there is very little 'they' can do for you, very little to fear, or hide, or not attempt brave and important things."

∞

It was during the fight for the Phoenix Indian School that John McCain—the representative of my interests specifically, and the representative of Arizonans in general—first attracted my attention. I was outraged over my own sheer powerlessness in the face of the unmitigated arrogance of our Arizona delegation—so far removed from us. Every one of them had turned his back on us as though we didn't exist, secure in the knowledge that they could get away with it because there was nothing we could do about it.

Hasn't this always been the root cause of rebellion, of revolution? What aroused my interest in McCain, our Republican senator in a Republican administration, was that he was the only one with any clout in the Arizona delegation who might have been able to help us with the Department of Interior or the White House, where the land-swap scheme was hatched. But he insisted that it was a done deal; that there was nothing he could do. He absolutely abandoned us, and carried on like a bantam rooster whenever anybody challenged him.

Never having lived in Arizona before he arrived to run for Congress, McCain hadn't even lived in Phoenix until he moved from suburban Tempe to the remodeled former home of his wealthy in-laws after he was elected to the Senate in 1986. He had no concept of the significance of the Indian School site in the context of a "Central Park" for downtown Phoenix, much less its importance to Phoenix and Arizona history.

I compare John McCain to Chance Gardiner in the book *Being There*, by Jerzy Kosinski. Chance, or Chauncey, as he came to be called, is a cipher, who through the misperceptions and misconceptions of those around him, is accidentally launched into celebrityhood—to become a media superstar, a household name, the man of the hour; perhaps even the next president of the United States. Just as Chance appeared from nothing out of nowhere, his persona created by myth and flack, so did John McCain. A candidate sprung fully armored from the head of Ares, the god of war.

The grandson and son of an admiral, he'd been a navy brat, born in Panama in 1936 with no place to call home—in fact, over the years, after being accused of being a carpetbagger in his first election, one of his most frequently cited lines was: "My friends [why must all right-wing politicians insist on addressing everyone as "my friend"?], my longest place of residence was the six years in my cell in Vietnam." Even though he was a legitimate hero who endured unspeakable brutality, he cheapened his heroism by exploiting it. By definition, real heroes don't brag.

After graduation from Annapolis, where he wore as a badge of honor his ranking in the lowest fifth of his class and boasted about his frequent infractions of the rules, he followed his father and grandfather into the Navy. After his release from prison, no longer able to fly, he returned to Washington where he was given a job with the Navy working on Capitol Hill. Becoming bored with his desk job and wanting to be where the real power was, he decided to become a United States Senator. But first he had to find a state to run in.

At first he set his sights on Florida, where he had once lived with his first wife. But finding no open seat available, in the time-honored tradition he looked west, to the state of his new young bride, who, in addition to beauty, as the daughter of the largest beer distributor in all of Arizona (a lot of beer in the land of the six-pack), was blessed with money as well.

And so John McCain, former prisoner of war and proud of it, arrived in Arizona. With his new wife's money he squeaked by in a four-way primary for the open congressional seat left vacant by Speaker of the House John Rhodes, who had stepped down after thirty years. It was a typically Arizona kind of thing: as the old song goes, "If you've got the money honey, we've got the time."

John McCain had found his home.

∾

As a parallel to the Indian School land swap, the Keating Five scandal unfolded. Both of Arizona's senators, McCain and DeConcini, were implicated, along with three other senators in the influence peddling of savings and loan financier-run-amok Charles Keating, and brought before the Senate Ethics Committee. To say that McCain and DeConcini were found to have committed no illegal act is not to say that they were innocent of unethical acts, no matter what their Senate brethren on the Ethics Committee decided. So here we were in Arizona, with each of our two senators having been hauled before the Ethics Committee, wounded and maintaining a low profile, rendering any Arizona presence in the Senate essentially impotent.

With AzScam rocking Arizona in 1991, and the blemish of the defeat of the Martin Luther King holiday (which McCain originally opposed), scandal-weary Arizonans had already endured the impeachment of a governor and the Keating Five affair. In April many Democrats were speculating like mad about who would

Part Three - Arizona

replace the ailing Mo Udall, set to resign sometime in the spring, and that it was pathetic that the party couldn't come up with a "name" to run against McCain, who, with less than a 50 percent approval rating in all the polls because of his Keating Five involvement, was so ripe for the plucking.

Then, in early summer, I was taken aback to read in the paper that someone I'd never heard of, an Air Force lieutenant general who had once lived in Arizona and who was now returning in retirement, had come out of the woodwork and announced that he was going to run in the Democratic primary for the nomination for the U.S. Senate. An echo, not a choice, to paraphrase Barry Goldwater's famous presidential campaign slogan—a clone of John McCain. And a guy without a clue about what had been going on in Arizona for the past twenty-five years.

Were we to be spared nothing?

∾

Politically, 1991 now seems positively quaint, the olden days, B.C.—Before Clinton. And technologically as well, before the proliferation and expansion of faxes, cellular phones, e-mail, and the Internet, bringing with them the instantaneous and incessant media coverage we now suffer from.

It was the days of the Gulf War; of unemployment and a disastrous economy with the highest deficit in the history of the Republic; of thirty-five million Americans without health care; crumbling schools; the Keating Five scandal; the Clarence Thomas hearings; Tailhook; the House banking scandal; the televised beating of Rodney King by policemen in Los Angeles; the fall of the Berlin Wall; the repeal of apartheid in South Africa.

And, finally, in August 1991, just days before Henry and I were to depart for Europe—to visit, among other places, a reunified Berlin—with a victorious Boris Yeltsen clambering atop a tank in Moscow, deluged by delirious throngs showering him with flowers, after forty-five years the Cold War was over.

Along with the convergence of all the other critical circumstances, to me this epochal event manifested conclusive evidence that a new world, so long aborning, had already dawned, completely passing Washington by, capping my idea that the times called for someone like me to run for the Senate. And this was even before Anita Hill.

~

My life has been the reverse of the one the baby-boomer women have lived. I essentially began my "career" on the verge of fifty, years before the boomers discovered menopause—the way they discovered "parenting"—and are beginning to discover that they are going to die. And as sure as night follows day, we will have to endure their discovery of the joys of grandparenthood.

More accurately, as my life worked out, I never even had a career. I've had a life. And being such a generalist is hard to put on a résumé, which is what the Washington women's groups insist on to be able to decide if you are "qualified" or not. And of course these groups are made up of the boomer generation and younger, a generation or two distant from mine, whose careers have been linear—on a track—fitting nicely into a category.

As a result of my work with displaced homemakers in helping prospective employers to understand that the qualities and skills necessary to survive and thrive as a wife and mother are transferable to the job market, I came to believe that my qualities and attributes as a mother, wife, and homemaker, and as a long-time community volunteer and political and civic activist, were equally as valid and valuable for elected office as a man's—and in reality much broader—whose only experience had been the military and/or a prisoner of war.

And it was about that time Cokie Roberts observed that Congress was like a bunch of two-year-olds that only a mother could deal with.

What about Margaret Chase Smith of Maine and Nancy Kassebaum of Kansas? They had never held public office before being elected to Congress. Senator Smith was first elected to fill the unexpired congressional term left by the death of her husband. And Senator Kassebaum's only "experience" had been as a homemaker and volunteer.

The list of men who never held elective office before they were elected to Congress is too long to include here. Although it does include John McCain.

With a liberal arts degree and a masters degree, I believed that my education, my life experience, my avocation, albeit not for pay, qualified me to run. The Constitution has only three requirements to run for the United States Senate: that you are thirty years old; a citizen of the United States for at least seven years; and a resident of the state you're elected in.

∞

One prominent Arizona Democrat, a lawyer and a boomer, who would later give me her support, at first wouldn't help me in the Senate race because I didn't have an answer to her question: "What are the newspapers going to put after the comma after your name?" I wasn't sure whether she was alluding to the fact that it might be "wife of," or that "community activist" or an equivalent would be equally lacking in weight. Familiar with the way political insiders and the Washington women's groups, of which she was one, looked at candidates, she was right, of course, because to their mind, having no label was the equivalent of having no existence. Even with two children, as a long-time career woman, it would never have occurred to her to identify herself after the comma with "mother," though since 1992 things are changing in that regard.

Consequently, the first time I went to Washington in October 1991 I was a real babe in the woods when it came to the Washington women's groups. I thought that because I was a woman they would open their arms and clasp me to their bosom. (It was a few years after the campaign, when I read *The Life of the Party*, the biography of Pamela Harriman, that I truly realized how vividly I had borne the stamp of "O" for "outsider." My beloved friend and generous contributor, Forest Burgess, an octogenarian who knew me as thoroughly as anyone, concluded after she read the same book, "My dear, I can see now that from the very beginning you never had a chance.")

I did not know the Washington ropes, but didn't know it. I didn't know that going by myself to Washington to find out what the ropes were was a flagrant demonstration of outsiderdom. But how else would you find out if you didn't ask? Well, you get somebody who knows to teach you, or even better, to open doors, so that when you show up you arrive with "attitude" and the right credentials. Whereas I thought that simply calling on the women's groups and declaring my interest was enough, and that they would tell me what I needed to know.

I didn't know that Washington ruled what went on out in the rest of the country, in every state, that what it boiled down to was when you wanted to run for national office, you had to have Washington's imprimatur, the approval of the national party as well as the political action committees that raised money for their causes. I thought they helped you because you believed in the same principles they did and, if elected, would help achieve their goals. Even if I had been elected without the help of the women and the PACs, their issues were my issues, and I would have fought for them because that was why I was running.

When I had telephoned in early October 1991 to set up appointments for the end of the month, no matter who I talked to the first two questions were always, "How much money have you raised?" and, "Have you done a poll?" When I answered, "Not a penny" to the first and "No" to the second, they all responded that they had no desire to see me without a poll and $50,000 in contributions.

But I insisted. I wanted to meet them, to find out what was expected of me, what I could expect from them, and how the game was played (of course, to them my timing was just a *teeny* bit late). And except for the National Organization for Women, you'd have thought I was Phyllis Schafly from the way they treated me. But I assume when they all realized that I was coming come hell or high water, I finally got appointments with Emily's List, the National Women's Political Caucus, the Women's Campaign Fund, the National Abortion Rights Action League, and NOW. And as it turned out—which naturally I took as a momentously auspicious, synchronous event—it just happened to be the week after the Clarence Thomas hearings, when all of the women of Washington, and America, were galvanized, in high dudgeon as never before.

Also, on that first round in Washington, I discovered another phenomenon. Nobody believes anything you say. The D.C. women questioned me closely about whether or not Hattie Babbitt (who after the 1992 election was appointed by the president to be ambassador to the Organization of American States), a lawyer married to

Part Three - Arizona

the former governor of Arizona, was going to run for the Senate. Wanting the answer to that question myself, I'd talked to Hattie a few days before leaving for Washington, and she had told me unequivocally that she was not going to run. And I believed her. When I relayed this information to my inquisitors, it didn't matter what I said, for in Washington, as I began to apprehend, truth is an alien concept. Nothing is definitive, all is a constantly swirling whirlwind of speculation, conjecture, rumor, a soupçon of truth sprinkled here and there, and legerdemain. Reported from one grapevine to another is the latest gossip, with the roots of all the grapevines sprouting from the soil of the same Washington vineyard.

With the exception of NOW, the purest in their support of women as sisters, the rest of the women played the game just like the boys—one of the biggest disappointments and letdowns of my entire campaign experience.

∾

I had been a member of Emily's List since its founding in 1985, joining after my campaign for the legislature. It was started to raise money for prochoice Democratic women candidates for the U.S. Congress and governor, to give them fundraising credibility that male candidates traditionally held by virtue of being male. When it started, there were so few women running for these seats its main purpose was to persuade women to run, and then to help them win by raising money. Raising money is a chicken and egg game, the old Catch 22. If you have money you can raise money. If you don't . . .

So how do you get it in the first place? Women never gave that question a thought until they started trying to break into politics, especially national politics. So Ellen Malcolm, a smart political entrepreneur—recognizing that if you want to elect more women to national office you have to raise the money up front to give them credibility—founded Emily's List, for "Early Money is Like Yeast—it makes the dough rise." In the world of politics, which was a male-only world until just yesterday, nothing speaks louder than money, the only thing men notice, and now the women, too. Money bestows instant credibility in the world of conventional wisdom, purveyed by politicians and pundits through the media, and finally to the masses. The old trickle-down effect.

By the time I went to see Emily's List in October 1991, they had learned a lot since they'd begun as, with Emily's help, more Democratic women had begun to run for—and be elected to—national office. And by this time, though the media hadn't picked up on it, Emily's List rarely even looked at a woman who wasn't running for an open seat, that is, a race in which there was no incumbent, since incumbency, according to the political handicappers, is the greatest ensurer of reelection. But even then, it had to be an open seat in what *Washington* deemed a viable state in a viable district. If that were then indeed the case, they wanted to help women whom they, the inside-the-Beltway seers, judged were "qualified."

With Emily's success in fundraising and getting women elected came power. When Emily spoke, the Democratic party, PACs, and politicos listened. An endorsement from Emily brought instant credibility. But, of course, the opposite was true. If you didn't have it, you were considered to be one of the unwashed by the people who counted, and your loss became a self-fulfilling prophecy: you can't win, even with our help, so we won't help you, and naturally you lose. If you can't win *with* their help, you sure can't win *without* it.

I'd met Ellen Malcolm two or three times on her fundraising trips to Arizona. Living in New York for twenty-two years, I'd met many women like her, confident, rich, un-glitzy East Coast. Many of these women can be snobs, but I gave Ellen the benefit of the doubt—certainly in her years of traveling all over the United States she surely must have long since transcended the East Coast elitist attitude, confronted as she must have been by the various accents and ethnic groups in the Democratic Party.

Ellen and her political director had both done their homework, as had all of the organizations I met with (the one exception being the young woman at the Women's Political Caucus I'd just fled from, who, it was perfectly obvious, hadn't even bothered to look at my résumé—and who since then, as is the practice, has moved on up the ladder of D.C. insiderdom. After allowing our discussion to be repeatedly interrupted by an intercom voice informing her of phone calls, even though she didn't take them, her advice to me was, "Go home and speak to groups. Get yourself known.").

After explaining that she'd examined all the aspects of the

Arizona Senate race—the Republican edge over Democrats in registered voters; Democrat Dennis DeConcini's conservatism; the results in McCain's last Senate race against the Democratic candidate; McCain's incumbency and the enormous amount of money he'd already raised—the political director at Emily's List confessed that she hadn't realized her job would be to counsel women *not* to run, as she believed she should me. And as she had just counseled a woman from Chicago who had preceded me—so upset over Anita Hill she had decided to run for the Senate—from the bureau of records or some such, who didn't have a chance, either. The woman who had either preceded or followed me wherever I'd been all day long.

I asked her name.

"Her name," she said, "is Carol Moseley-Braun."

∽

Finally, one day a few months later, when it began to sink in that nothing short of death or physical disability was going to derail me from what he considered my disastrous, destructive—and most of all, expensive—course of running against John McCain, Henry had had it. In a segment of an ongoing open-ended conversation about how I could not possibly be serious about this campaign, I could not possibly hope to win, I could not possibly raise the money, I knew nothing about running for the U.S. Senate, etc., etc., he stunned me with the question: "Claire, who in the world do you think you are?"

Remember, I said he realized nothing but death and physical disability would stop me. But now my mental faculties were being questioned, by my very own beloved husband, who I knew loved me and had always respected and admired my independence. Who called me Joan the Baptist, because my ideas and thinking are always ahead of the times, way out ahead of the curve—and then he would always remind me of what happened to John the Baptist, who brought the Good News before Jesus: Salome handed his head to King Herod on a plate.

Anyway, that question, Who did I think I was? stopped me cold. And hurt me deeply. And then, as is often the case when my feelings get hurt, I got mad.

"Who do I think I am? I think I'm a woman who's had it up to here with all these Democratic assholes out here who moan and groan and wring their hands because no one in this godforsaken place has the guts to go out and run against a corrupt, arrogant little pip-squeak who could give less of a good goddamn about the state of Arizona and even less about the people who live here. I'm sick and tired of hearing that no Big Name Democrat has the balls to run. Unless it's a sure thing, these so-called Heavy Hitters cringe and run for cover. There are no risk takers any more. These people are nothing but a bunch of wimps, afraid to take a chance, and now we have this general who popped up out of nowhere to run in the primary and the Democrats jump on him like a duck on a June bug. It's disgusting and disgraceful and I refuse to stand for it. That's who I think I am. This is America. I am outraged over what's going on here and I know that if I don't do something about it nobody else will. There's no righteous indignation in this goddamned state. Nobody ever rises up and says I'm not going to take it anymore. Well, that's what I'm doing and that's who I think I am."

And the next day I called a friend to get the name of a shrink.

∽

When your husband practically tells you you're crazy right to your face, you start to wonder if he may be right. Maybe I *was* nuts. Is there a test you can take to prove you're sane? Maybe I really had gone over the edge. Maybe I had some kind of personality disorder like delusions of grandeur, like those people who think they're Napoleon, or the character in *Arsenic and Old Lace* who thought he was Teddy Roosevelt. Or that they're God.

I'd never been to a psychiatrist. I didn't know what to expect, and was apprehensive, mainly because I was afraid I was going to find out I *was* crazy.

But as it turned out I wasn't seeing a psychiatrist at all. He was renowned worldwide, I discovered, for his reputation in hypnotherapy. And I needn't have worried. After I explained to him who I was, what I'd done, and why I was there, that I wanted to take a leap of faith to try to unseat John McCain—that I was fighting for a principle and wasn't afraid to lose. Well! Not only did he say that he didn't believe I was crazy, he told me that if I decided to run I could count on his vote!

And so, when I discovered that this wonderful man was a famous hypnotherapist, because the whole issue of crying is so touchy—especially for a woman candidate—I asked him if he could help me with an even bigger problem: Could he keep me from crying? I knew that crying could be more disastrous for me as a candidate than being crazy, since the United States Senate has always had its share of unsound minds.

"I can keep you from crying," the hypnotherapist said, "though I would never do that. You need to cry. But I can help you with some techniques to keep you from crying if you feel it's inappropriate."

I was fascinated by the hypnotherapy sessions, never dreaming I would be a good candidate, because I like to be in control; I discovered, however, that it had nothing to do with giving up control. It was more like imaging and visualization. It didn't take many sessions to achieve our goal, and I never cried in public during the whole campaign. (Though occasionally I tuned up in one-on-one interviews with a reporter, who never failed to mention it in the story.)

But the most extraordinary thing happened. In the waning days of the election, our children had come in from out of town to help me campaign. On election day we had driven to Tucson to thank my supporters there at the end of that last day, in a magnificent crisp, November twilight. At my campaign headquarters, surrounded by television cameras and lights and cheering supporters—and my children—as I ended my little speech I felt the tears beginning to well up for the very first time since I began the campaign. The polls were closing, the election was over. The therapist had told me he could help me get through it. And he had.

Since then I just cry the way I always have, and still make a damn fool of myself.

We've come a long way though. It's okay now for presidents, even senators, to cry. As long as they're men.

∾

Dino DeConcini is Senator Dennis DeConcini's older brother, Henry's old and cherished friend, who became my friend as well, after the first time we met at our wedding breakfast. He was among the first contributors to my campaign for the Senate, even though

Dennis was supporting my opponent. Henry's friendship with Dino—who some people, even Dennis, call the "smart" brother—dates back to their high school days when Phoenix was still a small town, after the DeConcinis moved to Phoenix from Tucson when the boys' father was elected state attorney general, later to be appointed to the Arizona Supreme Court. Henry was extremely fond of the senior DeConcinis, but didn't really know Dennis very well because he was three years younger. In those early years he was just "in the way," as kid brothers can be, and Henry remembers that Dennis used to run crying to his mother when the older boys kept him awake with their raucous poker games in the DeConcini kitchen.

So when I ran for the state legislature in 1984, I was pleased when Dennis offered to let me use his name for a fundraiser and made a little speech on my behalf. He and Dino and Ora, their mother—a woman of generous spirit and a former Democratic National Committeewoman who has always been warm and gracious to me—all made considerable contributions to my campaign.

When Dennis ran for reelection to the Senate in 1988 after saying he would serve only two terms and was then running for a third—even though he had never set the world on fire and always seemed to hold out on any key Senate vote until the end to milk it for publicity—out of loyalty and history Henry and I both contributed to his campaign. His opponent, an unknown Republican who came out of nowhere, made a surprisingly strong showing, reflecting Dennis's vulnerability. And that was *before* the Keating affair.

Though Dennis and I saw each other only at Democratic functions, our relationship had always been cordial, and true to my Southern roots, because of the family connection, I believed it to be based on a stronger bond than mere politics.

Hearing that Dennis was supporting the retired lieutenant general Truman Spangrud, I wanted to find out if it were true, because Dennis had a Midas touch when it came to fundraising and I would need his help if I decided to run. It was early October 1991—before my first trip to Washington—that I picked up the phone to call Dennis, two months after the Russian coup that brought an end to the Cold War, and during the time of the Clarence Thomas hearing, when Dennis's women constituents in Arizona were having a fit over his hard-nosed treatment (as a member of the Senate Judiciary Committee) of Anita Hill.

When I told Dennis that I was calling to let him know that I was seriously considering running for the Senate, and that I'd heard he was helping Spangrud, I figured, politician that he was, he would be just a little bit ingratiating. But, boy, did I get a wrong number!

He cut right to the chase: "Truman has $200,000 to put into the campaign. Do you? Not only is he committing $200,000," he practically gushed, "he's the perfect match for McCain. A *military* man, a *general*, and like McCain, he was a pilot who flew in Vietnam. And best of all, Claire, *he didn't get shot down!*"

I couldn't believe my ears. "The Cold War is over. Who in the world cares about that now? We need to look to the future, Dennis, not the past. And besides," I laughed, "that is the most macho thing I've ever heard!"

The conversation ended with Dennis saying to "be in touch if you can raise $200,000," leaving the door open. Not once did he ever say that he was definitely committed to Spangrud, and if there was one thing Dennis was respected for by friend and foe alike, it was keeping his word.

The next time I talked to Dennis was in January 1992, when I called to tell him that I'd decided to run, and once again asked for his support. I'd been elated when I'd seen that Spangrud had raised the grand total of only $2,000 by December 31, so even with the promise of a $200,000 pot, the general had obviously not raised the temperature of the party money folks.

As before, though, Dennis turned me down. "I'm sorry, Claire. You know I usually stay neutral in a contested primary, but I made a commitment to Truman before I knew you were thinking of getting in the race, and I'm going to have to stick by it."

"Tell me, are you helping him raise money?"

"Yeah, I am."

"I'm so sorry not to have you with me, Dennis, and that I'll have to do it without you. You know I have a constituency and Truman doesn't."

"Yeah, I know that, and I know you'll be able to raise a little money, but for a United States Senate race you need a quarter of a million just to think about it."

"That's what everybody keeps telling me. It's appalling."

"I know, but that's the way it is."

"I hope I can count on your help when I win the primary."

Apparently amused by my chutzpa, and in the face of such an improbable event, he laughed as he easily promised, "If you win the primary, you'll certainly have my support."

Dennis was true to his word to General Spangrud. He held a fundraiser for him in Washington that April and enlisted some fellow senators as sponsors. Until that time Hattie Babbitt had remained neutral, as had many other prominent Arizona Democrats. I called her to see if she knew about Dennis's fundraiser for Spangrud.

"I need your help. Have you heard about the fundraiser that Dennis is giving for Truman in Washington? It's going to be at the Monocle on April 1. He's got George Mitchell (then the Senate Majority Leader), Lloyd Bentsen, Joe Biden, Ted Kennedy, Pat Moynihan, Paul Simon—"

"How do I make out the check and where do I send it?"

At that time, a month before I officially announced my candidacy, I could truthfully state that I realized that senators were powerful. But those were mere words. Often I'd been challenged by some of those close to me, usually male, who said, "You have no idea what you're doing! You're trying to go after one of the one hundred most powerful jobs in the whole world! You can't imagine what that means!"

They were right. But until you have eyes to see and ears to hear, you aren't capable of fully comprehending the significance of the far-reaching tentacles of loyalty and power and influence of the United States Senate for one of its own.

But the implications weren't lost on Hattie Babbitt.

∽

When I asked him how I'd be able to recognize him, if he'd be wearing a red carnation in his buttonhole, he said he was fresh out of red carnations but would be wearing a dark brown leather jacket instead. I told him to look for a white Mustang convertible being driven by a woman with white hair, and since there's a lot of that in Phoenix, he had the wrong one if she didn't have a Southern accent.

Filled with curiosity and nervous anticipation, I circled the airline passenger terminal searching for a young man in the brown leather jacket that would identify Mark McKinnon, who was flying in from Austin, Texas. The way I felt evoked long ago memories of the days when someone would fix me up with a blind date and I had no idea what to expect, even though I had been given great assurances that we "really had a lot in common."

Even though the emotions were the same, this was like no other blind date I'd ever had. On the contrary, it was one of the most extraordinary, because Mark McKinnon was coming to see me at the suggestion of my older son.

When Henry had been fresh out of ideas about how to keep me from running, and aware that this son felt the same way he did, he said, "Why don't you ask Buddy if he can give you the name of someone who will tell it to you straight, whose judgment you can rely on to help you make the final decision whether to run or not." And so I had, and now here I found myself on a January Saturday in 1992 looking for this boy, only a few years older than my son, invested by me, of course, with all the psychological and emotional baggage that such an emissary would have to carry.

Mark McKinnon, the Democrat, and my son, the Republican, had worked as their opposite number on opposing campaigns in important races for governor and the Senate. As in any business, even if you're on the other side, you come to know who's respected and who isn't, and my son admired and trusted McKinnon. "He's a good guy, though don't let that fool you," he said. "He'll go for the jugular just like everybody else. But he won't give you the usual bullshit."

McKinnon was in his late thirties. In high school in Denver he'd sung and played guitar in his own band, and after graduation went to Nashville, where he worked at writing songs for Kris Kristofferson. He was twenty-two by the time he arrived at the University of Texas in Austin in the mid-seventies. During the Iran hostage crisis he became a hero as the crusading editor of the college newspaper, the *Daily Texan*, when he went to jail for refusing to hand over unpublished negatives of Iranian student demonstrators.

After graduation he did press work for a Texas governor and a Democratic Senate candidate before leaving for New York City to work with one of the top political consulting firms. After a few years, having had it with the Northeast and the Beltway and all it represented, McKinnon had recently returned to open his own media firm in Austin. And now here he was, flying in to Phoenix at my son's behest to spend a few hours to talk to me about my race.

I recognized him at once. Along with his dark brown leather jacket he wore jeans and cowboy boots, and over his shoulder was slung a worn leather bag. The minute he got in the car I felt like I'd known him all my life.

Driving to a restaurant in downtown Phoenix, which I knew would be empty of people I knew on a Saturday, making it easier to talk more freely, it was clear that since the time we'd spoken briefly on the phone he had done his homework. What was more, there was the unmistakable energy that is generated when only two political junkies are gathered together with the prospect of a new campaign—the fire bell for the Dalmatian—and I realized immediately that he was no more going to advise me not to run than fly to the moon.

Over lunch we discussed everything there was to discuss about the race, which according to McKinnon was contained in two questions, the Why question and the How question. The Why question, "*Why* are you running?" to satisfy the voters, and the How question, "*How* are you going to run?" to satisfy the insiders who are consumed with the process. Mainly we concentrated on the How question, which in the end always boils down to money.

"Your campaign would have to be lean and mean and run on a shoestring—an efficient guerrilla war. The money won't come until the end, which is late with the primary election in September. The whole primary will have to be spent raising money, and you'll have to make the most of free media.

"This year I believe money will be less important than ever before, that the message will be more important than money. I'm not saying money's not important and not necessary. You have to get your message out. And you will never match McCain's war chest.

"I'm in politics because I love it and because I want to get

Democrats elected. And I'm in it for the money. When I have enough big campaigns going, I occasionally get to do what I call my pro bono campaign, just because I believe in the candidate. Claire, let's face it, it's a long shot, you understand that as well as anybody. But one thing's for sure. You can't win if you don't run. And you'll have so fuckin' much fun doing it. What have you got to lose?"

As I was letting him out at the airport I thanked him and then, "McKinnon, I don't know if you can understand this, but as a mother, I'm so touched that it was my son who sent you to me."

"I do understand. It's come full circle, hasn't it?" he said. And grabbing his bag from the back seat, he got out and said through the window, "Let me know what you decide. I'll do whatever I can to help you," and hi, ho, Silver, he was off into the sunset.

As I drove away I could think of nothing I had heard in the past three hours to change my mind. In fact it had only galvanized my determination to run. Cynics would look at McKinnon as a hustler, urging me to run because it would be in his best interests. But how much could he possibly hope to make out of a bare-bones race like the one I would have to run, with everything having to come at the end, and only then if I won the primary? I knew it was a long shot, and how many times had I asked the question, What do I have to lose? and come up with the same answer every time: Nothing.

And it came to pass that on April 15, 1992, I announced that I was a candidate for the United States Senate in the Democratic primary. I was terrified, but not afraid.

Eighteen

"How soon can you start, O'Hara?"

It was mid-June, before the September 8 primary election, and I was driving Marc O'Hara back to Sky Harbor, the wistful name Phoenicians had christened their airport, after spending a full day together.

I am not possessed of the skills required to do justice to a description of Marc O'Hara. In the first place, he is larger than life, which lends easily to caricature, and with a name like O'Hara, to cliché. And second, he is a work in progress, as are we all, though he more than most.

Mark McKinnon found O'Hara for me. O'Hara had just come off a primary campaign for a woman who was running for secretary of state in Oregon. When I called him a few days after he had returned home to San Francisco, I realized I'd waked him up when I heard a groggy, suspicious morning voice, prepared to fend off nuisance callers. I went on the offensive.

"Wake up, boy, this is Claire Sargent calling from Phoenix to tell you your future is waiting for you in Arizona!"

Long silence.

"Is this Marc O'Hara?"

"Yeah, this is Marc O'Hara. *Who* is this?"

"Claire Sargent. I'm running for the U.S. Senate in Arizona. Mark McKinnon gave me your name. Said you might be interested in running my campaign, that you'd be perfect for me."

Silence.

"For a minute there, I thought you were pitching some kind of real estate deal." Long pause. "McKinnon gave you my name?"

"Yes. He said you were one of the best free media people he'd ever worked with. In-your-face and a true believer. Can I send you a ticket to come over here? I can't hire you until I look you in the eye."

More silence. Then, the mists beginning to clear, "Yeah, I remember now. McKinnon did mention something about a race in Arizona. Wait a minute. Don't you have a primary?"

"Yes. I'm taking on the whole establishment. It's going to be fun, and you should be part of it. If McKinnon recommended you, I have faith. Will you please come over here?"

"I don't know. Uh, what's your name again?"

"Claire Sargent."

"Sorry, Claire, I've just finished a rough campaign and I need some time off. I also have some other things going on in my life I need to work out. I don't know if the timing is right. I really need a break."

"O'Hara, this is the chance of a lifetime. A campaign for the United States Senate. How many people get to do that? If we win, you'll be a hero, and if we don't, which isn't going to happen, think of all the experience you'll have for your résumé. And at your age. By the way, exactly how old are you?"

"Thirty-two."

"I have a son that age. Where'd you live before landing in California?"

"I'm a fifth-generation San Franciscan. A graduate of San Francisco State, with a minor in film and a major in international economics."

"Wonderful! Just what I want! Somebody who's not cut from the D.C. cookie cutter school of campaign consultants. Come on over here and talk to me. Think how sweet it would be for a woman to beat John McCain. It can be done, but not if I don't get some help, and soon."

"I can't make any promises, but go ahead. Send the ticket."

When O'Hara had arrived in the early morning two days later, the first words out of his mouth were not original for first-time visitors to Phoenix in the summertime.

"God, I thought this was supposed to be a dry heat! I thought I was walking into a blast furnace. I've always heard about the heat, but you can't believe it until you experience it. I seriously doubt if I can take this for five months. Is there a bonus for hazardous duty?"

"It's all a myth, O'Hara. This *is* dry heat. It just depends on whether you'd rather be boiled or baked. They say you get used to it, but you never do. The older you get the harder it is. Just be glad you would only have to do it for five months."

When we arrived at my campaign headquarters, I sensed that O'Hara found it just as disenchanting as the dry heat had been. I had chosen the site because of its downtown location, which I considered important, being a downtown person. But also I was attracted to it because of its charm, an adobe bungalow shaded by a magnificent jacaranda tree at full bloom in a cloud of azure blossoms, nestled next to a small two-story complex owned by a Hispanic friend of mine (who, I was to discover, as one of McCain's staunchest supporters, is, as I write, ensconced in D.C. in a federal job!) Seeing all this anew through O'Hara's eyes I instinctively knew that he disapproved, that this was not his idea of the "look" for a U.S. Senate campaign headquarters.

But as we walked through the door, I was proud and excited, as I was each time I entered, by the energy that emanated from within. Several volunteers, collating papers, working the three phones and the sole computer, were accommodated in one room that could not be described as commodious. I had a small office off to the right, big enough for a desk and a couple of chairs, to which I led O'Hara, offering him some coffee and gesturing to a chair.

Then I launched into my spiel.

"O'Hara, I've been running this campaign for the past two months, and you know the old saying, she who runs her own campaign has a fool for a candidate. I saw it in a campaign I worked on once and it's absolutely true. But I'm doing this out of necessity, not choice, since the first guy I had when I announced didn't work out. No chemistry. I've been almost crazy trying to do it all myself because I haven't been able to find anybody here in this state who knows more than I do about running a statewide campaign who has the time to do it, or who isn't working on another campaign.

"I don't have to tell you it's late. The traditional political campaign people all have jobs. They were signed up months, even years ago, some of them. This whole system is sick. That's why when I heard you'd just lost your primary race I was delighted. Not that you'd lost—I feel bad for you about that, I know it's painful—but if we decide to work together it'll help you move on."

"First, tell me why you're running and then tell me how you're going to raise the money," O'Hara said.

"Why am I running? Because the Cold War is over and I didn't hear anybody talking about cutting the money going to the military and using it here at home to put our own house back in order. No country can be strong unless it's secure at its foundation. We need a house with a foundation built on rock, not on sand, as we have now.

"I'm running because America—America!—at the end of the twentieth century, has thirty-five million people without a doctor. People in the richest country in the world are sleeping in cardboard boxes in our streets, O'Hara. It's an obscenity. One in five in America has been unemployed in the last year. One out of eight is on food stamps. Our inner cities are war zones. Children are having children. Our air and water and land are being fouled. Our country is in debt, maybe bankrupt.

"And I haven't heard anybody say he CARES. Here in Arizona, I've only heard military men say they want to be elected or reelected. The world has changed. These guys are dinosaurs.

"The war is over. It's time to pay attention to what's been happening here at home. A generation has been shaped by the changing role of women. And now, with lightning speed, the end of the Cold War has turned our world upside down, and we need new leadership.

"I guess I'm an idealist, though I'm not an ideologue, and I like to think I'm a pragmatist as well, because I like to get things done. And I got mad. I got mad at the Democrats. Here we have a really scandal-wounded Republican incumbent in a deeply anti-incumbent year and none of the so-called Big Name Democrats have the guts to run against him. And that was even *before* Anita Hill!

"McCain is still a Cold Warrior looking through a rear-view mirror, one of the biggest supporters of the military-industrial complex in the Senate. Now that the Cold War is over we've got to have some leadership to figure out how to convert these companies that turn out war machines into machines for peacetime—swords into plowshares—into trucks and buses and high-speed trains instead of tanks and B-2 bombers. Into rockets for satellites instead of missiles. I heard in New England they're making electric cars in factories that used to make submarines. We need to rebuild our inner cities, repair our roads, bridges, and highways—our infrastructure.

"Jobs are the biggest issue in this campaign. If people have a job, education, and health care—those three things—they will have hope. These are the things I want to talk about, and I've wrapped it up into what I call my Strategic Domestic Initiative—economic conversion that includes job training; a domestic peace corps; universal health care; investment in education—to replace the Strategic Defense Initiative, "Star Wars."

"The debt and the deficit have grown more in the last twelve years than in the history of our country, and McCain is so tied to the special interests he will never vote to close any tax loopholes for those guys. If we don't get this country's debt under control, we can't do the things we need to do. But you can't run a campaign on that. You need to talk to people about things that touch them personally. And women are good at personalizing these things.

"Then, the final straw was this retired lieutenant general nobody's ever heard of who graduated from the University of Arizona the same year I graduated from college coming back to save us from McCain. I couldn't believe it! O'Hara, I'm fifty-eight years old. I have nothing to lose. I'm beholden to nobody. This election is about change and reform. I can run on what I believe and say what I believe and I'm not going to lose my job, and neither are my husband or my children. I happen to believe that's a gift that not many people are given. I can work to change the system because I'm not dependent on the status quo.

"McCain picked out this state to move to so he could run for Congress ten years ago because there was an open seat. He was nothing but a carpetbagger looking for a more powerful job back in Washington where he'd been since he came home from Vietnam. He's never really even lived here. And then what does the Democratic Party do? It supports a guy who hasn't been around for twenty-five years—another carpetbagger who has no idea what's going on here—so he too can stay in Washington where *he's* also been for years. Tweedle Dee and Tweedle fuckin' Dum! Give me a break!"

"What's this guy's name?"

"Truman Spangrud."

"Excellent!"

"But it was the Clarence Thomas hearing that clinched it for me, O'Hara. All those men, so officious and patronizing and condescending, bigger than life right up there on the TV screen, without a clue and so unaware of it, with all of America watching in their living rooms, for the first time getting a real close-up look at a United States Senate with ninety-eight men and only two women, when over 50 percent of our population is women."

"Yeah, that's all good stuff, but you haven't told me where you're gonna get the money."

"O'Hara, I don't have any money of my own. And my husband Henry and I don't 'have' money, in the old money sense, though Henry has a very good income. However, he's really unhappy about me doing this, mainly because he knows how much money a race like this costs, and he's not going to spend everything he's planning to retire on for a campaign he believes is quixotic. And I won't ask him to do it. I think I'll be able to get at least $50,000 for the primary, and after we win it, we'll take it from there.

"Two million is the figure they give me that it will take to run. So, how do I raise two million? It may seem crazy, but I think it's possible based on a crucial series of events taking place, but I am making logical assumptions. One, I get the support of Emily's List, which I've belonged to since it began. Two, I win the primary decisively. Then, three, the state party closes ranks behind me, and four, DeConcini and the Democratic National Committee help me raise money in Washington for the general election.

"In this state, because of my volunteer work, I have a constituency among women, the arts, prochoice advocates, some environmentalists, and some of the social justice folks. I don't mean they'll vote for me in a bloc or anything—there's no such thing as a monolithic group—but I have been active in all those areas. Of course they're the ones who have the least money, and most of the money I raise will have to come from small donors, from people who live in Arizona. And I don't think Truman Spangrud will have support from anybody except the hard core rank and file Democrats, who certainly don't have a lot of money.

"There's a big problem, though. The primary isn't until September and it's going to be hard to raise money from Democrats during a contested primary. The late primary leaves only seven weeks before the election to raise the principal money it'll take for the TV to go up against McCain."

And after observing the dynamics of what can happen on a big campaign, I was completely candid. "O'Hara, if you take this job, our relationship has to be like a good marriage. We have to trust each other completely. A campaign is a cauldron, and when it heats up people say things and act in ways they never would at any other time. We have to be able to scream and holler and not get mad when the pressure builds up, to clear the air. That's where the trust comes in. We each have to know we're for the other, and when we disagree, we need to say so. I need somebody to run this campaign, somebody I can delegate to, so I can be the candidate. It's bigger than each of us, so we'll just have to keep on growing into the job together as we go along."

I had invited three of my closest advisers to meet with O'Hara separately to get their assessment of him and for him to get a feel for those who were supporting me. While a volunteer drove O'Hara around to see the city, I met with the three, who with great relief, though not without some reservations, since he'd never run a Senate race, gave O'Hara a thumbs up. They too were anxious for him to get started to get the campaign focused and back on track.

O'Hara had not said he would take the job, but it was obvious that the old campaign juices had started to flow. And we had hit it off.

At the airport he opened the door to get out of the car, then shut it immediately when the heat of the summer inferno poured in. "I'd hoped I wouldn't be, but I'm definitely interested. I'll think it over and let you know in a day or two whether I can take the job. If I do, the first thing we're going to do is find a new headquarters!" Bracing himself, he pushed open the door and sprinted into the terminal.

In June 1992, three months before the Arizona primary election, I joined the other women senatorial candidates in Washington for the National Women's Political Caucus "Salute to the 1992 Women Candidates." The event was a big deal for which many women—led by long-time Caucus hand, Republican Maureen Murphy of Phoenix—had worked very hard to get me included, and I was grateful. I had Caucus women from Arizona working on my campaign who were some of my most ardent supporters, and I had Caucus women in Arizona who hated my guts. They were not a united front.

The "Salute" was my initiation into the show biz of politics. Outside the Beltway, especially between the coasts, is summer stock. Washington is Broadway. And no one had quite impressed upon me the importance and impact it could have. There were a lot of things that it was assumed I knew that, in fact, I didn't.

It was at the time of the national outrage over the House bank scandal and the subsequent focus on all the perks of Congress. And after my first foray in October 1991 as an innocent alone inside the Beltway thicket, from the window of my plane I took in once more our nation's capital outstretched below in the soft beguiling twilight. I remember thinking how still the dark waters seemed, while just under the surface the school of guardian sharks circled, sensing the promise of sweet fresh meat. Me.

As I rode in my taxi toward the hotel on that balmy summer evening, the Capitol, washed in light, glowed before us like the moon, a two-dimensional backdrop against the dark and cloudless sky. My taxi driver pointed and said, "See there ahead? That's the Capitol. It's a place so full of crooks they need to take a broom to it and sweep out everybody who's there." When I told him that I was running for the Senate from Arizona and was going to do just that, he turned around and looked at me and said, "What's your name, lady? So if you get elected I can tell people about the time you rode in my cab. We need some more women. I sure do hope you make it."

The next morning I met for the first time Jeanne Clark and Marie Morse, who worked for Anthony, Stanton and Gage, a firm specializing in women's campaigns. They were the first people in

Washington I'd met who seemed sincere and interested in really wanting to help me, to guide me through the labyrinthine paths and landmines of PACs and fundraising and the women's groups. For me it was as though I had been rescued by the cavalry and taken inside the stockade to be protected from the marauders. At last I was no longer alone.

I discussed with Jeanne my concern over what I was to say that night at a press conference when all of the candidates would be given a minute or two to speak, and telling me not to worry she said she'd write something. Marie had set up appointments with many of the "progressive" PACs: those concerned with social issues like abortion rights, gun control, the environment, education—my kind of people—and all of the women's organizations as well as the DSCC, the Democratic Senatorial Campaign Committee. Marie had programmed three full days of meetings from early morning to late afternoon, and we adhered to the schedule scrupulously. She was a very impressive woman: besides being smart, she was wise, elegant, and gracious, and of my generation, which was a comfort to me in the tidal wave of youth. She had a quiet strength and good judgment that I trusted completely.

Delighted and proud to have my daughter, Corinne, who lived in Washington, by my side on that auspicious evening, when the two of us opened the door to where the candidates were to congregate we were greeted by the din of total chaos. The room was dark against the banks of television lights focused on some risers at the other end of the room where the candidates were assembling. In the crush I spotted the face of Ann Lewis, a well-known Democratic operative, whom I'd never met, but felt that I knew because I'd seen her on TV, and reflexively reached out to her like an old friend. I'm sure she was startled. Harriet Woods, the Caucus president, appeared, anxiously guiding me like a mother hen up front, where I was thrust into the light among the other candidates. With a sense of esprit and exuberance we hugged each other or shook hands and introduced ourselves, all for one and one for all, or so it seemed that night.

Posing on our risers, smiling and waving, we all joined in a little cheerleader routine before the solid wall of cameras. Senator Barbara Mikulski of Maryland, our leader and putative den mother, gave a

Part Three - Arizona

rousing speech and then like the Pied Piper led us through the multitude, out the door, down the hall, and into the ballroom to an even greater assemblage. It was absolutely thrilling! People waving and cheering us on along the way. I had a sense of unreality that this could be happening to me.

Harriet introduced Senator Mikulski, who made another even more energetic speech, and then began introducing us one by one. The senator, who is under five feet tall, makes a point of having a box to stand on when she is behind a podium and microphones so that she can be seen. When the taller ones stepped up, they moved it out of the way. I had become concerned, panicky actually, that my speech was too long, and not in keeping with the cheerleading tone the others had adopted. While the others took their turn, I was mentally trying to pare it down to a few punchy remarks that I could shout out as the others seemed to be doing.

In my concern for what I was to say, when my turn came I completely forgot about the box, stepped upon it, and arose like Big Bird, almost two feet above the microphones and the podium. From my aerial view I spotted Corinne, who gave me a dazzling reassuring smile but with anxious eyes. My notes were so far below me on the podium that it was hard for me to look down to see them. So, improvising on what Jeanne had written, just before reaching the end my mind went blank. Long, deadly, silent pause—I knew my handful of friends in the audience were holding their breaths—before finally pressing on to close with a wonderfully funny line Jeanne had given me: "John McCain has more baggage than Samsonite." Bringing hoots of laughter and raucous cheers, I was allowed to finish with a little pizazz.

Quoted in the *Washington Post* "Style" section the next morning—"the" place to be I was informed—if people had only read the Post, I would have been deemed a hit. But I had a feeling that the C-Span-viewing powers-that-be were probably underwhelmed by my "presentation," though I never got any direct feedback except for that old conversation stopper, "I saw you on TV," its corollaries being, "I saw your picture in the paper," and, "You had your hair cut." I mean, how do you respond to statements like that?

The press singled out Barbara Boxer, Geraldine Ferraro, Lynn

Yeakel, and Carol Moseley-Braun, but that was not unexpected. Though Ferraro's primary was still ahead of her, Ferarro is Ferraro, and the others had already won their primaries in "important" states.

By the time we got to the convention in July, only a month later, however, we had been divided into two camps. The Emily's List anointed: Dianne Feinstein, Barbara Boxer, Lynn Yeakel, Patty Murray, and Carol Moseley-Braun. (The story—perhaps apocryphal—was that when late polling showed that she was going to win, having not lifted a finger to help her before, Emily's List had delivered a $5,000 PAC contribution to Carol on the weekend before her Tuesday primary election. Getting in on the action, however belatedly, they would be able to take credit for her victory.) And their rejects: Jean Lloyd-Jones, Geri Rothman-Serot, Gloria O'Dell, Josie Heath, and me.

∾

I was crazy about Barbara Mikulski, though in awe and intimidated at the same time. I believe the source of her pugnacity flows from a wellspring of outrage over social injustice and discrimination. Before the other women joined her in the Senate, I knew I could always count on her to fight for the things that I cared about.

As the only female Democratic senator, on every occasion during the election when all of the women senate candidates were gathered together, Senator Mikulski was our leader.

And so it was at the Democratic National Convention in July 1992 in New York City when I was quite excited to discover that all of the women Senate candidates were to have our picture taken by the *New York Times*. It was to be after a reception and rally at the Rihga Hotel on West 54th Street, an opportunity to corral us while we were all in one place at the same time.

As the reception wound down, on my way to the restroom I happened to pass by the room where two young men were setting up the cameras for our portrait, as they properly called it, and as I stopped to chat with them I was absolutely knocked out by an American flag so mammoth that it covered in its entirety a vast wall from floor to ceiling, so enormous that it had to be turned under at the bottom and at one end.

With the Stars and Stripes as the backdrop, a sort of stage set had been designed, using a platform, ladder, and stools, which had been covered by a cornflower blue cloth. Fred Conrad, the photographer, explained that he and his assistant had designed it weeks before and had spent the last two days putting it all together. It had been meticulously planned with a spot for each of the candidates, and, finally, they were now painstakingly angling and focusing several cameras. True artists at work.

When I returned for the portrait-taking, I discovered several candidates, some with their aides, already descending onto the set like wild horses, paying no heed whatsoever to Fred Conrad, who was trying quite diplomatically, though unsuccessfully, to position these strong-minded women into what he viewed as the most artistic arrangement. Finally, recognizing the futility of it all, he was smart enough to simply stand back and watch the chaos.

Liz Holtzman, a candidate in the New York Democratic primary, was there, having placed herself strategically in one of the seats in the front. When Geraldine Ferraro arrived, you could sense the tension between the two—Gerry was her rival in the New York primary—as Gerry sat herself down on a high stool behind Liz. And I was amused when, to the dismay of the photographers—Ferraro as auteur—she then began to direct the women to where she divined they should sit. The best laid scheme had most assuredly gang a-gley, and it was quite a deliciously madcap scene.

When everybody was settled at last into a spot, the photographers gently began to make suggestions, some successful, some not—I'd never before heard of the one being photographed giving the photographer directions—but then I'd never posed with a group of women running for the U.S. Senate either.

For the next half hour or more we were on good enough behavior to sit for what seemed to be at least a million shots until there were impatient shouts of "Enough, enough," and, as the photographers finally folded their tents, we all began to rise from our seats. As we did so, several candidates' aides swooped upon the scene like a flock of birds, hell-bent on plucking up their prey to fly away to the next event.

Suddenly above the din of our imminent departure there arose the unmistakable voice of Barbara Mikulski.

"I want the candidates to stay put and sit back down, and I want everybody else out of this room except them. I've got something I want to say to them, and I want to say it in private. Everybody else out of here, now! And I mean everybody but these twelve women!"

When no one made a move to leave, Senator Mikulski became one irritated senator. "When I say everybody but the candidates I *mean* everybody, and I mean *now*. We haven't got all day!"

And so after the hangers-on finally tore themselves away and shuffled sulkily from the room, the senator, hands on hips, standing in the spot that the photographers had just vacated, waited for us, like so many unruly students, to settle down. When complete silence enveloped the room, and she had our rapt attention, she began.

"I want you to know I have been waiting for you," she proclaimed, fists still planted firmly on hips, leaning slightly forward from the waist, like a coach before the big game.

"For six years I have been alone. And for six years I have been *waiting* for you.

"I want you to understand something. These next few months are going to be some of the toughest you have ever lived through in your life. Your opponents are going to go after you with everything they've got. They will say anything—they will do anything—to keep you from getting elected. You are not going to believe what is happening to you. But you can get through it! And when you do, it will be *worth* it. Because *I* need you and the *Senate* needs you.

"For those of you who have been in the House, the rules in the Senate aren't the same. It's a lot easier to get things done. It's not as complicated or as hard to attach an amendment to a bill to drive the boys crazy to get what we want.

"So I want you to remember! I am *waiting* for you! Together we can change the *Senate*. And together we can change *America!* Don't let me down!"

∽

It had been a long day. The apartment O'Hara and I were using was only one express subway stop away from Madison Square

Garden and the convention. It was no more than fifteen minutes after I'd left the convention that I walked into the apartment and immediately turned on the TV to catch Governor Ann Richards of Texas, who was next on the program as I left the Garden to come home.

From the moment we had arrived for the convention, O'Hara had been wild over what he called the DSCC's "Rube Goldberg" plan for servicing campaigns. The communications room, where on a daily basis you had to pick up a pass to the convention floor, was in a hotel twenty blocks north of the Garden, which because of convention traffic congestion was at least a thirty-minute ride by cab— each way—if you could find one.

The DSCC press operation, which O'Hara actually thought was pretty well-coordinated, was another twenty blocks back down town at the hotel across from the Garden. Luckily, because I am a veteran of the subway, O'Hara and I were able to get around as quickly as possible.

At no location—neither the communications room, the press room, nor the Garden—was there anyone coordinating the activities of the various campaigns, no central clearing-house for candidates, no check-in time, nothing.

Scouting out the communications opportunities, O'Hara discovered the "cattle call," an event taking place each day when senators and candidates could send live television interviews to their home states. It essentially amounted to signing up for a designated time for a satellite feed to a TV station in your state, and hoofing it over to Madison Square Garden and getting in line.

Before getting in line, you were directed to the makeup room, where all manner of exotic New York makeup artists were on hand to "do" you. The first time I availed myself of this unexpected perk, I was quite amused to discover that the only other occupants of the makeup room were rather cowed males, protected by capes and seated in front of mirrors, watching stolidly as the experts worked their magic. The makeup room was a great leveler.

I barely recognized Senator Harris Wofford of Pennsylvania, a former college president, whom, along with his wife, Clare, I'd enjoyed meeting the day before at a party at the Rockefellers' in

Pocantico Hills. When I spoke to him draped in his cape, he acknowledged my greeting with a sheepish grin.

Outside in line I recognized lots of senators, all as spiffed up as I was, and was pleased to get a chance to talk to Senator Paul Wellstone from Minnesota, whose upset election I'd researched as I was considering whether to run. Even Dennis was there, surprised, I'm sure, to find me doing the same thing he was.

Observing all this was a reporter for the *New York Times,* writing a story about how the Democrats were taking advantage of this latest up-to-the-minute communications technology. His article included a description of O'Hara, off-camera, throwing me "softball" questions for the audience back home. My first mention in the *Times*, a far cry from the not-so-distant notion of when a lady's name should appear in the newspaper: the day she's born, the day she marries, and the day she dies. When in politics, it's, "Be sure you spell my name right!"

During the afternoon we'd run into Jeri Rothman-Serot, the Senate candidate from Missouri. She said she'd heard something about Ann Richards introducing the Senate candidates at the convention that night, and we tossed around whether it was a real possibility, since the night before the Emily's List senatorial candidates had been featured in special cameo appearances televised nationwide. And according to the agenda for that evening, Ann was going to introduce the forty or so women candidates for the House.

But, aware of the inefficiency and the sheer lack of organization (the perfect spot for the old Will Rogers chestnut: "I don't belong to an organized party—I'm a Democrat."), and knowing that anything was possible, we both agreed that we would find out what we could and let the other know.

A few hours later, early in the evening at the VIP hospitality suite in the hotel across from the Garden, we ran into Don Foley, the director of the DSCC, who, after we asked him, told us that there had been some discussion about Ann introducing all the women candidates, but that it had been decided to stick with the Congressional candidates as planned.

"You're sure?" I asked.

"Yes, I'm sure," Don Foley replied.

Secure in that knowledge, when we saw Jeri at the hospitality suite we gave her the news, and left to go to the convention to pay a visit to the Arizona delegation.

The Super Bowl of party politics to which the faithful make a pilgrimage every four years, the convention is wired in favor of party stalwarts, who as a rule attend at great personal expense and discomfort. The privilege of attending is earned only after first deciphering the arcane rules of the state party, and then, over a period of several weeks, successfully clearing the hurdles of one of the most devilishly complicated processes ever devised. To be subjected to this ritual and to survive, becoming one of the chosen, is considered an honor.

Acutely aware that it was these party regulars who made up the Arizona delegation, and that probably 99 percent of them supported my opponent, I knew that their response to my appearance might be chilly and distant at best. Even so, I felt it was important to show up.

The climate was as I'd anticipated—though they weren't unpleasant. Not being a member of the delegation, I wasn't entitled to a seat, the number of which are strictly allocated by the convention and rigidly protected by each delegation. Therefore, while I visited I had either been sitting in someone else's seat or standing. After shooting the breeze with some friends for a respectable length of time, I felt it was time to leave as the hour for Ann to speak approached, and delegates began returning to reclaim their seats.

It was probably somewhere around ten o'clock.

I had a choice: since I had decided not to go to the party I was invited to after the event was over, and since we weren't part of the VIP contingent, I could either climb up to the nosebleed section in the rafters with O'Hara, where Ann would be no more than a speck in the distance and I would need binoculars to even know who she was, or I could stand around in the chaos down in the bowels of the arena watching the TV consoles. Neither of which appealed. Since a convention is so much better on TV than it is being there, I decided to go and watch Ann in the peace and quiet of the apartment.

With that, deciding to go hang around the press room until it was over, O'Hara walked me to the subway, and I was home in ten minutes.

In the apartment as the TV screen lighted up before me I saw the stage of the convention on the screen, Ann to one side, and women streaming in from both right and left as their names were being called by Ann, and then, as the phone began ringing, reeling with disbelief, I heard her say: ". . . and for the Senate, Claire Sargent from Arizona . . ."

I thought I was going to faint, or throw up. As the phone continued its insistent ring, it took everything I had to lift the receiver. I could barely speak. Then, as the light of remembrance of another night nearly forty years before began to flicker in the far reaches of my memory, I began to laugh.

∾

In Mississippi every May the Kappa Alpha Order celebrated their heritage and tradition with a weekend that was capped off by their grandest event of the year, the Confederate Ball. At Millsaps I was considered to be close to the KAs. My daddy had been one, though it wasn't anything I'd ever heard him talk about, and I probably wouldn't even have ever known it except that when my brother came to Millsaps, Daddy told him he was a legacy, and so my brother pledged KA as well. Some of the boys I grew up with were KAs at Millsaps, as well as some of the boys I'd graduated from high school with. So I had a lot of good friends there. And that's literally what I mean. Friends. Not "boy friends."

It was the last semester of my senior year, when I was going out with Sonny, who wasn't a KA. Several weeks before the Confederate Ball the KAs choose their KA Rose, usually the girl who is pinned to the president, and four KA Sweethearts, who are then presented at the ball amid great fanfare and pomp. About a month before the ball, somebody told me that I'd been chosen a KA Sweetheart. I couldn't believe it, and wondered if it were really true, since nobody I knew in the KAs had mentioned it. Or more to the point, I hadn't even been invited to the ball.

The days passed, then the weeks, and still no date. Since nobody else had said anything to me about it, I just assumed that whoever told me had been wrong. And of course it would never have occurred to me to ask anyone outright, because it would be unseemly, as though I might be hinting that I wanted to be a sweetheart. And on the other hand, it would embarrass both me and the person I might ask if it weren't true. I didn't even say anything to my brother, because I assumed he surely would have told me if it were true.

When someone asks me what words I want on my tombstone, I tell them: "Never assume."

On Thursday before the ball on Saturday I happened to run into my brother, who lived on campus.

"Say, have you heard anything about me being a KA Sweetheart for this ball that's coming up?"

"Sure. Why?"

"Well, I sure do hope you can take me because I don't have a date."

"Claire! You don't have a date?"

"No, I don't, and I can't believe yall are so unorganized that someone didn't make sure that all the sweethearts had one. Nobody ever let me know anything about it."

"Aw, this is awful. I already have a date. I'm sure everybody just took it for granted somebody asked you. I sure did. I'll go see what I can find out and let you know."

Friday, my brother reported, every KA within miles had been canvassed and had had dates for weeks. Even though I could have gone out and dug up a KA from somewhere, it just didn't seem fittin' that I should have to do that. If I was their sweetheart, then the KAs should treat me like one. If I'd been desperate, I suppose I could have scrounged up a date. But it was the principle of the thing.

So on the night of the Confederate Ball, rather than basking in the spotlight, this KA Sweetheart celebrated her sweetheart-hood in the time-honored way: playing bridge with the girls, late into the night.

"What did they say when I wasn't there?" I asked my brother the next day. "Did they even call out my name?"

"Yes, they announced that you were a sweetheart, but that unfortunately you weren't able to attend."

Miss Otis regrets.

ೞ

I heard O'Hara screaming my name, along with a stream of obscenities at whoever was with him. "Claire, Claire! Did you see it? Did you see it! Are you okay!"

And I was completely taken by surprise when the next thing I heard was a calm, quiet voice, "Claire, this is Don Foley." It was Don Foley with whom O'Hara had watched the disaster unfold. It was the head of the DSCC O'Hara had been shouting obscenities at.

I was completely drained, limp.

"Claire, there is no way I can ever make this up to you. I realize that you've had a triumphant moment stolen from you, and there's no way you can ever know how deeply sorry I am. I take full responsibility for what happened. It was an impromptu decision, and we tried to get in touch with you, but it was too late. Whatever I can do to help you, I'll do. Just tell me what you want me to do."

"Don, I don't care that I wasn't up there on that stage tonight. It's the principle of the thing. It was just so completely inept and it makes me look like a fool. Naturally I would have liked to have been up there, but it's not going to change my life whether I was there or not. It's just such a goddamned stupid thing to have happen. How in the world can I explain it back home when they ask 'Where were you? You were the only one not there?' What do I tell them?"

"I'll be happy to write a letter, talk to anybody you want me to."

"Thank you, but there's nothing you can do. I respect the way you're taking responsibility. But it doesn't change what happened and what a fool I feel like."

"I understand, and I wish I could do something to change that."

"Goodnight, Don. I need to speak to O'Hara again, please."

"O'Hara," I said when he was back on the line, "this reminds me of something that happened a hundred years ago when I was in college. I'll tell you about it tomorrow. I'm fine. Go out and have some fun. You need it after this."

Back in Phoenix, more people told me they'd seen me on TV that night than those who asked me why I wasn't there.

Can you beat it?

∽

I still laugh out loud when I remember an interview with the editorial board of the *Mesa Tribune* during the primary campaign, when I was asked what I thought was my most important accomplishment.

Part Three - Arizona

While the lieutenant-general-cum-Pentagon-budget-officer—answering first—droned on yet again about the numbers he'd crunched on some budget, I pondered my greatest accomplishment. Intuitively I wanted to respond, "My children," but remembering something I'd read many years before about housewives never being able to look at their lives as having accomplished anything beyond being a mother—which of course would have been the perfect response on this occasion—I decided to go with an answer that was symbolically related.

My reply—that the most important contribution I'd made (and naturally I meant since I'd come to Arizona) was playing a crucial role in getting the palo brea trees planted on Central Avenue—of course fell on ears long deafened by cynicism and ignorance. Anybody who might have read the story covering that occasion had to think I was a nut; and I was later described editorially, as I recall, as someone who "dabbled in xeriscaping."

(A lesson that had been hard for me to learn was that if you didn't explain even the simplest little thing to political reporters [with one exception, a reporter—now gone—from the alternative newspaper *New Times*], that—perhaps unused to my style: loquacious, free-associative, circular—they just didn't get it. Paradoxically, however, these *tabula rasas* believed they were the world's foremost authorities. I had mistakenly assumed that most such reporters were educated—that they might have read a book or two, perhaps even Joyce Kilmer in high school, or that they had even the suspicion of life experience beyond their narrow niche.)

I had been involved with planting the palo breas after Terry appointed me to a special city committee mandated to redesign Central Avenue, Phoenix's main thoroughfare, to be for Phoenix what "the Champs Élysées is to Paris." As a result of my experience with Desert Cities, I had definite ideas about the new design that I shared with the committee, the majority of whom were already of the same mind.

Never before having been a party to promoting creative ideas to the City Council, I hadn't realized just how difficult it would be to accomplish the seemingly obvious: to use desert landscaping in the desert. (We were forced to compromise with a pink water-guzzling non-desert plant when one city council member thought the burnt orange blossoms of the desert honeysuckle would "clash" with the rose-colored sandstone sidewalks!) And settling on the palo breas, a task I assumed would be a snap, proved to be a surprisingly sticky wicket after a group of Central Avenue businessmen, who had their hearts set on a boulevard lined with orange trees à la Palm Springs, California, threatened to bolt and refuse to pay their assessment if they couldn't have their orange trees. Pressure was brought to bear, arms were twisted, and we finally got the palo breas—a breathtaking desert equivalent of spring-blossoming native dogwood in the South and the East Coast—starting a run on that particular species that's been unabated ever since.

Is the final design perfect? No. But for a creative project executed by committee the result was extraordinarily successful (due in large part to the grit and drive of the newly-arrived Sheryl Sculley—now Assistant City Manager).

And because the trees symbolize the eternal for me, a rare instance to be found in this city, I considered them to be quite an important accomplishment.

How would you ever turn all that into a sound bite?

∾

The Tailhook incident, in August 1992—only a few weeks before the September primary election—was the first time I knowingly dipped my toe into the waters of hard-ball politics. Up until then, tough as it had been taking hits from a primary opponent who attacked me because of my husband's position as a utility executive—unfailingly referring to me as "Mrs. Henry Sargent"—his attacks had seemed almost juvenile if not non sequiturs.

But when I held a press conference to accuse John McCain of having been privy to the debauchery, drunkenness, and destruction that had been a feature of the Las Vegas Tailhook Association meetings for years, he came after me like Clinton & Co.—"attack and deny"—went after Gennifer Flowers, as did the press, matching McCain's ferocity over my audacity.

Dubbed by some the Navy's worst catastrophe since Pearl Harbor, "Tailhook" was the result of one woman's courage in going public with a story that would beam a spotlight into the dark, dank

Part Three - Arizona

recesses of Navy culture, tradition, and procedure. The story of what happened to Paula Coughlin on the "third deck" at the 1991 Tailhook convention in Las Vegas not only set off a chain of events that brought down some of the Navy's highest ranking officers, it shattered her own life in the process.

Since 1992 I've read several books about Tailhook '91—including *The Tailhook Report, The Official Inquiry into the Event of Tailhook '91*, published by The Office of the Inspector General (Department of Defense)—making everything I'd ever read about the event in a newspaper or seen on TV seem like a fairy tale compared to the real and ugly story that has still gone largely unreported. It is the story of the arrogance, corruption, wholesale lying under oath, cover-ups, and vilification of the Tailhook victims that took place to deny the debauchery that itself was integral to the culture and tradition of the Navy.

Tailhook '91, an annual reunion of the Tailhook Association held in Las Vegas and partially underwritten by defense contractors since the early sixties, brought four thousand naval officers to Las Vegas in 1991. The reunions were renowned for their "lewd and lascivious" behavior, centered on such creative activities as "ballwalking," "belly/navel shots," "butt biting," "zapping," and leg shaving, as well as binge drinking, hard-core pornography, public and paid sex, tens of thousands of dollars of destruction of hotel property, and the "gauntlet," where Paula Coughlin and others were assaulted. Tailhook '86 had even featured Ronald Reagan's Secretary of the Navy, a married man with three children. In the center of a throng of close to a hundred naval officers cheering him on, he lay on his back on the floor, his head between the legs of a completely nude woman, "eating whipped cream out of her crotch."

John McCain attended subsequent reunions, Tailhook '87 and Tailhook '90, as a United States Senator. And when I asserted at a press conference during the primary that the senator couldn't possibly have been innocent of the knowledge about what was going on, he responded angrily in his best bantam rooster style that the abuse of women guests at Tailhook conventions "was unheard of until 1991."

In *The Mother of All Hooks* William McMichael recounts that after Tailhook '90 (attended by McCain), a pre-1991 reunion letter was sent out to squadron commanders cautioning against "any resemblance to get-togethers of the past" (and after which, in the wake of Tailhook '91, nine women officially reported being assaulted).

"Those unfamiliar with the ways of Tailhook," writes McMichael, "would only have needed to read the first sentence of the letter's first few paragraphs to get an idea of what Tailhook was all about." He continues:

> As last year, you will only be charged for damage inside your suite. . . .
> In past years we have had a problem with under age [sic] participants. . . .
> Also, in the past we have had a problem with 'late night gang mentality.' . . .
> Tailhook will also have a flight surgeon on board this year.

Further, the official *Tailhook Report*, in addressing "The Failure of Leadership," concludes that "Tailhook '91 was not significantly different from earlier conventions," and that "most of the officers we spoke to said that excesses seen at Tailhook '91 . . . and other inappropriate behavior were accepted by senior officers simply because those things had gone on for years. Indeed [they] were a part of the allure of Tailhook conventions."

Ever the grandstander—and with his reelection coming up the following year—having been tipped off the day before the news of the Tailhook scandal would break, the next day, just fourteen days after the end of the contentious confirmation hearing for Supreme Court nominee Clarence Thomas in which Anita Hill had accused him of sexual harassment, John McCain took to the floor of the U.S. Senate to denounce the sexual harassment at Tailhook. (Though I was unaware of it, it was the exact same day that I was across town meeting with Emily's List and the National Women's Political Caucus on my first trip to Washington in October 1991). Calling for an immediate high-level investigation and demanding that the Navy temporarily suspend its participation "in the so-called Tailhook reunion," he also criticized Secretary of the Navy Lawrence Garrett III for dragging his feet.

According to Gregory L. Vistica's book *Fall From Glory—The*

Men Who Sank the U.S. Navy, some on Garrett's staff "were surprised by McCain's ambush and stricken by the irony that he would have the nerve to speak out on Tailhook. Several of the older aviators were aware of McCain's past reputation. 'He would fuck a pile of rocks if he thought a snake was in it,' said one former Vietnam POW who had served in the Navy with McCain."

In the investigation following Tailhook, McCain's Navy comrades lied under oath for the sake of their own personal records, as well as Navy tradition.

Even an Admiral.

∾

I doubt that the reporters had even bothered to read the investigative article in the August 10, 1992, issue of *Newsweek* that delved into the scandal that was "rocking the navy"—the basis of my attack—quoting a 1987 article in *The Hook*, a publication of the Tailhook Association, which reported immediately after the 1987 Tailhook convention in Las Vegas that McCain had "participated in the camaraderie of the third [floor]" at that year's convention.

In addition, my campaign called *The Hook* directly to get a copy of the relevant issue and discovered that the quote in *Newsweek* was only a half quote. The other half—"just such a pregnant, hugely provocative quote," in the words of O'Hara—reported that McCain had found that "the spirit of the third deck was alive and well," which I was to report at my press conference.

Before the conference, O'Hara had sent the pretty Rachel, his sweetheart visiting from San Francisco (now his wife), into the lion's den to schmooze with the reporters. When she came back, her eyes round with fear, she said that she had been petrified by the "vehemence" she felt in the room, the sense of them lying in wait, and that except for one woman it was all guys.

A *Phoenix Gazette* columnist, who, because of his age and years on the job, might have been considered dean of the local political press corps (and because of his ego considered himself its prince), asked the first question after I'd finished my statement. He couldn't figure out, he said, almost literally scratching his head, what I was accusing McCain of, since he hadn't been at the Tailhook convention in 1991.

Lightheartedly and, I thought, with humor, I replied, "You just don't get it, do you?" calling him by name.

With that he turned a hot fluorescent scarlet from collar to scalp, and after a few scoffing laughs from some of the other guys (who seemed delighted) had died down, there was only pin-dropping silence. Without knowing it, I'd committed the most unforgivable faux pas that a mere mortal can make: I'd embarrassed a reporter. Which I never meant to do, having no idea he would take it the way he did. But apparently, humorless misogynist and sexist that he later showed himself to be (to my surprise), he'd never in all his born days had to take such sass from a woman, and boy, did he take his revenge—far exceeding his pound of flesh—in his column the next day.

After the press conference, the lone woman, who had been taping the proceedings for a radio station, almost furtively stealing up to my side, whispered that she was shocked at how I'd been treated. And you were right, she said. I don't believe any of them got it.

They didn't. And they were all over me, savaging the messenger like a bunch of buzzards on a warm carcass in a meadow.

Even after it became clear that McCain had not told the truth, at first denying that he had ever even been there in 1987, and then changing his story three times in twenty-four hours, along the way revealing that he had attended in 1990 as well; and later, when pressed, yes, did seem to recall hearing something about some drunkenness, broken furniture, vomiting; even then the reporters never found it implausible that he might think that what had been going on all those years at Tailhook was just boys being boys.

For O'Hara, aghast at the way I was so viciously mau-maued and that the questions we raised were never pursued or refuted—that the press essentially had no idea of the significance of the story—the Tailhook episode became a defining, presageful event in my campaign. As far as the press was concerned O'Hara said, we would "always be up shit creek without a paddle."

❦

I can't imagine running for office if you don't like people. I don't mean that you have to be outgoing or even convivial. But if you don't have a genuine regard for the people you're going to represent, then to my mind you're in it for the wrong reasons.

With all my vitality, I know it's hard to believe, but as a fundamentally shy person I had to learn to be able to go up to perfect strangers and say hello and introduce myself. It's very difficult for me to make small talk, to speak at length about the weather like the Royals, so I've never enjoyed cocktail parties full of strangers.

On the other hand, Southern women are brought up to believe that it is their bounden duty to keep conversation going, that it is an ill wind that brings a silence. I remember with such fondness the sweetest Southern lady named Lucy, who was a member of my church in New York. One Sunday morning as I approached a small group of members, Lucy had her back to me, so I didn't hear her speaking and inadvertently interrupted her to introduce a visitor. When I apologized, she responded, "Claire, don't you think a thing about it. I wasn't saying anything. I was just talking."

But campaigning is as much listening as it is talking. I especially loved campaigning in the small towns across Arizona (where, if they were lucky to get it at all, "economic development" came in the guise of a new prison, and they were thrilled). It took me back to Starkville and Hattiesburg, to Ackerman, Sherard, and Port Gibson, the towns of my summers growing up in Mississippi, and reminded me of visiting in the homes and churches across the country on the Millsaps Singers tour when I was in college.

Far from the madding over-development of Phoenix, in the small towns and hamlets of Patagonia, Ajo, and Gila Bend ("the fan belt capital of the world"), Bullhead City, Miami, Globe, and Willcox, life is lived so much closer to the bone. I was filled with great affection for the people who live there, moved by their decency and their pride. They needed jobs, hospitals and medical care, education—the basics—and I wanted to help them.

The Navajo reservation's bleak eloquence in the north. The rolling Canero Hills dotted with pinon and manzanita, glinting burgundy and gray in the south. The red rocks of Sedona. The Mojave Desert's sere starkness. The wildflowers of the Apache National Forest and Picacho Peak. Even without the Grand Canyon, the diverse aspects of the incomparable grandeur of the state of Arizona unfailingly fill me with awe. After you've experienced this land of infinite horizons, you come to understand Westerners better.

From my years in Arizona I had come to believe that its people were always being ripped off, and not without the help of the boosters and the speculators who call Arizona home. This isn't an original thought, of course. In *Where the Bluebird Sings to the Lemonade Springs* Wallace Stegner, one of the West's most eloquent writers and defenders, describes this iniquitous state of affairs:

> Deeply lived-in places are exceptions rather than the rule in the West. For one thing, all western places are new; for another many of the people who established them came to pillage, or to work for pillagers, rather than to settle for life. When the pillaging was done or the dream exploded, they moved on, to be replaced in the next boom by others just as hopeful and just as footloose. Successive waves have kept western towns alive but prevented them from deepening the quality of their life, and with every wave the land is poorer.

I believed that John McCain was bought and paid for by the pillagers and promoters. To this day he has never even lived in the West. How could he have any sense of it at all from his vantage point in Washington, other than what the lobbyists for these people tell him?

Nineteen

Southern accent, white hair, and all, on September 8, 1992, I won the Democratic primary fifty-seven to forty-three, sweeping every county by 10 percent or more. Proclaiming it a surprising upset and noting the size of my victory—it had been a long time since anyone had won every county—most of the press, citing conventional wisdom, attributed my victory to my gender, though astute political analysis came to a far different conclusion

Most shocked, apparently, was my opponent, who never knew what hit him. I don't think it had ever entered his head that there was the remotest possibility that he could ever be beaten by a woman, least of all by me. In statements they made about me to the press after I won, and even during the general election, he and his supporters revealed themselves to be poor losers. A lot of soldiers have lost a battle and not handed in their swords.

After feeling for the past five months like Sisyphus pushing the boulder up the hill, it's hard to describe my feelings on that sweet night of triumph surrounded by a euphoric multitude. As someone who, putting it mildly, shows my emotions, on that evening I recall being filled with a great sense of serenity, as though I were removed from the scene, an onlooker. In the midst of the tumult of TV lights and cameras and press photographers and microphones, I do remember a fleeting moment with Mark McKinnon, who had flown in from Austin for election night with his wife, Annie. Unobtrusive observer of the scene, he casually drifted up to me and whispered in my ear, "Darlin', winning so becomes you!" And the next day, an old friend, a Republican who, along with his wife, a volunteer, had been at my headquarters the night before, called to tell me, "Claire, you were like a goddess!"

Is this heady or what?

There was only one jarring note on that remarkable evening. As my supporters congregated around the TV sets to savor the results, even before my victory was announced at the top of the hour, they were treated to McCain's first campaign commercial: McCain and his pretty young wife surrounded by all their little children—"Senator as Family Man"—the first shot across the bow of the seven-week TV blitz of his four-million-dollar campaign, though it wouldn't be until after the election that the voters would find out what a great family man he really was.

Intuitively, I always felt the Force was with me, and was the last to be surprised by my victory. But I was taken aback by a curious phenomenon that comes into play when you win—something I was not prepared for. Although I won the election, I was still the same person I was before the ballots were counted. But from the instant I was proclaimed the winner, a transformation almost palpable occurred in *those around me*. I was perceived differently, and treated differently as well.

The transformation from underdog outsider to "winner" brought a new deference. Certainly from the press, whether friendly or hostile, there was a new regard. Where before I had been largely ignored, they now hung on my every word before distorting them. Success has its own aura, as superficial as its shallow definition. It was quite unnerving, and I never got used to it.

Which was just as well.

∾

Two days after winning the primary the polls in the Phoenix newspapers showed me only ten points behind McCain: forty-four to thirty-four. Impeached governor Evan Mecham was getting into the race, and the momentum was with me. Fired up with the prospects of victory, prospector in search of El Dorado, I departed for Washington to raise the unbelievable sum of $850,000 in the next few weeks, and O'Hara was displeased when I was quoted in the newspaper as saying something to the effect that I was on my way to "grovel."

Now, depressed and disenchanted, just a week after the jubilation of victory I was on my way home to report that I had struck only fool's gold. That there would be no money coming out of Washington for my campaign.

Jeanne Clark, the political consultant who had helped me in June, accompanied me on this round as well. Smart as the dickens, she is wise in the ways of the Beltway without being *of* the Beltway, a distinction that's hard to explain. She is the compleat feminist, differentiating her from the organizational feminists; funny but deadly serious, wholly ethical and a wonderful writer, she has remained a good friend.

Though most Americans never have any reason or occasion to master the arcane and mysterious folkways of life inside the Beltway, it is an ignorance that is, in reality, deeply unhealthy for our country, part of the Beltway mystique, the better to demonstrate insidership. So I'll try to keep from getting too bogged down with jargon and acronyms.

Jeanne had set up appointments for me with the DSCC; all of the women's groups (except Emily's List), and some more of the progressive PACs. And, because political protocol apparently demanded that the senior Democratic official from Arizona serve as my shepherd, the most important appointment I had was with Dennis, who could turn on the money tap. And although I hadn't talked to him since I won the primary, I assumed that my appointment meant that Dennis was keeping his word to support me if I won.

His office had set up private meetings for me with other Democratic senators, some of the same names Dennis had hit up earlier in the primary for my opponent, engaging in the common practice of reciprocal fundraising, when one senator helps to raise money for another senator, and then the favor is returned. When this technique is employed in the incumbent senators' home states it amounts to the same thing as trading contributor lists.

With the distinction of sitting on more Senate committees than any other senator, Dennis was invested with immense power in the firmament of the Senate. These committee memberships and his seniority—and by extension all of the special interests in whose pies these committees had their fingers—formed the core of his prodigious fundraising prowess.

My first meeting was an issues briefing with Dennis's legislative director and her staff, each with her or his own area of expertise. Most of the family names of the staff were familiar, children of Arizonans, some prominent, both Republican and Democrat. Of course! Every senator's office must be this way. When I compared my minuscule campaign staff to the battalion arrayed before me, I fought back a rising feeling of panic. An encyclopedia of issues at the snap of the fingers, and this wasn't even the full complement. John McCain had this too.

༄

Greeting us the next day when we returned to meet with Dennis was his chief of staff and long-time aide, Gene Karp. Informing us that the Senate was in session and that Dennis would be along shortly, he ushered us into his office. Genial and low-key, Gene had been with Dennis the whole time he'd been in Washington, and as I subsequently discovered, seemed to sense and anticipate Dennis's every need and interpret his every nuance. They were a good team.

As we amiably chewed the fat Gene off-handedly took a card out of his desk drawer and handed it to me. I assumed it was one of his business cards, but it turned out to be one of those campaign volunteer cards for Dennis with a laundry list of items you check off: Yes, I will host a coffee; yes, I will volunteer at campaign headquarters, etc., with a line at the bottom where you sign your name, signifying that your name may be used publicly in campaign literature.

"Dennis hopes you'll be supporting him in his next election," said Gene, nonchalantly.

"I'll be glad to put up a yard sign," I quipped, handing it back.

With a small laugh Gene just dropped the card back in the drawer. It was all so casual I didn't think anything of it. I just figured it was Gene's way of letting me know for sure that Dennis would be running for a fourth term in 1994, since in his first run for the Senate in 1976 he had pledged to serve only two terms; and because of his obvious vulnerability when he broke the pledge to run a third time, there had been talk that he wouldn't seek a fourth because of his involvement, along with McCain, in the Keating Five scandal.

Part Three - Arizona

And besides, with Dennis not running until 1994, I'd have plenty of time and a lot more money to send a check after my own campaign was over.

When Dennis appeared—the first time we'd seen each other since I'd won the primary—I was reminded that many a person (of a certain age) often remarked on his strong resemblance to Bing Crosby, which can throw you off if you're expecting the bland, easy-going, Crosbyesque movie persona. Never bothering to congratulate me after I won the primary, he now did so, and after I introduced him to Jeanne, wasting no more time with the niceties, he began.

"Let me tell you how this thing is gonna work. At most we'll have only ten or fifteen minutes with each senator. Most of them are on the DSCC, and we want to try to get their help for your race and try to persuade them to go to their friends for money and to back a substantial allocation for your race from the DSCC. You also need to try to get a personal check from each one as well. I'm sure you've already found out that money is extremely tight, especially in Arizona because of the economy. Also, because it's so late, Clinton's campaign has already sucked up most of the money, not just in Arizona but around the country. There's only so much to go around."

The DSCC is a separate entity of the Democratic National Committee (DNC), the top of the Democratic Party organizational pyramid whose purpose is to elect a Democratic president and Democratic candidates for national office. The DSCC was created specifically to elect Democratic senators and serves primarily as a conduit for money to senatorial campaigns.

As a Democratic primary winner, I was immediately entitled to $17,500 from the DSCC, though I have no idea how they came up with that paltry amount. In a senatorial campaign that is but a gnat on an elephant, as Bob Dole liked to say. But for me it was like water in the desert, to pay my overworked and already underpaid staff who had worked as volunteers without pay for the last two weeks of the primary.

Closer to real money, above the $17,500, the DSCC allocates funds to each candidate on the basis, as I recall, of a state's voting-age population. In my case this would be $285,000. This comes from the so-called "soft money" that is poured into both political party organizations, the DNC and its counterpart the Republic National Committee (RNC), by single individuals or even corporations, money that does not have to be reported to the Federal Elections Commission. You don't receive this allocation automatically. You are entitled to this money *if* you are deemed by the DSCC to be worthy and *if* the money's there. If the DSCC detects the scent of a winner, however, no matter how long and how loud they've poormouthed that the well is dry, the funds miraculously appear.

I knew that now with only six weeks left before the election and victory in their grasp, the DNC was putting everything it had into taking back the White House, their first priority. Even so, it was a heady feeling to be taking part in the historical drama being played out.

With my expectations, and along with them my fervor, now diminished, the four of us—Dennis, Gene, Jeanne and I—trooped off at full trot through the halls of the Hart Building, supplicants to those dispensers of largesse, our duly elected senators of the United States of America. The political system at work.

Never very good at being a Southern Belle, at fifty-eight this flaw in my character had become even more pronounced. Being straightforward and forthright, and not a beater about the bush, it has always been difficult for me to "suck up" to people for favors. And I realized that this attitude might not be looked on with favor in a setting where deference and sycophancy were de rigeur. So, a virgin to the Hill, as it were, it was with this self-knowledge that I worked very hard to lower my tolerance threshold, tone down my candor, and brush up on my ingratiation techniques. Though precious little good it did me.

∽

Dennis and I developed a pitch, and though I was amused when he always opened with mention of Henry, I was rather taken aback that he had seized upon the Tailhook radio incident when McCain and I had really gone at it after my press conference, but it was obviously something he set a lot of store by.

His intro went something like this:

I've known Claire's husband for years. He's highly respected in the business community and an old friend of the DeConcini family. As you know I supported her opponent in the primary, but, boy, she really pulled off an impressive victory, and I sure want to do everything now that I can to help her. I wish you could have heard how she held her own with McCain on a radio talk show when he was going after her about her press conference on Tailhook. She's prochoice and she's got a real chance to beat McCain if she can just raise the money for TV, and she sure needs your help.

Then it was my turn.

I won an upset victory in the primary, fifty-seven to forty-three, taking every county, including rural Arizona. I need to get on TV right now, and am asking the DSCC for only $90,000, which translates into less than a minute of TV time in the LA media market. Also to underwrite a poll that the DSCC is dying to have. McCain started his commercials on the night of the primary election and is saturating the airwaves. He's been in office ten years and his approval rating is below 50 percent. We're only ten points apart, forty-four, thirty-four in the latest poll by the Phoenix newspapers. He's not prochoice and that could hurt him with a lot of Republican women. Even though I was outspent by my opponent I won the primary on $80,000 (each time I mentioned this there was a shocked murmur of disbelief). Our impeached former governor, Evan Mecham, is getting into the race and will split the Republican vote. Money goes so much further in Arizona than it does in the big media states, and if I can just have $90,000 now to get my commercials up and keep up my momentum, I have a real chance of winning.

After the pitch, I thought it curious that the question of issues never came up.

∞

The first call was to Senator Cranston, a recipient of $800,000 from Charlie Keating, who went to prison as the savings and loan debacle's chief thief, and with whom McCain frequently cavorted on a private island in the Bahamas. I liked Alan Cranston. I hadn't expected to, but I did. He had an air of wistfulness about him that touched me. Taking his ease in a big old worn leather chair, he was a man who in a few months, not seeking reelection, would be departing this pleasure dome for California, in the end made a scapegoat in the Keating Five affair by his colleagues on the Senate Ethics Committee.

Was he bitter, or did he accept it with equanimity as the rules of the game? I believe at a certain time and place in life one can and does. In the end Senator Cranston would be one of only two of the senators with whom I met who contributed to my campaign. It was not a lot of money in the scheme of things, but it was money he could have taken home to California, and I've often wondered what prompted him to help me.

Because Dennis had another commitment, only Jeanne and Gene were with me when I next called on Senator Bill Bradley of New Jersey, in whose office I encountered for the first time a woman as chief-of-staff. I was immediately drawn to Senator Bradley, who, warm and unpretentious and with a certain irreverence, showed us the view from his office through French doors opening to a small balcony, lovely in the amber light of the September afternoon. Covering one whole wall was a stunning abstract painting that reminded me of Helen Frankenthaler; when I admired it, his comments showed that it was clearly a work of art that gave him great pleasure, revealing another dimension, an awareness of something beyond the business of politics, of someone who values the human spirit, a quality so often lacking in politicians.

Without Dennis I was on my own to speak for myself.

"Senator, the DSCC wants me to do a poll, in the face of an absolute dearth of money. There's already a poll taken in the past week by the largest Arizona newspaper, which supports McCain, showing me only ten points behind. I need money simply to run my campaign and get my commercials up. I can't possibly afford a poll now. It's crazy."

"Conventional wisdom," he said. "A poll is a waste of money." Don't you always love people who agree with you?

For the first time I felt I could speak candidly, which led to a free-wheeling conversation about campaigning. "You know, Senator, I've never debated anybody in my life before. We found a letter from McCain pushed under my headquarters door the day after I won the primary challenging me to several debates, which we accepted immediately. But now he's changed his mind and is evading me because he doesn't want to give me the exposure. I'm not a polished debater, that's for sure. But I'm running on not being slick."

"Don't worry, you can do it. You just have to learn how not to answer the questions and say what you want to say. In my last race my opponent [Christine Whitman, now Governor of New Jersey] was great at it. I'll send you the tapes of those debates so you can see how it's done."

The most astonishing thing was that he actually appeared to be listening to me. There was a difference in the dynamics and spirit here which hadn't occurred before. My suspicion that this might be because Dennis wasn't along was later borne out when Jeanne related that Gene Karp had told her that my meeting with Senator Bradley was a side of him he'd never seen before.

Leaving Senator Bradley's office, I felt for the first time that attention had been paid. Captured by the spell that Bill Bradley had cast, however, I'd forgotten to ask him for a check. But the tapes arrived within days.

∾

Regrouping back at Dennis's office, after Gene Karp was called away Jeanne and I were joined by Dennis. In retrospect I realize that this tactic was well-planned—the old good-cop/bad-cop routine. And Dennis was the bad cop. He was once a prosecutor, and still was. "Claire, Gene gave you a pledge card to sign to support me in my next campaign. He said you didn't sign it, and I'm asking for your commitment in 1994."

This was the first mention that there might be any kind of a quid pro quo for his help. It had never occurred to me, so I was caught off balance by this demand so late in the game, and, naturally, reacted instinctively.

"That's two years away, Dennis, and two years is a lifetime in politics. I can't make that commitment to you today. Do you think two years ago that in my wildest dreams I ever thought I'd be in Washington, D.C., running for the United States Senate? I have no idea who'll be running in '94. You aren't prochoice and you voted for Clarence Thomas. And if a woman runs, I'll support her."

"I talked to Hattie Babbitt and she says she won't be running. I've supported WIC, family leave, Head Start. I've been a real friend to women and women's issues. I just held a fundraiser for Barbara Mikulski yesterday. I'm sick and tired of single issue politics."

"Prochoice isn't a 'single' issue. It is an overarching issue. Being against the right to control my own body is denying my rights, because I'm a woman, that it doesn't deny you because you're a man. Don't you understand that?"

Dennis was deadly serious when he said, "If you won't sign this pledge to support me, I'm not going to fall on my sword to raise money for you. I raised hundreds of thousands of dollars for Richard Kimball (the Arizona Democratic nominee for the U.S. Senate) in '86, here in Washington and from my friends in the Jewish community, the Catholic community, the Mormon community. I broke my back for him. But if it's not good for me, then I'm not going to break my back again for you."

"Do you mean to say that defeating John McCain is not good for you, for the state of Arizona, for the country? I thought that was the whole idea. That's why I'm running. Are you saying that you aren't willing to help me beat John McCain if I don't sign your pledge?"

"That's exactly what I'm saying. If it doesn't help me, then it's not worth my time to help you."

"Well, Dennis, you can't possibly know how deeply disappointed in you I am to hear that. I can't believe it. The best I can do is to make a commitment to stay neutral in the primary, not to support anybody else, and support you in the general."

"That won't be good enough."

"Then I'll have to think about it and let you know."

When Jeanne and I left Dennis's office and walked out into the wide hallway of the Hart Building, Jeanne stopped and turned to me, serious, but with a twinkle in her eye. "If we were anywhere else, I'd get down on my knees and kiss your hand! I'm so proud of you."

"For what?"

"For sticking by your principles. Claire, you just said 'no' to a United States senator. Anybody else would have signed on the dotted line without batting an eye."

"I just couldn't do it. I'm running because I want to change things. If I signed that pledge, my campaign would be a lie. I'd be just like everybody else. Doing anything to get elected."

"I'm just telling you, nobody else would have had the guts to do what you just did."

I didn't have time to dwell on the gravity of what had just taken place. In a campaign you can only concentrate on the moment and, as always, we were pressed for time. In fifteen minutes I was due at a reception for Henry Cisneros, the former mayor of San Antonio, and the Southwest Voter Registration people.

∾

The next day we were back in Dennis's office with appointments to meet with Senators Bob Kerrey, Jay Rockefeller, Ted Kennedy, and Richard Bryan. Business as usual, as though the conversation between Dennis and me hadn't transpired.

It was with enormous curiosity, almost a sense of occasion, that I anticipated my meeting with Senator Kennedy. His staff is reputed to be incomparable, the best on the hill. They had demonstrated that to me by being the first to send me congratulations after I won the primary. And they did not disappoint this day. It was just after lunch and the senator was due back momentarily. His aide chatted with us cordially until he heard the return of the senator, whom he went to fetch. (Aides have built-in senator-detecting radar.)

It is one of his inescapable burdens that being Senator Kennedy is being different from every other senator. I was greatly affected by a profound sense of world-weariness. Sitting directly across from him, I was transfixed by the size of his leonine head—even his *face* was big—and by his mane of silver hair. As testimony to fine staff work, after the obligatory pleasantries, Senator Kennedy recounted a trip to Arizona back in 1968. He was campaigning for Bobby, flying in a puddle-jumper in and out of five or six obscure Arizona communities, which he named precisely, with appropriate anecdotes, as though it were yesterday. Now this was impressive.

Dennis and I reprised our routine. He was neither more nor less spirited than the day before, in spite of our heated exchange. When we finished, I was elated to hear Senator Kennedy say, "I'm glad we were able to have this visit today. Tomorrow we're going to be drawing up the final list of recipients from our PAC. I think we'll be able to include you."

At last, a glimmer of hope!

Besides Senator Cranston, Senator Kennedy would be the only other senator to contribute to my campaign. And that was because of the incredible Dolores Huerta, a buzzsaw of energy who simply one day appeared in town and began to organize and rally the troops for my campaign, taking to the airwaves of the Hispanic radio stations. Dolores, a colleague of the late labor leader César Chávez, was standing with Bobby Kennedy when he was shot at the Ambassador Hotel, and maintains strong ties with the Kennedy family, though she never mentioned it to me during her visits to Arizona. She has an astonishing national network, and I'm sure she helped me in ways I'll never know. She was one of many people involved in my campaign who worked tirelessly and without fanfare, with the unlikely prospect of ever receiving anything in return. Crossing paths with people like Dolores is what makes it all worth it.

I know one thing: We would never have gotten Senator Kennedy's check without Delores. "We sure could use ten more Doloreses," O'Hara keened.

In the reception room of Senator Rockefeller's enclave we were confronted by a pack of the pin-striped, thousand-dollar-alligator-shoes crowd Ross Perot rails against: lobbyists on the prowl.

I had met the senator at the Democratic convention in New York in July at a fund-raising reception and brunch at his family's estate in Pocantico Hills in Westchester County, near the town where I had lived. Previously, the closest I had ever been to the Rockefeller compound was the gatehouse, when the guard called to tell me he had collared our family dog, Chumley, an English setter who knew no bounds when he was on the trail of a female dog in heat.

He was a cordial host then and a cordial host now. He is a very genuine man and I liked him.

"It's nice to see you again, Senator. I want to remind you of my promise to you when we met in New York at the convention, that I'd be knocking on your door for your help after I won the primary, and here I am!"

"Indeed I do remember, and congratulations! I like that can-do spirit. I wrote a check to Patty Murray in the primary on the spot because she had the same attitude."

Now I've never had a hard time asking for money. Although it may be difficult for many others, it's usually easy for me, though tougher when you're asking for yourself rather than a cause. However, I have to admit it just felt tacky to have to ask a Rockefeller to write a check. Isn't that what every other person in the world wants from him? Isn't that something he always has to live with, that people are after his money? I felt it a superfluous thing to have to do. But perhaps by not saying, "Then write me a check too," I failed his test. Test or not, I didn't get it.

Reiterating what I'd heard so many times, that most people were tapped out because it was so late, he added they were all working hard to campaign and raise money to help Terry Sanford (one of their own) who was having a tough Senate reelection race in North Carolina (which he eventually lost). That with the New York primary just a week away, they still needed money there, and in California as well—the two insatiable black holes of campaign contributions. We left with his words of kind encouragement and again the promise that he would "see what he could do."

With that and a dollar I could buy jack squat.

∾

I had met Senator Bob Kerrey several years before when I'd introduced him as our speaker at the Democratic luncheon club in Phoenix. When the president of the club called to ask me to introduce Governor Kerrey I thought he meant Governor Carey of New York. I'd never heard of Bob Kerrey. And the one-page bio I received from his office didn't tell me who Bob Kerrey was, revealing no essence of the man at all except for the fact that he'd received the Medal of Honor. Startled to see that he had a degree in *pharmacy*, of all things, I made haste to the library to do some research, and was naturally fascinated when the details of his life unfolded. Here was an uncommon man, and if his bio was any reflection, a modest man, unheard-of in a politician. Curious, I was looking forward to meeting him.

Over lunch on the dais before his speech, I was struck by the fact that he didn't appear to take himself too seriously, and by his openness. When I told him that in my introduction I wasn't going to mention Debra Winger, with whom he'd had a well-publicized relationship, he responded with a delighted, "Thank you, thank you!"

He did not disappoint. He clearly had charisma and delivered a good though not great speech. I didn't know then that he was considering a run for the Senate, but the locals were impressed and cheered that clearly here was a Democrat destined for greater things.

When he returned to Phoenix as the featured attraction at a fundraiser for the Democratic party in the spring of 1988 (Dennis's handiwork I was to learn later), I ran into him at the reception, where we chatted and he thanked me again for my introduction the year before.

I was pleased and not surprised when I saw that he'd won his election to the Senate that November. And then when he announced that he was going to run for president in 1992, I wondered what kind of campaign his would be. Knowing just the little about him that I did, I felt that it would be hard for him to get up like John McCain and brag about being a hero: about having his leg shot off in Vietnam and his Medal of Honor, and speaking publicly about the long ordeal of his recovery. It wasn't him. And I just knew that if his campaign consultants tried to make him do it, it wasn't going to work. And it didn't.

During the primary in the spring of 1992 he was in Phoenix for a fundraiser that Dennis was hosting for him in his campaign for president, and, as it transpired, it was on that visit that he also withdrew from the race. Once again he addressed the Democratic luncheon club, and in the crush of the phalanx that surrounds a presidential candidate, I was able to push through to speak to him only momentarily, on the run as he was leaving. I reminded him who I was and told him that I was running for the Senate and I needed his help.

He was surprised. "Are you serious? I thought there was some general in the race." (Obviously, Dennis hadn't told him.)

"That's right. But so am I!"

"Well, I didn't know that. Good luck to you. I wish I could help you, but you realize I can't get involved in a primary race. If you win, I'll see what I can do."

"I'm really going to count on you when I do."

He laughed (as they all did), "If you win, you can." And naturally I believed him.

Our path next crossed at Tavern on the Green in New York during the Democratic convention on our way into a party hosted by Paine Webber, the investment bankers. He was waiting for someone, and he was all alone, the wall of protectors and hangers-on gone, and I stopped to say hello. We had a good-humored exchange and, Johnny-One-Note, I reminded him I'd be coming to see him after I won the primary. Again, he laughed and wished me luck.

There's something I need to emphasize here. Encounters, however brief and obscure with people famous and not-so-famous, celebrities major and minor, even people just perceived to have some kind of recognition only slightly out of the ordinary, are frequently remembered as points of light by those whose paths they cross. I know this because it has even happened to me, that somebody who is the most total stranger will recall in great detail the time and place and conversation with me that I have not the faintest recollection of. So I was clear-eyed in approaching my meeting with Senator Kerrey.

Even so, on a more personal level than that of the others, I clung to the slim reed of hope that I could elicit his help. Believing that he was different, someone who was fighting the status quo, he would recognize that we had that in common and want to help me. If I could get him to Phoenix for a fundraiser, besides the money that it would raise, a senator who was a Vietnam veteran and a Medal of Honor winner would lend great credibility to my campaign against another Vietnam veteran.

I was placing a lot of chips on Kerrey's number.

The Senate was having a roll call, so we perused the watercolors by Nebraska artists on the walls of his office, a nice touch. And an offbeat note, what looked to be a well-read copy of the old children's book, *The Bobsey Twins,* lay on the table by the sofa next to where I sat. Seeing the book reminded me that in the presidential primary I'd read that when asked to name his favorite book, Kerrey had mentioned *The Movie Goer,* by the Southern writer Walker Percy, one of my favorite books as well as one of my favorite writers, which is why I remember it. ("To become aware of the possibility of the search is to be onto something. Not to be onto something is to be in despair.") Could a fellow Walker Percy-ite let me down?

The aide's senator-detecting radar was activated. She left and we heard footsteps approaching from the outer hallway, beyond the office. Amazing. This was what I call the Caesar, or deity, effect the senators have on everybody, when everyone in his wake (this was when there were only two women senators) snaps to attention. The only thing missing is a horse and chariot. You almost expect to hear, "Hail, Caesar!"

He and Dennis arrived together. Naturally, Senator Kerrey had changed in four years. He was older, more subdued, different. Had his campaign for president changed his sense of himself as well? Was he now just like the others? After congratulations on my victory and some small talk, I gave him an abbreviated rundown on my campaign and finished by saying, "I've been counting on you to come to Phoenix to do a fundraiser for me. I hope you won't let me down."

No one had bothered to tell me about what I heard next, but it buoyed my spirits considerably when he said, "Dennis has already asked me to come to Phoenix for a fundraiser for the Democrats sometime in October, but I'm still trying to get it on my calendar."

"Wonderful! If you come for them, you could work in an hour's reception for me before a dinner. Even a half hour will do. I really need your help."

"I'll see if I can work it out."

With my prospect of hope fulfilled I thanked him warmly, and as we left his office I was, as my children used to say, "psyched."

Within the week, however, my great esteem for this man would be displaced by stinging disillusionment, when this once uncommon man turned out to be just another common politician after all.

Part Three - Arizona

Back in the summer at the Democratic convention in New York all of the senatorial candidates were assigned an incumbent senator as a mentor to serve as her contact within the Democratic network of movers and shakers. I had been assigned Senator Richard Bryan, the former governor of Nevada. Senator Bryan was a pleasant enough fellow, and was billed as a good fundraiser, but they couldn't have chosen anyone with whom I had less rapport. I'm sure he felt the same about me; each knows when there's no chemistry.

I approached the meeting with Senator Bryan with little enthusiasm and even less confidence that he would have any interest in my campaign. As we entered his office, a buzzer alerted the senators for a roll call, giving Dennis and me just five minutes to do our shtick in fast-forward, and Senator Bryan enough time to also cop the tapped-out plea. But in an effort not to appear too impolitic, he volunteered: "There just might be an outside chance of some Las Vegas money being available at this late date."

Hearing those words, instead of raising my spirits, they plunged like a stone. I realized I was here asking for money, and getting desperate, but if there's one place I have to draw the line, it's with gambling. I'll never be convinced you can have legalized "gaming" without organized crime pulling the strings somewhere behind the scenes. The government has no business in the business of gambling. I believe it's a cop-out when our elected officials, without the backbone to raise taxes, turn to the lottery as a quick-fix gimmick for providing necessary government services. In the long term, I believe the presence of legalized gambling, including the lottery, corrupts and coarsens the spirit of the community.

With America's Indians it's a different story. Congress has failed to act to provide them with an adequate quality of life. If they want gambling on their reservations, which are their sovereign nations, that's their business and that's the law. Though I believe that with assistance a better long-term solution for economic development could be found.

So I heard myself saying, "I really appreciate that, Senator, and I hope you don't think I'm ungrateful, but that would be impossible. I just couldn't take their money. I could never support the interests of casinos."

There was an uncomfortable hush in the room. Everyone but Jeanne, who was used to me by now, was incredulous. Suddenly Dennis burst out laughing, leaped to his feet, and said, "Well, Dick, that's that. She doesn't want your money. Let's go vote!"

Politician that he was, and recouping with a true politician's spin, Senator Bryan responded, "You know, Claire, come to think of it, that is the best reason in the world for the Las Vegas folks to support you. They would be the last people in the world to want legalized gambling in Arizona." And out the door they went.

Leaving Bryan's office, the three of us—Jeanne, Gene, and I—walked for what was to be my last time through those corridors. On the way to the elevator at the end of that long, long day I told them I hoped they understood how I felt about the gambling money. They both laughed.

"I want to thank you, Claire, for two of the most unforgettable days I've ever spent in all the years I've been in Washington. It has been a quite an experience," Gene said, leading us into the elevator.

"So what have you decided to do about helping Dennis?" he asked as he was walking us out to the street. That this pleasant little stroll was part of the plan was transparent.

"I've been thinking about that a lot, Gene. Why can't Dennis have some sort of an epiphany and see the light on abortion? There are plenty of Catholic politicians who are prochoice. Mario Cuomo, Ted Kennedy, Geraldine Ferraro. Dennis has always bent with the political wind. Why can't he do it now?"

"Probably 95 percent of Dennis's staff is prochoice. But Dennis really truly believes abortion is wrong. It's just something he's not going to bend on."

"It's not a question of whether it's right or wrong. It's respecting my right to make that decision about my own body, my right to privacy. He's imposing his ideas of right and wrong on what all women can do with their bodies. Why can't he see that? Why can't he take the position that he believes it's wrong, but that it's unconstitutional to keep women from making this most personal decision for themselves? That's what Cuomo says. Dennis has never stood on principle before. Why is he taking a stand on this?"

Part Three - Arizona

"All I can say is that this is one time he's not going to change his mind."

"Then I'll have to think about it and let you know. The election is only six weeks away. I was really counting on Dennis's help, and without it I'll never be able to raise the money I need."

☙

Jeanne and I walked from the Hill to Union Station. The burnished russet colors of the flowers of early autumn, the pungent fragrance of fall in the long shadows of the late afternoon light as we walked under the majestic trees, just beginning to turn, heightened the perennial ache of melancholy that comes with the end of summer, the promise of winter and another year ending. The reality of not having Dennis's help overcame the exhilaration of the day, and the melancholy of the season began to afflict me as well.

We arrived at the station and had an early supper at the American Café. The same place I'd had lunch on my first trip to Washington to see the women's groups, not even a year ago, when I was still in swaddling clothes. Was it possible? How far I'd come since then! Jeanne and I rehashed the last two days as we comforted body and soul with a "mess of greens," mashed potatoes, and meatloaf.

Dennis held all the cards. Most people would tell me I was naive, a fool not to sign the pledge. That was the way the game was played. If I was going to win, I had to play by their rules. What did I expect? And playing by their rules, I could sign Dennis's pledge and later tell him I was sorry, I'd changed my mind since he hadn't changed his position on abortion; and playing by the rules, he'd understand. But these were the rules I was trying to change. And what did this say about Dennis's view of my chances of winning? Did he believe with his help I could win?

I didn't believe I was being intransigent when I made a commitment to Dennis to stay neutral in the primary and to get out and work hard for him in the general election against his Republican opponent. He'd helped my opponent raise money in the primary. Had Spangrud signed a pledge? Was that the reason for Spangrud's ridiculous campaign against the Keating Four instead of the Keating Five, presumably excluding Dennis, not McCain? This was nothing but extortion, coercion, blackmail, pure and simple.

And why me? Was he so desperate because of his treatment of Anita Hill and of his vote to confirm Clarence Thomas that he now needed the support of all the women he could get? Dennis's all-or-nothing strategy was so flawed, and this loyalty oath business was just such a ham-handed, dumb thing for him to do.

After saying good-bye to Jeanne I took the Metro to go to my hotel. As I came up on the escalator, a cab was letting someone out. It was still early and the evening was crisp and lovely, and on the spur of the moment I jumped in.

"Lincoln Memorial, please," I said.

I have absolutely no explanation for what prompted me to do this; it was completely spontaneous. Maybe it was because I had nowhere else to turn. It may have even sprung from a long-buried memory of Texas Representative Barbara Jordan going to the Lincoln Memorial the night before she had to vote on the impeachment of Richard Nixon. I can't say. But off I went.

I was troubled deeply by the stand-off with Dennis and what I'd seen these last few days in Washington, by the world according to the Beltway, totally cut off from America outside. I was running to change this. But the experience of the last two days only reinforced the old commandment that thou must go along to get along or not play at all. For the first time I had been taken seriously, yet I was still on the outside, and my intentions were being thwarted by the system. It reminded me of the mime encountering the invisible wall.

I had come to realize that the metamorphosis that takes place in a person after election to the Senate is not necessarily caused by a particular senator but by those who surround him. On a much smaller scale, just as I had been treated with a new deference after I won the primary, I could imagine that attitude expanded exponentially if I were to become a full-blown senator. Senators are deified, and they accept it. Why not? On the whole, these are not bad men. We wrap them in the mantle of Olympus, and they grow to like the cut and feel of it. We forget they're just like us. And so do they.

Nowhere is it written "You have to have at least a quarter of a million dollars just to think about it," as Dennis had said. How far we've come from the three bare-bones requirements to be a senator.

The taxi let me out, and I walked past the Vietnam Memorial, people there as always. I usually stop, but coming here to contemplate I couldn't allow the intrusion of any more anguish. I needed the serenity and awe and sense of history and continuity that emanates from the Lincoln Memorial, and as I walked up the stairs, I was moved once again by its brooding majesty.

I was drawn here by the need to be reminded. Reminded of why I was running for the United States Senate. I had lost my way, lost my perspective, as I'd gone through the grinder of the last two days. A campaign requires you to armor yourself to deflect the viciousness and meanness and pettiness of the process. But once you've been elected, there's no way you can let down your guard, there are so many people wanting a piece of you. You have to become inured. I wondered if any senators ever came here, to remind themselves, if they even realized that they needed reminding:

> *That this nation, under God,*
> *shall have a new birth of freedom;*
> *that government of the people, by the people, for the people*
> *shall not perish from the Earth.*

The power and simplicity of the familiar words cast their spell. This was why I needed to make the pilgrimage. And it was then that I got the notion of running for only one term in my head. That if you don't care about being reelected, you can serve and make decisions unencumbered. It would be the only way you could do that. It would take someone who wanted to *do* something, not to *be* something, as I would later say.

No more begging. No more whoring.

Twenty

A week later, the day before I was to leave once again for Washington, we had received over the transom a newsletter sent out by a group of hard-core Republicans. Up until that time in the campaign I hadn't read anything so mean, and couldn't believe that its members wouldn't be embarrassed to belong to a group that peddled such garbage.

Page one was devoted to a crude parody of Shakespeare's *Taming of the Shrew*—a dialogue between Petrucio and Katharina as a thinly veiled put-down of a female political columnist by a male political columnist in each of the Phoenix newspapers. Petrucio was the hero, an obvious reference to my unremitting antagonist in the *Phoenix Gazette*.

But I couldn't figure out why they attacked the 34-year-old Katharina, a registered Republican whom I called the *Reader's Digest* of political columnists because she'd be hard-put to turn out a column if she couldn't quote the national news magazines and those two other eminent sources, Jay Leno and David Letterman. She'd never written one word about me that could be construed as anything but negative, once even describing me as having interests that "run a mile wide, but unfortunately a half-inch deep." This from a "journalist" who throughout the entire campaign never interviewed me, never attended a press conference, or even talked to me on the telephone, who only parroted what the other local reporters wrote about me.

But the centerpiece of the newsletter was a long malicious depiction of the Democratic primary election as a Hobson's choice

Part Three - Arizona

between boring and stupid, and the Democrats had chosen stupid. Pushing it even further, I was characterized as, "Here, I've got breasts, vote for me."

When he got the "editor" on the phone, O'Hara began so amiably you'd have thought he was chatting over a beer (an exception to O'Hara's customary demeanor in such situations). Then, "I want to talk to you about the Democrats having a Hobson's choice, and this line about the breasts, which crosses the line and really stinks," O'Hara said, and as the editor responded, obviously embarrassed that we'd seen his rag, O'Hara twisted a favored lock of hair as was his habit when listening intently on the phone. After several minutes O'Hara said, "We consider this piece malicious, intended to embarrass Claire and impugn her character in a way that is tantamount to making jokes about Lee Atwater having cancer," and then telling him to put us on his mailing list, he hung up.

When I asked O'Hara about this after the campaign in a 1993 interview in San Francisco, he reminded me that people who send out newsletters like that are serious political partisans on the level of Rush Limbaugh. "But on a deeper level," he said, "I know it hurts to read that kind of thing and it's hard not to take it personally. Especially when the whole point of your campaign was to emerge beyond the box and the perspective that the male-dominated political world creates for you—that this is who you are and this is what you are. Time and time again in the primary Truman referred to 'Mrs. Henry Sargent,' et cetera. There was a constant reminder that somehow you haven't earned the right to run, even from our own Democrats, who felt that Spangrud was preferable—why, I don't know—because he sort of fit the bill better than someone who has an enviable record of achievement in Arizona.

"And I've come to realize that that kind of box or glass ceiling or whatever it is that you were fighting out of—that I have been a party to—is hard for me to appreciate at times when I'm not reading that kind of stuff. Because you really couldn't say that kind of thing about a man in the flippant sort of way that he did and get away with it.

"Other than just sort of taking the guy as kind of nasty and petty and meaningless, the only other way is just to slug the guy.

What do you say to somebody like that?"

See why there were times when I loved this boy?

～

The flight to Washington the next day was one of those rare times in a campaign, a chance to be alone, to reflect. And that tabloid stuck in my mind. The meanness of it, the tone.

"I've got breasts, vote for me" must have been picked up from *Newsweek* when a former Pennsylvania Democratic Party Chair commented on women candidates, alluding to Lynn Yeakel, his state's Democratic nominee for the U.S. Senate running against the incumbent Republican, Arlen Specter.

Would it never end? Can't you imagine the firestorm if a woman ever said of a male candidate, "I've got a penis, vote for me?" The best way to respond to this, I decided, was with humor.

I was on my way to two fundraisers: the Democratic Senate Majority dinner and the DSCC Women's Council luncheon. Each of the women senate candidates was to speak at the luncheon. It would be the perfect place for some levity.

When O'Hara and Jeanne Clark met me for breakfast the next morning, I told Jeanne about the tabloid and asked if we couldn't inject a humorous reference to it into what I was going to say at the luncheon. She loved the idea and came up with what is now known simply as The Joke.

Hearing the news that the luncheon was oversold and the hottest ticket in town, and that the DSCC was even deigning to provide me with a "candidate escort," I was a nervous wreck. This was going to be a Big Deal.

At noon, as Jeanne and O'Hara and I approached the Hilton, I immediately felt the wave of energy that pulsates when women gather, reminding me of the United Nations Women's Conference in Nairobi. I hadn't seen so many women spilling from one place since. Suddenly Linda Bird Johnson Robb appeared and took my arm to guide me into the throng to introduce me. I had met her at the Democratic convention in New York where she'd been gracious and kind to me on several occasions. Her husband, Senator Chuck Robb of Virginia, was chairman of the DSCC, and as is the custom of every properly brought up Southern lady, she had the good manners to quietly take charge of those of us who were candidates, taking care to introduce us and to see that we were treated cordially. She is a fine, bright, thoughtful woman whom I admire and to whom I'll always be grateful. Now *she* would make a *great* senator!

This was the drill: Senator Mikulski was the emcee. First, the candidate's TV ad would run. When that was over, Mikulski would introduce the candidate, who would then have one minute to speak. Then the candidate would leave the stage on the opposite side. Finally, after the last one had finished, we'd all gather back on stage for the finale.

No one had told me it was going to be the Academy Awards. But I was just so thankful I had an ad to show! I wondered if I were the only one who had only one, and I was so proud that my team had taken care of all these details, getting the tape here and all, and I hadn't even known about it.

Waiting in a private room where we could relax and have a bite to eat, accompanied by my superfluous escort as well as Jeanne and O'Hara, we heard there were twelve hundred people at the luncheon. This was my first time to ever speak before so many, and I really couldn't believe I was getting ready to go out there and do it. Jeanne and O'Hara told me no matter what I said, or how I did, this was my crowd, that they would be for me as no others would. I wrote a few lines of Jeanne's speech on two or three three-by-five cards, getting it down to the bare bones, and went off by myself to go over them.

In my two-year-old Ralph Lauren navy blue pin-striped suit and open-collared white shirt, a white silk camellia pinned to my lapel, I felt comfortable and looked sharp. I had practiced what I was going to say, and was pleased and secure with it written on the cards. In the beginning of my campaign, I said that I was terrified, but not afraid; and now, even though all kinds of flying things were turning somersaults in my stomach, I don't know what had come over me, but I realized that I was no longer terrified.

Since Gerry Ferraro had lost her primary race in New York, and Barbara Boxer wasn't able to make it from California, as Mikulski stirred up the troops with one of her trademark stemwinders there were only eight of us waiting in the wings, a good-lookin' gutsy group of gals!

As each woman was called forth we heard a mighty roll of thunder as hosannas rose from the crowd. I think I was fourth or fifth in the lineup, giving me a chance to watch the commercials, each one spunky and full of spirit.

Suddenly I heard my name, and there was my ad on the enormous screen. I froze, and thought my heart would surely cease to beat. It was so short. Was that thirty seconds? Then I heard Mikulski call my name. Off I strode out into the darkness, an astronaut propelling into space, into the light of the universe.

Cheers from the crowd as I crossed the stage to the podium. I think I remember a small light on it, which I had to move in close to, to be able to see my notes.

Nothing but darkness out there. And now an electric silence, waiting for me to begin.

It was simple and straightforward:

> I'm Claire Sargent, the stealth candidate!
>> Audience: *Yea!*
> I just won the primary 57 to 43 . . .
>> Audience: *Yea!*
> . . . against an Air Force lieutenant general!
>> Audience: *Yea!*
> Now I'm running against one of the Keating Five,
> John McCain!
>> Audience: *Yea!*
> Some of us have been accused of running because we're women!
>> Audience: *YEA!*
> In fact, some say we campaign on, "I've got breasts, vote for me!"
>> Audience: *YEA! YEA!*
> Well, I say it's about time we voted for senators with breasts . . .
>> Audience: *YEA! YEA! YEA!*
> You haven't even heard the punch line . . .
>> Audience: *YEA! YEA! YEA! YEA!*
> After all, we've been voting for boobs long enough!
>> Audience: *TOTAL BEDLAM!*

I couldn't believe my ears and eyes. It seemed the whole ballroom was on its feet yelling and screaming. It was pandemonium. At that moment I understood why people become performers. Adulation must be the highest high. And I understood something else. I had been good.

When I got to my seat I found myself next to Lynn Yeakel, the brunt of the original "breasts" comment, who, in stitches, told me, "That was great! I wish I'd said that!"

Then we were all there together on the stage and it was over. All of a sudden people started streaming forward to reach up and shake my hand, to speak to me, to thank me, Billy Graham at one of his crusades. Then there were Jeanne and O'Hara, twin grins below me.

Rescuing me, they threaded me through the crowd toward the wall of TV cameras and reporters for interviews. O'Hara, who had been standing at the back by the TV cameras, said that when I was on the cameraman was laughing so hard his camera was shaking, and he told O'Hara he couldn't remember when he'd had such fun at a political gig.

And that night, when we arrived for the reception before the Big Dinner, I experienced what I'm sure will be the closest I'll ever come to my fifteen minutes of celebrity. Senators, wives of senators, perfect strangers came up to me and wanted me to tell them the joke. It was incredible. The superficiality of it all. I wanted to say, Wait a minute! I've been trying to talk about cutting Star Wars, health care, the influence of special interests, and nobody pays any attention! Now everybody wants to hear a joke! It's nuts!

But I kept smiling through each retelling, realizing I just might as well accept it, and went on to meet practically everyone at the party.

The Democratic Senate Majority Dinner was the biggest fundraiser of the year for the DSCC, attracting one thousand of the devout, at least $1,000 a pop, though it could have been even more. Fifteen Democratic senators were up for reelection. There were thirty Democratic challengers.

O'Hara and Jeanne and I were assigned to a table in Siberia, as far away as you could be and still be on the floor. If we'd ever had any doubts about where we stood with the DSCC, nothing could have been a more obvious symbol of our status as outcasts. At an event whose sole purpose was to raise money by mixing with people who had it, our tablemates were all from the staff of the DSCC, except for a lovely man from Labor, with his wife, whom I'd met when I came to D.C. during the primary. During the dinner he most graciously and generously took me by the elbow and walked me all the way across the floor, threading through the sea of tables, up to a table square dab in the middle of the room in front of the band, so that I could speak to the most influential woman at the American Federation of State, County and Municipal Employees to ask for her help. (O'Hara had found out that morning that McCain was faxing labor leaders in Washington saying that I wasn't supporting them.)

On the way to the AFSCME table I chanced to spot the table where Bob Kerrey was sitting. The week before when I'd been with Dennis in Senator Rockefeller's office, when Dennis had said that he hadn't planned to come to the dinner, Rockefeller gently chided him, reminding him that he should be there to introduce me around. Since Dennis hadn't wanted to come anyway, with the standoff in our relationship I'm sure he couldn't think of a good reason to be there. So after I left the AFSCME table, I took it upon myself to corner Bob Kerrey to find out if his trip to Phoenix had been nailed down.

When I arrived at Kerrey's table I unexpectedly discovered that the seat next to him was vacant, and sat myself down. He was cordial, and when I asked if he were going to be able to work out a trip to Phoenix to help me, in the most congenial way, as though he were making a casual observation about the wine, he said, "You're not supporting Dennis. I can't help you."

When a cartoon character is knocked for a loop he has a halo of stars around his head. When I heard Bob's words I felt like I'd been slammed by a two-by-four, and I saw stars.

When I could speak I said, "You can't help me? Because I'm not supporting Dennis?"

"No."

"But Dennis isn't prochoice. I told him I'd support him in the general."

Part Three - Arizona

"I'm sorry, but if you can't support Dennis, I can't support you."

"You'll never know what this has done to me, Bob. I'm simply devastated. I thought that you weren't like everybody else. That you were different."

The occupant of the seat I was usurping had returned and was hovering over us, so I got up to leave. He owned one of the big rental car companies, Bob said, when he introduced us. I smiled. How nice.

In shock from the crushing assault on my spirit, I was suddenly drained, exhausted. By the time you get to be fifty-eight, you believe that you've experienced most of life's disappointments, and usually more than once. But I was unprepared for this at this time in this place.

On the way out I numbly recounted to O'Hara what had happened. Even though he realized I was lower than a snake's back—and he didn't feel so good about it himself—he told me I should rethink my decision about Dennis, but that we'd talk about it tomorrow. We'd just had one of the best days of the campaign and I should try to get a good night's sleep before my eight o'clock plane back to Phoenix in the morning

"Was that today? It seems like a million years ago."

The phone rang early the next morning. It was Corinne.

"Mame! You're mentioned once in the first section and twice in the "Style" section of the *Washington Post!* And you were on TV and radio."

"What!"

"About the boobs. You were great!"

"I had no idea. I was at a dinner last night and went straight to bed when I got in. I don't believe it!"

Back in Phoenix the loyal and true Roslyn Breitenbach picked me up at the airport and reported that things had been wild. After hearing my words played over and over on the radio talk shows, and Rush Limbaugh calling me a Feminazi, our phones had been swamped by people calling in, up in arms; even some of my friends were upset. But I was cheered to hear that one woman called to say she'd almost driven off the road she was laughing so hard, and that many others called to say they loved it too. I was astounded at the extent of the coverage, but especially of the vitriol and outrage.

You work so hard as a candidate to get your message out, to discuss the issues, and it's like talking into the wind. And then something that doesn't amount to a hill of beans gets blown all out of proportion and becomes "news."

Mollie Ivins, writing in her book *Molly Ivins Can't Say That, Can She?* about Ann Richards's campaign for governor of Texas, relates that

> one of Clayton Williams's television ads showed Ann Richards at the political highlight of her career, making the keynote address to the Democratic Convention in 1988, specifically the famous line on President Bush: "Poor George. He can't help it. He was born with a silver foot in his mouth."
>
> I was astonished at how may people objected to that line and held it against Richards throughout the campaign for governor. The line itself is already classic and will be used in every anthology of political humor published hereafter. Yet a surprising number of men are alarmed by the thought of a witty woman. They think of women's wit as sarcastic, cutting, "ball-busting": it was one of the unstated themes of the campaign and one reason why Ann Richards didn't say a single funny thing during the whole campaign.

She goes on to write, "Margaret Atwood, the Canadian novelist, once asked a group of women at a university why they felt threatened by men. They said they were afraid of being beaten, raped, or killed by men. She asked a group of men why they felt threatened by women. They said they were afraid of being laughed at."

∾

Excerpt from an Actual Tape Recording
oo oo
Republican Legislative District Meeting
Kingman, Arizona—October 1992

Male voice: . . . No one has mentioned John McCain here tonight. Claire Sargent is running against John McCain. How many here heard the remarks that Claire Sargent made the other day? It's been on national television. She says why don't you vote for the breasts? But you've been voting for boobs for years. If John McCain had said that, they would have crucified him and killed him before he ever got up the next morning. He probably wouldn't have lived, they'd have stabbed him. But yet she can say this. She is the most liberal broad—pardon me (laughter from audience)—the most liberal broad who ever sat on a toilet seat (laughter).

<u>Woman's voice</u>: How do you spell liberal? (laughter)
<u>Another woman's voice</u>: How do you spell broad? (laughter)
<u>Original male voice</u>: There was an editorial in Sunday's paper [the Arizona Republic] and it told what her beliefs are. She's against the death penalty, she thinks it archaic. She stands for every liberal idea that there is, and the editorial (inaudible) is an excellent rundown on her by Cheshire on the front page of the Perspective section. She would be an absolute insult (inaudible). She favors abortion for any reason, even to the selection of gender (inaudible).
<u>Another male voice</u>: You're preaching to the choir here.
<u>Original male voice</u>: Well, I know that. You've got to spread the word on her—because the feminist movement is a damn thorn in our side. And I love woman [sic]—but not over and a-, and if they're intelligent and have the ability to be elected to office and do a good job, that's fine. But just because they're a woman or a female doesn't give them access, or special access to an office. So, John McCain has got a tough fight ahead of him. But God, he has a terrible opponent, and we've gotta recognize he has a terrible opponent, so if the Democrats know what she is before they go into that voting booth—we've got about what, thirty-five days, thirty-eight days.

As I listened to this tape sometime in the last weeks of the campaign, I was so stricken, so revolted by its vulgarity, that I put it away and didn't listen to it again for over a year. When you've heard someone say something like this about you, you wonder what kind of person it is who crawled out from under a rock to speak such crude, vile words—words that give you the creeps and make your flesh crawl.

But then everybody says, "You can't take it personally!" Only in a political campaign are you told that you can't take it personally. And that's because a campaign is truly just a game. A game of trivia. One that trivializes the campaign, the candidates, the issues, the Declaration of Independence, the Constitution, government of the people, by the people, for the people. And until We, the People of the United States, take back our government, it will not end. And we will continue to get the government we deserve.

∾

It was a few days after my return from Washington and my devastating encounter with Bob Kerrey that word came down from on high that Dennis needed an answer about whether or not I was going to sign his pledge to support him in 1994.

It was by then almost three weeks after I'd won the primary and only four weeks to go until the election. McKinnon had shot some commercials, but in spite of a spate of frantic fundraising, I didn't have enough money to get them on the air.

In the meantime O'Hara and I, as well as some members of my staff and several hard-core supporters, had been around and around about signing Dennis's pledge. People were all over the place on why I should or shouldn't sign.

"Of course you should sign. First you have to get elected. Then you can tell him you've had a change of heart. That's how he would do it, as well as the rest of the Senate. That's how they always do it."

"Wait a minute! Why do you think so many people have come out of the woodwork to support you? Because they believe in you. That you're different. If you give in now, where are you going to draw the line?"

"Sign the goddamn thing. Why have you got a problem?"

"Nobody will ever have to know. It's the way things are done, Claire. You scratch my back, I'll scratch yours. I can't believe you didn't know that."

"I can see how she feels. It's extortion, pure and simple. And even if she signs, how can we trust Dennis?"

"Obviously Bob Kerrey and Paul Simon trust Dennis and are willing to withhold their support because of him. [Senator Paul Simon had informed me of this on the telephone when I called to ask for his help.] They're the only ones who've told you that to your

Part Three - Arizona

face. How many others are there? Claire, you need the help of every senator you can get. Do it!"

"Fuck Dennis. Fuck the whole system. Isn't that why you're running? To change the system? You've already taken the first step. Stick to your guns."

When O'Hara and I were alone later, he told me it was up to me, that he would accept whatever decision I made. But he wanted to be sure that I understood that if I signed, I still might have a chance. And that if I didn't, it was all over.

I never involved Henry in the day-to-day of my campaign. He received my schedule and knew when I would and would not be home, and, the opposite of many husbands I've heard about, was cheerfully self-sufficient when it came to meals and the details of domesticity that in normal times were my bailiwick. Besides his financial support, which in the end amounted to around $100,000, Henry's primary role was in helping me to maintain a sense of balance, as well as my sense of humor.

When I knew that my decision about Dennis had gotten down to the lick log, realizing that whatever I finally decided to do might profoundly change either me or my campaign, or both, I was anxious to talk it through with Henry, to get his thoughts. I'd related to him the reasons for my impasse with Dennis, though I hadn't had a chance to catch him up on the Bob Kerrey coup de grace. And so as I did, he listened closely and solemnly. What I really wanted to hear from him was if I was just too naive for words. Were all politicians really this way? Is this the way the world has always worked? Was I a fool not to know this, or more, to even let it bother me?

Because I believed, deep down, that I thought his answer was going to be "yes," when I heard his words, my love for him was reinforced beyond measure.

"You've come this far without selling out," he said. "It would be a shame for you to have to start now."

And, naturally, I burst into tears.

Here's the way the conversation with Dennis went when I called him at home:

"Dennis, I want to thank you for all you've done for me, though

I'm sorry we've gotten off on the wrong foot about this pledge thing..."

Dennis interrupted, "Claire, here's what I can do for you. I have two checks here for a thousand dollars each, one from me and one from my mother, which I am having delivered to you. If I get your pledge to support me in 1994, along with these two checks I'm prepared to go to the DSCC meeting tomorrow and ask for maximum support for your campaign, and to do everything I can to help you raise money from everybody I know. If I don't receive your pledge, you'll get the checks and I will ask the DSCC for $25,000. It's as simple as that."

"You won't accept my offer of neutrality in the primary and support in the general?"

"No, I won't."

"Then please tell your mother how much I appreciate her check, and I thank you for yours. We [this was definitely the collective 'we,' not the royal one] will really be counting on the $25,000 from the DSCC. It's too bad things turned out this way, Dennis. I'm terribly disappointed that we couldn't work something out."

"I am too, Claire."

In the end, the DSCC was so tukie they only scrounged up $21,000 out of that famous soft money pot—you send them your bills and they pay them direct. I realize that to some people to gripe about $4,000 sounds truly picayune, that it's not even walking-around money. But for a lot of folks, including us, it was somebody's unpaid salary.

∾

From that time on, more or less, I was only able to afford "free" media, that is, any sort of event or news angle my crew could concoct to try to entice the interest of TV, newspapers, or radio. Which—given the cast of characters covering my campaign, and the fact that I wasn't John McCain—took a lot of doing.

From the very beginning I'd said I was going to be a different kind of candidate, that I was going to run on who I was, the way I'd always been, to say what I believed. That I wasn't going to change to get elected. And because I believed it was wrong to "use" people, I wasn't about to start now.

Part Three - Arizona

So I admit that I didn't make it easy for my new press secretary, hired by O'Hara after I won the primary. On one occasion I had O'Hara and my press secretary positively frothing at the mouth, though I really couldn't blame them. I was completely unbending when it came to one issue in particular, which the press had been all over me about from the first day I announced my candidacy.

That was the fact that Henry belonged to a country club that had no black members—a club he had belonged to for many years, long before we were married, whose membership had originally been paid for by his company until the law was changed, prohibiting such things.

I had never been a member of any private club, and was especially uncomfortable the first time I visited the country club soon after I arrived in Phoenix, and was surprised when I realized that there was not one person of color to be seen. It bothered me that Henry belonged to such a place, and when I asked him about it he said that there were no rules restricting black members, it's just that none had ever been proposed, although there were Hispanic and Asian members. "So," I'm sure I replied at the time, "why don't you do something about it?" (In case you haven't figured it out, Henry and I have different styles. Where I take things head on, he prefers the background and a low profile, avoiding confrontation if at all possible. He is a moderate, and after all, moderates are, well, moderate. "Be not the first to accept the new, nor the last to cast the old aside," is the oft-quoted adage learned at his grandmother's knee.)

The years passed, but when Arizona began to be characterized as a loony bigoted backwater with the Mecham impeachment, AzScam, and the Martin Luther King holiday voted down, the timing seemed propitious, and Henry began thinking of how he would lay the groundwork to propose a black member.

So, months before he had any notion that I would run for the Senate, at a dinner at the ASU art museum we found ourselves at a table with Dick and Linda Whitney, where Henry and Dick quietly discussed the idea with the president of one of the banks, also at the table, who later took it to the newspaper publisher, though Henry and Dick never heard another word from either of them about it.

Until it came up during the campaign.

When I announced that I was running for the Senate, a reporter asked me about my membership in the country club, and though I knew then that Henry was planning to propose a black member, I naturally didn't say anything about it. It surfaced again from time to time—even from my Democratic opponent—and each time I countered that I wasn't a member.

Actually, I suffered one of the most painful encounters I've ever endured as a result of the newspaper articles about the country club. I was having lunch with Dick Whitney (amazingly), when we stopped to speak to a prominent black man, who, as he made no bones about, had been turned down after being proposed for membership in a different country club. Standing up at his table to shake hands with Dick, he turned to me and announced at the top of his voice for all the world to hear, "You sleep with a racist!"

I've forgotten the exact sequence of events, but sometime during the general election on a Friday afternoon—most Sunday stories, and therefore those that get the greatest readership, are written on Fridays, or even Thursdays—we got a call from the reporter with the *Mesa Tribune* I called "El Gordo" (the Fat One). Always hot on the country club trail, El Gordo's call was prompted by a report that the black ASU football coach, a local celebrity who had recently become controversial, had been accepted as a member of the club—proposed by the publisher and the banker—along with another black. Aware of this second man's name, which must have been leaked along with that of the coach, El Gordo wanted to know if it was true that Henry had proposed him.

On my way out the door to Tucson, and already late, I wouldn't stop to talk to him and told O'Hara to tell him to call Henry if he wanted to find out anything about the country club, since he was the member, not me. And when I wouldn't let O'Hara tell him the truth, I believed he might well quit on the spot, and couldn't blame him. But I knew that El Gordo, lazy ignoramus and cynic that he was, would write that it had been done for publicity purposes on my behalf, and make it all look like a cheap act of self-promotion. Further, knowing that the man being proposed was as averse to publicity as Henry was, I simply drew the line.

When he finally reached Henry, El Gordo was so officious and obnoxious, Henry told him it was none of his business and hung up on him.

In my 1993 interview with him, O'Hara reiterated the importance of the story, that putting Henry's personal sensitivities above the campaign wasn't his job. From O'Hara's point of view, the problem with the stories about Henry belonging to the club didn't match up with who I was and what I was saying. They obscured the real issue, he said, of the kind of campaign I was actually running, and didn't reflect the fact that my staff was multicultural—Asian, black, white, Hispanic, Jewish, gay and lesbian, senior citizens, the halt and the lame, people from all across the political spectrum, a coalition who just showed up out of necessity not through design.

"And," O'Hara added, "McCain's staff was almost entirely runny-nosed young white Republican Protestant university graduates, a pathetic cross-section of Arizonans. And I think that is a much more fundamental issue."

The other thing that was a fundamental element of the El Gordo story, according to O'Hara, was that no one had ever made references to my own associations, and that it would have been "beyond reason to expect that they would write the same story about Mrs. McCain, that it was just a very sexist attack on you.

"Another thing wrong about that coverage was the assertion being made that the club is racially exclusive. The distinction between racially segregated and no black members was not being made, and I think that has its own racial overtone to it. To not regard Asians and Hispanics as being members of racial minorities who warrant inclusion, if you're trying to make those distinctions, has a racist overtone to it. And I was simply unable to convince El Gordo that Asian members and Hispanic members by definition make it a multiracial club. Whether or not there are black members is a question that deserves consideration, but El Gordo is just not aware of the fact that he is a racist and a sexist."

The exquisitely ironic ending to the story was this: a week or so later someone sent us a copy of McCain's campaign newsletter. Featured prominently in the center of the front page was a photograph of McCain with the new country club member—the one proposed by Henry—and the member's wife. McCain was posed with an arm around each of them at a fundraiser they were hosting for him in their home!

~

Relatively early in the primary, a volunteer who had never before worked on a political campaign had begun computerizing my answers to the questionnaires from the countless interest groups who want to know a candidate's stand on the issues—to have it on the record—everybody from environmentalists and Concerned Women of America to gays and lesbians and the National Rifle Association. You name it, there's a questionnaire for single-issue voters. And in some cases, money, though the really *big* money folks don't bother with questionnaires. They have paid lobbyists who already have the answers.

Now what I wanted to do in my campaign was to tell the truth, tell the people what I believed. That was one of the things I was running on. Every candidate I'd ever seen had equivocated, danced around issues that were unpopular or around those on which he or she didn't agree with the questioner. Or they just wouldn't answer the question. Except for Barry Goldwater. And whenever I would use him as an example, I always got one of those "yes, but" responses: "Yes, Claire, but he had already been elected." Heck, I wasn't a politician, and said so up front, and then was tarred and feathered by the press for not being what I said I wasn't in the first place.

Anyway, Michael Walters, the volunteer, had all my answers, which he and I had gone over, but certainly not with the fine-tooth comb a crack political consulting firm or strategist would have. I mean, the usual senatorial candidate never even *sees* the questionnaires; it's his consultants who come up with the answers, and then only when their backs are against the wall, and then only after seeing what his polling data show he should say. Hey, not me. I just answered them as straightforwardly as I knew how, no bobbing and weaving. For not only did I not have a pollster, at that time I didn't even have a campaign manager!

It was after the aforementioned *Phoenix Gazette* columnist wouldn't let up with writing about how vague he thought I was on the issues. So Michael came to me with the document, "Claire Sargent: On the Issues—On the Record," which was about forty

Part Three - Arizona

pages filled with all my answers to the questionnaires. He suggested I send it to the columnist to shut him up, to show him I wasn't vague, and to be on the record. I thought that was a grand idea, and off it went.

You have to understand here that unbeknown to me, this simple little act of openness would embody any political consultant's nightmare from hell. And it was something that had been lost in the shuffle by the time O'Hara had gotten settled in, and I never thought to mention it to him. Alas.

To say that political consultants don't like surprises is litotes, the opposite of hyperbole. And Marc O'Hara was predisposed to show his dislike for surprises more than most.

The day after I won the primary, I was just devastated, literally stunned, when I read the column written by this same *Gazette* columnist in which, among other things, he described me as a "euphemism for bored housewife," a real *compliment* compared to his other characterizations. It was one of the cruelest, most hateful, negative, shrill, *ad feminam* attacks on me of the campaign—later to be quoted in McCain radio commercials, to further demonstrate the vicious circle of the media/campaign connection. It still stings even now when I read it, his first crack out of the box of what was to be a relentless stream of invective that lasted until even *after* the campaign. Even then he wrote a mean, petty column about Corinne and me, criticizing us for campaigning together at a freeway exit brandishing Sargent signs on election eve during the evening rush hour. It was BENEATH a Senate candidate to behave in such an unbecoming way.

Well. Just. Lah. Dee. Dah.

And to think I met this guy in church when I first moved to Arizona, when we were ushers together in a big Presbyterian church out in Scottsdale. It was after an assistant pastor of the church came to call on me as a new member, and I commented that I was surprised that there were no women ushers at the Sunday services. The follow-up was a gracious letter from the senior minister (whose sermons I greatly admired), thanking me for bringing up the issue and asking me to be an usher. *I* didn't want to be an usher; I just wanted women represented in the usher ranks. But I felt I couldn't say "no," and that I'd have to put my body where my mouth was. Maybe my fellow-usher had held it against me all these years, who knows? And this shall be a lesson unto you: Just because you meet somebody in church doesn't mean he's not a louse.

So! You can imagine the heart-attack surprise that seized O'Hara when he read all the ideas I'd expressed—that he had no earthly idea about—right there for all the world to see. My views on issues that wouldn't arise in a million years of campaigning, when you're only supposed to talk about the issues that your polls tell you to.

Kicking into damage-control mode O'Hara screamed, "*Where* did he get this! *When* did you say these things! *Why* did you say these things!"

And so I calmly proceeded to explain the innocent way in which it all had happened, and how long ago it had been, and then asked why after three months was he only now giving it any ink?

The obvious reason, according to O'Hara, was, first, many reporters are lazy, and, second, as a result of that, never believing I had a snowball's chance in the desert to win the primary, when this formidable document crossed his desk so long before the primary, he must have thought, "Why bother?" and dropped it into the back of his file, where it languished. Until now, when he'd resurrected it, discovering that the grain of sand had become a pearl in his oyster.

It was only a week before other reporters started calling O'Hara for their own personally autographed copies of The Document, as it came to be called. That's when we found out that the Gazette columnist had handed over a copy to McCain's campaign, after which a copy turned up on the desks of literally every newspaper in the state of Arizona.

O'Hara, who had studied journalism as well as film, became unglued, livid over what he called a breach of the "journalistic ethic." He could not believe the columnist's superiors could condone such a flagrant breach of ethics.

Two years later, in 1994, McCain repaid this columnist (along with an equally toad-eating *Mesa Tribune* columnist who will never live down the purple prose of his opening line in that report) with his wife's exclusive, rigidly controlled drug-addiction story, when it was revealed that McCain's wife, Cindy, had been addicted for years to the painkiller Percocet and had stolen the drugs from desperately deprived children in a Third World medical project she had set up. Her addiction went back even before the campaign, before she was depicted in the glowing "Senator as Family Man" television commercial introduced on the night I won the primary.

It is a cliché to say that the hypocrisy is breathtaking, because today hypocrisy is *expected* in our politicians, and John McCain belongs with the masters. The most pitiful part was that the news of her addiction apparently came as a *complete surprise* to him. When the cat was finally out of the bag (several people I talked to had known of her condition and how she maintained her habit), obviously afraid to tell him herself, Cindy McCain recruited their *lawyer* to break the news to her own husband. When you really think about it, isn't that just so *sad?*

True to form, like a leopard after an impala, McCain pounced on the doctor whom Cindy had pressured for the drugs. He can never practice medicine again anywhere in the United States. The last I heard, Cindy was still awaiting resolution to see if she could get into a diversionary drug-treatment program—rather than serving a mandatory jail sentence—as the senator remorselessly continues his votes for prison over prevention and treatment.

In one of the most ruthlessly extraordinary instances of managing the news ever witnessed, even for McCain, even for Arizona, thus did these pathetic excuses for journalists perform their services for the good senator yet again.

Why Americans hate the media, indeed.

Twenty-one

There were times when I felt like General MacArthur left to fight the war in the Pacific with his hands tied behind his back, while General Eisenhower had at his command all the firepower available to win the war in Europe.

Jettisoned by the Democrats, I still had my biggest battle ahead of me, and like MacArthur at Corregidor, I stood alone. In contrast to the way my own party regarded me, my opponent, as well as the Republican Party—all the way up to the White House—treated me with enormous respect, leaving no tern unstoned to pound me into the ground, fulfilling Barbara Mikulski's prophesy. Before it was all over, I was feeling like the coyote smushed flat under the monster road-rolling machine in the Road Runner cartoons, so much raw power brought to bear against me—me!—that in a perverse way I was flattered.

At the exact same moment I was begging for crumbs from the Democrats in the days just after the primary, here's the letter—using the same poll results I was quoting—with which McCain was badgering special interest lobbyists:

JOHN McCAIN
UNITED STATES SENATOR
517 2ND STREET NE
WASHINGTON D.C. 20002

September 21, 1992

"Sargent Gains on McCain, poll shows"
<u>Phoenix Gazette</u>, September 17

To paraphrase our leader Bob Dole, any incumbent running unopposed in 1992 is in for the race of his life . . . and I <u>certainly</u> am not running opposed.

Part Three - Arizona

Evan Mecham—Arizona's impeached Governor—appears to have qualified to be in the general election as an independent, although we're reviewing his petition signatures. Ultra liberal activist Claire Sargent won the Democratic primary, and joins us on the November ballot.

Mecham will attack from the right—Sargent from the left. I'll have to run a two-track campaign in a state where politics is a contact sport. Contrary to the thoughts of some political experts, it won't be a cake-walk.

Here's the latest indication. A post-primary poll taken of residents in the Phoenix area and published in the September 17th Phoenix Gazette tells this story:

> McCain   44%
> Sargent   34%
> Mecham   10%

I am confident of winning . . . but a 2-track campaign won't be much fun, and it won't be cheap. In fact, it will cost over $500,000 more than our original budget.

I ask for your consideration, your support—and your participation at my special reception on Wednesday, September 23rd. It will be held from 6:00 to 7:30 P.M. at the Powers Court Restaurant in the Phoenix Park Hotel in Washington, D.C. The requested contribution is $1,000 made payable to the John McCain Reelection Committee.

Please RSVP to Steve Gordon or Jerry Seppala at (202) 546-0900.

I will meet this challenge from an ultra liberal and a totally unpredictable independent if I have the resources. I look forward to seeing you on September 23rd.

Sincerely,
[signed John]

Senator John McCain

PAID FOR BY JOHN MCCAIN REELECTION COMMITTEE
DONATIONS ARE NOT DEDUCTIBLE AS CHARITABLE CONTRIBUTIONS FOR INCOME TAX PURPOSES

The *additional* $500,000 he's pleading for would raise his war chest to almost $4 million in contrast to the $300,000 I raised for my whole campaign. (Just imagine. Three hundred thousand dollars is a whole lot of money to some people.) And it only took him two days to put this little shindig together!

With his campaign commercials rolling morning, noon, and night on television and radio, and his volunteers covering the Phoenix area with four times the number of signs he had ever used before, McCain was reaping the rewards of no end of fundraisers and campaign appearances—by the president himself, General Colin Powell (which seemed inappropriate, since he was at that time serving in the United States Army), Nancy Reagan, Liddy and Bob

Dole, Alan Simpson, and Dick Cheney, among others I've forgotten—to withstand my juggernaut!

Without the DSCC and Emily's List, who declined to give me even their token $5,000 PAC contribution, I depended on the generosity of small contributors, the bedrock of my campaign. In senatorial campaigns anything under $1,000 is considered small change by the big boys, though whenever I got a contribution of $100 I was elated.

Big campaigns are won or lost with television commercials. And without the money to run my own TV commercials to define who I was and what I stood for, McCain did it for me, demonizing and marginalizing me and my positions as extremist in his own commercials, in any way he chose, having his way with me. As were the newspapers, and from them, the local television news programs, who do little more than parrot the stories that appear in the newspapers, with the small dailies and weeklies picking up the same stories.

Because Arizona is considered such a bedrock conservative state, when we so desperately sought the help of the Clinton campaign for an appearance by Bill Clinton on my behalf, we were told that Arizona had been placed in the bottom tier of states considered "possible," essentially written off by the Clinton campaign from the git-go. Even though his strategy was essentially correct, in the end I believe Clinton lost Arizona by only 1 or 2 percent, and if he'd campaigned here might very well have won.

∾

Throughout his whole presidential campaign Clinton came to Arizona only once, and as I recall it wasn't a long-planned event, more of a last-minute drop-in. It was before he'd won the nomination, during the time I was without a campaign manager, and it was a real fluke that I even met him at all, a small triumph that I relished.

Naturally, a Democratic presidential candidate, during the primary, would be scheduled to speak in a labor hall, and though it was the largest one we have, it didn't accommodate all that many people (Arizona is not what you'd call a real labor-friendly kind of place). At that time I was still leaning toward former Senator Paul Tsongas from Massachusetts, who had gotten my attention the year before

Part Three - Arizona

with his treatise *A Call To Economic Arms: Forging A New American Mandate*, by spelling out specifically where he stood on a whole raft of issues that seemed to me to be non-ideological, intellectually honest, and philosophically consistent beliefs that I basically agreed with. But what had ultimately sold me on him was his vow not to run a negative campaign.

When Clinton arrived, Tsongas was still in the race. I actually didn't know all that much about Clinton, though I'd met Hillary at a small luncheon when she'd come to Phoenix earlier in the year, and I was looking forward to seeing and hearing him, up close and personal, for myself.

As I remember it, I'd had other long-scheduled appointments—I may have even been out of town—and broke my neck to try to get there early, knowing full well that my opponent would be right up there in the front row. But even though I arrived in good time, the crowd was so huge and already so packed in, that the police and security had already closed off all the entrances, and by no entreaty, no matter how passionate or pitiful, would they be moved.

Turned away with no room in the inn, I was spotted by some of my own supporters who yelled and beckoned me over. Overjoyed, I quickly joined them and found myself amid a spillover crowd in what had become an orderly makeshift rope line, stretching almost ten deep from the back of the building where Clinton would exit.

When other friends in the crowd recognized me, I was pushed up to the front, where I stationed myself and passed out small "Sargent for U.S. Senate" signs.

You never know when what appears to be a defeat will turn into victory. For when Clinton soon emerged from the back door of the union hall at the opposite end from where I stood—beginning to work the rope—I glanced out at the parking lot and spotted leaning against a car my opponent's factotum, usually his constant companion, obviously waiting for him. When he spied me—our eyes locking—planted right there in the front row with my red, white, and blue sign, I'll never forget the expression on his face. A classic slow burn, as he realized that I would be the one in the circle of Clinton's spotlight—maybe get my picture in the paper, or even on TV!—not the general still trapped in the crush inside. Beside myself with such one-upmanship, I gave him my widest grin and a breezy little wave. When you think about it, could anything be more petty? And it felt so *good!*

This must have been after Gennifer Flowers. We'd all heard the rumors about Clinton and his women. And even though I talked to him for just a few minutes, he absolutely dazzled me. I'd never before felt such a powerful presence—like a force field—and I could certainly understand how women might be melted by his magnetism and riveting gaze.

What really impressed me more than anything, though, was his seemingly genuine connection with the folks he was meeting. A couple standing beside me had a photo of their son taken with Clinton that they brought for him to autograph. When he got to us, and they asked him for the autograph, looking at the picture and recognizing the boy without a moment's hesitation, he said, "Are you Joe's parents? You should be so proud of him!" and went on about how wonderful Joe was, relating an anecdote, asking what he was doing now, what they were doing in Phoenix. I mean, they had a five-minute conversation, with his concentrated attention, as though they were the only people in the world.

Then, turning his beam on me to inquire about my sign, when he heard my accent and that I was a Mississippian, well, he took off on that for a good long riff, allowing Kathleen Abernathy, one of the women who had called me over—who had brought her camera—to capture the scant few minutes I've ever had with the now President of the United States.

The next day back at my headquarters, I told everybody that I hated to admit it, but I was hooked. And when Paul Tsongas let me down by going negative against Clinton in the Florida primary, I didn't have to feel quite as guilty about being so fickle.

∾

In any account of the 1992 presidential race there has been the inevitable cry of "foul" by the Republicans against the liberal bias of the press. And by and large this has even been acknowledged to some extent. Unhappily, the opposite is true in Arizona.

Arizona's reputation for bedrock conservatism is well-founded. By the time I ran in 1992, however, Barry Goldwater was considered left-of-center by Arizona Republicans, as was pro-Clarence Thomas, antichoice Dennis DeConcini. So you can just imagine where I—prochoice and anti-Star Wars, and in favor of decriminalizing marijuana (a different approach to this idea was affirmed four years later when medicalization of illegal drugs was approved overwhelmingly in a statewide citizen's initiative)—was painted on the political spectrum by John McCain.

This attitude was reinforced and confirmed each day by the state's largest newspapers, the *Arizona Republic* and the *Phoenix Gazette*, the morning and afternoon papers, both owned by the Indiana-based holding company controlled by the Quayle family, and on whose board Dan Quayle now sits.

"What are you going to do about the Phoenix newspapers?" asked Terry Goddard at a meeting of my exploratory committee. Terry by then, through a quirk in the Arizona election laws, had a little more than twelve months previously been defeated in *two* elections for governor. He had been through hellish campaigns against Republican Fife Symington, who filed for bankruptcy after running on his record as a businessman and who later was forced to resign after being convicted on seven felony counts of bank and wire fraud. During the two campaigns the Phoenix newspapers' relentlessness in their strident attack on Terry was equaled only by their fierce, maddog support for Symington.

Just as day after day the Phoenix newspapers had unmercifully torn Terry to shreds in his first campaign for mayor, when the stakes grew as the power of the office expanded in the governor's race, the papers fired up to feeding-frenzy level.

I knew all this. But I thought that because they'd treated me so kindly in the past, they would be fair if I became a candidate for the U.S. Senate. Hadn't these same newspapers even contributed $20,000 to the Desert Cities Conference? Times had changed. They had new enlightened leadership. It would be different now.

Compared to the newspapers' treatment of me, Terry's was a day at the beach.

In late 1993 however, there was sort of a personal vindication when the editor of the *Phoenix Gazette* called to invite me to lunch. Even though he personally had never written anything negative about me, I was put off because of my past treatment by the newspaper. But curious about the invitation, I accepted. I was completely taken by surprise when he asked me to be among a group of "pundits" to take part in covering the 1994 elections, giving me carte blanche to write articles on anything I wanted to say about politics, which would be published on the Op-Ed Page.

When I accepted, I told him that either he had very low standards, since his very own editorials had asserted that I had "no grasp of the issues," or that this was an exoneration. A very engaging, intelligent man, he gave me a pithy description of what he thought of my treatment, but our conversation is off the record.

∾

"The power of the White House to aid a local campaign cannot be exaggerated," huffed my everlovin' *Gazette* columnist, alluding in a different context to Bill Clinton campaigning for a Democratic candidate in the 1994 elections. He might have written the same line to acknowledge the power of George Bush's White House behind John McCain's 1992 reelection campaign, though never would have, of course.

For starters, in the president's effort to showcase McCain, after they both spoke to a national convention of the Veterans of Foreign Wars in Indianapolis, Bush invited him to fly aboard Air Force One to Houston to the Republican National Convention. Using the occasion to reflect McCain's proximity to the White House, the two of them spent the flight time to Houston to call a local Phoenix talk-radio host—clearly beside himself—to take calls on Air Force One from the duly impressed locals. I mean, what is the phone on Air Force One good for if you can't use it to help your pal's reelection, no matter that the American taxpayer is paying for the phone call.

And later, toward the end of the campaign—yet once again with McCain aboard Air Force One—on the way to sign the North American Free Trade Agreement, the president arranged another talk-radio call-in; this time to Rush Limbaugh's station during prime time, after his station had criticized McCain for that first Air Force One call made to a rival.

But there's more. At President Bush's insistence, McCain's relatively minor role on the first night of the Republican convention in

Houston was rescheduled to a prime-time slot on the night before President Bush accepted his party's nomination. As a complement to President Bush's acceptance speech, McCain preceded former President Ford with a speech extolling Navy Lieutenant George Herbert Walker Bush, who, like McCain, was shot down in combat. (This pride in getting shot down *has* to be a guy thing.)

The self-same columnist waxed eloquent about McCain's speech as "mark[ing] the biggest buildup for an Arizona Republican politician since the heyday of Barry Goldwater—and a return from the political dead just two years ago."

Though I wear as a badge of honor the lengths to which the White House went in massing its awesome power against *me*, I honestly shudder to think at how far they would go when they are really *desperate*.

All of this pales, though, compared to the Big One to come. (Remember, in all this time I have no television commercials, so the only thing the voters are seeing and reading is McCain, McCain, McCain, extolling himself and bashing me, both in paid and free media. All is Wonderful! Counselor! The Mighty God!)

On the morning after I won the primary, O'Hara found a letter from McCain stuck under the door challenging me to a series of debates. And according to a newspaper story, at eight o'clock that same morning McCain issued a statement congratulating me on my victory and challenging me to a series of debates, as well as pledging he would run a clean campaign. "The voters in Arizona," McCain said, "deserve an opportunity to see and hear us on the same stage. I would hope that we could agree on dates and format for several debates."

Which was the last we were ever to hear from McCain about any debates. We could hardly get him pinned down for the one he finally realized he couldn't avoid.

I wasn't great in the debate, but McCain is no William Jennings Bryan, either. It was one of those expectation things. Folks aren't disappointed when they're not expecting very much, but thrilled if things turn out better than they thought. I'd never debated anybody in my life, and, never having been trained to think on my feet, can sometimes take a day or two to think about a response to a remark.

A truly blank slate in rhetoric and debating, realizing that excellence was a reach that would exceed my grasp in the few short weeks available to prepare, I felt if I could just hold my own it would at least be a draw. The formats for these things are so stilted and artificial that there's little room to maneuver, and since I'm more "spontaneous," as the political press describe someone who isn't "scripted," I'm much better one-on-one than in a formal question-and-answer format. The hardest thing for me to learn to do—which I never mastered—was *not* to answer the question, to say whatever I wanted to say, whether it's related to the question or not, an infuriatingly irritating practice I abhorred. To get me up to professional politician level in the time we had would have taken a Skinnerian behaviorist using electrical shocks.

We ended work on the debate early in the afternoon so I could go home to rest. When I left to go to the studio, I hadn't bothered to put on any makeup because our liaison with the debate people had been told that I should get there in time for them to make me up. Which I did. Roslyn and I were shown to a room to wait. And wait. And wait. Finally Roslyn went to find out what was going on, and when she returned she reported that there had been a monumental snafu. Not only were there no makeup people around, between the two of us we had nothing more than a lipstick and comb, and even a spot check of the audience members who were on my side could only produce a pale blusher. I couldn't let it get to me, and using what we had, colored up as high as I could—though I knew that bathed in the blazing lights of TV I would come across as a candidate pale and wan.

Entering the TV studios, the eye-squinting lighting giving it the look and feel of high noon, I spotted someone already seated at the table, and as I drew nearer, on closer inspection was startled to discover that it was McCain. He was so thoroughly and heavily pancaked (by his own people, I assumed) in the most scary death-mask pallor—not just his face, but to the very tip top of his bald pate—where wisps of hair had been carefully combed over the top of it from a very low part—down the back of his neck, under his chin, even including his ears and lips—making him resemble nothing so much as a cadaver prepared for "viewing." Biting my lip, it was all I could do to keep from dying laughing, and momentarily I felt sorry for him.

∽

I found that one of the most curious aspects of a campaign was that if you hadn't known your opponent before the campaign, you surely would never get a chance to know him during the campaign. The only time I'd ever met John Sidney McCain III, which came about in the unlikeliest of places—at a fundraiser for him in my own apartment building—was the result of a chance encounter.

It was fall of 1988. Our old friend Charlotte was visiting us for the weekend to attend the christening of Henry's granddaughter, which is how I can pinpoint the time. In our apartment building after picking her up from the airport, we happened to run into a neighbor, the head of a bankers' association, who suggested that if Charlotte would like to meet Senator John McCain, he was going to be at a party that he, the banker, was giving on our roof terrace that weekend, and he'd be delighted for us to come.

When we were alone and I told Henry I thought it was odd that the banker had invited us to his party out of the blue like that, he said that it must be a fundraiser. When I declared that I wouldn't be caught dead going to a fundraiser for John McCain, he said he was sure that Charlotte and I wouldn't be expected to make a contribution, and that he thought Charlotte would enjoy it.

Welcomed warmly and graciously by the host and his wife, everything was so highly discreet—no name tags, no list, no checks changing hands. If I hadn't known, there was no indication whatever that we were at a fundraiser. (So *this* was how the lobbyists did it!) But when I saw that there were maybe no more than ten or twelve couples, I was amused when I realized that, in theater lingo, we'd been invited to "paper the house."

After arriving alone, John chatted briefly with his hosts before they casually began to work the room together. When he got to us he was affable and friendly, not stiff the way he came across on TV. And when he heard my name he surprised me by mentioning Terry, which made me realize he'd been briefed. It was mildly flattering, and even though I'd never been part of Terry's inner circle, if you tell a politician that he won't believe you.

The sensation I had as I talked to John (besides the surprise that he was so much shorter than I thought he'd be, much shorter than I am) was of being transported back to a college fraternity party in Mississippi, bantering with a boy from the Delta—more Ole Miss than State, more Phi Delt than KA—with the same cocky confidence and gleam in his eye.

Discretion continued when a few days later Henry received a diplomatically worded note from the host requesting a check.

What I hadn't realized until I nailed down the date of this event (my recollection was that it had been for the 1986 Senate race) is that Henry's contribution that day in 1988, unsubstantial as it was, went into a war chest that would four years later be used to bring about my own defeat.

∾

I thought it poor form—well, bad manners, really—that John didn't stand up to shake hands with me, since this was the first time we'd met during the whole campaign. After all, he came from a family of admirals who set a lot of store by social graces—aren't Annapolis men supposed to be "gentlemen"? So I was rather surprised when he remained rooted in his seat—certainly a different John McCain from the charmer I'd met at his fundraiser.

Even so, it amused me, and I just figured—boys being boys—ignoring me was his clumsy way of trying to play some kind of childish mind game to throw me off. But when I sat down next to him and saw that he had placed a copy of "Claire Sargent—On the Issues, On the Record" practically under my nose in such an obvious effort to try to get to me (supplied to him by that fine fellow, the political columnist of the *Phoenix Gazette*), it was all so petty and heavy-handed that I got tickled and beckoned O'Hara over so he could enjoy the ludicrousness of it.

When O'Hara spied the infamous treatise, he leaned down and whispered sweet nothings in my ear to reassure me, and then, unable to resist playing the boys' game, seamlessly leaned over to whisper something in John's ear as well. I hate to have to admit it, but when I asked him after the debate what in the world he had whispered to John, he laughed and said, "Oh, I just called him a string of the crudest names I could think of, and he couldn't do a damn thing about it. I just wanted him to know what we thought of his lame stunt."

After the debate was over, John made a beeline for the exit, not even pausing to answer one single question from the press. Although it was reported that his handlers had told him not to lower himself to comment on the debate, an incident recounted in a book that I read after the campaign offers an additional explanation for why he shot out of there.

In *The Nightingale's Song*, Robert Timberg writes that during the first debate in his 1986 Senate campaign, six-plus inches shorter than his Democratic opponent (and appearing even shorter on TV because of camera angles), John had had to stand on a stool behind his podium to keep from looking "like a pygmy," in the words of his campaign operative. When his opponent pointed that fact out in the debate, John was furious. It explains why one of the conditions of our debate was that the candidates remained seated, and why John never budged out of his chair. At five feet eight in my bare feet I stand a good three inches taller than John McCain. Having me towering over him was something he just couldn't tolerate.

Making a strategic decision, my team chose to have me take the high road and leave the low road of attacking McCain over the Keating Affair to former Republican Governor Evan Mecham, also in the debate. For which, among a number of other mistakes, including "looking tired," I was roundly criticized. But on the whole, I felt I'd done okay. Not great, but okay. At least I hadn't died, as I'd thought I might.

No matter how well or how poorly I did in the debate, it gave me TV exposure, which I desperately needed and which I could not afford on my own. It was the first time voters had seen me on TV on the same level with John McCain. And the last.

Just eighteen days before the election, when President Bush sent John on a hastily arranged mission to Hanoi, it was simply politics as usual, and what a poor sport I was to point that out! By-passing Senator John Kerry, who was chairman of the Senate committee looking into the MIA question, the president instead "requested" McCain to join retired General John Vessey on an emergency trip to Hanoi to "resolve" the MIA issue after a "surprise" recovery of a cache of several thousand photographs. Not only did it gin up terrific national and international media coverage for him, it gave McCain the cover to avoid any other debates as well.

Stumping in northern Arizona after returning from Hanoi twelve days before the election, McCain joked, "While I was in North Vietnam I went up eight points in the polls, and my campaign staff has urged me to go on another trip somewhere in the next twelve days."

It was only *after* the election that the *Washington Post* reported that the MIA-POW photos had been purchased by the Department of Defense many months before McCain's trip to Vietnam.

These are but a few examples of the power of the White House in aiding a local campaign, which brings to mind an observation by the Confederate Civil War general George Pickett when he was asked to what he attributed the failure of the Confederacy in the war. Well, Pickett is said to have replied, I kinda think the Yankees had a little something to do with it.

∾

The day of the Bob Kerrey press conference dawned. At my headquarters all hands were at full tilt, reminding me of an ant farm where the ants bump headlong into each other as they scurry, heads down, in a straight line in opposite directions. I was barely in the door before I was hustled back to my car.

I was one of several speakers for an event in Sun City, the suburban retirement community—the first stop of one of the longest days of the campaign. There were one or two speakers ahead of me, and when the personage introduced me with a singular lack of warmth or grace, it warranted, I felt, as brief an encounter as possible with an audience I sensed to be equally as hostile. Still, I was pleased to see that the presence of a CBS crew taping my speech did create a fleeting flurry of attention, but when it was over I beat the hastiest retreat I could manage without appearing to run.

Outside in the bright October sunshine I encountered the CBS crew again, assembling their gear at a picnic table. I went over to introduce myself and instantly took to them when they expressed their sympathy about how unfriendly the crowd inside had been. Nearby an attractive man I'd never seen before, clearly not a local,

Part Three - Arizona

sat waiting patiently on a bench in the shade of a tree—for me—I discovered to my surprise.

His name was David Culhane, with CBS "Sunday Morning." I was embarrassed that I didn't know who he was, but because I don't watch much television—especially in the morning—I'd seldom seen the show. He was there to interview me as part of the segment being filmed, sort of "A Day in the Life of . . ." (the first time I was to hear of it!) that would be shown nationwide shortly before election day. And what a pleasurable change it was to be interviewed by someone with a combination of empathy and intelligence, a phenomenon I'd so rarely experienced.

One of the great mysteries of the campaign remains to this day unanswered. Constantly struggling as we always were for even a crumb of free media, we had absolutely nothing to do with our biggest TV coverage of all, the "Sunday Morning" story, and to this day have not the faintest idea as to how or where it originated. Like the Coke bottle in *The Gods Must Be Crazy*, it simply fell out of the blue into our lap.

One thing I had determined to do during my campaign was to remain as natural and down-to-earth as I could, eschewing the artifices of heavy makeup and perfect hair, even when I was on television, serving as my own "appearance coach." My staff accepted this as just another aspect of "letting Claire be Claire." They understood that I wasn't—and never could be—the female counterpart to all those plastic, blow-dried, every-hair-in-place male senators, nor one of those brittle cookie-cutter women draped in scarves and the ubiquitous necklace.

In the first place, I have so little of it there was no way I could ever have perfect hair; I just washed and dried it with a towel. And second, with the exception of the infrequently shown commercials filmed for the general election and the few studio TV appearances—with in-house makeup people whose makeup always made my face break out in a rash—I wore no more makeup than I normally did. I mention this here because when I later watched the David Culhane interview on nationwide TV, I realized that I had certainly achieved the natural look and need never have worried about looking too perfect.

The next stop, CBS crew still in tow, was an interview with an ultraconservative talk-radio host with a wide audience, a budding Rush Limbaugh clone, and I wasn't looking forward to it because of his reputation for being so obnoxious. To my pleasant surprise, however, considering what I'd expected, he treated me courteously enough, even though it had become real tiresome forever having to demonstrate that I most assuredly wasn't the wacko he and his ilk and McCain had made me out to be.

Actually his treatment of me was similar to the surprising response I'd encountered other times I was the guest of a supposedly hostile radio host.

The first time it happened was in Tucson during the primary. A real blowhard had made it his mission to badmouth me and got kind of a Limbaugh head of steam going, really trying to take me on, boxing me into a corner by extending an open invitation to me to come on the air with him. After being advised by my Tucson folks that nobody listened to him but the hardcore right wing—that even Dennis avoided him—I dug in my heels and told O'Hara to just forget it and to quit harassing me about it. I wasn't going to dignify the guy with my time. However, after I'd won the primary, and reading in a Phoenix newspaper that I was ducking this fellow—who, the article stated, admitted with no apologies to repeatedly referring to me as a "nitwit" and an "airhead"—O'Hara shifted into high gear and finally just plumb wore me down.

You've heard the old joke, "You have the perfect looks for radio." Well, I discovered, there's a lot of truth in that.

Radio, with its built-in protection, has produced legions of on-air personalities like this fellow, becoming profligate with them since the early 1990s, when Limbaugh became every radio guy's role model. All-powerful in the safety of the sound booth, they are naked and vulnerable without it. I read somewhere that before Limbaugh became Limbaugh he was taping a segment before a live audience for a New York television show, I believe it was *Saturday Night Live*, and when the audience started with catcalls and boos he was so cowed and undone that the audience had to be removed before taping could continue, without them. And even on his own

TV show he sits with a desk between him and the hand-picked all-white Kens and Barbies allowed into the studio. He remains nothing more than he was as a child that only a mother could love—an insecure, unattractive, overweight little boy who can dish it out but can't take it.

The opposite of tough.

Too full of misgivings to sit still in the cramped two-chair anteroom while I waited to go on the air—radio stations I've been in have notoriously little space for people who don't work there—as I stood leaning against the wall, there appeared a poorly toupéed, ordinary-looking late-middle-aged ol' boy, almost shouting, though good-naturedly, "Where's Claire Sargent?" Apparently it was my radio host, and astonished, I managed a bright smile as I stared wordlessly and put out my hand, hoping my surprise was concealed as I was thinking, "Ah, all is revealed."

Amusing me even more was what he said next: "But you're so attractive!"

"Well, what had you expected?" I asked.

"From what I'd heard I just assumed you'd be different."

And that went for both of us.

Except for dealing with the expected calls of McCain supporters (I had my own side calling in, too), with the host now transformed into a complete pussycat, the show couldn't have gone more smoothly or amicably. In his summing up at the end of the program, he even reiterated a second time on-air how attractive and charming I was. (It's so *easy* when you really want to turn it on, the old conditioning kicking in.) I would have done my mother proud.

༺

Still shadowed by the CBS team, after the radio interview it was on to a downtown hotel for the press conference with Kerrey, planned to coincide with the local five o'clock news. Considered by my campaign to be one of the most important events of the election, it also turned out to be the most perfidious.

Because of the details and insights that were not known to me at the time, I include here excerpts from Marc O'Hara's recollection of what happened at that fateful press conference, which he recounted to me when I interviewed him in San Francisco in July 1993:

"Our thinking was that Bob Kerrey's stature as a Vietnam veteran and national politician would lend great credibility to the campaign, that we were not being taken seriously. In addition to that, the whole thing was wrapped up in a much more fundamental desire to be involved with this man that we both regarded so highly. And we banked our emotional bankroll on it.

"His first resistance was that since Dennis wasn't getting your help in '94, he really couldn't help you. Eventually, bringing to bear pretty much everything we had, we got to the point we were telling Kerrey if he didn't help you we wouldn't be able to stop the feminist protesters who were gonna be out marching with signs asking why he wouldn't help.

"Kerrey finally relented. So we worked out a deal with his people whereby he would do a press conference for us prior to the activities he was doing for the party. And as these things sometimes do, they got down to a negotiation that took place between Kerrey's Washington office and our office while he was en route, in which we laboriously explained the circumstances we found ourselves, of the irony of the fact that McCain chose this day to announce that he was going to Vietnam. He put Kerrey in a tough spot. We all recognized the bipartisan nature of the MIA-POW Committee, their work together, their war buddy status etc., and then we started negotiating on what he could actually say given this new twist.

"The obvious thing, that McCain was using the thing as a political ploy, was out, so we finally negotiated it down to unless it comes up don't mention it. It was made more than clear that the McCain trip to Vietnam was a political grenade that we did not want to explode in our hand. And to continue the metaphor, basically what happened is that Bob Kerrey pulled the pin and shoved it up our ass.

"After a significant effort to get the Kerrey people to recognize just how much jeopardy this McCain announcement had put our press conference in, Kerrey proceeded to endorse you in *one sentence*.

"Finally, to really put the knife right in our heart, Kerrey elaborated for awhile on the unique nature of McCain's participation in the Vietnam mission, citing its importance, timeliness, McCain's unique relationship with the Vietnamese, and his necessity to the president.

"It was really a situation where the press couldn't come away with anything other than the impression that Bob Kerrey was very comfortable with John McCain serving in the seat that you were after. And the press reflected that. It was almost hard for them not to say Kerrey endorsed McCain. For a Democratic senator to come into a contested Senate race and, even if he hated you, for him to have left that impression was a failure of his partisan responsibility of a fundamental nature.

"There's only two ways to really evaluate what he did. The first and more nefarious is that he came in with an agenda to get the most out of it politically and that meant appeasing McCain, because McCain was already in the seat and it could be assumed from his perspective that McCain was going to keep the seat. The other is that he was just too stupid and unconscious of the circumstances he was in to do any better than he did. And I think it would be a gross underestimation of the subtlety of his mind to let him off the hook, that he just somehow misread that. That's like it's almost impossible to believe anyone who has been as successful as he's been in politics could go into a press conference and say the things he said unconsciously.

"It's hard to come away with any other conclusion about Bob Kerrey other than that he sacrificed your ambition to win that seat for a politically viable continuation of a relationship with McCain. And I can only tell you that if LBJ was the head of the DSCC, he would have had Bob Kerrey's butt in a sling and dick for dinner.

"If there's anyone who owed a debt to the kind of conversations that you were continuing in politics it was Bob Kerrey. He has made a political career out of contesting the general reality of the political arena and saying that he's not the same, that he's a new and different politician.

"I really think that Bob Kerrey demonstrated political ill will and short-sightedness, and that somehow this incident, which was a minor incident in a minor footnote in the history of politics could find its way into the *New Republic* [in an article by Fred Barnes, July 1993] demonstrates just how gross a failure of political etiquette that it is.

"It was just unconscionable. Were it not for the fact that I really felt that it would only damage us further, my first impulse was to tell Bob Kerrey to take off his artificial leg and shove it up his ass.

"Ultimately for both you and me there was a personal affront that was pretty hard to swallow, because both of us had respect for this guy. And for the reasons that you were running Bob Kerrey seemed to be kind of a sole dim light in the political wilderness that we could kind of hold onto: If he's there maybe we can be there. If he can validate us maybe we're okay."

∾

It's curious, the things you remember. When Bob Kerrey and I shook hands before the press conference in our initial greeting, I was instantly overwhelmed by what is now referred to, when used by men, as a "fragrance," and the notion flitted across my mind that had Debra Winger been along instead of the woman traveling with him, she probably would have told him to tone it down.

He did it all so well, played it so effortlessly, as if nothing were amiss—when everything was amiss. I felt as though I were playing a role, an accessory to the deception that all was sweetness and light, basking in his glory. So flattered and delighted that this dashing hero, this courageous Medal of Honor winner, had deigned to make an appearance on my behalf.

One of the first things they teach you about going on TV is that you should always smile. Not being an actor, I found that hard to do, to even think about smiling when I was talking about serious things. And making it even more difficult was that it was the opposite of the Southern Lady reflex I was working so hard to rid myself of, the automatic laugh or smile when it was completely uncalled for or unnecessary. It was just so ingrained, and whenever I did it, I would hear myself and despair.

But smile I did with the most glowing smile I could muster for the folks out there in TV land, as well as the media surrounding us, as I read the speech that had been written for me to introduce him. When I finished, another warm handshake for the cameras. Then he began. And after a one-sentence statement—I believe it was, "I endorse Claire Sargent for the U.S. Senate"—launched into what I thought must be his stump spiel about Clinton and Gore. After all, he'd run against Clinton in the primary, and I figured he needed to get on Clinton's good side in case he won, which by then it appeared was likely. Then he would surely return to me and how Clinton and I together could change America. But when that didn't happen, and he moved on to the glories of McCain, I knew that I most definitely was not going to remain standing there smiling like an idiot. Indeed, an honest reflection of what I was feeling was clearly apparent in my picture in the paper the next day, in which, like the mask of tragedy, the corners of my mouth were most decidedly turned down.

Desperately hoping that surely O'Hara or somebody would come to my rescue and end this fiasco, I longed for more experience as my mind raced through possible reactions and scenarios of how to seize the moment, to stop what was going on at once, or, failing that, to end it with humor, with a clever, subtle putdown. What, I wondered, would happen if I step up to the microphone after he finishes and simply tell the truth about what is going on, about his arrangement with Dennis? What would that do to the Democratic party, to Clinton, at such a crucial time in the election? I'd be crucified by the Democrats for not being a team player and probably accused of lying. Hey, but isn't it clearly obvious that Kerrey's not on *my* team? Who's team is it, anyway? I mean, here I am being *ravished* right here in public on television for all the world to see. Am I supposed to just stand here and take it? God, I wish I knew what to do!

And so, uncharacteristically, woman of action that I am, not knowing what else to do, I simply stood there and took it. It was the most humiliating experience of the campaign—nothing else I experienced equaled that moment of sheer helplessness. If it hadn't been so devastating, the timing might have been compared to farce, because it sure got a lot of laughs.

I suppose it comes with turning sixty and becoming more mellow, because I've long since put that incident behind me. And if I've learned one thing it's this: When you're in the political game, whatever happens, politics is politics. No whining allowed. You accept what happens and move on. Bitterness only corrodes the person who harbors it.

Martin Luther King, Jr. wrote in a letter from the Birmingham jail that unearned suffering is redemptive. I'm sure anyone who's ever run for office believes that her or his suffering was unearned, as I'm positive mine was, of course. Perhaps that's why on occasion so many of us may be possessed of those most lamentable qualities of all: self-righteousness and self-pity.

Twenty-two

Pat Schroeder and Gloria Steinem and Dolores Huerta were the only members of the political establishment who saw any value in me as a candidate. Pat and Gloria and Dolores didn't need a reason to be involved in my campaign. They had no personal agenda other than helping another woman get elected to the United States Senate. They made my cause their cause and gave me their power.

These three women must have been at a thousand things together, each with her own very distinctive style. When they were on the scene, they immediately and intuitively took up the cause with great intensity, each in her own way.

It's not a surprise that they're all women of my generation and all women who have fought long and hard against discrimination and for women's equality. Their relationship to the campaign was based entirely on their understanding that I was another foot soldier in a battle that they'd been fighting for a long time and they knew that I needed their help.

One of the great days of the campaign was the Pat Schroeder day. Pat did for us everything we had wanted Bob Kerrey to do, and more.

Her definition of me as a candidate was so enthusiastic and so independently arrived at, and, familiar from her own experience with all of the criticisms I was facing, she deftly dismissed them out of hand in a gracious, elegant way.

I don't know how many other candidates she's campaigned for, but I know she went all over the country, wherever she was needed. The day she arrived in Arizona she had to leave her home in

Colorado at 4:30 a.m. to get to Tucson in time for a breakfast fundraiser for Karan English, who was running for Congress for the open seat in our new congressional district.

I was filmed by the local NBC television station as I left my apartment in Phoenix at the crack of dawn in the Clairemobile, a blue van with "Sargent for U.S. Senate" signs on the sides and back. We were to pick up Pat at the Karan English fundraiser in Tucson and go on from there to my press conference. But before that we checked in at my Tucson headquarters.

Unfortunately.

My Tucson campaign manager, Kathleen O'Dea, was one of the most capable people I've ever met. She had four, actually five, jobs. Lawyer, puppet designer, wife, mother, and campaign manager. I can state unequivocally that it was her direction of the targeting, early voting, get-out-the-vote, and the publication and distribution of a last-minute tabloid that defeated Spangrud so overwhelmingly in southern Arizona in the primary. No one could have done a finer job. And she was still at it in the general—loyal and wholly believing in me—underpaid, understaffed, and overworked though she was. She had independently arrived at the notion of my serving for only one term—the idea I'd been chewing on since I made my pilgrimage to the Lincoln Memorial—and that I was going to announce shortly at my news conference with Pat.

It was not a difficult decision for me to make. I clearly realized that under the rules as they now stood the only way to break the choke hold of incumbents and special-interest money was to go back to the original intent of the Constitution and the citizen politician, who served a term or two and then went back to her life. A job in the Congress was never intended to be the lifetime occupation it has become. And since the election I've heard others speak to this same issue, that the store owner on Main Street or in the mall should be able to run for Congress if we're ever going to wrest control from the pros and put it back into the hands of the people. And the only way to do this is to take the money out of the campaign process.

I realized this was a controversial decision and had talked it over with many of my supporters and contributors to let them know

Part Three - Arizona 341

how necessary it was for me to do this if I truly wanted to change the system. This would be a symbolic first step. And if elected, I wouldn't accept a penny from anyone from the time I was sworn in until the day I left office. I would be free to make decisions based on what I thought was right, not from the pressures of the special interest groups from whom I would have to grovel for contributions each and every day until the next election.

The Schroeder event was less than two weeks before the election, and I had thought that the Dennis issue had long since been put to bed, but I was wrong. Kathleen pulled me aside into her small office and shut the door. Dear God. What new disaster had befallen?

She began. Very seriously and quietly. "I know this is a big day for you and you have a lot on your mind, but I need to talk to you.

"This is the first time in the history of Arizona politics that the Tucson Democrats haven't held an event for the Democratic nominee for the United States Senate. Everyone is asking me what's going on. Why isn't the party holding a fundraiser for you? Where is Dennis? Isn't he going to help you raise money?

"This lunch today will help me pay a few bills, but we might as well close the campaign office. We have volunteers, but I can't even do a mailing to the people I've ID'd as likely to vote absentee so they will at least have heard your name.

"Claire, you've got to call Dennis and make peace with him. It's still not too late. Who do you think you are [the old question again]? Don't you realize by being so stubborn and uncompromising with Dennis that you are letting down the women of Arizona? You are putting your own principles before those who most want you to win, who most need your help in the Senate by being very selfish and inconsiderate. I've spoken with one of his staff people and he said he was sure Dennis would be open to talking to you again."

She was in tears, barely able to finish.

I was crushed and sent reeling by this barrage of criticism, coming as it did so unexpectedly and from one so close to me. I had such respect for this woman. She'd worked like a dog—everybody had, making silk purses out of sows' ears for so long. She was worn out from fighting with her hands tied behind her back. She'd done such a brilliant job in the primary, and was so proud of trouncing Truman in southern Arizona. She hated losing. Now here she was beaten down by no money, no resources, and no hope of either. She was desperate. And I couldn't blame her.

I didn't have the time to give her the attention she deserved. I should be on my way to get Pat, and here I was having to deal with this perilously emotional, difficult situation. I didn't know what to do, what to say. What she said had cut me deeply, about being selfish and not caring about the other women. I could see how she could look at it that way. But I could do no other. What Kathleen was telling me was that I shouldn't be too proud to give in, that I was arrogant and egotistical. But I was goddamned if I was going to be tortured like a fly, having first one wing pulled off, then the other, leaving me finally pleading for my life with only two weeks left. The money wouldn't be there anyway at this late date. It was too late.

Caught as I was in this emotional whipsaw, I wanted to reassure Kathleen so that she wasn't left completely without hope, with no prospect of deliverance. How could I end this as soon as possible, and with as much grace and kindness as I could muster?

"I can't promise anything. It's really too late, Kathleen, but I'll see what I can do. I'm sorry you feel the way you do, that I've let you down. I respect you enormously. And I need you."

Later, she told me that she had been put up to being the heavy by several desperate members of my staff. That I might listen to her. I'll say one thing. It sure was rotten timing.

∞

Pat Schroeder proved a lot of people in Washington wrong, that you *can* be successful on your own terms. She never hankered after being a big deal in the hierarchy of the House. She put the concerns of her constituents and of women ahead of working her way up to the top of the House ladder. She never took herself too seriously—an alien concept to the boys—though she took her job deadly seriously, which is why she stepped on so many toes, somehow able to remain the outsider even as she was on the inside.

Her being there for me made us all feel that we weren't the idiots that in our dark moments we thought we must be from the way I was being portrayed. The point I'm making is that the feminists in Washington, the tough insider politically savvy crowd who have a prototypical idea of a candidate—one who appeals on a level of political sophistication to which I really didn't even aspire—to them I didn't compute. But to Pat Schroeder I did, and here she was giving me her imprimatur, and her blessing.

She was exactly as I had expected her to be. Down to earth, a twinkle in her eye, unaffected, and a pro. It was one of those times during the campaign—that I could count on one hand—when I encountered someone in a position to help me, whose only agenda was my agenda. Words fail me in trying to describe how rare, how unique that is in politics. All she wanted was more women in the U.S. Senate. She was there to help another woman get elected. As simple as that.

Pat and I napped in the Clairemobile on the way back to Phoenix for another fundraiser in the early evening. At my apartment we had a rare chance for some peace, and with our stocking-feet propped up, talked of shoes and ships and sealing wax. When I opined that she must have a lot of help to be able to do everything she does, I fell out laughing when she opened the double-breasted black jacket she wore, holding out both sides so that I could see the eight gigantic safety pins—they looked like diaper pins from days of yore—four on each side, anchoring her eight buttons in place. "If I even own a needle and thread, I wouldn't know where to find it!" she chortled.

∽

Gloria arrived on Saturday, three days before the election on Tuesday. It was Halloween.

I couldn't help thinking back to the Halloween one year before, when I was returning to Phoenix after my first round with the Washington women's groups. On my way home, as I trudged exhausted at midnight through the St. Louis terminal after my connecting flight to Phoenix had been canceled because of weather, I realized that this was what I would be doing a lot of if I were elected. Glamorous it was not. Under the harsh fluorescent lighting that cast a greenish, surreal glow, I was buffeted on all sides by airline personnel turned out in freakish, ghoulish masks and costumes, a

Fellini movie come to life. I'd forgotten it was Halloween, the perfect metaphor for my trip to Washington, where everyone wears a mask and nothing is as it appears. I was depressed after my meetings with the women's groups whose collective response had been, "Take two aspirin and *don't* call us in the morning." They didn't take me seriously.

Now, here I was, one year to the day later, waiting for Gloria Steinem, who was getting ready to walk off this plane to help me do battle.

I'd first seen Gloria in 1984, the year I ran for the legislature, when she was the featured speaker at a luncheon in Phoenix and I was introduced as a candidate. I was astounded by the number of women who appeared as if out of the woodwork—a huge, silent, feminist population, one thousand strong, as they waited in long lines to enter the event. It was the first glimmer I had that there were throngs of women in Phoenix just like me, and I hadn't known it until then. It was one of the most affirming moments I'd had since I'd arrived in Arizona.

Seven years later, in 1991, I heard that Mary Montalvo, a member of a women's issues group with the city of Phoenix, had gotten a bee in her bonnet to celebrate International Women's Day, with Gloria as speaker. Recalling the energy and excitement of Gloria's last visit, I called Mary to see if I could help. What they needed, as always, was money. So I helped put together a reception at $100 a copy, which for most women in Arizona is a lot of money. I think we cleared ten or fifteen thousand dollars, which all went for a women's education fund. But the most fascinating thing to me (besides the fact that we established International Women's Day as an annual event, observed on a bigger and grander scale every year since) was that once again Gloria was a catalyst for turning out close to twenty-five hundred determined women—on a week night in downtown Phoenix—who literally had to climb over concrete barriers (set up for a car race) to reach the convention center. It was the most astonishing turnout I'd ever seen.

Gloria doesn't just campaign for women she thinks can win, she campaigns for underdogs as well. She campaigned in Illinois for Carol Moseley-Braun in her primary fight when Emily's List—

deciding she wasn't "viable"—had turned her down. It is *because* all women have historically been underdogs that Gloria rallies to their side. It is *because* they have made a decision simply to enter the arena that she is there for them. It's not whether they can win; it's that they're in the game.

She hadn't flown first class, so she wasn't the first one off the plane. How many planes, I wondered, had she been on in her life, as I searched the faces of the arriving passengers. Spotting her, anonymous in the crowd, with only a single slouchy black bag slung over her shoulder, I marveled at her stamina and her ability to drop out of the sky into a foreign land without being completely disoriented.

In 1983, when I'd read Gloria's book *Outrageous Acts and Everyday Rebellions* and discovered that she and I were exactly the same age, each of us born in 1934, I couldn't believe it. Until then I had never known of another woman exactly my age who called herself a feminist. Never having studied women's history, I had little or no knowledge of heroines I could identify with. When I took history, on the infrequent occasion when Susan B. Anthony's name was mentioned it was a one-sentence description of her as a suffragette. Today when it's mentioned it's a complaint about the shape of the coin named for her. Whose fault was that, I ask you?

I had visions of Gloria growing up in Ohio during the war, climbing trees as I did, seeing the same picture shows, collecting tin cans and planting a victory garden as I had in Mississippi. Which, I discovered as I read the book, turned out not to be the case. Even so, I was fascinated to know that we shared the events of girlhood and history at the same time, only in different places and different ways; and then having taken such disparate paths, to have them cross now, at this time and this place.

The event was held in the Lath House in downtown Phoenix, a luxuriant, bowered outdoor space, in the long shadows of late afternoon. As Gloria and I entered from the back, making our way slowly through the sea of tables to the stage up front, the women rose to their feet in a wave as we walked by. Retha, one of my most steadfast volunteers, produced a large, ancient Indian drum, and began beating it rhythmically. Picking up the beat, the women clapped their hands, quietly at first, and then louder and louder as we finally reached the stage, in a crescendo of drumming, applause, shouts, and whistles. It gave me goose bumps, as it does even now as I write.

I knew it was for Gloria, that I was only basking in her reflected light. But I didn't care. It was fine. And my staff, led by Jesse, had done me so proud, producing this splendid upbeat evening the Saturday before election day. We were all in such desperate need of something positive, some affirmation of what we were about, especially after these last savage weeks.

There was a bizarrely hilarious note when the event was over. We'd had tens of thousands of a really terrific tabloid printed—in the end without money to mail it—prompting a woman on my staff to come up with the idea to haul them down to the Lath House and give each person fifty tabloids to take home to pass out to all her friends. It wasn't a bad idea. But on the Saturday before the election, there was no way it was going to change the outcome. Everybody had been so busy making sure that the event went smoothly that somehow the extra tabloids—one had been placed at each place—had slipped through the cracks, nowhere to be found.

Just as Gloria and I reached the edge of the crowd on our way out, I sensed more than I heard a great commotion, and turned to see the staffer red-faced and shrieking, having an absolute fit and falling in it when she discovered the tabloids hadn't made it. Going completely berserk, with O'Hara frantically trying to hush her up as unobtrusively as possible—so that at least Gloria wouldn't see or hear her—she drew quite a curious crowd, who had the good sense to shoo us away.

Later that night, the woman who had been so distraught showed up at a smaller gathering for Gloria on the roof terrace of our apartment building, flaunting a campaign button with a red slash through the names McCAIN and O'HARA. Fun and loathing on the ol' campaign trail.

After putting in the longest, most grueling day—leaving New York in the early morning, a five-hour flight to Phoenix, a press conference, three fundraisers (two for me and one for a prochoice group)—Gloria was taking the red eye out at midnight, to arrive back in New York early the next morning.

I'd planned for her to be able to have some quiet time to herself to recharge after her final appearance at the end of the last event—something I always needed—putting a bedroom at her disposal where she could be alone and rest before she had to go to the airport. To my surprise, apparently still as wired as I was, she chose instead to join my family and me in our small study where we were all mindlessly watching a re-run of *Saturday Night Live,* and after a few minutes, it was as though she'd been watching TV with us all our lives. Since you don't have to talk while watching, it was the perfect antidote she and I both needed.

And at midnight she caught the last stage out of Dodge.

Sic transit Gloria.

༄

If my campaign was jazz improvisation, election day included melodic intervals and chordal convolutions before taking off on a tangent of surreal stream of consciousness that finally ended in a crashing decrescendo.

As I recall, the only thing on my schedule was to go vote before I was to drive to Tucson to be there when the polls closed. Realizing a TV crew would most likely be at my polling place, I shamelessly asked Henry's darling four-year-old granddaughter Carolyn, who was in town with her mother, Kitty, if she'd like to go with us, knowing full well, of course, that she would be thrilled to death. And sure enough, there they were waiting for us as I got out of the car, holding her hand for TV land. I never saw it, but others said they did. And I was so ashamed. I remember thinking how I'd run the gauntlet of the whole campaign without subterfuge, and here on the last day, I'd stooped so low as to use a *grandchild.*

Sometime around mid-afternoon, Corinne, my son John, his wife, Elisabeth, and Kitty, along with one of my staff, boarded the Clairemobile for Tucson, the final stop of the campaign. I have no recollection of anyone ever mentioning preparing a concession speech, though I might have had a prepared speech for Tucson. But I'm not sure about that, either.

My memory is that when we got to Tucson we went straight to the Arizona Inn for an early supper, which I could hardly get down, and that while there spotted Republican Congressman Jim Kolbe dining with some friends. Confident of victory, he appeared to be thoroughly enjoying his meal and having a perfectly marvelous time.

I was not upset over losing the election. I knew that it had been lost long before, though I tried, probably unsuccessfully, not to show it, to keep everyone's spirits high, as well as my own. I just hated it so much for my troops, about whom O'Hara said later, "We had all been running on fumes in the last days, but in the face of clear defeat we did not retreat. We were like the Confederate troops marching into a phalanx of lead." And I'm telling you, they were. Warriors all.

As I've recounted, at my Tucson campaign headquarters on that final November evening, as I thanked those faithful warriors and bade them farewell, my tears finally flowed. The campaign was over. I had fought the good fight. I had stayed the course. I had kept the faith.

After some follow-up interviews we were driven to Democratic election night headquarters, where returns from the East Coast had been coming in for some time, as well as projections on races around the country. You have to remember, I'd had no preparation whatsoever for the events of this night. So when the first thing I heard—while I was being interviewed live on TV—was for my reaction to one of the networks' pronouncements that John McCain had won the election (when if the polls had closed, it couldn't have been even five minutes), I know I must have looked shocked, because I was. But with a bright smile, naturally, I just said something to the effect that it was clearly too early to tell, and after making nice a while longer, fled for the van to call O'Hara.

To no avail. Though for the whole story, you need to hear O'Hara's side:

At my Phoenix headquarters sometime between 6:50 and 7:00 that night someone had asked O'Hara to tape up a photo on a window where we had everybody's picture, and as he did, he "looked through the glass and saw McCain's bald head on a TV set. It just broke our heart, getting the news at ten to seven. The finality of it."

Knowing he was to meet me at the Democratic election headquarters at the Civic Plaza, he immediately left to go down there, where he "just wandered around," visiting, getting more and more lubricated with fire water as the night wore on. Among those he encountered was my former fellow church usher and *bête noir*, the McCain-flacking *Gazette* columnist John Kolbe, on whom he bestowed quite a large and vociferous—and very satisfying—piece of his mind.

The plan had been to drive me from Tucson to the Civic Plaza to meet O'Hara there. He would tell me where to meet him when I called in on my way back. When I couldn't get him, I told someone at my headquarters I'd stop by the Civic Plaza to try to find him and bring him back to our headquarters, where Henry was waiting for me. In the meantime, others would look for him too.

When I heard McCain claim victory on the van radio—I believe before eight o'clock—I was stunned. Apparently nobody had factored this in, that I'd be trapped on the highway when this happened, and I believe it was somewhere around nine-thirty by the time we got back to Phoenix, when I dashed alone into the election-night mob.

Having to stop and commiserate when I didn't know anything but what I'd heard on the radio, I was frantic when I realized I'd never be able to find O'Hara—it was like being caught in one of those recurring dreams of trying to get somewhere, and things keep holding you back and blocking your way—and hightailed it for the exit.

Never having found themselves in such circumstances, it was hard on our children, disappointed over my losing, and not sure how I was really taking it, and I hated this awful situation for them, too. It was probably after ten o'clock by the time we got to my headquarters, and Henry and everybody else were beside themselves. Especially the media.

Quietly Henry took me aside and asked me if I weren't ready to concede, and I told him I would not—could not—concede without O'Hara there with me. I just wouldn't do that to him. That people were looking for him and I was sure he would show up any minute.

Well, it was probably after eleven when Dave and Matt brought him in and whisked him into a back office. When I tried to talk to him about conceding, I realized that he, to put it in his words, "had pretty much mentally turned in his keys." So I went in to my press secretary—who was having a nervous breakdown trying to hold the furious press at bay, all over him because I wouldn't accommodate them with a concession speech—and told him I was ready. I honestly have no recollection of what I said, and after endless interviews, the last thing I remember is that it was after midnight by the time I asked my press secretary to get John McCain on the phone. To tell the truth, by then he was the last person I had on my mind. And, well, hell, he'd already claimed his victory hours before.

The final vote was 771,395 to 436,321, 56 percent to my 32 percent—$5.18 per vote for him, $.68 per vote for me—with Mecham getting 11 percent.

Never able to get through to the senator on election night, I called him the next morning, reaching an aide, and asked him to have the senator call me back. But he never did.

∞

I was not the perfect candidate. In fact, I can easily say that I may have been the most imperfect candidate—by conventional standards—who has run for the U.S. Senate in modern times.

I ran as myself. Isn't that an interesting concept? Have you ever thought about that before? If you don't run as yourself, who are you running as? When Barry Goldwater made his famous "Extremism in pursuit of liberty is no vice" statement when he ran for president, someone reportedly said, "Oh, my God, he's running as Barry!" But running as yourself is against all the rules laid down by those mutual parasites—Beltway consultants, TV talking heads, and the media—feeding off the host that is the candidate. And they will collectively savage you if you deviate from their prescribed libretto.

If you choose to play anyway, breaking all the rules, you get hammered. So though I may have been naive, I was never in any way a victim. In addition to being an imperfect candidate, I put my campaign staff in a bind when I effectively dried up most of the funding that might have been available. And they toiled on under circumstances most people would never have tolerated.

I called them the Dirty Dozen, since that's about the largest number we ever had on the payroll at any given time, and because they were such a disparate, wondrous collection of human beings, all totally committed to me and the campaign. Only three of them had had anything remotely close to any really big-time campaign experience, and some had no campaign experience at all. Poorly paid, sometimes not even paid at all, I'm still profoundly humble when I think about how much they gave for so little in return.

And then there were my volunteers. Unless you've been a candidate—at any level—it's difficult to understand what it's like to have people appear, unbidden, unknown, out of nowhere, because they believe in you and what you stand for. They accept you, feet of clay, warts and all. It is heady stuff, and there's a reason that people get hooked and become political junkies.

I always felt increased by my staff and my volunteers—by all of my supporters—who represented every spectrum of the rainbow of society. Until the day I die I'll be as deeply honored by having them with me, believing in me, as I was equally desolate at disappointing them.

I'll tell you one thing, though. I wouldn't have missed it for the world!

Twenty-three

After the election I learned that Karan English had refused to sign Dennis's pledge as well, and went on without his support—with the help of Emily's List—to win the new Congressional seat anyway, only to be defeated in 1994 after serving only a single term. Makes you wonder, though, doesn't it, about who all did sign Dennis's pledge? All those guys who ran that he helped raise money for? And what about all the appointments he made after Clinton was elected? Did he nail them too?

And you'll never guess who became the new chairman of the Democratic Senatorial Campaign Committee: Bob Kerrey, of course!

As for Emily's List, I know it's hard to believe, but I signed up again. Big time, too, to be a Majority Council Member. It was when Dennis, in October 1993—a year to the day after I'd told him I wouldn't sign his pledge—announced that he would not run for the Senate in 1994. Said he couldn't "put up with all the b.s." of fundraising.

I figured that if I wanted to keep on getting prochoice women elected I had to keep on putting my money where my mouth is. Cathy Eden had already announced in June that she was running against Dennis in the primary, and I believed that if she was going to get any help from Emily's List, she needed someone on the inside fighting for her. But it didn't do any good. I was never really on the "inside."

Not only did they not help Cathy, neither did they help Cindy Resnick, a Democratic state senator from Tucson, who also announced against Dennis. Coming in third in a three-way primary after Cathy pulled out, Cindy ran a scrappy grass-roots campaign that with Emily's List's money she would have had a good chance of winning. Neither did they raise a finger for Carol Cure, a congressional candidate in an open seat that same year, even after many Emily's List members in Arizona wrote letters—as they had for me—pleading for their support for all three. They did, however, continue to support Karan English in her second bid.

After that campaign cycle, when Emily's List started asking for money for their Women Vote! project in 1996, getting women out to vote for Democrats in targeted states (which would never include Arizona), they'd finally become nothing but an arm of the Democratic Party, only peripherally helping a select group of women candidates. And FINALLY I said to hell with them. I mean, I am *loyal,* and it takes a lot for me to let go!

In 1996 a friend sent me a clipping from a San Diego newspaper with an interesting story. After two years of tedious deliberations by the city of San Diego over the future of the 540-acre Naval Training Center on the edge of Point Loma, so went the story, the Barron Collier family was "abruptly plopped down" amongst them, still singing, it appeared, the old familiar Florida swampland tune. This time trying to swap its oil and gas rights in Florida's Big Cypress National Preserve for FOUR surplus military bases, including the Naval Training Center in San Diego! "I mean," the article concluded, "didn't we all outgrow Florida land swaps along with the Tooth Fairy?"

As for the Indian School, guess who got behind fundraising for the park—the Community Alliance guys! And though I would never claim any cause and effect, I found out not long ago that two weeks after I wrote them that memo, about them fiddling while Rome burned, they had indeed taken some action: They formed a committee to look into the situation. And eight years later, with all of the biggest guns in town now supporting it, they are well on their way to their goal of $13.5 million for a park. It takes 'em awhile, but God love 'em!

Oh, I almost forgot. Dennis stayed on in Washington after he left the Senate at the end of 1994, and became a lobbyist. James Reston, the late *New York Times* Washington bureau chief, trenchantly, but poignantly, captures such customs: "Yet the habits of the past like the bent figures of homeless former senators still haunt the capital."

And a few years later I saw this article in the *Wall Street Journal:*

> President Clinton has made the extraordinary decision to appoint former Senator Dennis DeConcini to the board of directors of Freddie Mac, the federally chartered corporation that handles residential mortgages. Mr. DeConcini is best remembered for being the ringleader of the Keating Five. They were the Senators backing infamous Savings & Loan high-flier Charles Keating. Having Mr. Clinton give Mr. DeConcini a cushy Freddie Mac job must astonish Bob Bennett, who is now Mr. Clinton's personal lawyer. In 1991, Mr. Bennett was outside counsel to the Senate Ethics Committee. He built a compelling case that Mr. DeConcini lobbied on behalf of Mr. Keating until the day before his Lincoln Savings was seized by the government. Mr. Bennett strongly indicated that the Senate should take disciplinary action against Mr. DeConcini, a move it declined.

∞

The week she turned forty, Katharina, the *Reader's Digest* of political columnists—the one who said my interests were a mile wide and an inch deep, the one who never even talked to me—was named editorial pages editor of the *Arizona Republic.*

And wouldn't you just know it? Now John McCain is bored with being a senator and wants to be president!

∞

Having now lived almost an equal number of years in Mississippi, New York, and Arizona—such disparate regions of this magnificent land—I am a part of all that I have met. Though Mississippi still retains its mystical, Gothic "holt" on me—my tap root is deep—and though I've grown to feel a genuine connection to Arizona—its desert, fiery sunsets, endless horizons, and deep friendships—New York City stole my heart the second my feet

Part Three - Arizona

touched ground on that New Year's Eve so many years ago. Every time I cross the East River and see the skyline as I'm coming in from JFK or LaGuardia, I know I'm back where I belong, where I feel truly free.

God has shed Her grace on America, and, for some reason, on me. And while I continue to ponder that—since my journey isn't over—I'm taking up tap dancing.

Epilogue

Rice pudding has always been one of my favorite desserts. I should qualify that by saying *Southern* rice pudding has always been one of my favorite desserts. Southern rice pudding is made with leftover rice (always available) mixed with milk and eggs and sugar and vanilla and baked with nutmeg on top, so it's like baked custard, only with rice in it. Served hot or cold it is delectable.

Back in 1956, when I first arrived in New York, I was delighted to discover this familiar favorite featured frequently on menus that were otherwise laden with food either foreign or strange to me. Which led to what I've come to refer to as The Rice Pudding Lesson.

At the time, I was still quite unnerved when I sat at the counter at Schrafft's for lunch and ordering a sandwich brought the impatient confrontational question: "What kind of bread?" Unfamiliar with having a choice of anything other than white bread and mayonnaise, I was mystified as to what my choices were, afraid to ask in the face of such animosity. So I always said, "White, please," until I got the hang of the whole roster of breads, toasted or not; with butter, mayo, mustard, or Russian; on the side, or not at all.

I give you this to illustrate where I was, assurance-wise, with intimidating waiters and waitresses, and the breadth of my cuisine experience.

So the first time I ordered rice pudding, I can't tell you how incredulous I was when a mass of cold, creamy white goo, sprinkled all over with cinnamon, and studded with black things that looked like what we called water bugs—which turned out to be raisins—

was placed before me. Screwing up my courage, I looked up at the waiter and smiled, "I ordered rice pudding."

"Yes, that's right," he said, and disappeared.

Throughout that first year, knowing full well that all rice pudding was not made the same way, I'd occasionally give rice pudding another try, and each time I got exactly the same thing. White goo.

Finally, one night when I was having dinner with my friend Marion who had recently arrived from Jackson, I spied rice pudding on the menu and asked her if she'd had the misfortune to order it.

"Yes," she said, "and I keep getting the same thing every time, rice mixed with cream and sugar and raisins."

"Me too. I can't tell you how many times I've ordered it. Should we try it, just to see if we might be lucky enough to get the real thing?"

"Why not? But let's ask the waiter what it's like before we do?" Clever girl, that Marion.

Well, we did ask the waiter, whose accent was as thick as ours, only in another tongue. "We were thinking about ordering the rice pudding, but we would like to know if it's baked like a custard, or if it's mixed with cream and raisins?"

Silence, as he stared at us with that glazed look you get when you know that not one word has registered. Then, smiling, a fraction of comprehension, "No raisins, no raisins."

Realizing we'd hit the top in communicating, we decided to go for it. What the heck.

The waiter was right. Raisins were absent from the creamy white goo he set before us.

Mystifying the poor waiter, Marion and I collapsed into a fit of hysterical laughter.

"Claire," she was finally able to gasp, "we've just got to face it! What we've finally got to realize is, we never learn from experience!"

Two or three years ago I stopped in for supper at the Cornelia Street Café in Greenwich Village, which I've frequented since it opened in 1978. In all the years I've been eating there, I'd never before seen rice pudding on the menu, but there it was. Having realized years ago that New York rice pudding was New York rice pudding, I said to the waiter, "Tell me about the rice pudding."

"It's different, not what you usually get around here. The rice is baked in an egg custard base with fresh vanilla bean and nutmeg on top."

With great outward calm, though aquiver inside with excitement, I asked, "Are there raisins?"

"No," replied the waiter.

"I think I'll try it."

"You got it," he shot back, and went off to fetch for me the most glorious rice pudding I'd put in my mouth since I left Mississippi.

GRATEFUL ACKNOWLEDGMENT is made to the following for permission to quote selected material:

Where the Bluebird Sings to the Lemonade Springs by Wallace Stegner. Copyright 1992 by Wallace Stegner. Reprinted by permission of Random House, Inc.

Molly Ivins Can't Say That, Can She? by Molly Ivins. Copyright 1991 by Molly Ivins. Reprinted by permission of Random House, Inc.

The Mother of All Hooks: The Story of the U.S. Navy's Tailhook Scandal by William McMichael. Copyright © 1997 by William McMichael. Reprinted by permission of Transaction Publishers; all rights reserved.

"Clinton Sleaze Factor" (Asides: 8-4-97), reprinted with permission of *The Wall Street Journal.* Copyright 1997 by Dow Jones & Company, Inc.

Writing A Woman's Life by Carolyn G. Heilbrun. Copyright © 1988 by Carolyn G. Heilbrun. Reprinted by permission of W. W. Norton & Company, Inc.

Fall From Glory by Gregory Vistica. Copyright © 1995 by Gregory L. Vistica. (N.Y.: Simon & Schuster. Inc.).

The Moviegoer by Walker Percy. Copyright 1961 by Walker Percy. Reprinted by permission of Random House, Inc.

The Utne Reader, "Trials and Transformation—A Conversation with Robert Jay Lifton," by Marilyn Berlin Snell, July/August 1995.

ying an el
at will it take
orpora
few women
GUEST VOICE
SARGENT
U.S. SENATE
Phoenix to
global
Collier
Collier
Collier
Claire Sargent, presi
1991 International
Sargent,
Phoenix feminist
beats retired general
LLACS
H BEHLEN